World Rule

World Rule

Accountability, Legitimacy, and the
Design of Global Governance

JONATHAN GS KOPPELL

THE UNIVERSITY OF CHICAGO PRESS   CHICAGO AND LONDON

JONATHAN GS KOPPELL is director of the School of Public Affairs at Arizona State University, where he also holds the Lattie and Elva Coor Presidential Chair. He is the author of *The Politics of Quasi-Government: Hybrid Organizations and the Dynamics of Bureaucratic Control* and was for ten years on the faculty of the Yale School of Management.

The University of Chicago Press, Chicago 60637
The University of Chicago Press, Ltd., London
© 2010 by The University of Chicago
All rights reserved. Published 2010
Printed in the United States of America

19 18 17 16 15 14 13 12 11 10   1 2 3 4 5

ISBN-13: 978-0-226-45098-8 (cloth)
ISBN-13: 978-0-226-45099-5 (paper)
ISBN-10: 0-226-45098-8 (cloth)
ISBN-10: 0-226-45099-6 (paper)

Library of Congress Cataloging-in-Publication Data
Koppell, Jonathan GS
    World rule : accountability, legitimacy, and the design of global governance / Jonathan GS Koppell.
        p. cm.
    Includes bibliographical references and index.
    ISBN-13: 978-0-226-45098-8 (cloth : alk. paper)
    ISBN-13: 978-0-226-45099-5 (pbk. : alk. paper)
    ISBN-10: 0-226-45098-8 (cloth : alk. paper)
    ISBN-10: 0-226-45099-6 (pbk. : alk. paper)   1. International organization. 2. International cooperation. 3. Legitimacy of governments. I. Title.
    JZ4839.K688 2010
    341.2—dc22   2010007677

⊚ The paper used in this publication meets the minimum requirements of the American National Standard for Information Sciences—Permanence of Paper for Printed Library Materials, ANSI Z39.48-1992.

IN MEMORY OF
JUDY GRUBER AND NELSON POLSBY,
MY TEACHERS, ADVISORS, AND FRIENDS

Contents

Illustrations

Abbreviations

ASTM	ASTM International (formerly American Society for Testing and Materials)
BCBS	Basel Committee on Banking Supervision
CITES	Convention on International Trade in Endangered Species
EU	European Union
FLOI	Fairtrade Labelling Organizations International
FIFA	Fédération Internationale de Football Association
FATF	Financial Action Task Force on Money Laundering
FIB	Focused Intermediate Bodies
FSC	Forest Stewardship Council
GGO	Global Governance Organization
IASB	International Accounting Standards Board
IAEA	International Atomic Energy Agency
ICAO	International Civil Aviation Organization
ICRC	International Committee of the Red Cross
IEC	International Electrotechnical Commission
ILO	International Labor Organization
IMO	International Maritime Organization
IMF	International Monetary Fund
IO	International Organization
ISO	International Organization for Standardization
ISA	International Seabed Authority
ISEAL	International Social and Environmental Accreditation and Labelling Alliance
ITU	International Telecommunication Union
IWC	International Whaling Commission
ICANN	Internet Corporation for Assigned Names and Numbers
MSC	Marine Stewardship Council
NGO	Nongovernmental organization

NATO   North Atlantic Treaty Organization
OMOV   one member, one vote
UC   Unicode Consortium
UN   United Nations
UPU   Universal Postal Union
WCO   World Customs Organization
WHO   World Health Organization
WIPO   World Intellectual Property Organization
WTO   World Trade Organization
W3C   World Wide Web Consortium

Introduction: The Organization of Global Rulemaking

Leaders gathered at the Group of Twenty (G-20) summit in April 2009 did not emerge with a plan to reorder the world economy as some had hoped or feared. In the wake of the global financial crisis, however, the participants did agree that the interconnectedness of the financial system necessitates global oversight. The form and function of international institutions was vague, as one would expect, but national regulatory efforts seemed futile in the absence of global coordination. Only a month later, the outbreak and quick spread of swine flu demonstrated that financial calamities are not unique in this regard.

Many of the most pressing problems confronting humanity require a global response (Weiss and Daws 2007, 4; Held and McGrew 2002). The causes and effects of climate change are distributed worldwide. Political unrest spills easily across borders, shaking seemingly stable institutions. Fluctuations in commodity prices cause unforeseen ripples in the markets for essential foods in seemingly remote corners of the world. Natural disasters often prompt mass emigrations, taxing the resources of neighboring countries. This is the unavoidable reality of the twenty-first century.

And yet, even as the need for global institutions is widely recognized, skepticism regarding international organizations remains deep. The United Nations (UN) General Assembly is routinely charged with incompetence and fecklessness (e.g., Bayefsky 2007; Hawkins et al. 2006, 3). And perhaps most damningly, it is dismissed as irrelevant (Morgenthau and Thompson 1993; Waltz 1993; Gilpin 2002; Huntington 1973). Because the

UN and other international organizations lack the coercive tools needed to compel obedience, critics say, they depend upon the goodwill of those they ostensibly control. This is a polite way of calling them useless.

Strangely, international organizations are concomitantly chastised for their unchecked power and lack of accountability, a critique that bundles several complaints in a single accusation (Chesterman 2008). The International Monetary Fund (IMF), an institution singled out by the G-20 leaders as a linchpin of future global financial oversight, is a frequent target of protesters' ire. Critics express unhappiness with the inaccessibility of the policymaking process to the general public, the apparent imbalance of influence among members, and the opacity of operations. It is often said that international organizations suffer from a "democratic deficit" (Keohane and Nye 2003; Falk and Strauss 2001; Verweij and Josling 2003; Porter 2001; Bodansky 1999). This phrase, seemingly linked genetically with global governance, is an all-encompassing indictment.

The persistence of both charges is puzzling but informative. How can global governance organizations (GGOs) be simultaneously accused of irrelevance and injustice? If international organizations don't matter, why would anyone care whether they are unaccountable? The criticisms may reflect poor performance by international organizations, but more profoundly, they reveal the multiplicity of demands and pressures facing the organizations generating rules for the world (Barnett and Finnemore 1999). In a single editorial regarding the requirements of a new global financial regulator, for example, Sir Howard Davies (2008) made the following two points:

> *[T]here is a big problem of legitimacy.* The Financial Stability Forum, which sits at the center of the system (without much formal authority), includes the Netherlands and Australia but not China or India. Ten of the 13 members of the Basel Committee, which sets bank capital ratios, are from Europe; there is only one Asian member. The crisis presents a good opportunity to make these bodies more representative. *If we do not allow China to participate in making the rules governing finance, how can we expect it to obey them?*

> *[T]he new system needs to move faster.* It took the Basel Committee the better part of a decade to design the Basel II standards that banks are just beginning to implement. That's right: These guidelines on leverage and capital are already out of date before coming into service. *Regulatory clocks must be speeded up.* (Davies 2008, emphasis added)

Each point is compelling, but in combination they are highly problematic. Including a broader range of constituencies is normatively and politically appealing, but it obviously will not speed up the standard-generating process. Indeed, it would almost certainly slow things down quite a bit.

Such internally contradictory imperatives make for a thorny administration problem, one that cannot be solved without leaving some (or all) interested parties less than completely satisfied. The tension between the normative expectations facing governance organizations and the practical demands of building and maintaining authority in the transnational context is the central theme of this book. The undemocratic features of global governance organizations are cast not as unsightly blemishes to be surgically removed but as evolved attributes that allow global rulemaking organizations to survive and function effectively in a difficult environment. To some, the implications of this conclusion may be unpalatable. Bureaucratic adaptations are required that are not merely unfamiliar but potentially at odds with some core beliefs regarding the requirements of legitimate democratic governance, including equity, impartiality, and disinterestedness (Rothstein and Teorell 2008). Effective international organizations will never fully satisfy normative expectations cultivated in the domestic context or even those moderated for the transnational context (Barnett and Finnemore 1999; Buchanan and Keohane 2006; Hurd 1999; Dahl 1999; Keohane 2002). Global rulemakers that *do* meet traditional norms of democratic legitimacy will struggle to wield meaningful authority. This is the uncomfortable reality of global governance.

Interlocking Questions

Two seemingly independent issues are addressed in this book. First, why do global rulemaking bodies look the way they do? There are many organizations undertaking the fundamentally similar task of crafting international rules, and yet they look very different from each other. How do we account for variation in their organizational design and rulemaking processes? Second, why do all of these organizations seem incapable of operating in a manner that does not engender criticism for accountability shortcomings? It turns out that these questions are inextricably linked. The same forces that shape GGOs also make accountability elusive. Indeed, the architecture of global governance is both a response to and cause of the accountability challenge.

The emphasis on the organizational design and administration of contemporary GGOs differentiates this study from many contemporary treatments of international organizations. Particularly distinctive is the idea that an understanding of accountability for global governance organizations can be broadened through an analysis of their structure. Most discussions of accountability for international organizations emphasize one of two approaches. One, international relations scholars often argue that normative expectations imported from the domestic arena are inappropriate in the transnational context. So they offer a novel or modified definition of "accountable" or "democratic" better suited to the environment. Two, analysts of accountability then offer organizational designs that will better satisfy normative expectations of democratic legitimacy (Keohane and Nye 2003; Grant and Keohane 2005; Benner et al. 2004). Such approaches treat accountability as a problem to be solved. We simply need to build a better mousetrap, so to speak, to get accountable global governance.

Here, the approach to understanding the accountability shortcomings of GGOs comes from the opposite direction. Existing organizations are examined with the goal of determining why these entities fall short of accountability expectations. By understanding variation in the design of GGOs, it is argued, the root imperatives causing the accountability deficits will be uncovered.

The conclusion offered herein, that the alleged failures of accountability spring directly from the inherent conflicts among the demands of global governance, is based on an empirical examination of twenty-five functioning GGOs. This set of organizations has been limited to bodies that develop, promulgate, and implement rules on a global scale. Treating this heterogeneous subpopulation of international organizations, essentially regulatory in character, as a class is a distinctive feature of this study. To some, it may seem implausible to herd specialized agencies of the United Nations into the same corral with nongovernmental standards-generating bodies, but the observed variation in approach to representation, rulemaking, enforcement, and interest group participation does indeed cut across conventional dividing lines.

Methodologically, the study combines quantitative and qualitative approaches. A systematic coding of structural and procedural features of each global rulemaking organization was carried out to build a unique dataset. This information is complemented by qualitative data gathered through interviews, providing a sense of the dynamics within the realm of each organization. In a sense, this study assumes an evolutionary perspective. Inferences are drawn from the collective characteristics of the population that has survived and thrived. It is not argued that all extant global governance organizations are, by definition, optimal. Rather, the goal is to ascertain whether patterns in the distribution of characteristics reveal drivers of organizational design.

The first three chapters lay the foundation. Two theoretical cornerstones are addressed at the outset, the many meanings of accountability and the tension between organizational legitimacy and authority. The empirical analysis is set up in chapter 3, which explains the selection of organizations included in the sample and introduces the key variables. In chapters 4–7, variation in GGO approaches to structure, rulemaking, adherence, and interest group participation are examined to uncover any patterns and determine whether the accountability challenge offers an explanation. In each chapter, analysis of the observations of GGO characteristics allows the identification of general GGO "types," providing a sense of the alternative approaches to balancing competing imperatives, different solutions to the accountability challenge. This analytic approach is carried through to the final chapter, wherein three overarching models of global governance are identified drawing upon the types identified in chapters 4–7. These three models of global governance—*classical* GGOs, *cartel* GGOs, and *symbiotic* GGOs—combine features in different ways to meet variants of the shared accountability challenge. Thus this book reveals similarity where it may not have been apparent and offers an underlying theory to explain variation: GGOs must create and implement rules to satisfy highly varied constituents, keep members (nation-states and/or nongovernmental entities) committed to participation, and do both without the coercive tools associated with the governmental bodies typically charged with such tasks.

It is important to be clear about what this book is not. This is not a replacement for the previous work on the international organizations discussed in these pages. For each individual organization included in this book, there are enlightening studies that dig into their history and relevant policy matters. The goal is not to provide a better understanding of any single organization. Readers who know a lot about one of the twenty-five included organizations are not likely to learn anything new about that single organization. The insight offered here concerns the *entire class* of GGOs. The dynamics of each GGO are undeniably unique in ways that will be glossed over here, just as studies of human behavior obscure the differences that make any generalization inapplicable to some individuals. Experts on, say, the World Intellectual Property Organization or the International Accounting Standards Board may justifiably take issue with the generalizations applied to "their" entities because this analysis attempts to draw comparisons among very different organizations.

Neither is this book an exhaustive digestion and response to the substantial international relations literature regarding international organizations or global governance. Instead, it provides a different theoretical lens through which empirical findings are analyzed, an organizational perspective that is underrepresented in the contemporary literature. Other frameworks of interest are engaged when appropriate but it is not a goal here to substantiate or debunk any one theory. This book complements multiple theoretical approaches to the study of global governance and offers data to test the hypotheses of those who have examined these issues.

Finally, although an explanation for the accountability failures of global governance organizations is offered, the book is neither defeatist nor a rationalization of accountability shortfalls. It offers a realistic assessment of GGOs against a backdrop that accurately reflects the constraints they face. It is a caution in the face of efforts to draw blueprints for more accountable global governance. The undemocratic features of global governance organizations are revealed by the analysis contained herein to be not random attributes but key elements of their strategies for survival and effectiveness. To some extent, in other words, GGOs are unaccountable by necessity. If meeting the demands of effective global governance compromises democratic administration, those demanding more transnational accountability will be disappointed or satisfied only by a very weak incarnation of global governance (Held 2004; McGrew 2002b).

This chapter is divided into three sections. First, contemporary global governance is sketched and a case is made for its significance. Second, the case is made for examining global governance from an organizational perspective. Third, the logic of global governance is explored as a foundation for discussion of the architecture of GGOs.

The Emerging Reality of Global Governance

Protesters may assail GGOs for their perceived failures to consider the interests of the world's citizens, but many academics merely shrug their shoulders. In the world of political science, the principal vice of GGOs is irrelevance (Kerwer 2005). Realists and their kin view international politics as fundamentally about relationships among states. National governments remain the key actors and to the extent that GGOs have any consequence, it is epiphenomenal (Drezner 2007). That is, the outcomes created by GGOs are merely the operationalization of bargains among powerful states (Ikenberry and Kupchan 1990; Mearsheimer 1995; Waltz 1993; Huntington 1973).

There is evidence to support this perspective, including this study of global governance. There are no proclamations of a postnational world to be found in these pages! Still, the state-centric view seems overly reductionist. It assumes that national governments are unitary actors with the time, ability, and desire to create and impose preferred positions across the full spectrum of policy domains. Or, in the alternative, it assumes that the effects of rules generated by global governance organizations are utterly trivial, mere details within broad parameters set by the world's great powers. Both assumptions are misplaced (Keohane and Nye 1974).

One reason for skepticism regarding international organizations is that people often look at the wrong ones. Although there is a natural tendency to fix attention on the United Nations, most global governance is not pursued through a single centralized legislature or bureaucracy. Substantively focused bodies, crafting rules for worldwide application and relying on other actors for implementation, represent the underwater portion of the global governance iceberg. This reality is not surprising; this "functional" approach was envisioned in the interwar era as a workable approach to global federalism even before the United Nations emerged (Mitrany 1966). Sixty years later, the triumph of functional global governance comes into better focus every day. Examples include the following entities:

- the International Accounting Standards Board, a private nonprofit based in London that creates a broad array of accounting standards utilized around the world;
- the World Intellectual Property Organization, a entity with members representing 184 states with responsibility for overseeing multiple international conventions on patents, trademarks, and copyrights; and
- the International Organization for Standardization, an organization that brings together representatives of 161 national standards bodies to oversee and manage processes that generate standards in a wide range of areas from screw threads to petroleum products to corporate social responsibility.

As these examples suggest, global governance is not the sole province of governmental institutions (Dingwerth 2005; Rosenau and Czempiel 1992b; Boli and Thomas 1999; Hassel 2008; Cashore et al. 2007; Bernstein and Cashore 2007; Rhodes 1996; Peters and Pierre 1998). Global rules do emerge from traditional intergovernmental organizations in the form of treaties and conventions, but they also (more commonly in the contemporary context) are promulgated by nongovernmental or quasi-governmental bodies that issues standards and/or recommendations (Held and McGrew 2002; Reinicke 1998; Cutler et al. 1999). And intergovernmental bodies are increasingly collaborating with nongovernmental entities in every phase of governance (Boli and Thomas 1999; Bull et al. 2004; Cutler et al. 1999; Hassel 2008; Borzel and Risse 2005). Any study of global governance that artificially circumscribes the universe of governance organizations on the basis of sector is doomed from the outset to misread and misrepresent the situation.

Taking Global Governance Seriously

The substantive narrowness of many of the most accomplished GGOs may lead to an underestimation of their significance. As suggested by the examples already mentioned, GGOs have made their marks within circumscribed arenas. The implications of their rulemaking activities may not be understood outside the communities that are intensely interested in bank regulation, Internet commerce, maritime safety, and so on. And, as mentioned above, many of the most dynamic global rulemakers are quasi-governmental bodies that combine the participation of states and interest groups or completely nongovernmental organizations using the rulemaking process to promote an industry or push a social agenda.

All in all, this is not the stuff of classical tracts on geopolitics even if the implications of such matters are far-reaching. The number of people with a passionate interest in the work of *all* global rulemaking organizations is limited. So contemporary "global governance" appears to be many disconnected activities; it is not typically experienced as a single phenomenon by one individual or institution. Taken together, however, the activities of global governance organizations can be seen as the early signs of a gradual shift in governance anticipated by functionalists but dismissed by realists and other skeptics (Held and McGrew 2002; Kahler and Lake 2003; Karns and Mingst 2004; Haas 1964). Some critics have been searching for a global state and thus have overlooked the reality that even the current set of GGOs meets two criteria to warrant serious attention. First, the activities of GGOs have notable economic implications for states and market participants. Second, the activities of GGOs increasingly appear to impinge upon the autonomy of national governments (Cooper et al. 2008).

ECONOMIC IMPLICATIONS. One way to validate the significance of GGOs is simply to point at the bottom line. In every substantive sphere in which established GGOs are active, they have the ability to create significant costs for economic actors (Braithwaite and Drahos 2000). Put bluntly, the actions of most global governance organizations are serious business. A few examples illustrate the point:

- The International Civil Aviation Organization (ICAO) sets baseline standards for national aviation safety programs. The *ICAO Safety Management Manual* establishes the parameters of a safety framework that is compliant with the organization's founding convention (ICAO 2006a). At a minimum, this necessarily imposes costs upon airlines and airport authorities to gather and collect data. The substantive recommendations produced by ICAO on issues such as equipment standards and staffing requirements have dramatic cost implications. Even seemingly arcane matters—such as the safe transportation of infectious substances—create burdens for airlines that must handle passengers and cargo in a more resource-consuming fashion (ICAO 2005b).
- The Basel Committee on Banking Supervision, part of the Bank for International Settlements, is best known for generating international standards on capital adequacy for banks. The standards, when implemented by national bank supervisory agencies, require that even the largest financial institutions keep a portion of their assets liquid as a cushion proportionate to their liabilities. These assets cannot be leveraged or used to generate returns consistent with funds that are put "at risk," and thus the consequences for each regulated entity's profitability are profound (Kapstein 1994; Porter 2001; Kerwer 2005). Some analysts of the 2008 financial crisis even pointed a crooked finger at the Basel capital standards (Coy 2008).
- The International Electrotechnical Commission (IEC) generates standards covering a broad spectrum of devices and components. The setting of standards creates significant "network effects" for manufacturers and thus can

be vital to the success of a business. By generating an *international* standard, organizations like the IEC greatly expand the scale of potential business opportunities. Moreover, the establishment of a standard can raise significant barriers to entry for firms that may now face markedly higher production costs or interoperability requirements. Thus the stakes in the setting of standards are quite high.

• Through its program on essential drugs, the World Health Organization (WHO) affects the demand and pricing strategies for various pharmaceuticals—and the terms under which they can be marketed—all over the globe (Irwin and Ombaka 2003). The same organization's "International Health Regulations" set requirements for governmental handling of disease outbreaks, including the impositions of quarantines and other restrictions on travel and trade. The economic consequences of the WHO's assessment of danger due to SARS outbreaks in China and Toronto surprised many and brought home the real financial impact of GGO activities and regulations (BBC 2008).

So it is not difficult to make the case for GGO impact on markets, even without the low-hanging fruit of the World Trade Organization (WTO). One could continue to list examples in areas as diverse as shipping, software design, and accounting. The position set forward by liberal institutionalists—that rules generated by GGOs can shape markets for goods, services, and trade—seems irresistible (Martin and Simmons 1998; Hawkins et al. 2006). GGOs mean business, whether one counts in dollars, euros, yen, or renminbi.

LIMITS ON STATE SOVEREIGNTY/AUTONOMY. For some skeptics, it is a minor concession to admit the financial significance of GGOs. These organizations are more or less meaningless in their eyes precisely because they are merely technical facilitators of economic exchange. That is, the contest for world domination is still waged by states, and GGOs are, at most, tools utilized by states to achieve their goals (e.g., Waltz 1993; Drezner 2007).

This position also resonates. It would be difficult to contend, for example, that any GGOs could be effective if the national governments of the world sought to eliminate them. Indeed, a central point of the analysis here is that in order to maintain authority, GGOs must carefully calibrate their attention to key powerful actors. But do GGOs have the ability to impinge on national autonomy? This seems a reasonable basic litmus test of GGOs "mattering" in purely political terms. Indeed, as a small sample indicates, there are numerous cases that satisfy it:

- The International Atomic Energy Agency (IAEA) is best known for its role as inspector charged with verifying compliance with nonproliferation agreements. But the IAEA also develops safety standards for the world's nuclear power plants. These standards are literally voluntary—and thus impose no burden on nations and the nuclear industries contained therein—but because all other interactions with IAEA require compliance with all standards they are effectively mandatory. This makes the international nuclear standard supreme and almost impossible to ignore. Its requirements are referenced extensively in the regulations of the US Nuclear Regulatory Commission (NRC 2004), for example.
- The Convention on International Trade in Endangered Species (CITES) establishes permitting and documentation requirements for the import and export of endangered species. These requirements, including verification of the species' status in the exporting country, are binding on signatories. The secretariat is regularly updating the species to which standards apply; the result could be unwanted regulation of transactions of previously unaffected species (CITES 2008).
- The Internet Corporation for Assigned Names and Numbers (ICANN) is an unusual entity chartered as a nonprofit corporation in the United States. It governs the domain name assignment and management for the Internet. Among the activities that seem to subordinate national authority, ICANN sets requirements for the practices of Internet registrars, regardless of physical location, and has the ability to delegate responsibility for country-level domain names at its discretion (Mueller 2002).

Consistent with any realist's expectations, the ability of a GGO to impose an undesired requirement upon a national government is inversely proportional to that nation's political power (Gruber 2005; Shaffer 2005; Lake 2007). Thus the standards promulgated by the International Accounting Standards Board (IASB) are likely to be adopted by the government of, say, Thailand (Deloitte 2008). Authorities in Argentina are more likely to comply with the International Labor Organization's new requirements on maritime worker safety (for fear that international shipping companies will avoid their ports of call) if they are ratified.

More powerful states have greater latitude to resist or ignore disliked rules and standards (Lake 2007). In the course of this study, it was observed that IASB would almost certainly not adopt a standard that was objectionable to US regulators, for example (Tamm Hallstrom 2004). But even the most powerful actors—states and firms—do accept some outcomes that clearly are *not* preferred by them. The WTO *does* rule against the United States. The ISO *does* adopt standards that are not preferred by industry. The International Whaling Commission *does* adopt policies hostile to whaling interests and their patron states (Young 1992). The underlying logic of the utility of participation in international organizations does not obscure the reality of particular outcomes.

One could rightly conclude that the powerful members of global governance organizations support the organization because the *net* outcome is positive, even when specific preferences are not met (Hawkins et al. 2006). That is, the existence of an international regime in shipping, for example, is preferable to the lack of such a regime even if one particular rule is not desirable. If the GGO *consistently* behaved in a fashion that upset this calculus, the powerful would cease to abide. This is likely true, but members must determine what course is in their overall interest—not a simple chore. There are innumerable small decisions made within the bureaucracies of GGOs every day. The idea that members are omniscient utility-maximizers, updating the payoff of participation on a daily basis, is misplaced.

The complex fabric woven by the interconnections among multiple GGOs make such calculation extremely difficult. Withdrawing from any single organization without upsetting others is awkward. And it is difficult to imagine how even the most enlightened official would calculate the net costs and benefits of every decision across all organizations. What can be observed are instances of powerful actors reluctantly going along with GGOs. By necessity, latitude is granted to GGOs even if it is not infinite (Hawkins et al. 2006).

Not One World Government but a Network of Multiple Global Governance Organizations

There is no centralized global state, of course, but the population of GGOs is not a completely atomized collection of entities, either. They interact formally and informally on a regular basis (Pattberg 2005; Jacobson 1979). In recent years, their programs are more tied together, creating linkages that begin to weave a web of transnational rules and regulations (Bull et al. 2004; Slaughter 2004a; 2004c; Rosenau and Czempiel 1992a; Zacher and Sutton 1996).

One nexus for GGOs is the agreements that are part of the WTO. Unique among the entities considered here due to its oversight of numerous bilateral and multilateral agreements, the WTO has authority to validate sanctions imposed by one nation upon another. This gives the WTO more independent bite than most GGOs (Keohane and Nye 2002; Barfield 2001; Esty 1998; Woods and Narlikar 2001). Combined with its adjudicatory functions, the WTO sets the terms for trade negotiation and, in effect, shapes the business models of countless firms engaged directly or indirectly in international trade.

GGOs try to use the power of the WTO to bolster their own influence. The World Intellectual Property Organization (WIPO) provides a classic example. WIPO's standards on intellectual property have been incorporated into WTO policies, specifically, the Agreement on Trade-Related Aspects of Intellectual Property Rights (TRIPS), granting them presumptive legitimacy in any trade dispute. This effectively makes WIPO standards on protected intellectual property the global standard.

Like the TRIPS accord, the WTO's Technical Barriers to Trade Agreement accords status to standards produced by GGOs including the International Organization for Standardization (ISO), the International Electrotechnical Commission (IEC), and the International Telecommunication Union (ITU). Although not singled out like WIPO, these bodies meet process requirements established by the WTO. Thus their standards, when adopted by national governments, are presumed to be acceptable technical requirements and not impermissible barriers to trade.

Other collaborations among GGOs have produced rules written and adopted jointly. For example, the International Labor Organization worked with the International Maritime Organization on a maritime labor treaty. The World Wide Web Consortium and the Unicode Consortium both have working groups that are recognized by the ISO, as do other GGOs. These types of linkages are likely to multiply as new technologies and products cross domain barriers.

There is also a connection among the many GGOs that are loosely affiliated with the United Nations (Koenig-Archibugi 2002; Karns and Mingst 2004). Although being part of the UN system has limited administrative consequences for each entity, it does create connections and commonalities (Karns and Mingst 2004). For example, the existence of an international civil service allows individuals to move from organizations to organization. This transfers norms, practices, and expertise between seemingly disconnected entities (Mathiason 2007).

The global governance network is not limited to intergovernmental organizations. Many of the most traditional international organizations collaborate extensively with nonprofit and for-profit nongovernmental bodies (Pattberg 2005a; Bull et al. 2004). In some cases these partnerships are explicit and formalized. In other instances, governmental bodies adopt standards promulgated by nongovernmental entities or rely upon them to provide the market pressure necessary to promote compliance (Higgins and Tamm Hallstrom 2007).

While the coordination among GGOs is a defining feature of global governance, the relationship among GGOs is not always cooperative. The lack of central coordination of global governance sometimes results in direct competition among GGOs. While the notion of government agencies competing for turf is very familiar in the domestic context, the phenomenon can take on a different cast in the realm of global governance. The ISO, for example, faces competition from the IEC and the ITU in staking out leadership on issues that cut across their respective mandates (e.g., Internet-related technologies, digital photography, etc.).

More profoundly, some go head-to-head, offering competing standards and seeking market dominance. And yet such competing GGOs invariably *also cooperate!* This is a distinguishing feature of global governance and receives full treatment in chapter 8. Consider another ISO competitor. ASTM International is a comprehensive standard-setting body offering standards in a wide swath of areas—many also covered by ISO. Both organizations rely upon fees derived from the adoption of their standards and thus their competition is not merely for prominence or prestige but for customers and revenue. Yet even as ASTM challenges ISO dominance in certain areas, the organizations cooperate in many others. In fact, ASTM is, indirectly, a member of ISO. The unusual dynamic of simultaneous coordination and competition also has its roots in the multiple demands facing global governance organizations.

This study provides insight into the dynamics and implications of the relationships described above. It is certainly true that the norms, understandings, and expectations that guide the behavior of participants are crucial elements of global governance networks (Krasner 1982). But the relationships among global rulemaking organizations and their place in a broader governance ecosystem are reflected in and influenced by their architecture. This observation underscores the value of examining GGOs as organizations.

What the Design of Global Governance Organizations Tells Us

The organizational perspective provides a lens through which one can ascertain how and why GGOs are arranged, an important means of understanding the general suspicion of global governance organizations and charges of nonaccountability (Burall and Neligan 2005; Kahler 2004). It allows greater precision in articulating and assessing allegations. Biases in the representational scheme or rulemaking processes that systematically exclude or advantage some actors, for example, are tangible claims to investigate. Although such analysis was central in seminal early work on international organizations (e.g., Jacobson 1979; Cox and Jacobson 1973; Haas 1964), scholarly study of international governance has moved away from the examination of the bureaucracies charged with the task of implementing agreements (Kratochwil and Ruggie 1986).

Contemporary research on global governance generally follows one of two paths: broad, theory-driven discussion or narrower, often policy-focused, examination of one or two organizations. Several fine edited volumes bridge the distance between these approaches by weaving together such work around core concepts like power (Barnett and Duvall 2005), delegation (Hawkins et al. 2006), globalization (Held and McGrew 2002; Nye and Donahue 2000; Kahler and Lake 2003), privatization (Hall and Biersteker 2002; Higgott et al. 2000; Cutler et al. 1999), and networks (Slaughter 2004b; Zacher and Sutton 1996; Jacobson 1979). The underlying relationships among nation-states and their incentives to participate in global governance regimes have been illuminated (Haas 1980; Kratochwil 2001; Keohane 2002; Hawkins et al. 2006). Through the investigation of specific GGOs, the detailed relationships between key parties, the evolution of landmark agreements, and the realities of implementation have been explicated in numerous areas including trade, environmental protection, and financial regulation (Bodansky 1999; Kerwer 2005; Porter 2001; Zacher and Sutton 1996). As the references throughout this book indicate, these studies provide great insight into the dynamics of global governance.

But a gap remains. Fewer steps have been taken to treat empirically global governance organizations as a *class of organizations*, functioning bureaucracies that carry out assigned tasks (Hafner-Burton et al. 2008). Scholars in the administration field have focused on domestic bureaucracies, with only limited attention to the structure and design of transnational bodies. This is understandable. Even among the twenty-five organizations that are the subject of this study, there is tremendous heterogeneity, notwithstanding their shared focus on rulemaking. With each organization operating in a unique policy domain, similarities are easily obscured by the distinctiveness of each entity. Still, as examples of work aimed at overcoming this obstacle demonstrate, this type of integrative study is necessary to build a fuller theory of global governance because it reveals the characteristics and dynamics common to all GGOs (Davies 2002; Karns and Mingst 2004; Barnett and Finnemore 2004; Murphy 1994; Bodansky 1999; Kerwer 2005; Porter 2001; Zacher and Sutton 1996; Hawkins et al. 2006).

The origins and implications of organizational structure are at the center of research in public administration and organizational theory. To such students of bureaucracy, understanding an organization from the inside out is a familiar approach. Of direct relevance to this study, for example, scholars have offered explanations of organizational structure as a response to environmental complexity (Scott 2008; Powell and DiMaggio 1991). And, more specifically, research has pointed to the sources of funding, the rules governing human resources, and the judicial environment as influential factors to explain the design of institutions. The basic logic of such investigations—seeing variation in the structure of organizations as a phenomenon to be investigated—is not limited to one methodological approach or type of organization. Fligstein (1990) and Williamson (1985) offer explanations for variation in the internal structure of firms from a sociological and economic perspective, respectively. Transnational organizations have not been subject to much analysis in this tradition, and they present an opportunity to move beyond the emphasis on domestic government organizations that exists in the administration literature.

The four empirical chapters at the heart of this book build on recent literature as well as earlier scholarship that factored aspects of organizational design into the analysis of global governance (Cox and Jacobson 1973; Davies 2002; Karns and Mingst 2004; Young 1992; Brunsson and Jacobsson 2000; Barnett and Finnemore 2004; Jacobson 1979; Koremenos et al. 2004). Features of organizational design are explored in four key areas that are central in the understanding of bureaucracy and governance: representational structure and administration, rulemaking, adherence (enforcement), and participation of interest groups. In each area, the empirical observations provide a picture of global governance in action and are interpreted through the theoretical lens provided in chapter 2.

Representation and Administration

The manner in which a member participates in an organization is a fundamental political consideration. In the governmental context, democratic systems display multiple approaches to representation, voting, division of power, and so on. Political scientists have shown how variations great (e.g., parliamentary versus presidential systems) and small (e.g., alternative committee rules) can influence substantive outcomes (Lijphart 1999; Linz and Valenzuela 1994; Shepsle and Weingast 1987). The design of representation for international organizations presents distinctive considerations. For example, a representational scheme that accords great weight to the concept of sovereignty would grant each nation an equal vote, but this would result in power out of proportion with population and, perhaps more critically, realistic accounts of national power and prestige. The architecture of each global governance organization reflects a consideration of such unavoidable dilemmas. Complicating matters, each structural choice is one of myriad determinations; examining any one in isolation invites misinterpretation.

In chapter 4, the analysis focuses on the channeling of representation (top-down versus bottom-up), the allocation of influence (both in terms of voting rights and the locus of decisionmaking), and the relationship between the representative bodies and the full-time bureaucracy. Insights are often gained from combinations of features that are prevalent. For example, it is observed that representational structures granting countries equal voting strength are typically paired with designs that place substantive responsibility in subbodies with unrepresentative composition. The existence of such structural patterns thus reveals the opposing demands that GGOs must satisfy.

It is critical also to look beyond the representational aspect of global governance to examine the often neglected bureaucratic dimension. Public administration scholarship has demonstrated that variation in bureaucratic structure can affect the substance and implementation of public policy (e.g., Wilson 1989; Horn 1995). Variation in the administrative structure of the twenty-five global rulemaking organizations studied here certainly has consequences but the distinctiveness of each presents a challenge. Fundamental issues, including scale of the bureaucracy and its role in the organization, were emphasized. To cite one specific insight offered in these pages, in many GGOs the bureaucracy serves primarily to support members' direct engagement in the rulemaking process. In other organizations, the professional staff plays a more traditional role, carrying out functions delegated by the representative bodies.

Again, clear patterns in the distribution of characteristics suggest different approaches to the accountability challenge of global governance (which will be explicated in the next chapter). Classifying GGOs based on the clustering of attributes renders discussion of such patterns easier. This descriptive exercise, identification of types through latent class analysis, is part of each chapter and helps link the empirical observations with the theoretical core. In chapter 4, GGOs are said to have a structure that is either *traditional* or *hybrid* in type. The traditional-structure type includes a representational and administrative design reminiscent of a domestic government, with an assembly made up of all members overseeing a permanent bureaucracy. The hybrid-structure type features representation based on substantive interests, with no "general assembly" of all members, and a more active role for members in the rulemaking process.

Rulemaking

The common function of the organizations included in this study is the generation and implementation of rules. Public administration scholars have been increasingly interested in the process by which rules are crafted. Studies have demonstrated that variations in the rulemaking process influence the content of rules (Kerwin 2003). It has been debated, for example, whether novel approaches to rulemaking that facilitate negotiation between government agencies and affected industries grant greater influence to interested parties (Coglianese 1997; Freeman and Langbein 2000; Langbein 2002; Langbein and Kerwin 2000).

The variety of approaches to rulemaking associated with GGOs includes the traditional, bureaucratically driven processes associated with government agencies and contemporary, participatory models that place rulemaking responsibility in the hands of interested constituencies. This analysis focuses on the degree of formality of the process (i.e., the procedural latitude available to the GGO), the nature of the rule-approval process (including the content of decisions and the standards for approval of new rules), and the accessibility of the process to interested constituencies. Once again, the most interesting findings concern the combination of features and the implications regarding the dynamics of global governance. It is observed that decisionmaking by consensus is a rather undemocratic practice that helps organizations overcome the potentially paralyzing effects of one-country / one-vote apportionment of influence. This constitutes a significant departure from previous work citing consensus as a normatively appealing paragon of democraticness (Cronin and Hurd 2008).

Once again, patterns in the observations were analyzed to define two general approaches to rulemaking. Each organization is characterized as either *forum* or *club* rulemaking type. *Club* rulemaking is a more exclusive approach that keeps decisionmaking in relatively few hands. *Forum* rulemaking is the approach familiar to students of rulemaking in most domestic governance systems, more rigid in its assignment of roles and expectations.

Adherence

The limitations of traditional approaches to enforcement have been documented. Coercive, state-based enforcement regimes have been found to be expensive, inconsistent, and subject to political manipulation (Scholz 1991; Shipan 2004; Scholz 1986; Stigler 1970). In recent years, attention has turned to alternative approaches, frequently those that emphasize market mechanisms (Freeman and Kolstad 2007). Understanding the full range of tools available to induce compliance is critical in the study of global governance because *all* these approaches are associated with implementation of GGO rules.

The term "adherence" is used because GGOs are distinguished by their lack of enforcement tools. Responsibility for implementation is almost entirely delegated by GGOs to both state and nonstate actors. Global governance organizations must therefore accommodate the traditional and market-based adherence strategies, an important consideration in explaining observed patterns. In this area, apparent differences in organizational design may be misleading. Seemingly great disparities are less consequential than is typically concluded. For example, intergovernmental organizations generally have international treaties behind their rules while nongovernmental rulemakers have no claim to the mantle of international law. But almost all treaties allow signatory nations to opt out of disliked provisions and, perhaps more problematically, do not formally sanction members that do not vigorously enforce international rules. Examining the design of adherence systems in practice reveals that formal inducements are not the prime drivers of rule implementation. Even when GGOs possess formal tools to compel vigorous enforcement, the market mechanisms inducing implementation seem more important. This is revealed by considering the relationship between the design of the adherence regime (including the nature of the entities charged with implementation, the tools at their disposal, and the mechanisms available to motivate their performance) and other aspects of the GGO design, particularly the mechanisms in place to ensure the satisfaction of market participants who will ascribe value—or not—to the adoption of international rules.

Two adherence types, *conventional* or *composite,* are differentiated on the basis of patterns observed in the agents and tools relied upon by GGOs to implement rules. From the perspective of the GGO, however, the *conventional*-adherence approach, which involves formal state-based regulatory mechanisms, is not dramatically different from the *composite* approach that relies predominantly on markets. Moreover, a key counterintuitive finding is that rules produced by nongovernmental GGOs are often adopted and implemented by governmental entities.

Interest Group Participation

The participation of interest groups is a fundamental issue in the study of political systems. Interest groups are key actors—representing and influencing the views of citizens, participating in the electoral process, collecting and disseminating information, and promoting public policies. Given the consequences of the rules and regulations generated by GGOs for multiple constituencies, the mobilization and effectiveness of formal interest-based organizations is likely a significant variable in GGO decisionmaking processes.

Comparative examination of domestic interest group activity has demonstrated that structure of interest group participation in the policymaking process varies quite a bit across national contexts with significant consequences (Ehrmann 1958; Thomas 1993). This variation appears to be directly related to the structure of political systems. When government authority is widely distributed and accessible at multiple points, for example, interest group power seems to resist concentration as well (Pross in Thomas 1993, 219; Cawson 1985). Limiting access to sanctioned associations, on the other hand, naturally leads to concentration of interest group authority.

This chapter moves beyond the scope of the internal structure of the global governance organizations in an effort to capture the nature of interest participation in GGO activities. Empirical observations of the mobilization and participation of interests groups in GGO rulemaking suggest that the two general models employed by political scientists to capture interest group participation in politics, *pluralism* and *corporatism*, are often inapplicable to the GGO ecosystem. The idea of *global concertation* is introduced to describe the common dynamic: interested parties are integrated into the rulemaking process as individual firms, not mediated by formal interest-based organizations.

Overall, the design of global governance organizations tells us about the dynamics of international rulemaking. Previous research on international bureaucracy is firmly in the rationalist tradition, to use Scott's well-known differentiation of "rational, natural and open" perspectives on organizations (Scott 1992). Administration of international organizations is implicitly understood as a conscious design, crafted in response to a set of logistical requirements. The careful examination of structure, rulemaking process, adherence, and interest participation in these pages jibes with more recent analysis showing the appropriateness of natural and open theoretical frameworks. The design of global rulemaking organizations, and the systems of which these organizations are a part, are adaptive and responsive to shifting environmental challenges and constraints.

The analysis presented here is based primarily upon a dataset composed of more than 140 variables per organization. The variables were chosen to provide a meaningful basis for discussion of variation in the four areas of analysis. The survey emphasized formal structural features of the organizations but included informal elements that provided a better picture. For example, the data collected with respect to structure included the form of representation, the allocation of voting power, the relationship between representative bodies and management, the number of employees, sources of funding, annual budgets, and so on. However, information was also collected on the identity of nations selected for critical subgroups within organizations and the background of the individuals participating in rulemaking (as a means of evaluating the substance of decisionmaking). Similarly, the survey captured formal elements of the rulemaking process, including requirements for approval of new rules, the organizational locus of final approval, and the decision rules, but records of *actual* rulemaking offered important information regarding organizational practice. Accommodating the broad range of institutional arrangements in a single research instrument was a critical challenge. Capturing all of the organizations using a single instrument required some simplification.

Information captured in the survey was complemented by interviews with GGO staff, members, and representatives of groups that interact with GGOs (appendix A). This qualitative data added considerably to the understanding of global governance provided through analysis of survey data. The dynamics of each organization are not captured in the rules and, in some cases, the rules are only loosely connected to the way "things get done."

In the concluding chapter, three overarching models of global governance are defined by drawing together the cluster analysis in each of the four areas. Just as correlations among characteristics were investigated and explored to identify structural, rulemaking, and adherence "types" that proved useful in drawing the connection between organizational design and accountability, the distribution of these types was examined in a search for patterns. Although three distinctive models of global governance are defined, this book argues that a singular logic guides the design and administration of global rulemaking organizations. Key interests must be satisfied with minimum deviation from normative expectations. The design of each GGO represents a sustainable expression of this logic under different environmental conditions. By unraveling their design, this fundamentally different approach to global governance shows that these solutions are imperfect (hence the persistent elusiveness of accountability) because GGOs are in an impossible position, unable to completely satisfy two sets of competing demands.

The Logic of Global Governance

Unlike individuals born into an existing governmental regime, members must make an affirmative decision to join and support a GGO. Why would an actor—government, firm, interest group—participate in, support, and obey a global governance organization? Most answers trace back to the actor's self-interest, but there are several ways to conceptualize this fundamental notion (Higgott et al. 2000; Nye and Donahue 2000; Sohn 2005; Koremenos et al. 2004; Cooper et al. 2008; Hawkins et al. 2006). One's approach is inextricably linked with an understanding of the international arena generally.

Many theoretical approaches start with the idea that the supranational context is essentially anarchic, but this can mean different things, from a lack of order to a lack of government (Axelrod and Keohane 1985; Lake 2007). Depending upon one's view, the propensity toward cooperation among states will vary. But one point of agreement is key for this project: all theories contend that cooperation must bring some benefit to the actors (Keohane 1983). This is most essential in exploring the demands of accountability even if, from such a starting point, students of international relations depart in different directions.

Realists see the resulting dynamic as a struggle among states for security and self-interest. Any resulting order reflects the hierarchy of power among states. International organizations are possible, of course, but they represent the outcomes of this ongoing contest, bureaucratic manifestations of the hierarchy. The arguments in this book are consistent with this view up to a point; GGOs must balance other considerations in their construction. The notion that international organizations, once created, have the ability to shape subsequent behavior or constrain states is *not* consistent with the realist approach.

Many others see greater variety in the objectives and motivations of states as actors in the international arena. Institutionalists of different stripes see participation in international organizations as a reflection of the rewards of cooperation among nations. This has been conceptualized as a solution to the "prisoner's dilemma" faced by nations in anarchic conditions (Axelrod and Keohane 1985). Or it might be seen as a means of facilitating cooperation by making commitments more credible, creating an infrastructure for monitoring and dissemination of information, and generally reducing transaction costs (Chayes and Chayes 1995; Keohane 2002; Abbott and Snidal 2000; Hawkins et al. 2006). There is no implication that such arrangements erase the disparate power of nations; international organizations certainly can perpetuate such inequity (Lake 2007).

There are those who see international organizations moving further from the anarchic condition. Such perspectives focus on the requirements of organizations created to pursue collective goods (Wendt 1999). To build a system of commitment and enforcement that makes the organizations something more than bureaucratic manifestations of the power distribution, intergovernmental organizations must "check power politics" (Karns and Mingst 2004). This resonates with the functionalist viewpoint, which emphasizes the potential of international organizations to "bring [nations] actively together" to address specific issues that transcend national borders.

In a way, this view accommodates Marxist interpretations that see the capitalist demands of the international market as drivers of transnational cooperation rather than of state interests (Murphy 2002).

The focus on rulemaking organizations—which excludes entities concerned with peace and security—narrows the gulf between theoretical perspectives. In the judgment of an organization considering membership in or support for a global regulatory body—or, more accurately, those making decisions on the organization's behalf—participation must produce some benefit (whether you are a realist or an institutionalist). The expected tolerance for the interests of other (less powerful) members would certainly vary depending upon one's model of international relations. The liberal perspective seems to provide more insight into the observations in this study inasmuch as members seem to place value on sustaining the organizations such that they are willing to bear costs in the form of concessions to weaker players (Barnett and Finnemore 1999). The emergence of varieties of nongovernmental and quasi-governmental governance organizations provides interesting examples of the power of functionalist and constructivist perspectives. State concerns are never absent, but such organizations and the regimes around them do depend upon and promote other transnational interests. To be clear, these are often superseded by national considerations, but these approaches clearly offer an explanation for the observed patterns.

Constructivist analyses of international organizations are also consistent with this study's emphasis on the importance of normative demands in shaping institutional design. Global governance organizations operate in contexts where, depending on the kinds of activities they undertake, they are exposed to varying normative claims about accountability.

With respect to most of the organizations discussed here, the benefits derived from the maintenance of a global framework and set of shared rules are economic (Braithwaite and Drahos 2000). Analysis of firms' behavior in the marketplace makes the benefits of common rules clear. Companies would like to see a single standard emerge for, say, compact discs because of the formidable network effects that would increase sales. With a single CD format, a disc manufacturer would expect greater sales and lower costs (because only one format would have to be supported). The costs of inputs would be lower because the manufacturers of blank CDs would be able to spread costs over all purchasers and the economies of scale would be maximized. Similarly, manufacturers of CD players benefit from the huge inventory of CDs that will work with any player. Consumers are more likely to buy players and discs because they do not have to worry about the compatibility of a CD with their current (or future) player, thus eroding a potential barrier to purchase. To see the inefficiencies of a market in which a standard has *not* emerged, look no further than the modest adoption of high-definition DVDs in the face of two competing standards.

Manufacturers of any number of products—from bicycle parts to oil pipelines—will thus be very eager to see the most widely adopted standard emerge. This means their products can be sold in any of those places. This logic carries over to financial products and services. The desirability of global accounting or capital standards is driven by the desires of capital market participants. Those seeking capital prefer a single standard so they do not have to present the same information in multiple formats in order to reach investors around the world. Investors want to make investments in multiple markets without the uncertainty associated with unfamiliar rules. Does a balance sheet in Brazil mean the same as a balance sheet in Germany? Do they treat accounts receivable consistently? Answering such questions is *much* easier in a world with global standards and thus the investment opportunities multiply. Moreover, firms hungry for capital can now look around the world and reassure potential investors that their financial statements mean the same thing as those back home.

Governments obviously have an interest in the economic well-being of their states. But the logic of international organization is not merely about markets and money. Ensuring the health and safety of the world's people is easier with the creation and adoption of global rules. The World Health Organization (WHO), for example, defines the characteristics of communicable diseases. This facilitates cooperation; it means that an individual attempting to travel from one country to another can be flagged as, say, a SARS carrier, and there is limited dispute about its meaning. With shared standards for the safe operation of oceangoing vessels, ports can comfortably allow ships to enter their waters with reduced fears of disastrous spills or accidents.

When Is a Global Rule Preferable to No Rule?

If the promulgation of international rules and standards were as wonderful as the preceding paragraphs suggest, one would wonder why there are not more global governance organizations, each one churning out wealth-maximizing, safety-enhancing rules to the delight of every concerned party. The answer, of course, is that while a shared standard or common regulation *may be* beneficial, it does not *have to be.* All rules are not created equal.

Investigating the nonemergence of rules and institutions that create rules is as challenging as it is important (Keohane 2002). We are not only looking for dogs that didn't bark, we are trying to ascertain *why* they didn't bark. From most theoretical vantage points, any answer is found in a consideration of each potential organization member. For every actor, a calculation is required regarding the development and acceptance of new international organizations that generate global rules. One might reduce this question to the very straightforward: are we better off with this rule than without it?

The realist would likely point out that a hegemon has no need for such an entity because its dominance renders the rules it promulgates global standards. This judgment might be tempered if participation in the organization offered advantages in implementation or enforcement. The legitimacy bestowed upon a rule generated by a global governance organization may reduce the costs of implementation significantly (Suchman 1995).

A potential member uncertain as to the outcome of the rulemaking process would be wary of any international organization. It might be nice to have a standard for high-definition DVDs but if that standard is the one patented by my competitors I'd just as soon maintain the status quo, thank you! While it would be lovely to adopt universal accounting standards, if the chosen standards make the companies in my country look very poor relative to those in other nations, we'll just stick with our way of doing things. While we're all for enhanced public safety, if the new global health rules make it difficult for us to export our products, we will object strongly.

There are very few, if any, truly neutral rules—rules that affect all parties equally—so there will inevitably be some unhappy actors in every sphere of global governance. Still, the convergence of interests required to build an international regime, or even an organization, need not be absolute. Members may continue to support the GGO and even abide by rules they do not prefer because they make the calculation that the *net benefit* of a global regime is significant enough to warrant acceptance of a specific undesirable rule. This resolves the problem if *more often than not* the rules generated by GGO are desirable.

Can that be guaranteed? And, more to the point, can that be guaranteed for *all participants* even when the interests of the many different actors are divergent? The answer is, quite simply, no. The net benefits of global governance cannot be guaranteed . . . at least not to everyone. This begs the question, who should the GGO try to keep happy? The answer traces back to the logic of global governance: parties adopt and abide by global rules because they benefit from so doing. But those benefits, like the costs, are not distributed evenly, nor need they be. Consider one of the examples:

Smaller nations may gain more from globalization of accounting standards than large, wealthy nations. Consider that the companies in the smaller nations have a very small pool of domestic capital and thus opening doors to American investors has great value. Indeed, many nations simply adopt American GAAP accounting standards (as a realist might expect). From the American perspective, the marginal gain achieved by ceding authority to a global accounting standards body seems relatively modest because the domestic market is already pretty rich with sources of capital and opportunities to invest (or, at least, it was). American accounting standards are utilized so widely that most global investors already understand them. The fact that there is a vibrant international accounting standards organization, and the United States is an active participant, has important implications.

First, less-powerful members accept the disproportionate influence of Americans (and EU representatives) because they have much more to lose by walking away from a global regime than accepting a nonpreferred rule. Second, the attractiveness of a global regime—even to less powerful actors—is greatly reduced by the nonparticipation of the "more important" actors. Third, this dynamic is recognized, at least implicitly, by all actors such that the disproportionate influence of the powerful players is accepted. Fourth, the maintenance of international rules under these conditions is of sufficient value to keep those powerful players at the table.

It is vital to recognize that these observations explain the participation of the less powerful *even on unequal terms.* Why adhere to global accounting standards if these standards are different than those employed by investors in the wealthiest markets? Why bother adopting a technical standard if consumers in the richest countries do not purchase products consistent with this standard? Why follow global health guidelines if in most attractive destinations these standards are not given any weight in making immigration or importation decisions? There are no compelling answers to these questions. Thus, more powerful countries not only have the most power to walk away from international organizations; the harm to other members of the GGO (and the organization itself) if these members do walk away is also the greatest. The departure of key members dramatically erodes the incentives of all actors (regardless of their level of influence) to participate and follow the GGO rules.

An important aside is required. It is easy to imagine that the "powerful actor" is always the United States of America. This is not true. First, there are other significant nations with great influence particularly in some GGO spheres (e.g., EU countries, Japan, China). Second, there are unique dynamics in some arenas that lead to different alignments. In shipping, for example, the leading nations in terms of vessel registries are Venezuela, Liberia, and Greece. As a result, ensuring that these countries are on board with any new rule is vital. Third, the situation is dynamic. The agreement of the United States is less important than it once was and is likely of declining centrality. Finally, while it is convenient to speak of nation-states, many GGOs are not organized around governmental members. The World Wide Web Consortium (W3C), for example, has corporate members, but the logic still fits. Keeping Microsoft satisfied with the work of the W3C is vital to maintaining its authority and credibility as a rulemaker.

No GGO can make everyone happy, and the organization that strives to do so is likely to disappear. For their own survival and effectiveness, global rulemakers must satisfy (in net terms) the most important actors. Or, at a minimum, the GGO has to ensure that whatever it does, the crucial actors are not worse off than they would be in the absence of the GGO. That is, the GGO cannot create conditions inferior to the status quo for key actors. To do so would risk the complete unraveling of the organization. Alas, clearing this bar is necessary but not sufficient to avoid accountability pitfalls.

Plan of the Book

The initial chapters lay the foundation both theoretically and empirically. Chapter 2 develops the theoretical lens through which the empirical findings are interpreted. First, the idea of accountability is deconstructed. There are actually five different conceptions of accountability to be disentangled. Second, the idea introduced in this chapter, that the demands of legitimacy, normative and pragmatic, can be in conflict, is expanded. The case is also made for a switch in the language of legitimacy, allowing that authority can be illegitimate, as is the case in common usage.

The third chapter lays the groundwork for the discussion of the empirical research. The population of global governance organizations is introduced by culling global rulemakers from the population of all organizations. This exercise not only identifies the research subjects, it calls attention to the implicit classification scheme that categorizes organizations on the basis of characteristics that are assumed to be most fundamental. In the process, our understanding of GGO distinctiveness is sharpened. The third chapter also introduces the five "core characteristics" of global governance organizations—sector, rule type, funding, membership, and technicality—that were used in case selection and the analysis of gathered data.

Each of the subsequent four chapters is devoted to a different facet of GGO design—structure, rulemaking process, adherence (a term used in place of the more typical enforcement), and interest group participation. These empirical chapters have the same internal structure. Key areas of variation are identified, and the alternatives in each area are laid out. The data is then examined in a search for patterns across the sample of GGOs. Explanations for the observed patterns are sought first in the "core characteristics" (identified in chap. 3) of each GGO. In each of the four empirical chapters, GGO types are identified based on an analysis of the patterns in variation (if they exist) and the clustering of characteristics across GGOs.

Chapter 8 delves into the complex relationship among global governance organizations with an emphasis on the distinctive dynamics of simultaneous coordination and competition. The concluding chapter 9 first draws together the empirical analysis, identifying three overarching models of global governance—*cartel, classical,* and *symbiotic*—based on organizational profiles created using the types identified in chapters 4–7. The tension among the competing demands of global governance is managed differently under each model.

Finally, the concluding analysis returns the reader to the issues identified at the outset of this chapter. Unlike many analyses of accountability and global governance, this book offers an explanation for the structures and processes adopted by GGOs that create accountability deficits. Each of the three models represents a different solution to the global governance puzzle, with distinctive strengths and weaknesses. *Classical* GGOs lean in the direction of responsibility-type accountability, meeting normative expectations imported from the domestic government context. These organizations sacrifice responsiveness, however, and risk alienating powerful members. *Cartel* GGOs represent a rare breed that can flaunt democratic conventions and maintain authority nonetheless because of the unique coercive tools at their disposal. It is posited that the third model, *symbiotic* GGOs, enjoys an evolutionary advantage by leaning toward responsiveness rather than responsibility-type accountability. *Symbiotic* GGOs seem less burdened by unattainable normative legitimacy expectations, reflecting a mistaken belief that these organizations are less public than others because they are less governmental, a distinction that will be revisited in the conclusion. In essence, these organizations trade fidelity to democratic norms for greater authority. By asking *why* global governance organizations are unaccountable instead of trying to fix them, this dynamic comes into relief.

Accountability and Legitimacy-Authority Tension in Global Governance

E ven the cleverest organizational design cannot mask the compromises required to make global governance work. Dissatisfaction is inevitable. Some members of the organization will object to the inequity of influence, the blatant disparity that grants a select few de facto veto power and disproportionate influence in the rulemaking process. Others, on the other hand, will chafe at the ability of weak members to impede progress on key issues because of objections in unrelated areas. Moreover, there are many constituencies—businesses, civil society groups, international organizations—harboring deep concerns regarding global rules that will complain that they are excluded from global rulemaking bodies and unrepresented in deliberations.

The disparate shortcomings are all branded failures of "accountability," a word offering a tent broad enough to accommodate the divergent demands of myriad GGO constituencies. Accountability functions as a catchall complaint because it is a remarkably plastic concept. It can be used to convey a range of standards against which organizations are judged (Mashaw 2006). An accountable organization might be characterized as transparent, revealing its behavior and the consequences thereof to the world. But an accountable organization might also be spoken of as one that is punished for poor performance or misbehavior. Or an accountable organization might be subject to regular inspection and performance review. Notwithstanding this murkiness, scholars and critics of global governance have persistently focused on accountability because it is a matter of fundamental importance. It is a gateway to core matters, including the very legitimacy of the organization in question. An unaccountable government is seldom, if ever, thought to be legitimate (Held and Koenig-Archibugi 2004; Woods 2003).

Indeed, critics of international organizations routinely question their legitimacy, pointing to the lack of elections, undue process, inequality of influence, and so on (e.g., Held 1999; Held and Koenig-Archibugi 2004; Zurn 2004). Overcoming such legitimacy problems is necessary for global governance organizations, it is argued, because it is necessary to secure authority (Beisheim and Dingwerth 2008; Hurd 1999; Grant and Keohane 2005b; Buchanan and Keohane 2006; Esty 2006). Organizational authority is the ultimate goal: the ability to promulgate rules that are implemented and followed. And so the critique that GGOs lack accountability is more than cosmetic; it speaks to the sustainability of their power.

Scholars and critics operate on the unstated assumption that GGOs can meet two very different sets of requirements for building and maintaining authority: the requirements of normative legitimacy and the interest-based demands of the governed. As GGOs endeavor to meet both the normative and practical expectations, however, it is apparent that these imperatives are sometimes in conflict. Global rulemakers sometimes cannot satisfy the interests of participants without violating norms of democratic governance.

Some would describe the tension between normative expectations and pragmatic considerations as a clash between multiple forms of legitimacy. Notions of legitimacy rooted in moral judgments regarding the proper assignment of power (*normative* legitimacy) are running into justifications of obedience based on assessments of interest-satisfaction (*pragmatic* legitimacy). In this chapter, an alternative language is suggested that pulls apart the normative and pragmatic notions of legitimacy in a fashion more consistent with popular discourse. Regardless of the vocabulary employed, however, the essential problem is the same: the logic of global governance described in the previous chapter puts GGOs in an awkward position betwixt normative expectations and practical interest-based demands. Satisfying the latter will, at times, require violations of the former, and vice versa (Risse 2004). This not only breeds disappointment among governments, interest groups, NGOs and other concerned parties, it imperils each organization by jeopardizing the basis of authority.

The accountability shortcomings thus are the expression of near-inevitable failure of global governance organizations to digest this brew of incompatible expectations; it is the way we "experience" the struggle for legitimacy in global governance. Organizations that compromise principles to maintain the support of key members are not accountable. But GGOs that lean the other way, maintaining their fidelity to principle in the name of normative legitimacy while infuriating key constituencies, are not accountable either.

This chapter serves as the foundation for the empirical investigation, establishing the theoretical prism through which observations are interpreted. The variations in the structure, rulemaking process and adherence regimes of the twenty-five GGOs studied can be understood as responses to the accountability challenge and legitimacy-authority tension described here. Thus the empirical component provides an opportunity to assess the accuracy of the dynamic hypothesized in this chapter.

The theoretical foundation is laid in three sections. First, the concept of accountability receives special attention. An inventory of accountability concepts is offered, grouped into five broad categories: *transparency, liability, controllability, responsibility* and *responsiveness* (Koppell 2005). The categories are broad, and are not mutually exclusive; organizations can be accountable in multiple senses at the same time. It is argued, however, that there is a particular tension between *responsibility* and *responsiveness.* In this sense, the seeds of the GGOs' accountability shortcomings lie in the nature of the concept itself; the many meanings of the word imply a set of contradictory imperatives.

The second section focuses directly on the concepts of legitimacy and authority for which accountability is pivotal. The bases of organizational legitimacy and authority are examined with particular emphasis on disentangling their normative and pragmatic bases. It is argued that the disparate notions of accountability specified in the first section map quite naturally onto the concepts of legitimacy and authority. The abstract concepts of legitimacy and authority are then translated into the concrete demands confronted by GGOs. The conditions under which these demands may conflict are specified. Finally, the conclusion emphasizes the distinctiveness of the challenge faced by global governance organizations. It is important to be clear why the clash of accountability, legitimacy and authority expectations is particularly vexing for this set of organizations.

Five Concepts of Accountability

Bovens, Schillemans and 't Hart have made the astute observation that accountability has two broad meanings that seem to reflect linguistic and cultural differences (Bovens et al. 2008). Among Europeans, accountability generally refers to the mechanisms by which social control over bureaucracy is exerted. In the American context, however, accountability is used more normatively. It is a virtue which organizations are said to possess or lack.

The international relations literature has generally employed the European conception with respect to global governance organizations (Grant and Keohane 2005b; Benner et al. 2004; Keohane and Nye 2003). Discussions focus on the effectiveness of various accountability *mechanisms*—electoral, market-based, hierarchical oversight, reputational, legal—in the transnational governance context (Held and Koenig-Archibugi 2004). The appropriate accountability virtue—the sense in which GGOs ought to be accountable—has mostly been approached in negative terms. It has been pointed out, for example, that electoral accountability for international organizations is impractical and thus inappropriate (Dahl 1999; Keohane and Nye 2003). Relying on the awkwardness of certain accountability *mechanisms* to determine which accountability *virtue* is desirable seems counterintuitive.

Developing an affirmative notion of the accountability virtues appropriate for global governance organizations requires an inventory of accountability concepts. The many meanings of accountability as a virtue can be grouped into five broad categories: *transparency, liability, controllability, responsibility* and *responsiveness* (Koppell 2005). The categories are broad, and they are not mutually exclusive. Organizations may be accountable in more than one sense. Indeed, the first two notions of accountability (*transparency* and *liability*) can be thought of as foundations, concepts that underpin accountability in all its manifestations. The three substantive conceptions of accountability sketched below—*controllability, responsibility,* and *responsiveness*—can be at odds, however.

The idea of tension within accountability may seem peculiar but it reflects a fundamental challenge of public administration (Gormley and Balla 2008). As the five conceptions of accountability are described, it will become clear that maximizing all virtues simultaneously is not possible. For GGOs, the greatest tension is between responsibility and responsiveness. This is a reflection of the logic of global governance described earlier in this chapter. The connection between accountability and legitimacy is intro-

TABLE 2.1 **Five Conceptions of Accountability**

Conception of Accountability	Key Determination
Transparency	Did the organization reveal the facts of its performance?
Liability	Did the organization face consequences for its performance?
Controllability	Did the organization do what the principal ordered?
Responsibility	Did the organization follow the rules?
Responsiveness	Did the organization fulfill expectations?

duced following the description of different notions of accountability, and investigated fully in the next chapter.

Transparency

"Transparency" is the literal value of accountability, the idea that an accountable bureaucrat and organization must explain, or account for, its actions. An accountable organization cannot obfuscate its mistakes to avoid scrutiny. Transparency is most important as an instrument for assessing organizational performance, a key requirement for all other dimensions of accountability (Benner et al. 2004). Thus transparency is critical for its instrumental value but belief in the openness of government to regular inspection is so firmly ingrained in our collective consciousness that transparency has innate value, particularly in a democratic society (Grigorescu 2007; Florini 2003; March and Olsen 1995).

In practice, transparency requires that accountable individuals and organizations are reviewed and questioned regularly. Alleged wrongdoing or perceived failure must be investigated and explained. A transparent public organization grants access to the public, the press, interest groups and other parties interested in an organization's activities. In the American context, transparency has been institutionalized in the form of Freedom of Information requirements, sunshine laws and other regulations that open up the governmental process to review. In the international context, there is no similar body of administrative law prescribing transparency requirements but the general expectations follow the same outline (Grigorescu 2003; Grigorescu 2007). Private-sector organizations are subject to similar requirements, especially those that are publicly traded or issue securities. Transparency here requires presentation of truthful information to stockholders, creditors, analysts, customers and regulators in required reports, prospectuses and filings.

Liability

This conception attaches culpability to transparency. In this view, individuals and organizations must face consequences for performance, punishment for malfeasance and reward for success. The liability dimension of accountability, although seemingly alien in the public sector, is quite familiar with respect to elected officials. Elected representatives are said to be accountable because they can be "punished" by removal from office at the hands of voters (Goodin 2000). Bureaucrats and judges are sometimes said to be unaccountable. Obviously this charge is applicable to GGOs as well.

Liability for unelected persons or organizations can involve alternative forms of punishment. In the public and the private sectors, bureaucrats are criminally liable for stealing funds, misappropriating resources, or abuse of authority. Organizations too can be held criminally liable for illegal activities. Witness the indictment and plea bargain of the Arthur Andersen accounting firm for its actions related to Enron. Negative consequences do not have to involve criminal penalties to fulfill the liability vision. Poor performance evaluations with consequent impact on compensation are consistent with this dimension of accountability. This also applies to organizations. For example, some education reforms require that schools failing to meet performance standards should face budget cuts (Scales 1999).

Remunerating managers based on their individual or organizational performance is consistent with the liability vision of accountability. This is, of course, most familiar in the private sector. Employees in a host of jobs receive bonuses tied to their performance. Many employees receive compensation based on performance (e.g., sales personnel that are compensated on a commission system). This approach has been imported into the public sector. Some government agencies provide cash bonuses to employees that are cited for outstanding performance. New York City school superintendents, for example, are now eligible for bonuses (NYC Dept of Education 2002). Even more expansively, a provision of the 1996 welfare reform law in the United States granted twenty million dollars to the five states most effective in reducing the number of children born to unwed mothers (Healy 1999).

The animating principle of liability as an element of accountability is that mere revelation of wrongdoing or poor performance is insufficient. Consequences must be attached to performance in the form of professional rewards or setbacks, added or diminished budget authority, increased or diminished discretion, reduced or increased monitoring.

Controllability

Three substantive dimensions of accountability are built upon the foundation of *transparency* and *liability*. The dominant concept of accountability revolves around *control*.

If X can induce the behavior of Y, it is said that X controls Y—and that Y is accountable to X. Although few relationships between bureaucratic principals and agents are so straightforward, this understanding is the starting point for many analyses of organizational accountability. The plausibility of "bureaucratic control" has been the subject of debate from the early days of public administration (Barnard 1938; Selznick 1957). Wilson (1887) and Goodnow (1900) offered the normative ideal of a politics / administration dichotomy. In their vision, elected officials should reach consensus on public policy objectives and rely upon bureaucrats to implement their chosen policies.

Consistent with this conception, Herman Finer, in a seminal dialogue with Carl Friedrich, laid out the case for indirect popular control of government bureaucracies as the critical element of accountability. He argued that government bureaucracies should carry out the will of the people as expressed through their elected representatives. An accountable government, according to Finer, is one in which the people possess "the authority and power to exercise an effect upon the course which the latter are to pursue, the power to exact obedience to orders" (Finer 1940). Thus the accountability of an organization depends on the answer to this key question: Did the organization do what its principal commanded?

The contemporary public administration literature reflects a more nuanced understanding of *controllability*. Romzek, for example, differentiates four "accountability relationships," eschewing dichotomous outcomes for characterizations of degree (low vs. high) and source (internal vs. external) of control over organizations (Romzek and Dubnick 1987).

Controllability is increasingly represented in the discussions of accountability for global governance organizations. Viewing the construction of international organizations as a principal-agent problem, scholars have probed the mechanisms used by member-states to control GGO bureaucracies (Hawkins et al. 2006; Koremenos et al. 2004). *Control*-type accountability is particularly challenging in the global governance context because no population or institution has a clear claim to control. The mechanisms available to secure control may be less effective because of practical difficulties in monitoring international organizations although there is evidence to the contrary (Hawkins et al. 2006).

Responsibility

Bureaucrats accountable in the *controllability* sense are constrained by the orders of principals. Alternatively, bureaucrats and organizations can be constrained by laws, rules or norms. This dimension of accountability is labeled "responsibility." Of course, the broadness of the responsibility dimension provides for many alternative visions.

Fidelity to principle and law is the most straightforward manifestation of *responsibility*-type accountability. As Mashaw notes, it is typically associated with government for it "reinforce[s] the normative commitments of the political system. In a liberal democratic polity, for example, we expect governance accountability to reinforce the mechanisms of consent and to ensure that collective judgments (legal standards and public policies) are impersonally applied. Put in conventional terms, governance accountability is meant to reinforce democracy and the rule of law" (Mashaw 2006, 153).

In terms of *responsibility*-type accountability, adherence to the law is preferable to bureaucratic allegiance to a principal. Accordingly proponents of the public law approach to public administration object to novel institutional arrangements that diminish responsibility (Leazes 1997; Moe 1994, 2000). Programs that place more discretion in the hands of officials are highly problematic from this perspective. Far preferable are legal requirements regarding organizational behavior, incorporation of policy and program objectives into legislation, and elimination of plural executives (commissions, committees, etc.) that confuse lines of authority (Moe and Gilmour 1995).

Responsibility can also take the form of formal and informal professional standards or behavioral norms. Such standards may encourage better behavior and set expectations against which bureaucrats can be evaluated (DiIulio 1994; Kearney and Sinha 1988; McKinney 1981). This notion of responsibility is a key element of the alternative notion of accountability articulated by Carl Friedrich (1940) in his debate with Finer. Accountable bureaucrats ought not simply follow orders, Friedrich argues, but utilize their expertise constrained by professional and moral standards. Critics argue that professional standards can, in fact, hinder accountability by substituting professional interests for public concerns but this complaint seems to switch the focus to control (Tullock 1965; Piven and Cloward 1971; Mladenka 1980; Hummel 1987).

Responsibility can pertain to internal standards of behavior and performance *not* set by legislators. For example, Bernard Rosen (1989) outlines responsibilities to "make laws work as intended," to "initiate changes in policies and programs," and to "enhance citizen confidence in the administrative institutions of government." Sometimes such obligations are explicit, as in the case of oaths. All federal employees pledge to "support and defend the Constitution of the United States." In other instances, obligations are moral or implicit. Thus we would expect an individual not to steal even if ordered to do so. These general responsibilities may differentiate the accountability of a public bureaucrat from the accountability of a private bureaucrat but there are identifiable analogs. For example, corporate directors have a general fiduciary obligation to shareholders and doctors are obliged to protect their patients' well-being.

All these variations on *responsibility* boil down to a core question quite different than the one at the heart of *controllability*. Did the organization follow the rules?

Responsiveness

Another alternative to the hierarchical *controllability* approach to accountability is, in a sense, more horizontal. *Responsiveness* is used here to differentiate an organization's attention to direct expressions of the needs and desires of an organization's constituents. This element of accountability has been emphasized in recent years in the "customer-oriented" approach suggested by reforms aimed at "reinventing government" (Sensenbrenner 1991; Osborne and Gaebler 1992). Responsiveness, as used in this typology, turns accountability outward rather than upward although it is sometimes used to connote *controllability*-type accountability (e.g., Rourke 1992; Romzek and Dubnick 1987).

Responsiveness focuses attention on the *demands* of the constituencies being served. An organization can attempt to satisfy *responsiveness*-type accountability demands in different ways. An organization might poll "customers" to determine their preferences, solicit input through focus groups, or establish advisory councils with key constituent group represented.

Organized interest groups also serve the function of aggregating and articulating preferences of affected communities. Profit-seeking organizations must be accountable in this sense or they will perish. Companies carefully track consumer preferences through analysis of the market and allocate resources accordingly.

Responsiveness in the global governance context emphasizes the organization members and the entities responsible for adopting and implementing the rules promulgated by GGOs. These constituencies—which often but not always overlap—can effectively deprive the global governance organization of its power if not satisfied. This makes achievement of *responsiveness*-type accountability a critical organizational goal. But as noted in the previous section of this chapter, it does not mean that the organization will pursue the objectives of all constituencies with equal vigor.

The standard of evaluation with respect to responsiveness: Did the organization meet expectations? Note that this does not include the normative question of means. How the organization met expectations would be a matter related to *responsibility*-type accountability.

With recognition of the multiple meanings of accountability, it is hardly surprising that GGOs do not fulfill accountability expectations. For one thing, it is difficult to translate some concepts given the realities of international organizations. Controllability is a tricky matter, for example. The identity of the appropriate "controller" is often in doubt. Most important, however, is the clear conflict between *responsibility* and *responsiveness* in the orientation of global governance organizations. The failures of accountability for which GGOs are chided often reflect the contradictory imperatives identified here. *Responsibility*-type accountability requires keen attention to normative demands; GGOs must abide by rules of due process and remain a neutral disinterested party to rulemaking. But *responsiveness*-type accountability pulls in exactly the opposite direction. GGOs must accommodate the needs of vital constituents. Indeed, the very logic of global governance sketched in the previous chapter—that the outcomes must not offend the interests of key parties—sacrifices *responsibility*-type accountability (i.e., fidelity to principles of equity and fairness) for *responsiveness*-type accountability.

Of course, when organizations are faulted for failures of accountability, the sense of accountability in which the organization fell short of expectations is rarely specified. But the charge of nonaccountability represents

a significant challenge nonetheless. Complaints about a lack of accountability ultimately call into question the basis for the power wielded by an
organization or individual. In an era when democratic norms are almost
universally accepted, the notion of a rulemaking body that is not accountable is an anathema. It is illegitimate on its face. In the next section, the
connection between accountability and legitimacy is made explicit. This
requires an initial discussion of the relationship between authority and
legitimacy.

Disentangling Legitimacy and Authority

Authority is a quirky word; individuals or organizations are said to "have
authority." Yet authority is revealed only through the behavior of those
who choose to obey. Disobeying the putatively authoritative individual or
organization can effectively deprive them of authority—or at least reveal
a lack of authority. Yet authority is something more than submission in
the face of power. Authority is the routinization of submission, the institutionalization of power, a crucial step in the development of modern
societies (Hardin 1987). Organizations and individuals rely upon authority
to deal with complexity of all sorts. Establishment of routines and "standard operating procedures" makes for much greater efficiency. Without
such authoritative rules, every action would require decisions regarding
the optimal course of action. Obedience to authority allows the simple
path to be followed: do as required.

Within societies, within markets, and within organizations, deference
to authority is required to reap the benefits of specialization. The authority of expertise allows us to "obey" others who know more than we do.
The engineering department of automobile manufacturer does not have
to justify every decision to the marketing or personnel departments. Without accepting the expertise of others, incalculable time would be spent re-
learning skills possessed by others or second-guessing the actions of those
who have performed tasks in our stead. On a societal scale, this type of
authority allows some individuals to devote themselves to medicine while
others specialize in growing food or manufacturing housing. Without such
specialization, societal progress would be impaired. On the most basic
level, establishing rules (and rulers) allows societies to enjoy tremendous
efficiency in everyday interactions and eliminate significant sources of

uncertainty including the behavior of others. We are safer by virtue of the obedience that comes with firmly established authority (whether it is philosophical or martial in origins).

The mysteries of obedience and the institutionalization of power are core considerations of social and behavioral sciences. Why do people submit to authoritative organizations and individuals? Why do they follow laws, norms, orders, etc? People and organizations go along with the rules, follow the commands of people in uniform, accept conclusions of experts, respect posted notices, and do so every day of their lives (Pfeffer 1992). Of course, sometimes they do disobey, but modern society functions effectively in large measure because obedience, acceptance of authority, is so widespread.

One answer that has emerged from the social sciences has broad acceptance; obedience is linked to the legitimacy of the individual or organization wielding power (Franck 1990). Usually citing Max Weber, many scholars even define authority as "legitimate power." This can cause confusion because in common speech, authority implies acceptance of the need to comply with a set of commands or rules but it contains no inherent judgment regarding the *legitimacy* of the authoritative institution. In its everyday use, authority most certainly exists in the absence of legitimacy (Knight 1958). Many political regimes lack democratic legitimacy—or even some other form of normative legitimacy—yet possess authority. That is, the population is obedient, follows the laws, accepts and abides by the dictates of the government—even though the legitimacy of the regime is highly suspect. Contemporary regimes in North Korea and Burma (Myanmar) are widely viewed as lacking in legitimacy and yet the authority of each nation's government is undeniable.

It is not clear that Weber himself would subscribe to the authority-as-legitimate-power view attributed to him—especially given the contemporary use of the word legitimacy (Wrong 1988; Weber et al. 1978, 943–48). The translation from German into English causes a bit of uncertainty regarding the correct interpretation of the relationship among power, authority, and legitimacy in Weber's work (Cohen et al. 1975; Uphoff 1989). Weber does classify authority relationships based on types of legitimacy claims but does not clearly declare that all authority is legitimate. Weber writes of *Herrschaft,* which is sometimes translated as "domination" and sometimes as "authority." Talcott Parsons uses "domination" for *Herrschaft* and, in turn, translates *legitime Herrschaft* as "authority" but it is not certain that Weber would have drawn that rhetorical distinction (Cohen et al.

1975; Parsons 1942; Uphoff 1989). Indeed, if *legitime Herrschaft* is translated as "legitimate authority," there is a strong implication that there is such a thing as illegitimate authority. Nevertheless, Parsons and Lasswell, two seminal thinkers, used the term "authority" to cover only power relationships deemed legitimate (Uphoff 1989, 298; Parsons 1942; Lasswell and Kaplan 1952). Several scholars argue persuasively that the subsequent intertwining of authority and legitimacy was emphasized by others more than Weber himself (Uphoff 1989; Wrong 1988; Easton 1958).

The issue of what Weber had in mind is obviously of secondary importance. The conflation of authority and legitimacy, even if the definition is correctly derived from Weber, is problematic. It creates an intellectual dead end, sealing off access to important intellectual terrain. Institutionalized power in the absence of normative legitimacy is an undeniable feature of the world around us. Indeed, governments lacking in legitimacy are often referred to as "authoritarian," a practice that speaks to general separation of legitimacy and authority. Adopting a tautological definition of authority that invokes legitimacy makes it literally impossible for people to submit to an illegitimate authority. Indeed, critics of Weber insist he has done just that. Grafstein writes that "Weber virtually identifies legitimacy with stable and effective political power, reducing it to routine submission to authority" (Grafstein 1981).

The rhetorical construction of authority as legitimate power is inconsistent with the common use and understanding of the word legitimacy. Legitimacy is widely regarded as a word with normative content. As Buchanan and Keohane conclude, "legitimacy, understood as the right to rule, is a moral notion that cannot be reduced rational self-interest. To say that an institution is legitimate implies that it has the right to rule even if it does not act in accordance with the rational self-interest of everyone who is subject to its rule" (Buchanan and Keohane 2006, 409). On the other hand, self-interest—even self-preservation—does motivate people to accept authority in the political context and beyond. Obedience of this sort, Wrong calls it "authority by inducement," does not speak to the justness of the assignment of power that ought to be embodied in the idea of legitimacy (Wrong 1988, 45). As described below, authority is used in this book to capture institutionalized obedience driven by both legitimacy *or* inducement.

Failure to disentangle authority from legitimacy leaves important questions impossible to articulate. For instance, how do institutions (and individuals) acquire and maintain authority in the absence of legitimacy? Can organizations be legitimate and yet lack authority? Conflating legitimacy and authority renders such questions—critical in the analysis of global governance organizations—nonsensical. Specifying the sources of legitimacy and the sources of authority helps clarify boundaries between the two concepts. It is argued that legitimacy is, of course, one basis of authority but not the *only* basis.

The Bases of Legitimacy

Legitimacy offers an explanation for the power institutions have over individuals by tying obedience to a set of beliefs regarding the justness of a power assignment. The concept of "legitimacy" is not confined to politics, of course, contributing to ambiguity regarding its meaning, including conflation with "authority." In a review of the diverse body of work on legitimacy across disciplines, Suchman (1995) provides an expansive definition: "Legitimacy is a generalized perception or assumption that the actions of an entity are desirable, proper, or appropriate within some socially constructed system of norms, values, beliefs and definitions" (1995, 574). He seeks to capture and order the many uses of the word by dividing disparate notions into three basic categories:

- *Normative* (or moral) legitimacy is a function of beliefs about what entitles an individual or institution to wield power. An institution is legitimate because it is the just holder of power by the standards of an affected or concerned community.
- *Cognitive* legitimacy emphasizes the psychological, the degree to which an institution is unquestioned. An institution is legitimate because we accept and cannot even imagine its absence.
- *Pragmatic* legitimacy, as the name suggests, emphasizes the "interest-based" acceptance of an institution by the most affected parties. An institution is legitimate because the affected parties find it in their interests to accept it as such.

The *responsibility* and *responsiveness* concepts of accountability map easily onto these notions of legitimacy. In particular, *responsibility*-type accountability is a manifestation of normative legitimacy. Adherence to the rules and principles that underpin a legitimate regime is the essence of *responsibility*. Indeed, the connection extends beyond the political realm. One is legitimate as a physician or scientist to the extent behavior is consistent with the accepted norms of the profession. Thus failures of *responsibility*-type accountability directly undermine *normative legitimacy*.

Responsiveness, on the other hand, is linked with idea of *pragmatic legitimacy.* The organization failing to meet the demands of constituents can hardly be getting passing grades on any test of interest satisfaction. Such failures of *responsiveness*-type accountability are experienced as losses of pragmatic legitimacy. The organization is not satisfying the demands of constituents undermining its desirability.

Suchman's specification brings comprehensiveness to the discussion of legitimacy. He is explicit about the many different meanings employed whereas most writers wrongly assume (or assert) that their definition is shared by all. But including all definitions under one broad tent highlights the analytical problem posed by treating legitimacy as a catchall. The inclusiveness undermines the meaning of legitimacy. Grouping normative concepts (from democratic legitimacy to the divine right of kings) along with pragmatic legitimacy (interest-based obedience) and taken-for-grantedness (thoughtless acceptance of power that is the product of habit) blurs the essential meaning of legitimacy. In this book, legitimacy is used to reference the normative element. It is suggested that the logic of Suchman's "pragmatic legitimacy" is more comfortably accommodated within the non-normative concept of authority.

Normative Legitimacy

Contemporary beliefs regarding political legitimacy emphasize the process by which the leaders are chosen and the procedures followed in the exercise of state power. The hallmarks of a just process include transparency, predictability according to a set of well-known rules, equality before the law or in any governmental proceeding, objectivity and disinterestedness in the arbitration of disputes. Popular control of the government, through fair and meaningful elections, renders the state the legitimate holder of power. Of course, democracy has not always been the foremost basis of governmental legitimacy. The "divine right of kings" represents a notable alternate account of government legitimacy. Under this theory, the power of the state is legitimate because the ruler has been chosen by God to rule on earth. Pretenders to the throne are illegitimate because they lack this mandate from Heaven.

Political thinkers have contemplated this question of government legitimacy for centuries without resolution. The "social contract" metaphor, with its well-known variants offered by Rousseau, Locke, and Hobbes in the eighteenth century, presented an idea at least as old as Plato. Namely, that power was acquired by virtue of a bargain between individuals and the state. The purpose of the contract—to enhance the good of the whole, gain physical protection or secure natural rights—depends upon which political philosopher you ask. In the versions of the social contract offered by all three this exchange entitles the state to wield power over the individual as long as it fulfills the bargain. But each started with a different view regarding the underlying logic of governance.

Thomas Hobbes's formulation of the social contract is predicated on the observation that, in the absence of government, every man lives under constant threat of violence. Life in this state of nature, he famously wrote, is "solitary, poor, nasty, brutish, and short." Only because he is constantly at risk does man accept the dangerously powerful Leviathan and its protection. In his view, then, the question of state legitimacy is eminently consequential: the legitimate government is one that fulfills the agreement. That is, the government has met its obligation if the population surrendering absolute liberty is protected. Rousseau did not have the same fears of physical violence in the state of nature but he regarded individual pursuit of self-interest as a threat to the general good. He emphasized collective welfare over the individual but still required that the general will be abided by the state suggesting same participatory requirements for governmental legitimacy. John Locke's expression of the social contract emphasized the protection of property rights as a central function of the state because this was most lacking in the absence of government. A legitimate regime must respect this foundation as it administers the state. Failure to do so—substantively or procedurally—undercuts any regime's legitimacy.

Emphasis on process can be seen in nongovernmental contexts as well. The legitimacy of a scientist or a scientific institution, for example, depends in large measure on demonstrable consistency with norms regarding the scientific method. If a scientist does not follow accepted practices regarding collection of data, research design, and so on, the community will not regard the results as legitimate. In the realm of public policymaking, procedural legitimacy is shaped by political *and* scientific considerations. Legitimacy requires that the process be open and in accordance with legal requirements (such as the Administrative Procedures Act in the United States). Transnational governance organizations struggle with this because there is no agreed upon procedural standard to which they can refer (Esty 2007). If analysis informing policy decisions is not carried out in a fashion consistent with professional norms or if it appears to be manufactured to support a predetermined outcome, the resulting policy will also lack legitimacy.

Hobbes's social contract theory makes clear that legitimacy is not limited to procedural considerations. Organizational legitimacy may also be tied to results. This has be likened to "outputs" in contrast to the procedural "inputs" (Scharpf 1997). From this "consequentialist" perspective, the legitimacy of an organization depends upon its success in providing the public goods it is charged with delivering. A hospital is legitimate because it takes care of the sick. The military's legitimacy depends upon its ability to defend the nation. Even in the context of democratic governance, process does not always trump consequences. Repeated failures to provide public services will undermine governmental legitimacy.

Consequentialist legitimacy is definitely important to global governance organizations. The effectiveness of an organization, the acceptance of the rules it generates, are critical to its credibility (Held and Koenig-Archibugi 2004, 125). The International Maritime Organization is legitimate (in this sense) when it maintains safety in oceanic navigation. This output legitimacy is not a substitute for input legitimacy but the two can reinforce each other. GGOs with more input legitimacy seem more likely to be effective which, in turn, bolsters their output legitimacy. Both the "outcome"- and "process"-oriented approaches to legitimacy are critically important (Held and Koenig-Archibugi 2004). It is important to be clear that consequentialist legitimacy is *not* the same as pragmatic legitimacy, which emphasizes the benefits to a single actor rather than the general fulfillment of mission (Suchman 1995).

There is general agreement that the bases of legitimacy in the transnational context cannot simply be transferred over from domestic settings (Franck 1990). There is no consensus, however, on what is appropriate (Bernstein 2004). Some look at the voluntary nature of participation in global governance regimes and deem the whole subject of legitimacy moot. Voluntary participation constitutes consent, thus ending the legitimacy discussion (Rosenau and Czempiel 1992b). But this conclusion is not satisfying—particularly to those who have *not* given consent and question the legitimacy of GGOs. So the search for the foundation of legitimacy for international organizations continues. One roadblock is the lack of coherent community. To have meaning, normative legitimacy requires a shared set of beliefs. Without agreement among the global constituencies of the GGO, moral legitimacy is effectively impossible.

A second problem is the mixed nature of many international organizations. Straddling boundaries—public and private, domestic and international, government and nongovernment—renders the applicability of particular elements of normative legitimacy ambiguous (Cashore 2002; Bernstein and Cashore 2007). The importance of elections, for example, is disputed. Some theorists maintain that elections are required and that until international organizations provide for direct participation their legitimacy will remain in question (Held 2004; Falk and Strauss 2001; Mc-Grew 2002b). Others argue that this standard is inapplicable in the global governance context for logistical and theoretical reasons (Buchanan and Keohane 2006; Dahl 1999). Only one of the GGOs examined (ICANN) experimented with direct elections and soon abandoned the idea (Mathiason 2008). An election requirement would put legitimacy out of all GGOs' reach for the foreseeable future.

Fortunately, the core argument of this book needn't make reference to one solution or solve the puzzle of legitimacy for international organizations. There is a general pantry of "good stuff" from which the chefs cooking up such solutions select their ingredients. An inventory of the demands of legitimacy is offered in the middle section of this chapter. Each ingredient is at times ill suited to the recipe for organizational authority. All approaches to legitimacy set expectations that inevitably conflict with the requirements of authority.

Taken-for-Grantedness (Cognitive Legitimacy)

Some organizations are accepted features of a system, unquestioned by affected parties and legitimate as such. Suchman labels this "cognitive legitimacy," a tag that seems more confusing than his straightforward "taken-for-grantedness." An organization's taken-for-grantedness may be grounded in a historical record of normative legitimacy but whose active evaluation implied by that label ended long ago. An institution might acquire taken-for-grantedness and retain it even as it deviates from its historical legacy. Arguably, taken-for-grantedness is not terribly substantive, an echo of normative legitimacy, but it may be the most desirable form. All tests or validation requirements associated with normative legitimacy are short-circuited, and there is no burden to satisfy the interests of the governed. Such acceptance is the Holy Grail for global governance organizations.

Some international organizations have, by virtue of their longevity, achieved a measure of taken-for-grantedness. The International Telecommunication Union, for example, was founded in 1865 (as the International Telegraph Union) and is treated as the default authority for resolving issues regarding the harmonization of telecommunications standards (Murphy 1994). As the importance of such longstanding entities increases, however, the limits of established taken-for-grantedness are tested (Cooper et al. 2008). Organizations that previously melted into the landscape are suddenly cast in deep relief. Recent events highlighted the dynamic nature of this type of legitimacy: the SARS crisis shone a spotlight on the World Health Organization (WHO). When the WHO's travel advisories hit hard the economies of Canada and China, its institutional legitimacy became an issue (e.g., Gazette 2003). Similarly, the World Intellectual Property Organization toiled in relative obscurity until the importance of intellectual property in communications and pharmaceuticals attracted the interest of governments and NGOs; a diverse range of critics raised objections to the organization and questioned its legitimacy (Koch-Mehrin 2006; Maitland 2002; Williamson 2006).

Consistent with the theory of institutional isomorphism, many new GGOs assume forms, utilize nomenclature, and adopt policies that resemble those of governance institutions with which constituents are comfortable (DiMaggio and Powell 1983; Cooper et al. 2008). In the long run, such attempts to acquire taken-for-grantedness by emulating organizations that already possess it may create obstacles to maintaining normative or pragmatic legitimacy. By taking such forms, new international organizations saddle themselves with expectations commensurate with the impression they are creating.

Pragmatic Legitimacy

Individuals and institutions often recognize and submit to organizations based on a calculation of their interests rather than moral compulsion. This submission reflects the "pragmatic legitimacy" of the ruler. The parameters of this calculation are not constrained. If obedience is chosen because disobedience might lead to death, the regime is "legitimate" because the populace has calculated that submission is the best way to maximize utility. Suchman is careful to differentiate this notion from "output legitimacy" described in the previous section. Unlike normative legitimacy focused on outputs, which hinges on the fulfillment of organizational purpose, pragmatic legitimacy is more narrowly focused on the particularistic interest of a single actor. Authority without legitimacy (in this pragmatic sense) seems syllogistically impossible.

As an empirical matter, however, this doesn't ring true; institutions generally regarded as illegitimate sustain authority in a variety of contexts. Returning to Burma, the violent ruling junta, formerly known by its memorably creepy acronym SLORC, has maintained authority in the face of unfavorable election returns, domestic protest, and global condemnation. Few would defend the regime's "legitimacy" notwithstanding the ruling body's rebranding as the State Peace and Development Council. In a different context, organized crime syndicates maintain remarkably stable authority over geographic and substantive spaces with little regard for legitimacy.

It is always important, of course, to emphasize concepts over words. Employing Suchman's typology, this book focuses on the tension between the demands of normative legitimacy and pragmatic legitimacy. This statement is consistent with the common academic language that defines authority as legitimate power. The discussion seems much clearer using the proposed terminology, treating "authority" and "legitimacy" as distinct concepts. Still, the claims presented in this book do *not* depend on the proposed language.

The Bases of Authority

Authority is in evidence any time one must accept the institutionalization of another's power (Spiro 1958). Our boss has authority to give orders by virtue of her formal position. Our doctor has authority to diagnose and set treatment due to his specialized knowledge. Our mechanic has authority to tell you what is wrong with your car and how much it will cost to fix it because, really, do you know whether the alternator is bad? In each of these cases, our acceptance of authority reflects a mix of motives that includes legitimacy.

Broadly speaking, there are three sources of authority: formal, psychological, and pragmatic (Simon et al. 1991). Brief sketches of each show these are not mutually exclusive. Obedience may be explained by the logic of all three and they may reinforce each other (Levi 1997). Courses of action prescribed to acquire authority by formal, psychological, or pragmatic means may sometimes conflict. With the goal of distinguishing authority and legitimacy, sources of authority that can be disentangled from legitimacy, which typically receive less attention from political scientists, are emphasized in this discussion.

FORMAL SOURCES OF AUTHORITY. Obedience is offered to organizations possessing legal or formal authority because they occupy positions or perform functions that convey function and responsibilities. Their placement within a larger bureaucratic or governmental context may confer certain powers and status. Traditional language of authority frames this conceptualization in legalistic fashion. As Herbert Simon put it, "He who possesses authority, in this sense, has the *right* to demand obedience; while he who is commanded has the *duty* to obey" (Simon et al. 1991). Many organizations have this type of noncontroversial authority, most obviously in the governmental context. Prosaically, one follows the rules of the Department of Motor Vehicles because it is the designated organization for acquiring a license to drive.

Some nongovernmental organizations possess such formal authority by virtue of state delegation. The American Bar Association (ABA) is a private organization, but to practice law every prospective attorney in the United States must submit to the ABA's requirements. The organization's authority trickles down from the government; the state-imposed requirement is the ultimate source. Many GGOs are structured around representative bodies with nation-states as the unit of representation, a design that may similarly build authority through legal connections to the member states. Still, the transferability of governmental authority from many nations to a single GGO is hardly certain (Grant and Keohane 2005a).

Formal authority is "always traceable back to some fountainhead of legitimacy" (Simon et al. 1991, 181). Institutions are accepted and obeyed because they are part of a larger regime that satisfies some criteria of normative legitimacy discussed above. Yet we must be careful not to dismiss the very real effect of coercion (or the threat of coercion) on individual and institutional behavior. An organization's ability to punish those who disobey is an invaluable source of authority. One is compelled to acquire a license to drive or practice law, after all, by the state's sanctioning power.

Coercive tools are not reserved to states. Some nongovernmental organizations with formal authority are completely detached from governments, such as the FIFA (Fédération Internationale de Football Association), which governs "soccer" globally. Entities like FIFA have a "gatekeeper" function (or perhaps goalkeeper is more appropriate) with respect to a desirable good (e.g., participation in the World Cup). Access to the good requires acceptance of the organization's authority. There is a small set of global governance organizations with analogous power. ICANN, the Internet Corporation for Assigned Names and Numbers, effectively controls access to the root servers that are the de facto switching room of the Internet (Koppell 2005). Market-driven organizations like the Forest Stewardship Council (FSC) attempt to create this authority with the promotion of a distinguishing mark as a desirable good (Cashore et al. 2004). Use of the mark requires demonstrable acceptance of FSC authority (i.e., adherence with FSC standards for sustainable forestry).

PSYCHOLOGICAL SOURCES OF AUTHORITY.   This category captures the broad set of explanations for deference to institutions that hinge upon our active beliefs or unconscious patterns of behavior (Milgram 2004; Pfeffer 1992). Some organizations induce high levels of confidence, for example, because of their record of previous performance or status. Thus, people are inclined to obey their orders or recommendations. At a hospital where your health has been restored in the past, you are more likely to follow their prescribed course of actions in the future. This dynamic is understood and utilized by organizations seeking authority. A significant portion of marketing is intended to make the consumer—or citizen—feel that their obedience has been earned in this way.

Organizations try to win the confidence of those who have not had direct experience by publicizing their record and offering testimonials. Establishing markers, licensing or certification requirements that can be read as signals of quality or expertise builds upon this approach. One may not have personal experience with a particular, say, nail salon, but we can see that the shop is licensed by the state and infer some measure of confidence in the establishment. Storefronts often bear stickers indicating membership in trade associations—yet another tactic intended to win the confidence of potential consumers. These gestures reinforce the authority that comes with specialized expertise. We defer to the judgment of an engineering firm, for instance, because it is presumed that such an organization has a staff qualified to make requisite calculations and judgment. This is communicated by listing strings of professional degrees after names on the letterhead. Majone makes the point that regulatory bodies—including nongovernmental standard-setters—often invoke their expertise as a means of building authority and establishing legitimacy (Majone 1984). Some GGOs frame their authority in this light, depicting their activities as largely scientific and properly in the realm of experts rather than interest-driven public discourse (Koppell 2005; Porter 2001).

Legitimacy is essentially a psychological source of authority as it hinges on a set of beliefs regarding the just assignment and utilization of power. Obedience is deserved because the institution was created and is operated in a just fashion and / or its dictates are the product of a just process. These beliefs are ultimately subjective and contextual but nonetheless prompt obedience in matters great and small. Everyday occurrences—such as following the orders of a crossing guard or a flight attendant—reflect an acceptance of authority because those making demands of us are seen as legitimate in their position and demands. A collective group decision— say, what movie to go see—is accepted if the choice was made in a "legitimate" fashion (e.g., vote). Of course, the "costs" of obedience in situations like these are extremely low; thus our willingness to accept "illegitimate" individuals may be higher than in more critical areas.

It is difficult to determine whether general law-abidingness stems from belief in governmental legitimacy or fear of sanction, but there are instances where belief in institutional legitimacy seems to be a motivating factor (Hurd 1999). Franck uses one episode to illustrate dramatically the phenomenon. In 1998, the US Navy wanted to intercept a ship bound for Iran with dangerous silkworm missiles, but this action was never taken because the State Department prevailed in a dispute over the appropriate course of action, arguing that "under the universally recognized rules of war and neutrality, [this action] would constitute [an] aggressive blockade tantamount to an act of war against Iran" (Franck 1990, 4). Franck concludes that the outcome demonstrated "deference to systemic rules," a reflection of their legitimacy. One cannot prove that legitimacy was determinative in this or any other case of obedience to authority. Still, given the improbability of meaningful enforcement in a wide variety of situations, it is reasonable to assert that the psychological impact of legitimacy is at least a compelling contributing factor in many situations requiring obedience to an institution.

PRAGMATIC SOURCES OF AUTHORITY. The obedient individual or organization may calculate that deference to authority maximizes utility; the potential costs of disobedience outweigh the gains (Wrong 1988). This reasoning was discussed already under the heading of "pragmatic legitimacy" in Suchman's catalog of legitimacy conceptions. As obedience driven by a calculation of interest does not suggest moral judgment, it seems more comfortable here, clearly divorced from normative content. Indeed, self-interested recognition of authority does not even suggest that obedience is the ideal course of action, only that it is the best available alternative (Dahl 1990). Repressive regimes that instill fear in their subjects to win obedience have established authority on pragmatic grounds. Acceptance of governmental authority implies nothing regarding the absolute desirability of the government to the governed. Nor does obedience speak to the justness of the assignment of power, the government's legitimacy.

There are multiple approaches to an assessment of the benefits of obedience. It may be based on a single situation; obedience at one moment says nothing about obedience in the future. This type of "exchange-level analysis" would lead to an examination of specific policies or demand a decision on whether to comply based on a calculation of the costs and benefits of obedience or disobedience. For example, a nation submits to judgments of the International Court of Justice only when the body rules in its favor. This is a rather narrow, conditional sort of authority that would be difficult to see as "institutionalization" for it collapses whenever an undesirable command is given.

A broader approach would look at the net consequences of obedience and disobedience over many situations, incorporating the expected behavior of other actors, rather than confining analysis to a particular situation. Obedience to an institution might be guided by the practical value of supporting an overarching authoritative organization rather than a calculation based on a single decision or action. Thus interests are not necessarily served on an exchange level but on a systemic level. For example, the United States does accept the authority of the World Trade Organization even when it rules against American interests because US policymakers have determined that maintaining an international trade regime is in the national interest. Of course, a governor consistently hostile to the interests of the governed cannot sustain authority of this type without some coercive force to back it up. Sanctions alter the calculus of the party considering which course of action maximizes utility. If a penalty must be paid for *dis*obedience, the effective benefits of obedience increase. Therefore, the ability of the organization seeking authority to impose costs upon disobedient parties has a large effect.

Sanctions are not necessarily hierarchical or controlled by the state. Acts of retribution from ill-treated employees, for example, are a non-hierarchical type of sanction that give subordinates a form of pragmatic authority over their superiors. The manager might not make unwelcome demands of employees because she knows the cost—a petulant, unproductive staff—would be too high. On a grander scale, the pragmatic authority possessed by labor unions runs counter to the typical model of employer-employee relations. The threat of a strike, slowdown, or even unrest forces the executive to meet some demands from the union. In the context of global governance, the ability of a minority of members to effectively stall an organization—a phenomenon reported by interview subjects leading many GGOs—gives relatively weak members some authority over the powerful.

Some pragmatic authority stems from practical necessity. Monopolistic organizations that perform vital functions leave little choice but acceptance of their rules and decisions. We may be logistically at the mercy of others. Relying upon a contractor to perform a service, for example, one is forced to accept representations regarding the situation and work performed (or assume the costs of verification). Lack of expertise creates a similar asymmetry. The authority of the all-powerful auto mechanic is exemplary. Rarely does one leave the garage confident they have paid a reasonable price for a necessary service. We defer because we have no choice, not because we are filled with confidence.

Complementary and Conflicting Demands

The legitimacy of a regime can reinforce the other bases of authority and vice versa. Bureaucratic agencies of Western democratic governments, for example, have significant power to sanction or withhold benefits from disobedient individuals and firms. The authority of such agencies is buttressed by their legitimacy, a widely shared belief that they are the properly delegated agency of a legitimate government. In such cases, it is hard to envision any tension whatsoever. The agency performs functions that are valuable, and citizens are willing to obey. The resulting effectiveness reinforces the normative legitimacy, and so on. This ongoing circular reinforcement of authority and legitimacy is recognizable for some GGOs, such as the International Civil Aviation Organization, as well.

At times, however, GGOs' pursuit of legitimacy is very much at odds with the pursuit of authority. Put simply, there are situations in which organizations must take actions that undermine normative legitimacy in order to preserve authority or vice versa. To set the stage for the specification of the circumstances in which such clashes are likely, the theoretical bases

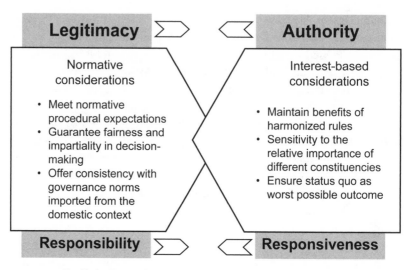

FIGURE 2.1. Conflicting Demands of Legitimacy and Authority.

of legitimacy and authority are translated into a more concrete set of demands.

The Demands of Normative Legitimacy

Even in the governmental context, the basis of legitimacy remains a moving target over time, geography, and context. The notion of "divine right" was entirely plausible in bygone eras and remains so today in some nations and, of course, in the religious context. The very fact that global governance organizations must be legitimate to constituents from varied backgrounds compounds the legitimacy challenge. Still, the catalog of normative legitimacy demands associated with Western democratic practices is, for better or worse, predominant. This is a function, in part, of the increasingly universal acceptance of these norms. Even nations typically judged inadequate in such terms attempt to meet these "accepted" standards. Singapore, for instance, maintains that it is a competitive democracy though few international observers would characterize it as such. In addition, the countries with the greatest influence in many international organizations share these norms. Specifically, the United States and developed nations of Western Europe created and support many GGOs; thus it is hardly surprising that the norms common across these countries have been adopted in this context. Finally, many of the most vociferous critics of GGOs also come from this cultural background and thus their critiques reflect these values and expectations. (An irony related to the central argument of this book is that the norms of democratic legitimacy are likely to be violated to satisfy the very nations from which these ideals originate.)

The set of features identified by scholars fall into general categories: representation, participation, equality, impartiality, due process, and efficacy. These demands might seem most applicable to primary government organs (such as the legislature), but these normative requirements extend to administrative agencies. Interviews with GGO leaders confirmed their concern with all of these "demands" as they face the administrative challenges of global governance.

The idea of *representation*—the normative belief that the governed should have a voice in the political system—was broached with the earlier discussion of elections. Of course, there are a host of structural approaches to the problem of representation that satisfy standards of legitimacy in different contexts. Thus the idea of indirect representation (i.e., the representative government selects an official who is part of the GGO) is not inherently invalidating (Buchanan and Keohane 2006; Dahl 1999; Grant and Keohane 2005b). There is typically some notion of *equality of representation* associated with normative legitimacy in a democratic system. Granting veto power only to permanent members of the UN Security Council undermines legitimacy on this dimension (Caron 1993; Hurd 2008). The difficulty of determining the proper unit of representation (i.e., individual, country, interest group) complicates this issue in the international context.

Participation is another core expectation that extends beyond representation or elections and is vital to bureaucratic legitimacy as well (Bernstein 2004; Borzel and Risse 2005). It is not enough to make the proceedings visible to interested groups. They should have the opportunity to be heard through hearings, submission of written comments, and contact with the governing organization (Bodansky 1999; Beisheim and Dingwerth 2008). The denial of such access suggests a lack of opportunity for the "governed" to shape the laws that will bind them and, as such, seems antithetical to democratic principles. Legitimate governmental organizations ought to offer all constituents the opportunity to observe and comment upon the activities of the organization. This may take the form of open hearings and sessions, release of published transcripts, or regular opportunities to testify or comment (Esty 2006).

These requirements might be seen as components of a general demand for rigorous standards of *due process*. All activities of legitimate organizations must be governed by a set of rules and procedures that are known to all and upheld vigilantly (Esty 2006). Ad hoc policymaking is a prima facie violation of this requirement. An organization that does not operate according to a constitution or fixed set of rules is quite suspect, particularly in the realm of rulemaking. It suggests that power is vested in the individuals running the entity rather than the institution itself. Deviations in the process should invalidate the output of the organization.

Transparency is generally considered to be vitally important to maintain organizational legitimacy (Grigorescu 2003; Grigorescu 2007; March and Olsen 1995). It ensures compliance with requirements and bolsters the perception that the governance of the organization and the rulemaking process are consistent with declared standards (Dingwerth 2005; Beisheim and Dingwerth 2008; Grigorescu 2007). Thus the legitimate rulemaking body should make its interactions with interested parties known to all other such parties (Woods 2003, 79). It publishes an account of deliberations, comments, and responses.

This "rule of law" also extends to the application of organizational requirements to individual members and nonmembers. Organizations must be constrained; inconsistency or whimsical decisionmaking undermines bureaucratic legitimacy as idiosyncrasies signal arbitrariness at best and corruption at worst. Most important, the general demand for *impartiality* or *neutrality* in the system must be met (Rothstein and Teorell 2008; Castells 2005). Each individual or organization should be treated consistently by a legitimate governance organization, with no one party receiving special consideration.

This requirement implies also that the decisions of a rulemaking body have a *rational* basis and are in the *public interest*. Legitimacy requires a rigorous analytic component to rulemaking process with ultimate emphasis on collective welfare in deliberation rather than the narrow interests of one constituency (Risse 2004; Hurd 1999). Lacking this component implies an arbitrary, capricious, nonsubstantive and possibly self-serving basis for rulemaking.

Finally, several approaches to legitimacy emphasize organizational output, as discussed above. The legitimate GGO must live up to its functional promise, producing a state of affairs better than that which would have existed in the absence of the organization (Buchanan and Keohane 2006; Young 1992). Focused on collective goods rather than self-interest, it is important to remember that this criterion is different than the notion of pragmatic legitimacy (Hurd 1999). Here the demand of legitimacy is that the organization fulfills its mission, meeting the objectives that are shared by *all constituents*. In practice, the divergence of preferences facing GGOs is often significant, however, rendering the output basis of normative legitimacy relatively weak. In situations where the standard of organizational performance is contested, interest satisfaction becomes a matter of authority (or pragmatic legitimacy, in Suchman's schema) because performance is about particularistic objectives rather than shared goals (Buchanan and Keohane 2006). As discussed below, the practical need for international organizations to put more weight on some members' preferences underscores the awkwardness of judging organizational outputs in normative legitimacy terms.

The Demands of Pragmatic Authority

Granting authority puts power in the hands of others without certainty regarding its use. Individuals (and organizations) are understandably reluctant to promise such obedience. As described in the section on the bases of authority, the functional and psychological reasons for obedience to global governance organizations are not terribly compelling. This results in emphasis on the interest-based rationale—the pragmatic basis of authority—which must be solid for a GGO to thrive.

Acceptance of an organization's authority on a pragmatic basis does not require satisfaction of each individual's *ideal* preferences. It may be the best possible choice given the alternatives presented. Extending this logic, one can see that authority is sometimes secured through manipulation of the interests of the governed, which may include the use of coercive tactics. Totalitarian regimes—those with unconstrained power reaching into every aspect of life—depend upon violence to maintain their authority. Given the dire consequences of rejecting the regime's authority, the population's calculation of self-interest in such societies clearly leads to obedience. This is an extreme illustration of the problem in treating coerced submission as the equivalent of obedience based on normative legitimacy. For states regarded as normatively legitimate, the coercive power of the government is a complementary source of authority.

Many nonstate organizations have a nonviolent ability to influence the interests of others to reinforce their own authority. For example, the Walmart in a small town with few alternative job opportunities wields profound influence over the population; acceptance of the company's authority is the only course consistent with self-interest. In theory, the population is free to "disobey" in their employment and purchasing decisions. In practice, the firm's authority is unquestionable. Indeed, the authority of a private firm may be so great as to arouse calls for state intervention based on normative considerations. This is another use of "voice" as a protest strategy when "exit" is not feasible.

Consistent with this general discussion, members of global governance organizations—be they nation-states or individual firms—calculate their assessment of the pragmatic basis of GGO authority in a particularistic fashion (Hurd 1999, 387). They do not look at the total welfare effect but their own expected conditions with and without the GGO. They do so with a long-term perspective. That is, countries rarely drop out of a GGO due to a single ruling contrary to their interests. The benefits of maintaining a global regime are factored into any assessment of a particular action contrary to an actor's preferences. So, for example, even when the American position on an International Telecommunication Union standard does not win the day, the United States may remain an active participant and even adopt the suboptimal rule.

The flexibility provided to global governance organizations is not unlimited, of course. Participants in any global governance system may—at some unknown point—decide that the costs are simply too high and walk away entirely. This is not an idle threat. An interesting example involved the World Intellectual Property Organization (WIPO), which was frustrated in its attempts to revise the international rules on patent recognition by member demands regarding a tangential set of economic development issues. Rather than concede on the contested issues, several nations (including the United States, members of the EU, and Japan) met outside the WIPO structure to negotiate a multilateral treaty (interview 2). This is less desirable to them than a WIPO agreement but preferable to capitulation. Even without formal exit of any members, the extraorganizational treaty would dramatically undermine WIPO with negative implications for its future authority.

Using coercion to establish organizational authority by altering the interest calculus of the governed is a strategy used broadly. But most GGOs do not have access to such tools. A novel set of global governance organizations attempt to simulate this tool by endowing a standard with market value as a means of inducing compliance. These "non-state-market—driven" governance organizations (NSMDs) are best known in environmental policy arenas. Entities like the Forest Stewardship Council and the Marine Stewardship Council establish standards for sustainable industry (Cashore et al. 2004; Cashore 2002; Bernstein 2007). The strategy involves creating a linkage between an environmentally preferable behavior (such as sustainable forestry) with a market premium for products bearing a stamp of certification. One might view this as a type of "soft coercion."

Other NSMDs are less subtle in the application of coercive techniques to make participation in global governance organizations a self-interested proposition. The Rainforest Action Network compelled Citigroup to participate in the establishment of environmental standards for developing-world projects financed by Western banking institutions. After being subjected to a particularly effective and embarrassing campaign targeting the company and its chairman, Citigroup joined the effort rather than resisting it (Conroy 2007). Granting authority to the rulemaking entity had become more consistent with Citigroup's interests than resisting it.

Reduced to its essence, then, the core demand of authority is to make the institutionalization of power in the interests of the governed (Bayles 1987; Hardin 1987). Relationships between the governed entity and the would-be governor in the realm of global governance rarely resemble the domestic model. Granting authority to GGOs must offer advantages specific to participants (Hurd 1999). If the particularistic interests of the governed are not served, nations or companies may simply walk away. This denies the organization authority regardless of any normative legitimacy achieved through the adoption of democratic structure and processes. Note the potential downward spiral, swirling together legitimacy and authority, confronting the GGO. Every time another member walks away, eroding the legitimacy of a GGO, the rules being offered are that much less universal, which in turn further undermines organizational authority.

Circumstances of Clashing Demands

Conflicts between the demands of legitimacy and authority are inevitable given the logic of global governance. The very premise of global governance sketched earlier in this chapter—that the outcomes must not offend the interests of key parties—represents a prima facie violation of the norms of democratic governance and administration (Krislov and Rosenbloom 1981; Buchanan and Keohane 2006; Castells 2005). Any pretense of neutrality or equality is shaky at best. If constructing an effective global governance organization simply required violating norms of democratic governance until the "big guys" are satisfied, however, there would likely be many more potent GGOs. One can push too far, sacrificing so much legitimacy in the name of authority that the entire endeavor is undermined. This helps explain why not one of the global governance organization included in this study has adopted the Security Council model or a structure that makes the power asymmetry so starkly apparent. Even if it is in the rational self-interest of weaker parties to accept lopsided outcomes, at a certain point, offenses to norms of democratic legitimacy become too much to bear (Ikenberry 1998). Global regimes can be undermined from the normative side of the legitimacy equation. Thus there are structures and processes in place that make satisfaction of every demand impossible. Conflict is most likely when (a) the distribution of interests among the population to be governed is heterogeneous; (b) the GGO does not have coercive tools at its disposal; and (c) the GGO lacks control over a valuable resource. Alas, these conditions are almost always present.

The consent of all nations does not have equal marginal effects on a GGO's authority. Some members (nations, companies, interest groups) are more critical to the establishment and maintenance of a global governance organization's authority. Any global rulemaking body that is not accepted by key actors offers minimal benefit to other potential members. Consider a few examples. The standards generated by the International Accounting Standards Board are intended to make it easier for investors (and others) to assess the financial reports of companies the world over. Accepting the IASB's standards creates real costs for those who must adapt current accounting practices. If the United States or EU rejects such rules, the benefits will not justify the costs because any effort to enter those markets will require restatement of all reports according to *another* set of standards.

Without the acquiescence of key nations or organizations, an international organization will be marginalized. Its value to the less powerful organizations is derived from the acquiescence of all parties (including the most powerful). If the GGO's rules are ignored by the most significant market participants, there is little reason for the less powerful to go along. Moreover, once ignored, the GGO may even lose its substantive legitimacy as it no longer achieves the very goals it was created to pursue.

If the most influential nations *do* grant a GGO authority, the less powerful face a stark choice. Although the typical transnational governance organization cannot coerce the rich and powerful, smaller and less wealthy nations face high costs for rejecting or ignoring the rules propagated by international organizations. The consequences could be dire both politically and economically. A nation out of compliance with International Civil Aviation Organization requirements for international air traffic, for example, would be effectively inaccessible to the world (including tourists and investors). A country choosing to flaunt the regulations of the International Maritime Organization risks losing the ability to export its commodities to world markets. A nation that fails to adopt the accounting standards of the IASB makes it that much more difficult for its companies to raise capital. These are real costs.

Even the largest and wealthiest nations sometimes face this dynamic. The SARS episode illustrated this potential most dramatically because it involved two powerful nations confronting the surprising power of the World Health Organization. Although the governments of China and Canada strongly objected to the conclusions that their cities were unsafe to visit, both countries nevertheless worked to satisfy the WHO requirements because the economic implications of WHO travel advisories were dire. For parties in this situation, the authority of the GGO is effectively coercive. Opting out of the international system is self-defeating.

If one took the logic presented above to its extreme, the conclusion would be that the most powerful members can simply impose their will upon each GGO in every situation. The GGO would have to satisfy such members because failure to do so would threaten the organization's authority. This reasoning is wrong. Representatives of less-influential member-states acknowledge and accept the power differential among GGO participants, but there is a limit to their tolerance for inequity (Woods 2003). The breaking point is a function of normative and practical considerations. Pushed beyond this limit, less-powerful actors will simply walk away, an outcome that serves no interests. For even the most powerful actors, widespread global adoption of rules created by GGOs is a significant part of the value proposition for participation in international organizations.

The capacity to accept apparent unfairness is bounded for less-powerful players *even if the net benefits of participation remain positive*. Studies of behavior in "ultimatum games" reveal this facet of human psychology. Such games place two individuals in a situation where they must share a finite good, one dollar. The first individual proposes how to divide the dollar. The second has only a take-it-or-leave-it choice: accept the proposed allotment or reject it, leaving both with nothing. In theory, the second individual should accept any positive amount (e.g., 1 cent) no matter how unequal the division. But it turns out that most people reject a grossly inequitable division (less than twenty cents) even though that leaves them with nothing, less than they would have received under the unjust division (Camerer 2003, 43). Moreover, most people occupying the first position do not try to impose "too unfair" a division, suggesting an internalized sense of fairness or an intuition that the person in the second position would choose nothing before accepting a grossly inequitable distribution.

Practical considerations also explain weaker members' intolerance for excessive inequity in the distribution of power within a global governance organization. At times, GGOs may stretch or even violate the expectations of democratic legitimacy, but the wholesale violation of such norms makes participation in such organizations a "hard sell" back home. If the GGO merely institutionalizes the preferred policies of the key actors in a given arena, the costs of participating in the GGO (which are not insignificant for a developing country or small firm) cannot be justified.

The need to meet some standards of normative legitimacy imposes real limits on the ability of GGOs to satisfy the demands of key actors. Consider the example of the stalled WIPO patent treaty referenced earlier. The ability of members to hold up negotiation on the patent treaty is a function of procedures adopted by WIPO to lend normative legitimacy. Like many global governance organizations, WIPO operates on a consensus basis. Consensus can be surprisingly ambiguous, but in this instance, agreement on the organizational agenda was required of all participating members (i.e., countries). This normatively appealing approach to decisionmaking now threatens to undermine WIPO authority because the lack of agreement prompted some members to convene outside the organization. Consistent with the logic of this chapter, the WIPO secretariat actively worked to resolve the conflict to keep patent negotiation.

Herein lies the tricky balancing act required of GGOs. If WIPO or any other GGO is to maintain stability, balance cannot be established on an ad hoc basis. The practical value of the governance organization—in the short or long term—must be manifestly obvious to all of the nations and organizations that must "opt in" in order to confer legitimacy and authority. Core members must be satisfied with the fundamental attractiveness of the global governance regime, meaning that the design of the GGO must build in the necessary reassurance to ensure commitment. Calibrating the organization to meet the very different demands necessary to achieve authority—while keeping in line with the expectations of normative legitimacy—is the challenge. The empirical research demonstrates that in both structure and process, GGOs do just this by incorporating "safety valves" that give greater influence to some members.

Normative Legitimacy or Bargaining Game?

One might frame the dilemma of global governance as a clash of interests, a struggle pitting the interests of large (i.e., powerful) against small (i.e., weak) members, without any reference to normative considerations. To maintain their place in an international system, GGOs must keep all parties sufficiently satisfied. The situation represents a complex asymmetric multiparty bargaining situation. Nations have varying levels of interest in a global rulemaking system (and each nation's interest varies by substantive area and issue). Each member contributes different levels of value to the system and thus commands different payments in return for their participation. Consequently, the United States extracts more preferential treatment than, say, Malawi, because a global accounting standard that is not adopted by the United States is essentially meaningless, while Malawi's adoption is only marginally significant (if at all). Collectively, however, the less-influential nations can undermine a global regime by opting out of the GGO. If the preferences of one member (or set of influential members) are satisfied at the expense of "weak" members at every decision point, eventually the weaker members may leave the organization. This would undermine the GGO, thus proving self-defeating from the perspective of powerful members hoping for a global regime.

One could formally model such a dynamic in the hopes of discovering the equilibrium at which the powerful members—or the leadership of the GGO itself—satisfy the preferences of stronger and weaker members (Shepsle 1996). The conclusions derived from such a model would be largely derivative of the utility assigned to any given set of outcomes as well as the value of a global governance regime for both the powerful and weak members. These assignments would be essentially arbitrary as the value of worldwide rules and any given decision are difficult to discern under the best of circumstances, let alone generalized across disparate policy areas.

Still, bargaining among interested parties is obviously central to global governance. The interests of weaker members are factored into the calculations of GGOs not simply to satisfy normative considerations but to maintain the balance of interests. In the discussion of particular cases and the facets of GGO organization including structure, rulemaking, and interest group participation, it is always clear that the weaker members are able to assert their claims based on some ability to deny the GGO its authority. Expressing the entire dynamic of global governance as a bargaining game internal to the authority side of the equation, however, misses an important element. Every GGO shows an interest in normative legitimacy independent of the interest-based satisfaction of powerful and less powerful members. That is, global governance organizations pursue legitimacy for instrumental *and* normative reasons. This raises an interesting question: what is the value of legitimacy in the absence of authority? Or, more practically, why would an organization worry about the demands of legitimacy *if it did not bring authority?*

This situation could arise in two ways. First, an organization may possess authority for reasons unrelated to normative legitimacy (e.g., the repressive regime). Second, an organization could be so hopelessly lacking in authority that it is ignored even as it checks off every requirement of normative legitimacy. (Some cynics argue that the UN General Assembly is the most visible example of such an entity.) In both cases, legitimacy seems to get the organization nothing; it has authority already or it never will. And yet, few if any organizations seem ready to write off legitimacy.

For the organization already possessing authority, legitimacy may be a relatively inexpensive means of maintaining authority (Hurd 1999). Dahl and Lindblom note that "lack of legitimacy imposes heavy costs on the controllers" (1992, quoted in Hurd 1999). The population must receive significant benefit from the maintenance of the regime or the organization must maintain sufficient coercive power—and deploy it when necessary—to make submission the preferable course. To the extent normative legitimacy can be a substitute for pragmatic bases of authority—without endangering the regime—it represents a huge potential savings for the governing organization. Of course, there are those who reject the very premise of the question in the context of global governance, arguing that legitimacy has no substitute; its demands must be satisfied (Bull et al. 2004; Dingwerth 2005). Buchanan and Keohane articulate this practical value of legitimacy arguing that "the perception of legitimacy matters, because, in a democratic era, multilateral institutions will only thrive if they are viewed as legitimate by democratic publics" (Buchanan and Keohane 2006, 407).

A second explanation lies in the values of the members and staff of governance organizations. The people running global governance organizations are acculturated to the values of Western democracy (for the most part) and *want* to conform to expectations of legitimacy. They do not see themselves as interest-driven servants nor do they particularly relish the idea of imposing the collective will by virtue of resentment-inducing coercion. To challenge the wisdom of another great political thinker, they would rather be loved than feared. Measuring this motivation for the pursuit of legitimacy is impossible, but that does not make it any less real. The men and women who make GGOs function are not comfortable with the idea of forgoing legitimacy, even if doing so were not deleterious to their organizations' effectiveness.

Finally, even organizations with authority solidly secured are likely to face questions regarding legitimacy. One might argue that an individual doubting the legitimacy of an authoritative organization ought to express this view by ignoring its authority. Practically speaking, however, individuals do not always have the luxury of disobedience. Vocal objection may be the strongest response available. This situation resembles that of a worker unhappy with the terms of his employment. Given the asymmetry of power, the option of "exit" is not practically available and thus "voice" becomes the primary means of objection (Shapiro 1999). Objection to the legitimacy of the individual, group, or organization with authority is possible without suffering draconian consequences. Consider the WHO-SARS example cited earlier. Like the residents of a company town who have no choice but to accept the dictates of the dominant firm, the Canadian and Chinese governments vigorously questioned the legitimacy of the WHO actions even as they complied. This puts the onus on the authoritative organization to identify the sources of its legitimacy. In the aftermath of the incident, the WHO worked to formalize its procedures for handling such situations for fear that these critiques could undermine the organization in the future (interviews 10, 11, 44).

What Makes GGOs Different?

The conflict between the demands of legitimacy and authority is particularly vexing for GGOs, but the need for organizations to maintain both is universal. For most organizations, legitimacy and authority are mutually reinforcing, as discussed earlier in this chapter. Legitimacy is a psychological source of authority. Authority leads to organizational effectiveness, which, in turn, provides normative "output" legitimacy. This legitimacy-authority circle is interrupted when organizations must violate legitimacy expectations to build institutional authority or vice versa. Although all organizations face this tension to some extent, three characteristics of global governance organizations set them apart: limited sanction powers, lack of taken-for-grantedness, and lack of an established community to provide consensus approval of organizational legitimacy.

Lack of Coercive Tools

The lack of sanction authority makes it difficult for global governance organizations to influence the calculation of interests of those considering obedience (Franck 1990). That is, most governance organizations can alter the interest-based calculation of the governed such that authority is secured; the organization is accepted because rejecting it is too costly given the consequences. With limited exceptions (most notably the WTO), GGOs lack the ability to alter the calculus of the governed in such a manner (Chayes and Chayes 1995). To build authority, therefore, the GGO must "give in" to the demands of influential members, compromising normative legitimacy in the process.

The lack of sanctioning tools renders GGO authority more conditional than it is for other governance organizations. Even when a global governance organization is exercising broad influence, it must factor in the limits of tolerance for its authority in ways that most governing bodies do not. This makes a sacrifice on the legitimacy front much more likely.

This is highly problematic, for the lack of coercive tools also logically makes legitimacy more important as a basis of organizational authority! As described already, organizations will attempt to build pragmatic authority by satisfying key parties in noncoercive fashion. The compromised foundation of pragmatic authority will inevitably turn attention of other bases of authority including legitimacy, a psychological source of authority. It is thus ironic that the steps required to build pragmatic authority threaten to undermine normative legitimacy.

Lack of Cognitive Legitimacy

Most GGOs are relatively youthful and lack the "taken-for-grantedness" that underscores the authority of venerable governance organizations. Even those international organizations that have achieved the much-valued "taken-for-grantedness" have a historical profile defined by organizational weakness. Global governance organizations that functioned as glorified trade associations or forums for international meetings are evolving from conveners into rulemakers and regulators. The World Health Organization, for example, recently created and enacted a comprehensive policy on smoking and the standards defining regulation of cigarettes on a global scale. WHO's work on SARS and avian flu pushed its taken-for-grantedness to the limit. It's as if the corner crossing guard asserted wide-ranging police powers.

Most GGOs do not enjoy lengthy histories of even low-level acceptance. This leaves them in an archetypical "Catch-22" situation. Without a track record of achievement, it is difficult to establish cognitive legitimacy, but without legitimacy it is difficult to build a record of reassuring performance.

Lack of Community

The worldwide reach of GGOs exacerbates the legitimacy and authority challenges. Among the constituencies served by global rulemakers—members and nonmembers—values and interests are heterogeneous in the extreme. Governance organizations typically struggle with conflicting expectations but for the GGO, the lack of shared beliefs and interests pose a significant obstacle.

Legitimacy remains a relativistic concept. The appropriateness of an organization's assumption of authority requires some agreement among the members of the concerned community (Suchman 1995). For global governance organizations, this is particularly troublesome, because the constitution of the relevant community is ambiguous and contested (Hurd 1999; Taylor 2002). GGOs are products of and responsive to a community of nations and interests with widely divergent views regarding the proper relationship between the governing institutions and the governed populace (Carr 1942; Taylor 2002). The participation of national governments in the governance of international organizations also varies, resulting in different expectations. Many communities of interest are not evenly distributed geographically. Moreover, influence within communities is not evenly distributed among the various subpopulations.

GGOs also serve a community of interest groups (including profit-seeking companies) that are deeply affected by the rules, standards, and regulations generated. Serving the interests of these parties is important, too. These organizations have owners and / or members with political influence scattered around the globe. Their concerns vary widely, and their relationships with the national governments are also heterogeneous. Conflicts among domestic interest groups often carry over to the international arena, leaving GGOs to sort out domestic conflicts along with transnational ones. Finally, there is a global community of individuals who are governed by, and have an interest in, international organizations. Cosmopolitan critics call for organizational legitimacy that satisfies this global community notwithstanding widely varied cultural and political expectations (Held 2004). Even in the absence of the legitimacy-authority tension, universally acknowledged legitimacy would be elusive because all these different constituencies maintain (but do not necessarily articulate) different standards.

Theory and the Empirical Analysis

The conflict between authority and legitimacy may seem esoteric and removed from the daily activities of GGOs. It is not. To the surprise of the author, several interview subjects described the challenges of their jobs in terms that could have been lifted from this chapter. Most commonly, the legitimacy-authority tension is experienced as accountability failure. As the discussion has shown, accountability represents the same legitimacy-authority minefield under a different name (Koppell 2005). With its emphasis on fidelity to principles regarding representation and process, meeting the demands of legitimacy calls for *responsibility*-type accountability. Granting special deference to key players as means of building authority—what would be seen as *responsiveness* in accountability terms—is anathema. Just as the distinctive challenges of global governance make it difficult for organizations to maximize legitimacy and authority, GGOs will struggle to be regarded as accountable because in one sense or another they will inevitably fall short.

Understanding the conflicting accountability imperatives and their relationship to the demands of legitimacy and authority helps make sense of the seemingly contradictory aspects of GGO structure and process. Each organization has adopted a distinctive approach to global governance, but patterns do emerge in the analysis of the empirical data gathered for this study. Drawing together the findings in chapters 4–7 on structure, rulemaking, adherence, and interest group participation, the concluding chapter offers three models of global governance: *classical*, *cartel*, and *symbiotic*. Each model represents a different solution to the inherent legitimacy-authority challenge of global governance identified in this chapter. As a result, each presents distinctive accountability shortcomings reflecting the demands each organization faces. Severe critics of global governance organizations might argue that the common element of global governance is a chronic lack of accountability, but they overlook this important variation.

A final word regarding the terminology employed in this analysis: the manner in which the words "authority" and "legitimacy" are used in this discussion should not deter readers who object to the definitions offered here. The core argument of this book concerns the conflicting pressures that shape GGOs. The choice of words used to describe this dynamic is of secondary importance. Employing Suchman's delineation, one could say that "normative legitimacy" is at odds with "pragmatic legitimacy." Normative legitimacy demands consistency with principles regarding the design and operation of the organization (or *responsibility*-type accountability). Pragmatic legitimacy places satisfaction of member demands (*responsiveness*) at the forefront, grounding legitimacy in self-interest rather than justice. Regardless of the rhetorical formulation, the essential argument is the same. GGOs are (sometimes) faced with conflicting demands. Because they typically lack the tools to figuratively twist the arms of the governed, they must contort themselves to satisfy two divergent sets of expectations. But no global governance organization is flexible enough to satisfy the contradictory demands of accountability.

CHAPTER THREE

Introduction to the GGO Sample and GGO Core Characteristics

D efining the group of organizations to be included in a study of global governance is surprisingly difficult. There is no bureaucratic equivalent to the Classification of Living Things introduced by Carolus Linnaeus in 1735, so one cannot simply choose all members of a particular kingdom or phylum of organizations. Creating such a hierarchical taxonomy requires identification of characteristics that are most fundamental to understanding an organization's behavior (Scott 1992, 127). Is it scale? Is it sector? Is it structure? Lacking answers to these questions, we are left with ad hoc categorization that lumps together organizations on the basis of characteristics we assume to be most important. By focusing on organizations with the same geographic jurisdiction (global) and function (governance), this study accepts two such assumptions. But a third characteristic often treated as equally fundamental—organizational sector—is examined critically. Indeed, it is argued in the pages that follow that governmental and nongovernmental global governance organizations have much in common.

This chapter first establishes the definition of a "global governance organization" (GGO), explaining the selection of entities included in this study, and, in the process, offering an approach to sorting the universe of organizations that explains the focus on rulemaking entities. In the second section, the sample of twenty-five GGOs examined is described. (A brief background on each GGO is offered as an online appendix). Finally, the third section of this chapter introduces five core characteristics of global governance organizations, each hypothesized as a predictor of GGO structure and process. These five core characteristics— SECTOR, RULE TYPE, MEMBERSHIP, FUNDING, and TECHNICALITY—serve as reference points in the search for patterns among the GGOs examined.

Sorting Out the Universe of Organizations

The nation-state has long been a dominant unit of political analysis, conforming to recent experiences in which national governments have played a leading role in human events. Separating organizations that transcend individual nation-states from those that do not is reasonable. But "international organization" is a broad category of entities grouped together on the assumption that a common trait, jurisdiction spanning national boundaries, is supremely important. The diversity of entities herded into IO Corral indicates that this grouping is more like a kingdom than a genus. "International organization" is used to describe everything from the European Union to Greenpeace to NATO. The diversity of the population of international organizations leads one to reasonably conclude that insights applicable to the whole class are scarce. Identifying a subset of international organizations with shared fundamental characteristics makes larger-*n* study plausible.

Geographic Jurisdiction

Finer division on the basis of geographic scope helps analysis of international organizations. They can be sorted among those that are bilateral, regional, multilateral (but not regional), and global. This book is focused on those that have or seek global jurisdiction. One might argue that separating global organizations from other international organizations is merely an artifact of conventional use, reinforced by divisions of academic subfields. Still, limiting the set of studied organizations to those with global scope satisfies methodological considerations as much as theoretical ones, increasing the internal validity of this study by reducing concern with contextual variation relevant to understanding regional organizations (Crozier 1964; Scott 1992, 137). Moreover, by examining *only* global governance organizations, a higher percentage of the total population is included in the sample.

The worst possible consequence of circumscribing the analysis by excluding regional governance organizations is that the significance of the findings may be *understated*; the conclusions of this book may apply to nonglobal transnational governance organizations. This leaves a rich vein of data to be mined in the future. This book provides testable hypotheses applicable to any number of international and domestic governance organizations.

Organizational Function (or What Do Organizations Do All Day?)

James Rosenau insightfully distinguished between government and governance (particularly in the international context), calling attention to the reality that many organizations that are effectively "governing" are not part of any government (Rosenau and Czempiel 1992). Organizations performing governance functions in the international arena may not resemble a domestic government bureaucracy. The essential point can and should be generalized: organizational function is not determined by organizational sector. Marketing is not limited to privately owned entities, for instance. Nonprofits do not have a monopoly on providing assistance. Organizational *function* may be the most meaningful dimension of variation among organizations but we do not have a standard taxonomy. In the interests of parsimony, it is proposed that every organization is engaged in one of four activities: *production, service, mobilization*, or *governance*. The first three are sketched briefly before turning to governance.

PRODUCTION. Organizations that make or create goods or commodities are engaged in production: growing, manufacturing, or generating something of value. For-profit organizations undertake such activities in the hopes of creating an economic surplus. Government organizations also produce a wide range of public goods including roads, sewers, housing, and other infrastructure. In many contexts, government is a market participant, offering goods through state-owned enterprises. Nonprofit organizations also engage in production. Cooperatives cultivate crops and commodities as well as engage in manufacturing. Many charities produce public goods, including housing and medical care. If one were to subdivide this category, producers of public goods and producers of private goods might be the first differentiation.

SERVICE. Organizations that help individuals or groups achieve their goals or satisfy their needs are service providers. The services provided by nonprofit organizations typically fall into a subcategory of assistance or aid (e.g., disaster relief or tutoring). Social welfare agencies are included in this category as well as entities that provide health care, postal service, and education. Religious and military organizations are included in this category, as they help people find spiritual salvation and provide national security, respectively. (These functions are so distinctive, they might deserve dedicated categories). There is a wide range of for-profit service providers, of course, including those carrying out tasks mentioned above (e.g., medical care) that are frequently associated with nonprofits. For-profit service organizations perform maintenance functions, prepare food, care for children, and offer entertainment as well as provide legal and financial services.

MOBILIZATION.　Activating people, groups, and organizations in a collective effort aimed at influencing others is deemed mobilization. Political parties are primarily involved in this activity as are many advocacy groups, consumer groups, interest groups, and labor unions. This category is heavily associated with nonprofit entities. One might take issue with the placement of certain organization types. For example, religious organizations might be considered mobilization- rather than service-oriented. The tempting digression into the categorization of different entities shall be resisted as the differentiation is offered for the purposes of distinguishing the final organizational function: governance.

GOVERNANCE.　Governance is about creating order. Definitions of governance generally touch upon the processes, systems, and structures (formal and informal) by which behavior is regulated and constrained (Peters 1995). In this expansive sense, every organization is engaged in governance. All organizations have internal distributions of power and authority, mechanisms by which decisions are made and implemented, and so on—though it may not seem like it at times (Pfeffer and Salancik 2003; March et al. 1993). To create an organization is to create order. An organization with a governance function seeks to impose order beyond its own boundaries.

Even construed broadly, most organizations are not engaged in governance in this sense. They do not seek to set the processes, systems, and structures of society generally. For-profit firms, for instance, generally work within market institutions whose rules are defined by other bodies. They may try to influence the organizations that set the rules of said institutions, but (for the most part) they acknowledge the power of a governance organization to create and maintain order.

This definition of governance emphasizes what Majone calls "regulatory" governance, as distinct from positive governance (1997). Regulatory governance calls for the enactment of rules, norms, or standards and demanding compliance with the goal of altering another entities' behavior (to reduce or compensate for negative externalities or compel production of some public good). Positive governance calls for an organization to assume responsibility for creation and distribution of some public good. These "positive" activities include key functions like provision of vital services (e.g., fire, national defense), implementation of social programs (e.g., education, housing, medical care), and operation of collectively consumed services (e.g., parks, transportation). Each of these activities induces behavior among those who partake in the goods and services produced. In the typology of organizational function suggested here, however, these tasks are better categorized as *production* or *service* than *governance.*

Even with this clarification, activities defying easy classification remain. Provision of subsidies intended to induce desired behavior blends *production* and *governance,* for example. Imposition of conditions to be satisfied in order for an organization to receive some benefit (e.g., a subsidy or loan) has the same effect. Still, the basic distinction between organizations that are positive and regulatory is robust. One might not accept the argument that budget pressures are forcing governments around the world to shift from positive to regulatory governance, for example, but the claim has meaning because the distinction between the two types of activities is comprehensible. There are, of course, organizations engaged in activities of both regulatory *and* positive character (i.e., production or service delivery). Organizations included in this study have rulemaking, a fundamentally regulatory activity, at their functional core.

Most conventional governance organizations are well known and, more often than not, governmental. Regulatory agencies make rules regarding everything from advertising to bookkeeping to construction to driving to employment, and so on. In this sense, legislatures are the ultimate governance organizations in the democratic context, for they typically produce the laws governing these (and innumerable other) areas. Bureaucratic organizations often add specificity to laws by crafting regulations clarifying the requirements for compliance with such laws.

But governance takes other, nongovernmental forms. Many entities try to shape the context in which other organizations operate without altering laws or regulations. In recent years, for example, nongovernmental organizations have encouraged consumers to consider various standards in their purchasing (Conroy 2007). This is a form of governance, as such standards can become de facto rules, constraining profit-seeking companies by making certain behaviors economically prohibitive (Brunsson and Jacobsson 2000; Greenstein and Stango 2007). The use of standards puts such NSMD governance organizations alongside other standard-setting bodies. The International Organization for Standardization (ISO) is perhaps the best known, producing standards for an enormous variety of industries ranging from oil drilling to cosmetics to environmental engineering (Higgins and Tamm Hallstrom 2007).

Some organizations perform a governance function (arguably) unintentionally. Credit rating agencies such as Moody's and Standard & Poor's effectively create rules for companies and governments that enter debt markets (Sinclair 2005). Because the ratings attached to their debt will affect the interest they must pay to lenders, entities endeavor to satisfy the ratings agencies' criteria. These criteria thus start to resemble rules with a penalty—higher borrowing costs—attached to disobedience. Organizations that rank institutions, such as colleges, can have a similar effect. College administrators seeking to raise or maintain their ranking must satisfy the criteria established by the ranking's creator, whether they believe it enhances their institution or not (Martins 2005). Indeed, there has recently been some backlash among American universities against ranking for precisely this reason (Marklein 2007).

Returning to the matter of immediate importance, the parameters of a "global governance organization" take shape. An organization has to be actively engaged in attempts to order the behavior of other actors on a global scale. This eliminates some organizations that operate globally but without the intention to create an ordered space in which other actors operate. Karns and Mingst (2004) provide a list of the roles performed by international organizations that clarifies how the definition of "governance" was applied in selecting the sample organizations for this research. There is a substantial population of international organizations, governmental and nongovernmental, that serve *one* of these functions:

1. informational,
2. forum,
3. normative (standards of behavior),
4. rule-creating (legally binding treaties),

5. rule-supervisory (monitoring and enforcement), and

6. operational

Only organizations devoted to three of Karns and Mingst's six activities—normative, rule-creating, and rule-supervisory activities—compel
changes in behavior of other parties. The other three functions—informational, forum, operational—complement the *governance* activities but
are less consistent with the use of "governance" set forth above. Examples
help clarify the application to real organizations.

The International Committee of the Red Cross (ICRC), an institution
created to provide "humanitarian protection and assistance for victims of
war and armed violence," is not a GGO (ICRC 2007). It is a service organization providing aid to needy populations. Obviously, the ICRC governs
itself, generating rules, procedures, standards, etc. to guide the behavior
of members and staff. Its mandate, however, is not to set general rules
governing ordinary behavior of people and organizations outside the organization. Contrast it with the International Civil Aviation Organization
(ICAO), which establishes rules applicable to actors around the world
operating within its substantive sphere of influence. Clear statements of
ICAO's ordering function are contained in its foundational documents
and publicly available descriptions that clarify the organizational mission.
The ICAO, for example, seeks to create rules that bring safety and security to international air traffic (ICAO 2008). Note that a major category of
international organizations is excluded from this study: transnational security organizations. NATO and other alliance-based organizations have
been central in the study of international organizations but *governance*, as
defined here, is not their core function.

One additional criterion was applied in selecting organizations for this
study: substantive scope. Many international organizations have wide-
ranging substantive jurisdictions. The European Union (EU), for example,
is involved in almost every conceivable area of public policy. Indeed, the
EU resembles a nation-state, with its own representative body, multiple
bureaucratic units and specialized personnel devoted to particular issue
areas. The UN system is, of course, equally broad in scope. Unlike the EU
and the UN, most GGOs are focused in a relatively narrow policy realm
such as air traffic control, intellectual property, or health. It is reasonable
to hypothesize that the dynamics of rulemaking for a multipurpose entity
are different than those of a narrow regulatory body. This project consid-

ers organizations that are narrow in both senses, function (rulemaking) and scope.

The substantive broadness of an organization's mandate is highly correlated with the broadness of its functions, making it straightforward to select organizations on this basis. Organizations with wide-ranging responsibilities are more likely to be engaged in positive governance (i.e., production). Both the EU and the UN employ positive and regulatory approaches, for example. Focusing exclusively on the narrower organizations has methodological advantages. Observing the institutional players, the interest groups, and the policy dynamics is easier with respect to narrower organizations. Bargains are more difficult to strike across issue areas, and thus the conflicts and means of resolution are somewhat easier to observe. Also, if history is any guide, the proliferation of narrow GGOs is more likely than an increase in the number of entities with wide scope. Narrower organizations are easier to construct and, by virtue of their circumscribed authority, seem less threatening to national autonomy (Cooper et al. 2008). Both of these points are consistent with the overall themes of this book and shall be revisited in subsequent chapters.

Aside from the UN, the two most prominent international organizations not directly included in this study are the Bretton Woods financial institutions, the World Bank and the IMF, although both are referenced throughout the text. These organizations are both substantively and functionally broader than the twenty-five GGOs examined in this study. Moreover, the nature of their activities is not as plainly in the regulatory governance mode as the included entities. There is no reason to assume that the findings offered are inapplicable to these important organizations, but certainly one would have to be cautious given the differences.

Finally, there is a small set of private firms whose market power is such that they effectively order the environment. Microsoft's Windows operating system is so universal that it takes on the characteristics of governance, establishing a common set of rules, definitions, and standards that make interactions much easier. Still, characterizing Microsoft as a governance organization by virtue of this reality feels odd because this effect is a by-product—albeit a formidable one—rather than the organization's core purpose. This project focuses on organizations that are straightforward inclusions in the governance category—organizations created and administered to generate rules—rather than wading into the substantial gray area. Interestingly, many organizations engaged in governance are vehement in denying that they govern anything. This project provides insight into the reasons why an organization would actively resist the governance tag.

GGOs Included in This Study

You won't find anything in the telephone book under "global governance organizations." There are quite a few international organizations, but most do not engage in "regulatory governance" on a global scale (as defined above). Of those that do have a rulemaking function, many have other roles more central to the organization's mission. The twenty-five organizations discussed in this book were chosen to offer variation on the core characteristics described in the third section of this chapter. Also, the selected organizations seem to "matter" to individuals and firms operating in the relevant spheres of activity. This evolutionary success provides an opportunity to draw inferences based on the observed patterns of characteristics for this sample. For this set of relatively effective organizations, what features seem correlated? There may be biases in the sample, but the analysis never treats the distribution of characteristics in this sample as representative of the distribution across the entire GGO population. There is never any implication that the percentage of the sample population displaying a characteristic is a strong predictor of the percentage of the total GGO population with the same trait. The analytic focus is always on the relationship among organizational characteristics.

Selection emphasized global governance organizations engaged in substantive arenas with straightforward public policy significance. The financial rulemakers included—the International Accounting Standards Board, the World Trade Organization, and the Basel Committee on Capital Standards—shape international commerce and global credit markets, for example. International sports federations, created to establish rules for competition in games like badminton (Badminton World Federation) and soccer (Fédération Internationale de Football Association), do create rules applicable beyond the membership of the organization itself on a global scale. In spirit and significance, however, they seemed distinct and a possible distraction to consideration of policy-oriented organizations. Of course, the findings may be relevant to these entities.

One might be surprised by the range in variation on commonly observed attributes of organizations. The average age, for example, is forty-nine years with a high of 142 (International Telecommunication Union) and a low of 8 (Marine Stewardship Council). The range in size is equally broad. The average GGO has about five hundred employees, but the largest (World Health Organization) has thousands, while the smallest (Unicode Consortium) has only three paid staff. Given the lack of a GGO census, it is difficult to determine whether the proportions of the total population are accurately reflected in this sample (as noted above), but GGOs were selected to ensure variation on the five core characteristics described in the next section. These characteristics (including member-ship, funding, and the type of rules produced) are evaluated as predic-tors of the approach to rulemaking and organizational structure among GGOs.

Global governance organizations that disappeared (or never came to be) are not included in the study. Identifying these "dogs that don't bark" is even more difficult than finding extant GGOs. The emphasis is squarely on that which *is* rather than that which *is not*. The goal is to learn from the existing ecology of global governance but certainly the issue of GGO formation is an important topic for further inquiry.

Core Characteristics of GGOs

Bringing an organizational perspective to the study of global governance entails an examination of the factors that might explain variation in or-ganizational structure and process. The literature on international or-ganizations generally separates intergovernmental organizations from nongovernmental entities. This separation presumes that organizations sorted into these two categories are fundamentally dissimilar, a notion that is contestable and examined in this study. SECTOR is, in fact, one of five core characteristics that theory suggests should have great consequences for GGO structure and process. The five variables—referred to as the "core characteristics" throughout the book—were identified based on the-ory regarding the nature of complex organizations. In the analysis of each aspect of the GGOs, the first hypotheses tested considered whether pat-terns in the distribution of variation were linked to the five core character-istics: SECTOR, RULE TYPE, MEMBERSHIP, FUNDING, and TECHNICALITY.

The twenty-five organizations were selected to offer variation on all five of the core characteristics. Naturally, there is not an even distribution

TABLE 3.1 **Sample of Twenty-five Organizations Studied with Core Characteristics**

Organization	Acronym	Sector	Rule Type	Membership	Funding	Technicality
ASTM International	ASTM	Nongovernment	Standard	Open	Revenue	Higher
Basel Committee on Banking Supervision	BCBS	Government	Standard	Closed	Member Contribution	Higher
Convention in the Trade of Endangered Species	CITES	Government	Regulation	Open	Member Contribution	Lower
Fairtrade International	FLOI	Nongovernment	Standard	Closed	Member Contribution	Lower
Financial Action Task Force on Money Laundering	FATF	Government	Multiple	Closed	Member Contribution	Lower
Forest Stewardship Council	FSC	Nongovernment	Standard	Closed	Mixed / Other	Higher
International Accounting Standards Board	IASB	Nongovernment	Standard	Nonmember	Member Contribution	Higher
International Atomic Energy Agency	IAEA	Government	Multiple	Closed	Member Contribution	Higher
International Civil Aviation Organization	ICAO	Government	Standard	Closed	Member Contribution	Higher
International Electrotechnical Commission	IEC	Mixed	Standard	Closed	Mixed / Other	Higher
International Labour Organization	ILO	Mixed	Multiple	Open	Member Contribution	Lower
International Maritime Organization	IMO	Government	Multiple	Open	Member Contribution	Lower
International Organization for Standardization	ISO	Mixed	Standard	Open	Revenue	Higher
International Seabed Authority	ISA	Government	Regulation	Open	Member Contribution	Lower
International Telecommunication Union	ITU	Mixed	Standard	Open	Member Contribution	Higher
International Whaling Commission	IWC	Government	Regulation	Open	Member Contribution	Lower
Internet Corporation for Assigned Names and Numbers	ICANN	Nongovernment	Regulation	Closed	Revenue	Higher
Marine Stewardship Council	MSC	Nongovernment	Standard	Nonmember	Mixed / Other	Higher
Unicode Consortium	UC	Nongovernment	Standard	Closed	Member Contribution	Higher
Universal Postal Union	UPU	Government	Regulation	Open	Member Contribution	Lower
World Customs Organization	WCO	Government	Multiple	Open	Member Contribution	Lower
World Health Organization	WHO	Government	Multiple	Open	Member Contribution	Lower
World Intellectual Property Organization	WIPO	Government	Multiple	Open	Revenue	Lower
World Trade Organization	WTO	Government	Multiple	Closed	Member Contribution	Lower
World Wide Web Consortium	W3C	Nongovernment	Standard	Closed	Member Contribution	Higher

on all five dimensions, but in this respect the sample likely does reflect the population. Expectations regarding the importance of these characteristics were not met uniformly in the empirical analysis. Organizational ownership (SECTOR) does have the most predictive power across areas of analysis, just as one would expect, but TECHNICALITY, MEMBERSHIP, and RULE TYPE are also good predictors of particular GGO structural and procedural features, oftentimes overriding SECTOR.

SECTOR

Fields of study, even whole schools within universities, are differentiated on the basis of organizational ownership. Business schools instruct students in the management of nongovernmental organizations (typically for-profit companies), while schools of public policy and public administration offer management training for the leaders of governmental organizations. For such institutions, this division makes more sense than dividing on the basis of geographic scope. For-profit companies that are domestic likely have more in common with international for-profit companies than they do with domestic government bureaucracies. Still, organizations on either side of the sector divide can confound expectations. As described above, organizational function is not perfectly correlated with SECTOR. Government routinely produces goods and provides services, and nongovernmental organizations are engaged in governance.

Confusing matters, differentiation on the basis of ownership is typically conflated with differentiation with respect to pursuit of profits. Organizations are conventionally spoken of as being either in the "public sector" or the "private sector." These are considered synonyms for government and nongovernment but a third sector, frequently labeled "nonprofit," or sometimes, "nongovernmental," is often added on. This typology is unclear, because the categories are not exactly parallel. Nonprofit organizations are generally construed to be nongovernmental, but governmental organizations do not typically pursue profits either! Similarly, "private sector" is generally taken to refer to profit-seeking businesses, but nonprofits are also "private," if by that we mean nongovernmental. And "public" is generally construed as "part of the government" making "private" applicable to nonprofit and for-profit nongovernmental organizations! For conceptual clarity, the public / private terminology is avoided.

One cannot simply rely upon "for-profit" and "nonprofit" as an alternative, because that dichotomy lumps together nongovernmental and governmental organizations, both usually nonprofit. To make matters more confusing, there are governmental entities that are for-profit, if we take that to mean generating an economic surplus. And no clear distinction exists between nonprofits and NGOs! In popular use, NGOs appear to be international and more interested in mobilization and advocacy than the typical nonprofit, which is generally involved in production or service delivery. Whether or not an organization pursues profits does not determine its ownership and vice versa.

To avoid confusion, SECTOR is used in these pages to communicate ownership only. Organizations are "government," "nongovernment," or "mixed." The third category is included because some organizations are owned jointly by governmental and nongovernmental actors. Some have argued that two categories are sufficient because *any* state ownership distinguishes an organization (Perry and Rainey 1988; Koppell 2003). This approach is examined at times to determine whether any results are driven by the three-category coding.

Even with the meaning of SECTOR clarified, application in the transnational arena presents challenges. What makes an international organization governmental? The UN and affiliated organizations seem the most governmental of international organizations. Yet by the definition of Rosenau (among others), the "governmentalness" of the UN is still ambiguous. The UN can and does utilize physical force to carry out its mission, but it does so under a very limited set of conditions. In terms of its "police powers," the UN is a rather weak cop. But the standard implicit in these denigrations seems to set the bar too high. The UN and affiliated entities exist by virtue of treaties signed by national governments. The UN General Assembly is made up of government representatives, and UN entities are funded (primarily) by payments from the governments of the world. The UN is as state-owned as could reasonably be defined in the absence of a global state. And, to the extent one uses governance function as a proxy for SECTOR, it communicates its governance function in the opening paragraphs of the first chapter of its charter. The organization's purpose is:

> To maintain international peace and security, and to that end: to take effective collective measures for the prevention and removal of threats to the peace, and for the suppression of acts of aggression or other breaches of the peace, and to bring about by peaceful means, and in conformity with the principles of justice and international law, adjustment or settlement of international disputes or

situations which might lead to a breach of the peace. (United Nations Charter, chap. 1, art. 1, in United Nations 2008)

Although the UN, in its entirety, is not addressed in this book—it is quite broad in both functional and substantive terms—many governmental GGOs are part of the "UN system" of organizations. This has far less meaning than organizational charts imply. Entities in the UN system do not "report" to the secretary-general or the General Assembly in the fashion that we associate with, say, American government agencies answering to the US president and Congress (Weiss and Daws 2007). Various forms of UN affiliation were included as variables in the data collection, but none have explanatory power beyond association with GGO sector. There are governmental GGOs that are not affiliated with the UN, of course, but organizations that are "governmental" are more frequently associated with the United Nations than nongovernmental GGOs. Thus any correlation between SECTOR and another characteristic shows up in the UN variables at some level.

The UN provides something of a guidepost for assessing other international organizations. By enumerating the caveats regarding United Nations' "governmentalness" (relative to domestic contexts) and spelling out the features that argue for its inclusion in the governmental category, the criteria used to determine whether an international organization is governmental emerges:

- created by national or subnational governments through treaty or other formal agreement,
- nations are members and participate in governance of international organizations through the appointment of government officials,
- funded by payments from governments, and
- endowed with some powers delegated by member governments.

Many international organizations meet these criteria, but there are also many entities performing the "governance" function that are not governmental, even by these modest standards. They were created by nongovernmental individuals or institutions. They are funded through revenues or contributions by nongovernmental bodies. They are incorporated, owned, and operated by nongovernmental entities. Two organizations in the sample are prominent examples of nongovernmental GGOs.

The nongovernmental International Accounting Standards Committee Foundation is incorporated as a nonprofit organization based in London. It is the parent entity of the International Accounting Standards Board (IASB), a body that creates rules governing a wide range of accounting issues. The IASB has developed and maintains the International Financial Reporting Standards, which is widely recognized and accepted globally (Tamm Hallstrom 2004). Although these standards are adopted by financial regulators around the world, the IASB is not formally affiliated with any government.

The Internet Corporation for Assigned Names and Numbers (ICANN) is incorporated as a nonprofit corporation (in California), but its power is derived primarily from an exclusive contract it has with the US government (Mathiason 2008). Were it not for the control over the Internet's root servers that has been delegated it by the US government, ICANN's claimed authority would be meaningless. Other mixed bodies are incorporated privately, but governmental entities are members. The International Organization for Standardization (ISO), which generates standards for products and business processes is incorporated as a nonprofit in Geneva, but its members are representatives of national institutes of standards (most of which are affiliated in one way or another with their governments).

RULE TYPE

Rule is used generically to refer to three mechanisms employed by GGOs in this study to codify requirements or expectations in a variety of fields. To provide more analytical leverage and, once again, make some generalization possible, the goal in distinguishing the approaches to global rule-making was to create the smallest possible number of categories. Three rule types are identified: treaty, regulation, and standard.

TREATY.   Sometimes called conventions or conferences, treaties are formal agreements between and among states. In the context of this study, only those treaties that call for the implementation of a set of rules applicable to nonstate actors are of interest. The ICBM Treaty, for example, is not germane because it does not require the state to impose requirements on external entities (i.e., bodies not part of the government agreeing to the treaty). Note that treaties meeting this definition often require the national government to create laws and regulations more specific than the terms of the treaty itself; this common feature helps distinguish treaties from international regulations.

Many of the global governance organizations described and examined in this book were, in fact, created by international treaties, so it may seem odd to speak of treaties as a form of rule promulgated by GGOs. The language may be awkward, but it is consistent with the practice of global governance. GGOs created by international treaty typically oversee the revision of existing treaties or the creation of new international agreements among member nations that fall within the substantive purview of the GGO.

Treatymaking by GGOs is a two-stage process. The first stage is the drafting and approval of the treaty within the organizational context. In this phase, the rulemaking is familiar. The proposed treaty will go through several stages of drafting, comment, and approval by committee until subject to final approval by the organization. This "final approval," however, does not give the agreement legal meaning (Aust 2000). It merely moves the agreement to the second stage of the process, and this is the distinctive aspect of treatymaking as a rulemaking process.

Treaties include a requirement for acceptance by national governments in order to take effect. In the absence of such consent—and the founding treaty typically establishes a minimum threshold of members for a new treaty to take effect—the proposed international agreement has no legal force. Revisions or some specifications of a treaty (sometimes called protocols) generally go through a similar procedure. Thus treatymaking as a means of making is highly dependent upon the consent of member nations, a feature discussed in chapters 5–6 on rulemaking and adherence.

REGULATION. Regulations are more specific in the definition of requirements than a treaty and can be applied to the ultimate target of regulation as written. That is, they do not require specification by the implementing organization for application to entities carrying out some transnational activity (e.g., shipping, communication). Many treaty-based GGOs are given the power to create regulations (or standards, defined below) that fill out the more general requirements laid out in the agreements. The International Health Regulations issued by the World Health Organization, for example, specify requirements under several foundational treaties.

Regulations do not require ratification or consent by member states to gain force. This does not mean that they are simply generated by the GGO without member approval. Rather, the approval process is complete at what is the end of the first stage of the treatymaking process—with a vote of the membership or some subset of the membership, always procedurally mandated. But the nation-by-nation ratification inherent to treatymaking is not required. Regulations are often specifications of fairly general requirements written into a treaty that the GGO is empowered to promulgate under the terms of the treaty itself.

Only in a few cases does the GGO have the ability to implement the regulations itself. In most cases, adherence with the regulations must be compelled by another actor—often the members of the organization— as discussed in chapter 6. The regulations produced by GGOs may be adopted by domestic or subnational governments, for example.

STANDARD. Treating standards as a type of rule will strike some as a misunderstanding of the very meaning of a "standard." The International Organization for Standardization, perhaps the most well-known standard-producing entity, defines a standards as "specifications and criteria to be applied consistently in the classification of materials, in the manufacture and supply of products, in testing and analysis, in terminology and in the provision of services" (ISO 2007b). The acceptance of common standards can open markets, create efficiencies of scale, promote competition among suppliers, and yield dramatic network effects in the sales of products (Brunsson and Jacobsson 2000). Customers can gain assurance regarding the interoperability of products and conformity with safety and quality requirements. Finally, governments are given a ready-made set of requirements that can be incorporated into law and regulation.

The choice regarding adoption of said specifications is left in the hands of a firm or state; thus standards are not, in the minds of standard-setting bodies, rules per se. But, as the discussion of international treaties and regulations indicated, the nonbinding nature of standards is hardly distinctive. Most treaties provide nations with the latitude to lodge reservations or otherwise disregard certain "requirements." In the global governance context, therefore, the discretionary nature of adherence with standards is unremarkable. Also, as discussed in chapter 6, the market pressure for adherence with standards is often stronger than the legal authority behind GGO-created regulations or treaties. Even ISO, which points out clearly that it does not "regulate or legislate," acknowledges that "although ISO standards are voluntary, they may become a market requirement" (ISO 2007b). This reflects the value every industry places on standardization.

Moreover, standards sometimes *are* given force of domestic law when they are incorporated into legal frameworks. And international standards are often integrated into other international regimes. The World Trade Organization's Agreement on Technical Barriers to Trade, for example, makes reference to international standards in explaining the rules for adjudicating conflicts between member nations. Standards produced in line with the WTO's requirements (including those promulgated by ISO, IEC, ASTM, and others) are presumed to be legitimate national requirements and thus not violations of free-trade agreements.

GGOs adopt and promulgate standards for practices in a wide variety of policy domains (from accounting to manufacturing to protection of intellectual property). They have proven so powerful a tool that activists seeking to promote a social agenda have created organizations to promulgate standards that go beyond technical standardization as conventionally understood. The NSMD governance organizations create standards to define a socially desirable behavior for participants in particular industries such as forestry, fishing, coffee production, and manufacturing (Cashore 2002; Cashore et al. 2004; Conroy 2007). International standards of this type—including those promulgated by organizations included in this study, the Forest Stewardship Council, the Fairtrade Labelling Organizations International, and the Marine Stewardship Council—are significant only to the extent adherence has market value. Each NSMD attempts to create value in its proprietary "mark" or logo such that consumers are willing to pay a premium for products bearing this sign or avoid entirely products that do *not* carry the identifiable symbol. When successful, the creation of such standards may have more impact on firms operating in these industries than governmental international rules (Conroy 2007).

Multiple Approaches under One Roof

Several global governance organizations create more than one type of rule. The World Health Organization (WHO), for example, promulgates treaties, regulations, and standards. The WHO recently pushed through the Framework Convention on Tobacco Control, an international treaty committing signatories to reduce smoking and other tobacco consumption. It has previously published (and amended) the International Health Regulations, covering a variety of subjects, and it issues standards covering levels of care and lists of drugs that are deemed essential to human health. Most

GGOs focus on one approach or another. For example, standard-setting organizations, discussed above, do not create treaties or regulations.

MEMBERSHIP.   Unlike domestic governments, most GGOs have "members." Traditionally, we think of the membership of international organizations in terms of nation-states. The UN is, of course, the exemplar of this type of international organization. Many contemporary GGOs have memberships that are not limited to—or even open to—government members. This difference is captured by the sector variable ("governmental," "nongovernmental," and "mixed"). The membership variable is concerned with the nature of membership itself, whether the organization is open or closed.

Many GGOs allow any organization that accepts the terms of the organization's founding agreement to participate as a member. GGOs frequently rely on the United Nations to define eligible members (i.e., UN members are eligible to join). GGOs granting membership to organizations clearing such a *de minimus* requirement are considered open. Essentially, anyone who wants to join, can join.

Closed-membership GGOs are more selective. They typically admit members according to criteria determined by the organization itself. Aspiring members must apply to the GGO and receive approval, giving the GGO—and its members—control over parties who participate in rulemaking and organizational decisionmaking. Two GGOs in the finance area—the Basel Committee on Banking Standards and the Financial Action Task Force on Money Laundering—have very small memberships limited to the wealthiest developed nations. Both organizations nonetheless promulgate rules with global applicability, hence their inclusion in this study (Barr and Miller 2006).

There is a third, very small set of GGOs that are not membership organizations at all. This is not because they resemble traditional national governments, with direct participation of the citizenry. On the contrary, these GGOs are organized as nonprofit, nonmembership entities, governed by self-perpetuating boards. Nonmembership GGOs do typically provide mechanisms for interested parties to participate in the organizations. The composition of governing bodies indicates that care is taken to ensure representation of industry and geographic groups, but the approach is different. For example, members of the International Accounting Standards Committee Foundation—the umbrella organization of the International Accounting Standards Board—are individuals appointed by the Board of

Trustees for three-year terms based on an assessment of their professional expertise. Individuals do not represent their employers and participate only as individuals. The Marine Stewardship Council is the other non-membership GGO represented in the sample.

FUNDING. There are essentially two models of GGO finance. Some rely largely upon contributions from members, while others generate significant revenue by charging fees for services and goods provided. Naturally, there are also organizations that mix contributions and revenues. Assuming that GGOs have an interest in maximizing—or at least maintaining—its financial support, the different incentives associated with different revenue models seem likely to influence organizational structure and processes.

GGOs take different approaches to contributions. In some cases, each member pays uniform dues. In other cases, the contributions are proportional based on some type of formula. Many GGOs apply standard international formulas for division of financial burdens, which typically link the size of contribution to the wealth of the member country. Several GGOs have unique formulas that are linked to the substance of the organization. For example, contributions to the budget of the International Maritime Organization are based on the tonnage of each nation's merchant fleet. Thus the top five contributors are Panama, Liberia, Japan, the Bahamas, and Greece (IMO 2000). In a few cases, members have the discretion to set their own contribution level (e.g., ITU).

Other GGOs generate revenue sufficient to support their operations. International standards organizations are most likely to be found in this category. The industry-oriented standard-setters charge users for copies of the standards. This income is split with the national bodies that are members of the organizations (Knight 2008). The socially oriented standard-setters frequently charge fees for the use of the recognizable mark and / or for certification of compliance with standards (Cashore et al. 2004; Conroy 2007). The revenue model is not limited to the nongovernmental GGOs as one might assume. The World Intellectual Property Organization generates revenue sufficient to support the organization through management of its international patent and trademark registry (WIPO 2006).

TECHNICALITY. It is impossible to treat the substantive area in which the GGO works as an independent variable because there would be one case in almost every category. This is unfortunate because it is reasonable to suspect that the substance of the organization's work has some impact on its structure and processes. To take this dimension of variation into account, the notion of technicality is incorporated into the study. The technical complexity of an organization's task is thought by students of bureaucracy to be a critical characteristic (Scott 1992, 2008).

Merriam-Webster's Dictionary offers that something "technical" has "special and usually practical knowledge especially of a mechanical or scientific subject" (Merriam-Webster Inc. 1998). This definition is consistent with the common understanding of the idea; something technical eludes understanding by those who are not trained in the subject matter. But TECHNICALITY is not intended as a synonym for "specialized." Most GGOs preside over fairly narrow substantive domains where the issues require a level of background knowledge and understanding. For some GGOs acquiring the requisite background knowledge is approachable for a wide array of individuals. Provided they are sufficiently briefed in the matters at hand, an average well-informed individual can participate in discourse on the rules generated by such GGOs. In other cases, the level of discourse, particularly in the rulemaking phase, is out of reach of even the sophisticated layman. Such GGOs are considered higher-technicality entities.

Assessing the "technicality" of each GGO's activities is difficult and somewhat subjective. The Organisation for Economic Co-operation and Development (OECD) has struggled with the challenge of determining technicality in its classification of industries (Hatzichronoglou 1997). Its solution focused on the investment of resources in research and development. On this basis, they sorted industries into four categories (high-technology, medium-high-technology, medium-low-technology, and low-technology). These classifications provide some guidance with respect to GGOs; aerospace and electronics were considered "high-tech" while shipbuilding and mining are considered low-tech. But these assessments do not extend to nonindustrial GGOs, like those dealing with accounting, health, and intellectual property. In recognition of the vagueness of the concept, TECHNICALITY is captured in an intentionally crude fashion. A simple dichotomous outcome—*higher* or *lower* technicality—is employed to sort the population. The approach has the virtue of transparency in its inexactness. This rough characterization sacrifices precision but offers greater confidence. TECHNICALITY is intended to capture the degree to which issues considered by the GGO and the rules it generates are scientific and / or otherwise inaccessible.

Most GGOs make some claim to high levels of technicality, a point discussed in subsequent chapters, particularly chapter 5 regarding rule-making. Self-characterization as a technical body appears to be a strategy intended to rebuff calls for greater participation and transparency (Porter 2001). More broadly, there is an implicit argument in the self-description of many GGOs that as the substance of GGO work grows more technical, the importance of public access declines. Higher-technicality GGOs do present more formidable barriers to participation through the very substance of their work. Scientific or technically sophisticated background may be required to understand issues, language, and ramifications of proposed rules. In these cases, technicality is a barrier because the underlying information is inaccessible to those lacking requisite knowledge. Indeed, the broader implications of higher-technicality rules may elude untrained eyes.

The technicality dimension provides an avenue of access to a critical area of variation. TECHNICALITY serves as a proxy for the degree to which the rules generated by the GGO are intended to achieve "pure coordination" or impose an outcome that favors one set of interests over another. This distinction is explored in great detail in subsequent chapters. The more technical the organization, the more likely the rulemaking process is generally aimed at straightforward coordination. That is, there is a need for a common rule, but parties demanding such a rule are relatively indifferent as to its content. The best example of pure coordination is a rule determining which side of the street everyone should drive on. Agreement is all that matters.

In contrast, there are domains in which coordination is highly desirable but each party seeking coordination has very different preferences regarding the agreed-upon course of action. In game theory, such a situation is referred to as a "battle of the sexes," typically exemplified by a situation in which a couple wants to go out together but the husband prefers boxing while the wife prefers ballet. Coordination is desirable by both parties but each prefers one outcome to the other (Furth 1993).

TECHNICALITY is a viable proxy for coordination. The best example in the set of organizations studied here is the Unicode Consortium, which sets rules determining the representations of linguistic characters in computer code. The existence of such a standard makes it possible for programmers around the world to ensure that characters are represented accurately wherever software is utilized. Programmers do not care whether an "A" is encoded as 11101101011 or 11001100010, only that everyone knows which is the correct string. Participants in Unicode Consortium activities are engineers or programmers deeply enmeshed in the technical aspects of computer-based communications through their work in academe or the private sector. The actual standards generated by the Unicode Consortium are incomprehensible to the average well-educated individual (including the author) and the implications of one approach to another are not immediately obvious to the layman.

The well-known World Trade Organization (WTO), in contrast, implements negotiated trade agreements, hears disputes regarding trade, and sets rules for the implementation and settlement of trade agreements. While the disputes may hinge on fine legal points, the disagreements are well understood by a general audience. Moreover, the implications of rules under consideration are quite transparent—and hardly neutral—in contrast with the more technical work of some GGOs. There is little doubt that rulemaking at the WTO is much more a "battle of the sexes" than a pure coordination game.

The consequences of technical matters can be profound (even if they are not obvious). Thus one must be wary of *assuming* that arcane, highly technical rules are inherently more neutral than those that can be read easily understood (Winner 1977). As noted above, organizations seem eager to characterize themselves as highly technical. One reason for this common claim is that the presumptive neutrality of the highly technical rules eases—at least by the logic of such GGOs—the need for rules guaranteeing access, participation, etc. Thus the cautionary note regarding the non-neutrality of high-technicality rules is necessary even as it undermines the value of technicality as a proxy for coordination.

In the empirical chapters that follow, these five core characteristics are explored as predictors of the structure and process adopted by global governance organizations. The relative analytic power of these characteristics provides insight into the underlying dynamics of global governance. SECTOR does prove important, as one would predict, but the provocative claim offered in the concluding chapter is that the emphasis on this characteristic may result in a net loss of accountability in global governance.

Structure and Administration of GGOs

G lobal governance organizations are at once captive to a set of normative beliefs regarding the proper structure of representation and bureaucratic process in democratic systems and, at the same time, compelled to violate said norms. Failure to meet normative expectations brings scolds of disapproval or, even worse, outright rejection of the entity. But fastidious adherence to democratic principles can render GGOs peripheral. On the surface, GGOs lean decidedly in the direction of the normative beliefs regarding democratic legitimacy, emphasizing member equality in voting rights, for example. Closer inspection reveals mechanisms that serve as "safety valves" for key members. The selective bodies most engaged in oversight and administration, for example, guarantee inclusion only of the most powerful.

This chapter explores the structural alternatives for GGOs. Combining a well-defined legislative (representational) body and an executive (bureaucratic) function within the overall organization, most global governance organizations resemble self-contained narrow-purpose governments offering two areas of variation. First, the political-representational structure is considered. How do members participate in the governance of the GGO? What are their rights and privileges? How is power divided? Second, the administrative structure is examined. What is the function of the bureaucracy? How does it relate to the representative body? How is it organized?

The political and bureaucratic aspects of global governance organizations are intertwined—the role of the participating members shapes the responsibilities of the bureaucrats—making the blurriness of the line separating the two a key variation. How clearly are the functions of the members and staff distinguished? How are members represented within the apparatus of the organization? How difficult is it to make a sharp distinction between the bureaucratic and representative elements of the entity? What is the balance between legislative and bureaucratic power in the organization?

It is argued that the answers to the questions raised in the preceding paragraphs do not have purely "rational" bases (Scott 1992). That is, global governance organizations are decidedly "natural" systems, reflecting the sometime-conflicting soup of imperatives identified in previous chapters. This study of structural features suggests, however, that the responses to the challenges of global governance are not random. Many of the characteristics are highly correlated, yielding the two general GGO structure types, *traditional* and *hybrid,* based on the analysis of the twenty-five GGOs in the sample.

Traditional and *hybrid* GGOs are differentiated by clustered variation on three dimensions: representational structure, apportionment, and bureaucratic function (table 4.1). GGOs with *traditional* structure adopt a conciliar approach to representation (i.e., a representative body that endows a selective council with day-to-day power), one-member, one-vote apportionment, and a centralized, functional bureaucracy. The *hybrid* structure deviates from the *traditional* type by channeling representation through specialized bodies, grouping members according to their interests, or organizing without explicit representation. The permanent staff of *hybrid* GGOs plays a supporting role to members who are deeply engaged in the rulemaking process.

TABLE 4.1 **GGO Structural Types and Accountability Emphasis**

Variable	GGO Structure Type	
	Traditional GGO	Hybrid GGO
Representational structure	Conciliar	Special., nonrep.
Apportionment	OMOV	Nonrep./1M1V
Bureaucracy	Centralized, functional	Distributed, supporting
Strongest predictor: sector	Government	Mixed / nongov.
Accountability emphasis	Responsibility (legitimacy)	Responsiveness (authority)

The bases of these structural types are laid out in the first section of this chapter. The alternatives on six dimensions of variation are identified and explained. This establishes a framework and vocabulary for discussion. In this chapter, this descriptive section covers both the representational and administrative structure of GGOs. The second section of the chapter presents and analyzes the distribution of characteristics. Patterns are identified within the observations for all organizations. Explanations are presented that link these patterns with the core attributes of GGOs described in chapter 2 (i.e., SECTOR, FUNDING, TECHNICALITY, MEMBERSHIP, and RULE TYPE). Patterns are identified based on a cluster analysis of the gathered data. As one would predict, the SECTOR of the organization is the most powerful predictor of GGO structure type. All governmental GGOs adopt the *traditional* structure (as do several nongovernmental GGOs), but there are subtleties to the variation that demonstrate why looking across sector is so important.

The concluding third section of the chapter offers implications of the observed patterns. This discussion ties the observations back to the theoretical core of the book and connects the specific findings to the other areas of focus (rulemaking, enforcement and interest groups). The *traditional* structure clearly leans in the direction of normative legitimacy, meeting the demands associated with governmental rulemakers. The *hybrid* structure, on the other hand, provides these GGOs with greater flexibility to satisfy powerful interests and build authority. The *hybrid* approach thus provides *responsiveness*-type accountability but leaves these organizations wanting in terms of the *responsibility*-type accountability emphasized by the *traditional* structure.

Six Variations in GGO Structure

Six dimensions of organizational structure are analyzed in this chapter. Table 4.2 defines each variable as a key question regarding the structure of global governance organizations, three regarding political-representational structure and three regarding bureaucratic structure. To allow for comparative analysis of GGOs, variations are reduced to the limited number of alternatives notwithstanding great differences within categories. Explication and analysis of the observed distribution of GGOs on these variables is presented in the second section of this chapter.

TABLE 4.2 **Six Dimensions of GGO Structural Variation**

Area	Question	Options
Representation	How is the participation of members structured?	Conciliar; specialized; nonrepresentative
Apportionment	How is the formal influence of members distributed?	One member, one vote; proportional; select powers; nonrepresentative
Balance	What is the primary locus of decision-making?	Legislative-centric; bureaucracy-centric
Bureaucratic Role	What is the core purpose of the bureaucracy?	Functional; supporting
Centralization	How is the bureaucracy organized?	Centralized; distributed
Scale	How large is the organization?	Small, medium, large

Three aspects of the political-representational structure of global governance organizations are considered: model of representation, apportionment of formal influence, and the balance of legislative-bureaucratic power. Each of these areas subsumes variation on specific aspects of political structure, and inevitably some differences among GGOs are overlooked in the aggregation. In some instances, variation within the categories is noted and explored when it adds to an understanding of GGOs.

Models of Representation

Notwithstanding the potential for myriad variations in the structure of participation, most of the organizations examined have adopted variations on the same model. Part of the explanation lies in the purpose in choice of representational scheme. The "conciliar" model satisfies normative demands more effectively than the other two observed types: the specialized representation model and the nonrepresentative model.

CONCILIAR MODEL OF REPRESENTATION. The "conciliar model" of the GGO structure is so named because its defining characteristic is a governing council drawn from a general assembly of all organization members (McLaren 1980, 42). The conciliar structure thus has three layers: a representative body, an intermediate body (the "council"), and a permanent bureaucracy (see table 4.3). These terms serve as generic labels; each organization uses its own terminology for each layer. The conciliar model is the overwhelmingly dominant structure among GGOs.

The representative body, comprised of all members, is the overarching entity responsible for the organization. This responsibility does not extend to day-to-day oversight of the GGO's affairs. Representative bodies typically meet rarely (70 percent meet annually or less frequently). Thus the parallel is inexact between the representative body of the typical GGO and a national parliament or other domestic legislative body.

The responsibilities of the representative body vary across organizations. Among the more common are final budget approval, formal selection of the management leader, determination of the general goals of the organization, admission of members, and consideration of amendments to the organizational charter or constitution. Nearly three-quarters of the representative bodies are also responsible for selecting members of the smaller, intermediate body.

The World Health Organization has a prototypical conciliar structure. The World Health Assembly is the representative body for the entire membership of 192 nations. It meets for several days once annually and delegates many responsibilities to its intermediate body. Thirty-four countries are elected to three-year terms as members of this executive board. Each country designates an individual board member (Stein 2001). On average, twenty-five percent of general GGO members are members of the intermediate body. In two-thirds of the sample organizations, there is some formal requirement guiding the selection of intermediate-body members. These requirements ensure representation of certain members or certain types of members. There are also informal "requirements" that are well known to members that guide selection in many cases (interview 14).

TABLE 4.3 **Elements of the Conciliar Model of GGO Representation**

Entity	Description
Representative body	Body composed of all organizational members that typically gathers infrequently.
Intermediate body	Body composed of subset members typically selected by the representative body according to terms laid out in organizational charter.
Focused intermediate body	Intermediate body with responsibility for an area of substantive activity of the GGO (as opposed to general oversight role of standard intermediate body).
Secretariat	Permanent staff of the GGO managed by a fulltime executive that is typically not the leader of the representative or the intermediate body.

Intermediate bodies are more actively involved in the oversight of the organization and meet more regularly than the representative body (though the average is still only three meetings per year). The intermediate body is more often engaged in the routine decisionmaking of the GGO, consulted on policy matters and is commonly charged with regular oversight of the permanent staff. This includes reviewing and approving GGO budgets, appointing the chief executive of the organization, considering specific policies and proposals, and establishing committees to concentrate on specific matters. In some cases, intermediate bodies act as the final approving entity in the rulemaking process.

Consider an illustrative example. The intermediate body of the International Labor Organization is called, appropriately enough, the "governing body." If the name did not make the body's function clear enough, the ILO's website provides a summary description: the governing body "takes decisions on ILO policy, decides the agenda of the International Labour Conference [representative body], adopts the draft Programme and Budget of the Organization for submission to the Conference, and elects the Director-General" (ILO 2006). This is fairly typical, although one might note that this intermediate body chooses the leader of the bureaucracy, a function that is typically reserved for the representative body (at least formally; Sands et al. 2001).

An alternative to the single intermediate-body model is to have multiple intermediate bodies. Many GGOs have organs with specialized functions, often defined by a substantive division of the organization's responsibilities. These entities are referred to in this text as "focused intermediate bodies" to distinguish them from the standard intermediate body with generalized administrative oversight responsibilities. Focused intermediate bodies (FIBs) complement the standard intermediate body; they do not replace it. FIBs provide a formal venue for members to participate in matters within a particular substantive sphere. Through a focused intermediate body, members can be deeply engaged in the day-to-day work of the organization. This is different than the typical intermediate body, which is generally more concerned with oversight of the general administration and activities of the whole GGO. It also should be regarded as something different in kind than bodies with responsibility for a particular administrative area, e.g., budget committee), because the focused intermediate body is concerned with the substantive activities of the GGO.

Several GGOs have multiple intermediate bodies with the responsibilities divvied among them on a substantive basis. The Convention on International Trade in Endangered Species of Wild Fauna and Flora (CITES) has three FIBs, the Animals Committee, Plants Committee, and Nomenclature Committee. The members of each committee are selected as individuals (rather than countries who then designate individuals) according to a formula that ensures weighted representation of all regions. The International Civil Aviation Organization has a similar arrangement, organizing member work on specific issues through the Air Navigation Commission (technical matters), the Air Transport Committee (economic matters), the Committee on Joint Support of Air Navigation Services, and the Finance Committee.

Focused intermediate bodies often differ from the typical intermediate body in terms of participation. Many GGOs have FIBs that are open to all members rather than an exclusive subset. The World Trade Organization, for example, has three councils: Council for Trade in Goods, Council for Trade-Related Aspects of Intellectual Property Rights, and the Council for Trade in Services. All members participate in all three. The International Maritime Organization also includes all members in its FIBs including the Maritime Safety Committee and the Marine Environment Protection Committee.

The final piece of the conciliar GGO model is a permanent bureaucracy often referred to as the "secretariat." Led by an individual typically appointed by the intermediate body (with or without the ratification of the representative body), the bureaucracy carries out the day-to-day operations of the organization, takes a lead in setting the organizational agenda, crafting policy, and managing the rulemaking process (Davies 2002; Mathiason 2007).

As explored later in this chapter, the breadth of the permanent bureaucracy's responsibilities varies widely. This helps explain the variation in the size of the organization and the bureaucracy's relationship with the representational bodies. In smaller GGOs, the top-level executive function of the organization is essentially the entirety of the bureaucratic apparatus. CITES and IMO are examples of GGOs in this category that have strong secretariats of this type (Reinalda and Verbeek 2004; Sands et al. 2001). In other instances, there is a large nonexecutive bureaucracy beneath the executive body. The WHO and ILO both have substantial permanent bureaucracies with thousands of employees (not all of them are engaged in

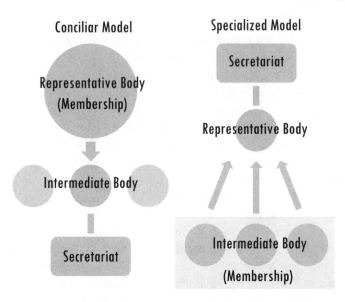

FIGURE 4.1. Conciliar and Specialized Models of GGO Representational Structure.

the rulemaking function; Taylor and Groom 2000, 52; Sands et al. 2001, 97, 99).

SPECIALIZED MODEL OF REPRESENTATION   Some GGOs reverse the top-down conciliar model, providing for representation through "specialized bodies" defined by substantive commonalities among a subset of organization members. These bodies then send delegates to an organization-wide representative body (often called the board of directors). For organizations adopting this "specialized model," the first level of representation is the intermediate body. This implicitly emphasizes the interest-based associations of each member because, in contrast with the conciliar model, members with common interests or industries are grouped at the organizational entry point. As discussed in chapter 7, GGOs adopting this structure actually assume some of the functions typically attributed to interest groups such as aggregating preferences and providing a venue for negotiation.

Specialized bodies are different than the FIBs discussed as a component of the conciliar model, although they may look similar on organization chart. Focused intermediate bodies are drawn *from* the representative body of a conciliar organization. The primary level of representation is still the *representative* body. The specialized model does not have a general representative body akin to the conciliar model, so there is no forum where all members convene as a whole. Reinforcing the members' identification by interest, the specialized bodies send representatives to an organization-wide governing body, a small group performing functions associated with representative bodies and intermediate bodies in conciliar organizations. Intermediate bodies in the specialized model are not ad hoc committees but formal parts of the organizational structure, the building blocs from which the whole is constructed.

ICANN utilizes a specialized representation model. Its primary constituent bodies are the three "ICANN organizations": Address Supporting Organization (ASO), the Country Code Names Supporting Organization (ccNSO), and the Generic Names Supporting Organization (GNSO). In ICANN's version of the specialized model, some intermediate bodies include members from multiple sectors with an interest in the same set of policy issues. For example, the Address Supporting Organization draws organizations concerned with Internet registry issues. Participation in this body is actually channeled through three regional bodies, adding a geographic component to the representation. In response to outcry from some concerned individuals, ICANN added an intermediate body (with somewhat circumscribed authority) to serve as a venue for individuals interested in ICANN policy. This At-Large Advisory Committee is unique in the population of GGOs (Lowi 2001; Marsden 2000).

ICANN's supporting organizations elect members to a board of directors that oversees the entirety of the organization. This board, which includes other members selected through a nomination process, performs many of the functions carried out by a representative or intermediate body under the standard model. A "nominating committee," constituted according to a complex set of requirements, selects eight of the fifteen board members to complement those selected by the specialized intermediate bodies (ICANN 2006). Like many organizations, ICANN explicitly stipulates that the board members are individuals rather than representatives of their employers or other organizations: "Directors shall serve as individuals who have the duty to act in what they reasonably believe are the best interests of ICANN and not as representatives of the entity that selected them, their employers, or any other organizations or constituencies" (ICANN 2006).

NONREPRESENTATIVE GGOS. Some GGOs take the notion of nonrepresentation even further by eschewing all affiliation in constructing organizational governance structure. "Nonrepresentative" GGOs do not have organizational "members" at all or, if they do, the governing body is made up of individuals who do not (formally) represent an institution or even a specialized body. It is analytically challenging to consider this organizational type alongside other GGOs; even speaking of the "model of representation" is awkward because members are not represented per se in the governing body. Understanding the drivers and implications of this structure is clearly necessary.

The International Accounting Standards Board (IASB) provides an illustration of the nonrepresentative model. The IASB is actually subsidiary to an entity called the International Accounting Standards Committee Foundation, which is governed by its board of trustees. This self-perpetuating body not only selects its own members, it appoints members of the IASB board, a separate entity. Both sets of board members are explicitly not to be seen as representatives of any organization with which they are professionally affiliated. The guiding criteria for the trustees in choosing IASB board members is *that the board* "will comprise a group of people representing, within that group, the best available combination of technical skills and background experience of relevant international business and market conditions in order to contribute to the development of high quality, global accounting standards. [Paragraph 20]" (IASC Foundation 2006). In practice, however, selection of Board members seems guided by representational considerations. Current members hail from, among other countries, the United States, France, Germany, the United Kingdom, Japan, and China. There are numerous individuals with careers in accounting but a regulatory, industry and academic perspective can also be found.

One must maintain a healthy skepticism regarding the distinction between a nonrepresentative arrangement and a more standard model. All nonrepresentative organizations, in practice, resemble the IASB. Board members are drawn from a variety of regions. At a minimum, then, members of these governing bodies seem to represent, in some vague sense, a geographic constituency. The inclusion of individuals associated with key industries is also universal (though again, the guarantee is not always explicit), suggesting that an interest-based representation is expected as well.

The "nonrepresentative" model can mix with the specialized model. Recall that members of ICANN's specialized bodies do not formally represent member organization per se although they sometimes do represent smaller constituent organizations (such as a regional subgroup of ICANN). Analysis shows that in practice the most important distinction based on political structure is between conciliar organizations and everything else.

Apportionment of Influence

A critical issue for any democratic political system concerns the distribution of influence. Systems of representation and voting can create winners and losers, remedy imbalances, or create them where none exist. The distribution of voting power is thus a vital element in understanding GGOs and a lens through which influence can be examined (Brauninger 2003; McIntyre 1954). Voting power should never be conflated with actual influence. Formal institutional arrangements represent only a portion of the story. There are subtle ways—and not so subtle ways—in which the influence of GGO members can vary that are not reflected in the organizational bylaws. Mapping power within an organization is a notoriously difficult task.

Looking at voting rules is an accessible means to assess the differential power of organizational members. It is readily observable, unambiguous, and reveals variation. Through the qualitative research that complemented this approach, the informal distribution of power was also observed, allowing integration of the formal and informal perspectives. Four models of voting apportionment cover the population of international organizations: one member, one vote; proportional voting; special powers to select member; and nonrepresentative voting (table 4.4). Nonrepresentative

TABLE 4.4 **Models of Apportionment**

Model	Apportionment
One member/one vote (OMOV)	Each member has equal formal voting power.
Proportional representation	Voting influence is scaled to some characteristic of each member (e.g., financial contribution, share of activity, etc.).
Special powers	Voting power is equal but some members are granted extraordinary powers (i.e., veto).
Nonrepresentative	Governing body is comprised of individuals rendering the notion of "representation" inapplicable.

GGOs are separated because the voting rights of the members of the governing bodies are disconnected from the member institutions, making it awkward to impose a judgment on institutional influence based on the voting apportionment.

The subject of voting and apportionment of influence also arises in chapter 5 on rulemaking. In that chapter, the focus is on the decision rules used in the processes involved in the consideration and adoption of a new rules, standards, or regulations. This chapter looks more broadly to capture general organizational governance decisions outside the rulemaking process (e.g., budget).

ONE MEMBER, ONE VOTE (OMOV).   The majority of GGOs treat the nation-state as the unit of organization (March and Olsen 1998). Even nongovernmental GGOs typically have structures that reflect national affiliation as an organizing element. The ISO and IEC, for example, are made up of national standards-setting bodies. This approach reflects the most widely shared political view of the world: a whole made up of countries (Nye and Donahue 2000; Higgott et al. 2000). There is no reason, of course, why global governance organizations must adopt this convention, and some GGOs have experimented with alternatives. In such cases, general geographic representation usually has some role; continents retain some significance even when nation-states are deemphasized. GGOs have memberships made up of a variety of entities: for-profit and nonprofit organizations and even individual members.

Apportionment of influence on a one member, one vote (OMOV) basis requires assignment of equal voting influence in the representative body and other decisionmaking situations regardless of differences in population or wealth. Note that some organizations have different "classes" of membership, with voting power differentiated for each class. Organizations that scaled voting power to membership level were coded as utilizing a proportional system of apportionment. "Members" with no voting power were not considered members for coding purposes.

Formal apportionment of voting strength does not, of course, indicate parity of actual influence. Smaller nations may be inclined or pressured to follow larger states. Countries with a disproportionate interest in a certain area may take the lead within the relevant organization. Apportionment of voting power in the OMOV fashion does establish a dynamic of member participation, but it should never be considered the final word.

The *rules* of voting may affect the actual power of a single vote. The one member, one vote apportionment can be associated with very different voting rules. Many organizations require a supermajority to approve some or all actions. The value of a single vote may, in effect, be greater under such a system than a simple-majority voting system, for example. The decision rules employed by GGOs are examined in the chapter 5.

Almost all global governance organizations seek consensus on all decisions although, ironically, understanding of consensus varies quite a bit. Often equated with unanimity, other common notions of consensus include "lack of strong disagreement" or "an overwhelming supermajority." The essential point is that the consensus decision rule provides flexibility and reduces the significance of OMOV apportionment because some members' agreement is more important than others. Thus consensus is normatively and pragmatically appealing, a point elaborated in the discussion of decision rules in the rulemaking process.

PROPORTIONAL VOTING. An alternative to equal assignment of influence to each member is a proportional system that differentiates among members in the assignment of voting power. There are many possible variations in the bases for the assignment of influence. One theoretical approach is to link representation to population, although none of the GGOs studied apportion power in this fashion. The avoidance of population-based apportionment is striking because it is straightforward and accepted as the normatively desirable arrangement in the domestic political context (Dahl 1971). In the United States, for example, there is a lengthy history of debate and litigation that has bolstered the requirement for population equality in legislatures.

Given that the most economically and militarily powerful nations of the world are considerably "outpopulated" by other countries, the avoidance of population-based systems is not surprising. Most obviously, the United States has less than a quarter of the population of China and India. The G-7 nations all rank behind such developing countries as Indonesia, Brazil, and Nigeria. It is difficult to imagine the acceptance of a governance system—in particular for organizations creating rules affecting commerce—based on population distribution. Neoliberals are just as unlikely as realists to suggest that such a system could be viable. The practice of apportioning voting power on a nonpopulation basis is widely practiced and accepted. Indeed, malapportionment is the overwhelming norm not the exception (Samuels and Snyder 2001)! The well-known example of the US Senate, which assigns equal voting influence based on state boundaries rather than population, represents a common model employed under federal and bicameral systems around the world.

As a matter of practice in proportional systems, influence is not apportioned as a function of population but rather in relation to members' importance in a substantive area. This can be measured in different ways. Votes can be scaled to each member's monetary contribution to the organization's budget, an effective proxy for importance. This is the approach used at the World Bank and IMF.

In some cases, the budgetary contribution is determined by a measure of the country's size or share of relevant market. The UN scale of assessment is widely employed. Other GGOs, however, make size of the contribution discretionary. That is, each member determines its own level of contribution. Thus the level of influence for each member is a direct function of its own determination regarding the importance of the GGO. Members seeking greater influence can increase its contribution and wield proportionately more power. The International Telecommunication Union allows for such a choice, and on its website the organization advertises the enhanced influence that comes with higher levels of membership.

Practically, proportional systems grant greater influence to the wealthier, developed nations. The United States' dominant voting power at the World Bank gives it the right to select the bank president, for example. This is not, however, *always* the case. The contributions to the IMO, for instance, are scaled to the size of each member's merchant fleet. The top five assessments were charged to Panama, Liberia, the Bahamas, the United Kingdom, and Greece (IMO 2000).

SPECIAL POWERS.   A third model of representation blends features of the first two by providing equal weight to each member's vote as a general matter but reserving special powers to a select set of members. The most familiar expression of this model is the UN Security Council. The Security Council has five permanent members with veto authority (the United States, the United Kingdom, Russia, France, and China) that is not possessed by any other country, even the rotating members of the council (Cronin and Hurd 2008).

The "special powers" model creates a two-tiered system of membership with the implicit premise, of course, that such a differentiation exists in reality. The apportionment of influence merely reflects this fact. There are informal ways in which special powers can be conferred without the bluntness of the Security Council model or even the guarantee of places on an intermediate body. By the account of participants in the governance of all GGOs, the "special powers" arrangement is, to some extent, a fact of life. Global governance organizations cannot move forward when pivotal members object. When the leader of CITES proposed that the International Whaling Commission allow hunting of nonthreatened whales, he was greeted the following day by representatives of the United States, Australia, and the United Kingdom, all of which have vocal antiwhaling activists, with the very strong suggestion that he back off. This ended the matter (interview 39).

As noted in the discussion of "consensus," the objections of one member may be deemed a lack of consensus while another member's objections may not. These observations of formal and informal special powers resonate with the core claim of this book: organizational authority depends upon the consent and support of key actors thus requiring violations of equality norms. One might also think of guaranteed membership in the intermediate body (described above) as a form of "special powers." It does differentiate a select number of representatives; membership in the intermediate body certainly grants more influence than membership confined to the representative body.

NONREPRESENTATIVE APPORTIONMENT.   As noted earlier, a number of GGOs have governing bodies that are not formally "representative." There is a supreme board or council but the members of this body are recognized as individuals rather than representatives of some other entity (country, firm, interest group). As these individuals do not stand for countries or organizations, their power cannot be regarded as an apportionment. The International Accounting Standards Board (IASB), for example, shows the inapplicability of the first three models to a nonrepresentative GGO. Therefore these organizations are acknowledged as a type that does not conform to any of the previously described models.

The nonrepresentative apportionment is another formal structure that does not reflect the informal realities of the organization's governance. The IASB is a case in point. Each board member has an equal vote, which suggests an equal apportionment of influence. But it is widely recognized that several concerned bodies—regulators and accounting bodies from the United States, the European Union, and Japan—wield significant influence over the IASB. Indeed, some would argue that in practice the IASB represents a de facto *special powers*–model organization.

Balance of Power

The balance of power between "branches" varies for global governance organizations as it does among governments. Naturally, the typical distinctions do not map perfectly onto GGOs. Generally, we speak of "strong legislatures" in contrast to "strong executives," but the GGO chief executive is not analogous to the leader of a domestic government. The GGO chief executive is not independently elected; she or he is typically selected by the members through the representative or intermediate body. So in this context, the "executive" truly refers to the administrative staff (including the leadership) of the organization.

In some national political systems, analysis of the balance of power brings the judiciary into the equation. This is inapplicable to GGOs because (with the exception of the WTO) these entities do not have an internal judicial function (Shaffer 2005). Entities such as the International Court of Justice or even domestic courts provide for reconciliation in a judicial venue, but this does not influence the administration of the organization.

The balance between the legislative and administrative sides of each GGO is intended to capture how the business of governance is actually carried out and in whose hands the day-to-day decisions rest. Even when the legislative body retains core decisionmaking authority, GGOs that display a bureaucratic-centric model have vested a large amount of control in the permanent staff. This includes agenda-setting power, fact-finding, identification of policy alternatives, deployment of resources, and control over communications. The IMO is one GGO that fits this description (see McLaren 1980).

The balance between legislative and bureaucratic power also provides insight into how the members regard the organization itself. One might infer that within bureaucracy-centric GGO, the members are content to let the entity run on "autopilot" and watch only for signs of unwanted activity. They may rely upon interest groups to alert them when something goes wrong. This has been likened to a fire alarm in describing it as a method of legislative oversight of the bureaucracy (McCubbins and Schwartz 1984).

The alternative to the fire alarm is the police patrol. It implies a more attentive legislature engaged in active oversight of the bureaucracy. This level of legislative engagement suggests an ascription of importance that justifies a significant assignment of finite resources necessary to participate on a more engaged level. The same analysis is applicable to GGOs. If members are willing to grant the bureaucracy wide latitude in shaping the organization's agenda and operations, it does suggest a lower level of engagement and interest.

As with all the areas discussed thus far, the legislative or bureaucratic bias of the organization may be reflected in the formal organizational structure, but it is also revealed in the informal operations of the organization.

LEGISLATURE-CENTRIC SYSTEMS. Attempting to characterize governmental systems with the broad brushes implicit in this variable is challenging. Every case—even the most seemingly clear-cut one—presents ambiguity as a result of aberrant examples or subjective sets of facts. The term "legislative dominance" is sometimes used to suggest that the locus of power lies in the legislative organ of a government, but "legistlature-centric" is not here intended to communicate absolute control or "micromanagement." Even the GGO, with the most active legislative organs will place a significant share of responsibility and authority in the hands of the bureaucracy and senior leadership of the entity. GGOs are termed legislature-centric when initiative for organizational activities is found in the representative bodies, when the administration and routine activities are closely monitored, and when all significant decisions are considered by the representatives of members without dispositive influence from the administrative establishment.

The International Labor Organization has one of the most interesting and unique representational structures in the GGO universe. This is classified as a conciliar organization because it has a general representative body (International Labor Conference) structured around nation-states and an intermediate body ("Governing Body"). The ILO is unique in that each national delegation includes representatives of government, employers (business), and workers (labor). The conference selects members of the Governing Body, which also includes, as permanent members, the representatives of ten "States of chief industrial importance." There is a significant permanent bureaucracy (International Labor Office), but a large segment of the staff is tasked with supporting the representatives and facilitating their everyday engagement.

GGOs in which members play an active role in performing rulemaking functions through working groups or focused intermediate bodies send individuals who possess high levels of expertise in the relevant fields. In some cases, the delegation of representatives to a GGO will include multiple individuals who have specialized in a particular aspect of the organization's activities. Therefore the representatives are highly informed and, one would expect, at no disadvantage when interacting with the permanent staff. The generalized expectation is that the more expert the representatives are, the less likely bureaucratic dominance will hold (McLaren 1980).

BUREAUCRACY-CENTRIC SYSTEMS. The conventional conflation of bureaucratic dominance and executive control is misplaced in the context of GGOs. There is no model of an elected chief executive set up as a rival to the legislative bodies. In the universe of GGOs, unlike most governance systems in which the legislature and executive are both elected, the leader of the GGO is generally chosen by the representative or intermediate body. This distinguishes GGOs from parliamentary systems because the leader is not a member of the legislative body.

It makes more sense to consider bureaucratic dominance as a function of the latitude granted to the bureaucracy (including the leadership) by the members. This means that bureaucracy-centric systems should not be seen as situations in which the administrative side prevailed over the legislature. The observed structure more likely reflects members' preferences regarding the role of the bureaucracy and its leader.

The leader of the bureaucracy, often holding the title secretary-general or director-general, is regarded as the head of the organization even when the representative body elects a nominal chairman who is formal chief of the organization. Although there is variation in the powers delegated to or assumed by the leader, the classic British television show *Yes, Minister* may exceed any academic prose as a working description of the "dominant bureaucracy" model of government. The program depicts all-knowing career bureaucrats bemusedly tolerating the elected official ostensibly placed in charge of the ministry. The legislature carries on making noise and smoke but achieving little, while the truly knowledgeable and understandable career civil servants keep the home fires burning.

This notion translates easily into the global governance realm. Some of the governmental officials appointed to represent member states at GGOs have limited background in the substance of the issues before them. For representatives of smaller countries, responsibilities often include participation in multiple GGOs clustered in Geneva, compounding the difficulty in staying well-versed in all the issues confronting each GGO. The permanent staff of the GGOs does seem, in many cases, to possess the true ability to "make things happen" and understand "how things work" in a way that the "legislators" do not. There is often a formal quality to this type of balance. The representative bodies might be at such a disadvantage under the best of circumstances, but the arrangements in some cases seem to preordain such an outcome by limiting the representative body to very few meetings, limiting the type of issues that come before the representatives, and granting the bureaucracy wide latitude to take action without permission of the assembly.

Administrative Structure

Students of politics have long understood that the institutional arrangements defining the rights and responsibilities of members can have significant implications for the substantive output of the organization, but administrative structure and the design of bureaucracies can be as important to understanding the creation and implementation of policy (Goodin 1996; Peters 2005). Indeed, it may be more important (particularly in the context of global governance) because the representative body is often quite removed from the operations of the organization. Discussions of global governance have provided an understanding of the mechanisms of several GGOs (Davies 2002; Tamm Hallstrom 2004; Karns and Mingst 2004; Murphy 1994). But most studies do not tie analysis of the GGO bureaucracies to the puzzle considered in this book. Administrative structure shapes the processes through which policy is made—including rulemaking—and establishes the terms by which interested parties participate and attempt to influence outcomes.

The diversity of organizational structure among global governance organizations is such that it is impossible to analyze every difference observed across the population included in this study. Like bureaucracies within a single governmental system, each GGO has developed its own patterns of administration with respect to human resources, budget, procurement, workflow, communications, and so on. Data on these features were collected in the GGO dataset; thus, patterns on these microelements were observable and reported where relevant. These differences appear to be of secondary importance and as a practical necessity attention is focused on broader considerations (McLaren 1980, 83). Three core aspects of GGO administrative structure are analyzed: the *role* of the bureaucracy and its *centralization* and *scale*.

Bureaucratic Role

In the world of global governance, the role played by the permanent staff of GGOs leans in one of two directions. For GGOs in which members have a more engaged function, carrying out much of the substantive work of the organization through committees or working groups, the administrative staff's primary function is to support their work. In contrast, the staff of GGOs in which members are less engaged in the day-to-day decisionmaking are performing the functional work of the organization under supervision of the members.

The dichotomous characterization ("functional" or "supporting") obviously glosses over significant variation and gray area. The most functional bureaucracies still engage members regularly in the rulemaking process. And the permanent staff of *supporting*-type organizations plays a highly significant role in the crafting of rules. The dichotomous characterization is intended only to provide a sense of the administrative dynamic.

FUNCTIONAL ROLE. Many global governance organizations look and "feel" like traditional government bureaucracies. These organizations are relatively fixed, and the assignment of roles and responsibilities is set by formal requirement. The functions of such organizations have been routinized and are carried out without the direct involvement of members— or even senior leadership. Most important, bureaucracies of functional GGOs, the regular staff of the organization, perform core tasks. Many of the venerable GGOs fit this model, including the World Health Organization and the World Intellectual Property Organization. Both have sizeable secretariats that collect data, track implementation, develop new proposed rules, bring together members for purposes of education and negotiation, and generally drive the process.

Note that the assessment of the bureaucracy's role is focused on the rulemaking function of the GGO because of the variance in mission scope across the GGO population (Feld et al. 1994). Many of the GGOs do have other responsibilities where the permanent staff plays a different role. The International Telecommunication Union (ITU) is an exemplar. The ITU is divided into three sections. The rulemaking function is performed in the Telecommunications Standardization Sector, referred to internally as ITU-T. It also has sectors devoted to radiocommunications and development. The bureaucracies of these two segments of the organization generally perform in a functional role. The staff of the ITU-T, however, is essentially acting in a supporting capacity (Cutler et al. 1999, 116). To be consistent across cases, the focus remains on the rulemaking part of each organization for this analysis.

SUPPORTING ROLE. The most striking characteristic distinguishing global governance organizations from domestic analogs is the widespread participation of members and interested parties in the rulemaking process. The nature of this participation and the general implications of it are taken up in chapters 5 and 7. Here the focus is on the structural embodiment of a process that places a great deal of day-to-day rulemaking responsibility in the hands of members through focused intermediate bodies, technical committees, or working groups. This approach naturally shifts some responsibility away from the permanent bureaucracy relative to the functional GGOs. It is tempting to assume that this also results in a loss of bureaucratic influence, but it is more accurate to say that such an arrangement alters the role of the bureaucracy without necessarily diminishing its importance.

In a supporting role, the principal responsibility of the bureaucracy, particularly in the rulemaking process, is to provide the member-driven committees with guidance on the procedural requirements and the proper format of rules. The bureaucracy often participates in the textual drafting and editing of rules, ensuring the compatibility of proposed rules with existing ones, and facilitating interaction with the other bodies of the organization that must review new rules (Tamm Hallstrom 2004).

Standards-setting organizations such as the International Electrotechnical Commission (IEC), the International Organization for Standardization (ISO), the ASTM International (ASTM), and the ITU offer a clear view of this model. In each of these organizations, technical committees have been established with specific areas of responsibility. Some of these committees are relatively new, but others are essentially as old as the organizations themselves. Technical Committee 1 of the IEC, for example, was created to come up with standards for "terminology," a good starting point for any standards-setting body! In all of the these organizations, there are also more general representative bodies and intermediate representative bodies (Cox and Jacobson 1973, 59; Feld et al. 1994, 109; Sands et al. 2001, 107).

Individuals who perform the support functions have significant influence in the rulemaking process. As sources of institutionalized knowledge for the members of working groups, the permanent staff serves as advisers and guides. In standard-generating GGOs like the ISO and IEC, the permanent staff members are typically more familiar with rules and procedures associated with rulemaking than members of technical committees. As the rulemaking process proceeds, staff may suggest the superiority of one approach over another or warn members away from certain issues that have proven difficult in the past (interviews 7, 8, 18, 29).

The permanent staff member often acts as a mediator, helping to resolve conflicts among participants in order to reach a consensus. It is a political process, and the reconciliation of interests is an important element that can often be best facilitated by the nonmember staffer (interview 29). In some cases, the permanent bureaucracy functions as a liaison between technical committees of the same organization and other GGOs. The IEC and ISO, for example, have significant collaboration—even running some joint technical committees—that requires administrative skill.

Aside from their support for rulemaking groups, the bureaucracy plays a large role in shaping the agenda of the organization in ways both obvious and subtle. The most obvious example is that the meeting agendas for the rare assemblages of the representative body are generally controlled by the administrative entity. Of course, members have influence (particularly those that are part of the intermediate body), but the initiative is clearly bureaucratic. Less apparent is the influence had by virtue of seemingly small choices regarding data collection, research, and scheduling.

Note that two forms of substantive member participation in the operations of GGOs have been identified in this book. Both create a supporting role for the bureaucracy. First, as just described, many GGOs rely upon working groups comprised of members that generate the actual rules to be adopted by the organization. Second, there are the focused intermediate bodies (FIBs) that were described in the section on representation. The FIBs also require the support of the permanent bureaucracy. They are often part of the rulemaking process (usually in a slightly more detached capacity than participants in working groups). They may play a role in assessing the implementation of rules and determining the priorities for the organization as it moves forward.

By virtue of their deep embeddedness in the rulemaking process, members of GGOs that have working groups and focused intermediate bodies assume a mixed role. On the one hand, the participation of members in the rulemaking working groups should be thought of as a variant of member representation. It is highly specific, because the bodies through which this "representation" takes place are substantively oriented with fairly narrow scope. But because members can participate most actively in areas of greatest concern, participation in a working group may be more valuable than participation in a representative body.

On the other hand, for organizations that rely upon members to essentially carry out the rulemaking process, the distinction between organization member and staff becomes a bit blurry. Most working groups or committees are not "ad hoc" or temporary. They are formal parts of the organization explicitly recognized and enshrined in the governing documents. GGOs add additional working bodies as necessary, thus opening new avenues for participation and representation as the organization tackles new fields.

This renders the notion of legislative versus bureaucratic dominance a bit murky. The formal structure of the organization may indicate that the representative body has little power over the bureaucracy. But the members may not be terribly interested in the general organizational issues because their participation in the working groups ensures them influence in the areas where it matters most. And, more to the point, if the members themselves are carrying out the core function of the organization, the division of staff from member loses some meaning.

Centralization

This straightforward notion requires little description. Some GGOs have a "centralized" headquarters where most of the permanent staff is based and most operations are conducted. Other GGOs, in contrast, have a more "distributed" model with work carried out in multiple offices around the globe or even virtually through the Internet. Distributed models present a relatively formalized version of the policy network that is of great interest in contemporary international relations research. Centralized and distributed structures offer two very different way of carrying out organizational tasks. It requires different strategies for parties seeking to influence the organization, alters the relationship between the executive and organization staff, and affects GGO relationships with other international organizations.

CENTRALIZED. The collection of monolithic edifices in the international section of Geneva has a familiar feeling to anyone who has navigated the governmental districts of the world's capitals, from Washington, DC, to New Delhi. The physical manifestation of centralized bureaucracy is only part of the story. Centralization implies a process that more often than not requires participation and approval of central authority. It is typically associated with more rigid administrative rules. It demands uniformity across subunits and iterations. It yields a distinctive organizational culture.

As one would expect, some of the oldest GGOs are the best examples of centralized administration and all but one GGO associated with the United Nations is of this type. The Universal Postal Union has a relatively small staff based in Berne, Switzerland, that carries out most of the functions of the body. The International Labor Organization (ILO), a much larger Geneva-based GGO, also carries out most of its activities internally. Still, there are similarly venerable entities such as the ITU and IEC that have a distributed structure. Reliance on distributed networks is nothing new in international administration. The World Health Organization is distributed, although its rulemaking function is centralized (Stein 2001).

DISTRIBUTED. The distributed organization relies upon a geographically dispersed network of individuals and institutions to carry out the mission of the organization. This structure is better suited to an organization in which members sprinkled all over the world participate in the rulemaking process through working groups. They may convene occasionally but much of their activities are now carried out through electronic communications. In the cases of the ISO and the IEC, each working group has its own secretariat based in the home country of the member that is serving as committee chairman.

The "distributed" label does not suggest that the organization is without a central office. All of the working groups and technical committees that make up distributed organizations work through organizational headquarters (many of which are also located in Geneva alongside the traditional centralized bodies). The rulemaking processes inevitably call for some clearance process back through headquarters.

The Basel Committee on Banking Standards is the only organization in which the supporting model is centralized. This entity creates standards for minimum levels of safe operation of financial institutions. It resides within the Bank for International Settlements, and its function is carried out through member committees and by staff seconded by member governments. Most of the individuals involved in this work (including the

members' representatives) are located in Basel, Switzerland, the organization's headquarters (interview 36). Thus both the support staff and the
"network" are centralized in this city.

Scale of the Bureaucracy

The "bigness" of a global governance organization is conceptually straightforward but empirically challenging. Scale is measured here by the number of organizational employees. At the large end of the size spectrum are
the formidable bureaucracies associated with some of the most venerable
GGOs such as the World Health Organization and the World Intellectual
Property Organization. These entities pale in comparison to many national government bureaucracies but with several thousand employees,
they are quite a bit larger than the average GGO. In contrast, many of
the organizations have tiny permanent staffs. The Unicode Consortium is
an extreme case with only three full-time employees, but thirteen of the
GGOs reported fewer than one hundred employees.

Using staff size is an imperfect measure because it is impossible to
determine precisely how many employees are engaged in the rulemaking function. The problem posed by larger organizations is the breadth
of their functions. Although GGOs included in this study were selected
because their primary activity is rulemaking, several of the organizations
do have substantial staff performing non-rulemaking tasks. The WHO,
for example, has a broader mandate than most of the GGOs discussed
here, and many WHO employees have nothing to do with rulemaking
(Taylor and Groom 2000). Another concern is that many GGOs rely upon
members to carry out the work of the organization. When only the GGO
employees are counted to determine scale, a misleading picture is inad-
vertently created. If one included the members participating in working
groups in the calculations, the numbers would be immense (but probably
even more misleading).

Even with all the noise created by these measurement problems, the
finding that scale is not perfectly correlated with the role and centralization of the GGO is counterintuitive. One would expect that the more an
organization relies upon members to carry out core responsibilities, the
fewer bureaucrats it will employ. And, conversely, one would expect functional GGOs to have more employees because it bears primary responsibility for carrying out the work of the organization. Neither intuition
holds true.

Patterns of GGO Structure

The patterns of variation observed in this study of twenty-five global governance organizations reveal that the goal of satisfying normative demands of democratic legitimacy take precedence in the design of GGO structure. Adoption of a one member, one vote apportionment, for instance, cuts across all categories of GGOs. But interpretation of the findings also suggests a more complicated story than the surface emphasis on democratic norms suggests. GGOs temper expressions of member equality with devices that render some members more influential than others. Most prominently, key GGO members are typically guaranteed inclusion in the more engaged "intermediate bodies" that have more impact than the full-membership "representative bodies." This indicates that the demands of authority—as manifested in structures that ensure *responsiveness*-type accountability—are never ignored.

Nongovernmental GGOs show more structural variation, suggesting that governmental GGOs face more explicit normative demands. A second, more novel, explanation lies in the connection between nongovernmental membership and the technicality of a GGO's substantive arena. TECHNICALITY proves to be the characteristic with explanatory power second only to SECTOR when identifying patterns among the set of GGOs. This is particularly true for variations in the approach to administration. More technical issues are more likely to be tackled by a distributed organization, the bureaucracy playing primarily a supporting role, with members carrying out much of the rulemaking function themselves.

Looking comprehensively at all six characteristics, two distinct GGO "types" emerge based on the clustering of characteristics. The *traditional* and *hybrid* structure types are introduced at the end of this section.

Political Representation

The most noticeable pattern in the representational structure is the lack of variation. More than two-thirds of the GGOs surveyed employ a conciliar model and one member, one vote apportionment. The two features are highly correlated, as indicated in table 4.5. This suggests the common pressures experienced by all GGOs. Among the alternatives, each is the most consistent with normative expectations for democratic governance. The force of institutional isomorphism bolsters this dynamic; GGOs will seek to emulate other GGOs that are regarded as legitimate and adopt similar structures. There is enough variation, however, to suggest that some characteristics are particularly powerful as drivers toward this norm.

SECTOR IS LINKED TO CONCILIAR MODEL, OMOV APPORTIONMENT. The dominance of the conciliar model is particularly overwhelming among governmental GGOs. This strong connection between GGO sector and structure is entirely consistent with the theory offered in chapters 1 and 2. First and foremost, governmental GGOs face the clearest demands for consistency with norms of democratic representation, particularly from those communities with democratically organized political structures. Conciliar structure is most consistent with core norms of democratic governance imported from the domestic sphere, making this relationship a clear illustration of constructivist logic. The reliance on one member, one vote apportionment among the same set of GGOs underscores the purposive value of structural features (table 4.5).

Organizations made up of national governments are especially keen to maintain the clarity of national sovereignty in their design, avoiding any implication of supranational authority. By structuring representation around nation-states with equal voting strength, the primacy of the state as a political institution is reified. By the same constructivist logic, dividing voting power in any other way would be to acknowledge the differential power of nations, effectively communicating that some nations are more sovereign than others. All countries are understandably loathe to do this, particularly in formal arrangements, if unnecessary.

TABLE 4.5 **Sector, Representational Structure and Apportionment**

Sector	Apportionment				
	OMOV	Proportional	Select powers	Non-represent.	Total
Government	13	0	0	0	13
Mixed	3	0	0	1	4
Nongovernment	2	1	1	4	8
Total	18	1	1	5	25
Fisher's exact = .003					
Representational structure	OMOV	Proportional	Select powers	Non-represent.	Total
Conciliar model	17	0	0	2	18
Specialized	0	1	1	0	3
Nonrepresentative	1	0	0	3	4
Total	18	1	1	4	23
Fisher's exact = 0.000					

The GGO sector is a more powerful correlate of structure than affiliation with the UN. Even governmental GGOs with no UN affiliation are almost certain to adopt a conciliar model and OMOV apportionment. The governmental character of non-UN GGOs like the International Whaling Commission, the World Customs Union, and the Convention on Trade in Endangered Species, as well as the accompanying pressure to conform to democratic norms, is the source of isomorphic pressure, not the administrative requirements of the UN.

An interesting inverse relationship between TECHNICALITY and structure is also captured in the analysis. GGOs dealing with more technical subject matter are *less likely* to adopt a conciliar model. This is not surprising given the statistically significant negative relationship between SECTOR and TECHNICALITY. More technical subject matter is more likely to be handled by a nongovernmental GGO, a pattern discussed below.

None of the other core characteristics used to sort the global governance organizations has independent explanatory power. Entities that make treaties (RULE TYPE) always have a conciliar model because they, by definition, are always organized around member states; governmental GGOs that make other types of rules also adopt a conciliar model. Organizations funded by contribution (the norm for governmental GGOs) are more likely to adopt a conciliar model, but again the connection is not robust beyond the FUNDING / SECTOR correlation.

NONGOVERNMENTAL GGOS ARE MORE LIKELY TO BE SPECIALIZED OR NONREPRESENTATIVE. Nongovernmental GGOs are far more likely to adopt a specialized or nonrepresentative structure than GGOs generally (table 4.6), but several nongovernmental GGOs also employ a conciliar structure. Thus the full explanation for the distribution has to account for the greater heterogeneity of representational structure among nongovernmental GGOs. Several characteristics distinguish GGOs that employ specialized representation or a nonrepresentative structure.

Having nongovernmental members instead of (or alongside) governmental members alters the requirements of the representative apparatus. Corporate entities that join nongovernmental GGOs have narrower interests, focused on particular issues and rules, compared with member governments. Their participation in a GGO is less contingent upon diplomatic and strategic considerations elsewhere. Thus their primary interest will be in the rulemaking process rather than the overarching governance structure. Nongovernmental GGOs are structured to facilitate this inter-

TABLE 4.6 **Sector, Technicality, and Structure of Representation**

	Representation			
Sector	Conciliar	Specialized	Nonrepresentative	Total
Government	13	0	0	13
Mixed	4	0	0	4
Nongovernment	2	2	4	8
Total	19	2	4	25
Fisher's exact = .006				
Technicality	Conciliar	Specialized	Nonrepresentative	Total
Higher	7	2	4	11
Lower	12	0	0	12
Total	19	2	4	25
Fisher's exact = .015				

est. This interaction of factors underscores the degree to which GGOs are "open organizations," adapted to meet the specific environmental demands they face (Scott 1992).

The members of ASTM International, a standards-setting organization based in the United States, participate in working groups similar to those employed by other standard-setters (e.g., ISO, IEC, ITU). This is the primary avenue for involvement. It has a "nonrepresentative assembly" composed of the voting membership of the organization, but this body never meets. Indeed, the leader of ASTM notes that most participants likely view themselves as members of a specific technical committee rather than as members of the organization as a whole (interview 38).

Nonconciliar approaches channel participation through substantive bodies that better satisfy demand for issue-based representation. The conciliar structure is suited for member participation in the broad policy debates facing the GGO. It does not, however, facilitate member participation in the rulemaking process. There are adaptations to the conciliar structure (discussed below) that facilitate this type of participation, but the conciliar approach, in its essence, emphasizes broader representation.

Viewing representational structure through a second core characteristic, the TECHNICALITY of the subject matter, provides an alternative way to observe the same dynamic. Nonrepresentative organizations are disproportionately working in higher-technicality subject areas. This is consistent with the previous observation regarding SECTOR and STRUCTURE. These highly technical organizations are more likely to attract members with a narrow interest in the outcomes on a particular issue or rule. For technical organizations, then, general representation is secondary to representation in the form of participation in the substantive work of the GGO (see table 4.6). The W3C, the Unicode Consortium, and ICANN all reflect this pattern. In each of these cases, the need for representation based on nation-state is not acute. On the contrary, it is more important that the specific constituencies interested in the policy area have influence. This is best accomplished through a nonconciliar framework (Gould 2000; Marsden 2000; Keohane and Nye 2000).

The emphasis on the relatively apolitical nature of rulemaking in the highly technical issue areas is underscored by the distribution of nonconciliar GGOs. By treating members of the organizations and their governing bodies as *individuals,* not representatives of organizations, the nonrepresentative GGO reinforces its apolitical character. All such GGOs operate in areas classified as highly technical. In addition, other governance bodies that do sometimes identify members by institution (such as Internet governance organizations, ICANN and the Internet Engineering Task Force) generally downplay institutional / national affiliation in their governance. This is an attempt to both satisfy a normative expectation of nonrepresentation for this subset of the GGO population and escape the expectations faced by more political organizations (Lowi 2001).

The patterns thus reflect two aspects of global governance. First, the normative expectations derived from domestic governance institutions and the state-based norms of international relations are imported into the general representational structure of GGOs. Among governmental GGOs, the adoption of both a conciliar structure and OMOV apportionment is a virtual requirement of *responsibility*-type accountability. Second, an industry-driven membership is more concerned with substantive representation with respect to technical matters of great concern. For such representation, a nonconciliar structure is preferable. Nation-states have more generalized interest in GGOs, making the conciliar model more suitable.

UTILIZATION OF FOCUSED INTERMEDIATE BODIES AS A SUBSTITUTE. Organizations with conciliar structure may seek substitutes for the substantive representation facilitated through specialized and nonrepresentative structures. Both the FIB and the working group offer some of the advantages of the nonconciliar models. Under the conciliar model, an intermediate body comprised of a subset of all members is delegated responsibility by the representative body to monitor the day-to-day management of the organization and engage policy matters as they arise. As noted earlier, however, this oversight is general. It supervises the organizational leadership, monitors the budget, authorizes decisions on new policy matters, and in some cases, approves new rules.

The International Atomic Energy Agency, best known for its role as inspector under nuclear nonproliferation treaties, produces standards related to nuclear power generation and handling of nuclear materials. It uses a standard intermediate-body approach. Its General Conference meets once a year, but it designates thirty-five member states to serve on the Board of Governors. The Board of Governors meets five times a year and has primary responsibility for budget review, selection of the director-general and, critically in terms of this study, final approval of safeguards agreements and safety standards (Sands et al. 2001, 113).

The focused intermediate body offers a complementary structure that permits substantive engagement. Like the standard intermediate body, the FIB is more directly engaged in the activities of the organization than the representative body. The difference is that the prototypical FIB is typically organized around the substantive responsibilities of the GGO. So, for example, the International Maritime Organization has FIBs devoted to maritime safety and maritime environmental protection. The International Civil Aviation Organization has committees on air navigation and air transport. These organs allow members with particular interest in those subject areas to engage with the bureaucracy (Sands et al. 2001, 86).

Conciliar organizations are more likely to employ FIBs. For the non-conciliar organizations such organs would be duplicative and unnecessary. Interested parties already have substantive access through specialized bodies or working groups. In fact, two-thirds of conciliar organizations employ FIBs providing the substantive access required by concerned members. Thus GGOs employing FIBs replicate a key feature of GGOs utilizing the nonconciliar approach to representation. Both sets of organizations guarantee members direct access to the core function of the organization—development of rules—and, by extension, influence over matters of deepest concern.

Apportionment of Influence

SPECIAL POWERS AND PROPORTIONAL REPRESENTATION ALMOST UNIVERSALLY ESCHEWED. SECTOR has a significant relationship with apportionment of influence, on par with the connection to representation. In formal construction, GGOs with governmental membership all employ a OMOV system. In this respect, the distribution of voting power resembles the most familiar international organization, the United Nations. In another crucial respect, however, the GGOs diverge significantly from the UN model. Contrary to expectations, there are no GGOs that provide a formal veto power to a select set of countries or members.[1] Thus organizational structure appears to grant equal influence to all members (in stark contrast to the Security Council, which makes the inequality quite explicit).

GGOs also eschew another familiar apportionment structure that provides for an unequal distribution of formal power. The proportional model of voting is often associated with the World Bank and the IMF. In both of those organizations, the voting power of each member country is tied to its financial contribution, and this arrangement does, in fact, give wealthier nations more influence (Feld et al. 1994, 135). The GGOs studied also do not typically adopt this approach to apportionment of voting power. This is not because the financial contributions are equal for all organizations. Like the UN, most GGOs, especially the governmental ones, employ a proportional system of contribution. The lack of proportional voting systems seemingly contradicts once again the intuition that the world's most powerful actors would insist upon differentiation in power before participating in international organizations.

The truth is more complicated.

SAFETY VALVES THROUGH INTERMEDIATE-BODY SELECTION AND DECISION RULES.   The provision of equal voting rights to all GGO members allows the organization to satisfy core legitimacy expectations in this sphere. But overall, GGO structure does not sacrifice the protection of key players' interests as the price of *responsibility*-type accountability. The guarantee of responsiveness, influence for pivotal members, is crucial to maintaining GGO authority. And this requirement is met. Still, the incorporation of "safety valves" into the design of global governance organizations is sufficiently subtle; resentment that could undermine the GGOs' hard-won legitimacy is not aroused.

This is a realist's problem that requires a neoliberal solution. Two mechanisms provide disproportionate influence to key participants and, more

1. ICANN represents a special and unusual case. By virtue of ICANN's contractual relationship with the United State government, the US Congress has a de facto veto over ICANN activities.

importantly, protect these critical members from undesirable outcomes. First, the selection of members of the intermediate body (or bodies) is structured to ensure inclusion of key organization members. Second, the decision rules (particularly in the rulemaking process) provide checks against undesirable outcomes.

Intermediate bodies perform the crucial governance functions within GGOs. Under the conciliar model, the representative body is relevant—particularly in situations that require ratification of a treaty—but it is restricted to decisions that can be handled on an annual, biannual, or even quadrennial basis. This typically translates into ratifying decisions made in the intermediate body: electing the chief executive, approving organizational budgets, adopting strategic plans and sometimes casting "yea / nay" votes on proposed rules that have been crafted in other venues. The representative body simply cannot engage in the ongoing decisionmaking.

The intermediate body is the locus of almost all critical decisionmaking across the GGO conciliar population. For illustrative purposes, consider the agenda of the General Assembly and the General Council and Technical Management Board (two intermediate bodies) at the annual conference of the International Organization for Standardization (ISO). The General Assembly, comprised of representatives of 159 member countries, heard presentations from the permanent staff regarding the accomplishments of the organization, current issues, the budget, and so on. They had limited voting responsibilities—electing of five of six candidates to the council, for example—as well. The intermediate bodies, however, considered more sensitive topics, such as collaboration with other international organizations and whether to take up standard setting in new arenas (Higgott et al. 2000, 128).

Democratic principle would give all members an equal opportunity to participate in the all-important intermediate bodies. But this is seldom the practice. Governmental GGOs in particular provide for the representation of specific members in the intermediate body (table 4.7). In this sample, thirty-five percent of GGOs guarantee intermediate-body membership to key members, and thirteen percent ensure that vital interests are represented. Another 17 percent require geographic representation. The guaranteed seats on intermediate bodies are obviously not randomly distributed. As a matter of practice, for example, it is unusual to see a selective body—whether it is called a council, a board, or something else—that does not include the United States and other economically powerful nations. This is true even when organizations do not formally call for

TABLE 4.7 **Sector and Intermediate-body Selection**

	Intermediate-body Selection				
Sector	Ensures key members	Ensures geographic representation	Ensures interest representation	No distribution requirements	Total
Government	6	3	0	2	11
Mixed	2	1	0	1	4
Nongovernment	0	0	3	5	8
Total	8	4	3	8	23
Fisher's exact = 0.008					

such representation, suggesting that this is a well-known informal practice.

Inclusion of key states in intermediate bodies can be a sticking point in a nation's decision whether to join a GGO. For many reasons, the United States has not ratified the Law of the Sea Treaty or joined its administering body, the International Seabed Authority. One of the issues was the lack of a guaranteed spot on the ISA's intermediate body. Interestingly, negotiations by the Clinton Administration did secure this privilege— although it is cryptic, because the text of the convention was amended only to ensure representation of the "the largest consumer" of "commodities produced from the categories of minerals" under discussion (UN 1982, 4[c]161.1a). Note that the language is careful to single out the consumer not of the minerals but of the commodities produced from the minerals, a strange formulation intended to guarantee US membership without saying so. This has not yet been enough of a concession to prompt American ratification, but it does provide an indication that inclusion in the intermediate body is a valued check on the organization. Interestingly, the treaty with the amended language is posted on the UN website, but *not* on the ISA website.

Decision rules can also be employed that limit the potential for negative outcomes. These will be discussed more fully in chapter 5. Of particular importance is the emphasis on consensus in decisionmaking. Consensus is an appealing notion that seemingly embodies principles of equality, but it is also a useful device for reassuring key players that may be skittish about the downside of GGO authority.

Remember that safety valves are intended to give powerful players the ability to stop undesirable outcomes more than the ability to secure desired outcomes (Rosendorff and Milner 2001). Participation in the GGO can never leave a key member worse off than the status quo. The guaranteed inclusion of key members in intermediate bodies and the operation on a consensus basis help provide assurance that this is the case without calling attention to the undemocratic aspects of these features.

SAFETY VALVES SEEM LESS CRITICAL IN TECHNICAL, CLOSED-MEMBERSHIP ORGANIZATIONS. Among the nongovernmental organizations and the more technical organizations, the dynamic is different. Protection of members from undesirable outcomes does not appear to be nearly as important. Neither representation nor apportionment is structured to provide the same safety valves to members.

Less protection from negative outcomes is required in highly technical organizations because in such arenas the rulemaking process is closer to pure coordination (Gruber 2000). Coordination is the objective of all organizations created to develop common rules, but the degree to which members are indifferent regarding any actual rule is highly variable. Members of the more technical organizations tend to have less intense preferences regarding the substance of said rule. The benefit lies in the coordination made possible by agreement on a single standard. This contrasts with "battle of the sexes" coordination characteristic of more political areas. These situations feature participants that are not indifferent as to the chosen rule or standard. It is termed "battle of the sexes" because the prototypical situation involves a husband and wife determining their plans for an evening out (Furth 1993, 355). They want to go out together but they have different preferences. The mutual interest in coordination is strong, but each spouse derives different benefits depending on the choice of activity. Thus the joint desire for coordination does not diminish the desire for greater influence in determining the outcome. Substantive domains in which the objective of GGO members is pure coordination will yield GGOs different than those operating in more contested arenas because fears of undesirable outcomes are less intense.

The clearest example from the sample of organizations examined here is the Unicode Consortium. The Unicode Consortium established standards for the representation of characters in all computer code. This important function dramatically increases the interoperability of computers around the world, ensuring that characters appear properly regardless of software or operating system. All participants have a strong interest in the creation and maintenance of common rules, but it is not terribly important what the rule actually says. As long as everyone agrees what string of numbers produces an A and what sting produces an α, the purpose of the rule is met.

In contrast, organizations that create rules in a "battle of the sexes" environment face more pressure to accommodate key players and provide the aforementioned safety valves. The International Labor Organization (ILO) produces rules that are very controversial on a range of subjects, from worker safety to the use of child labor. In this highly contested area, safety valves are very important. Thus it is not surprising that the ILO ensures representation on its intermediate bodies and employs FIBs (Taylor and Groom 2000; Zweifel 2006)

The expectation that membership rules would interact with structural safety values in a similar fashion was also supported in the analysis. One would expect that the need for protection is lessened in closed-membership GGOs because control over outcomes is already exercised at the membership stage. Fellow members are less likely to have divergent preferences. Qualitative evidence supports this reasoning, giving some indication of the gap between formal structure and actual practice.

The two GGOs with the most restricted memberships both illustrate the hypothesized dynamic well. The Financial Action Task Force on Money Laundering and the Basel Committee on Banking Standards both have memberships limited more or less to the G-20 countries. They are included in this study of global governance organizations, however, because the intended (and actual) application of their standards is worldwide, not regional. In both organizations, there is little concern regarding potential outcomes that would be violently opposed by members (interviews 36, 48). This is partially a reflection of the general agreement in the subject areas but also a consequence of the structurally ensured homogeneity of their memberships (Hulsse 2007; Hulsse and Kerwer 2007). The only safety valve employed is the use of the consensus norm in decisionmaking (Simmons 2001; Kirton and Von Furstenberg 2001, 71; Held and McGrew 2002, 60). Indeed, Barr and Miller (2006) observe with some surprise that the Basel Committee has increased transparency and participation but such procedural openness is palatable precisely *because* the structure is closed, a dynamic that will be considered in the next chapter.

Balance of Power

Examining the balance of power in GGOs brings the administrative function into the picture. Measurement poses a challenge in this area for much of the dynamic is informal. To create a standard measurement, several characteristics of the representative side of the organization were utilized as proxies for member engagement in the governance of the organization. The frequency of meetings for both the representative body and intermediate body were considered along with the length of terms of office for the leaders of these bodies. More frequent meetings and lengthier terms for leaders put the members on a more even footing with the permanent staff in terms of knowledge and understanding.

The inference is that an intermediate body that meets only once a year (or less) is weak relative to an intermediate body that meets more often. Infrequency of meeting requires more delegation of discretion to the permanent bureaucracy. Organizations in which the intermediate body (or bodies) meets more often, often under the leadership of long-serving elected chairmen, suggest a more balanced relationship (or even one of legislative dominance).

GOVERNMENTAL GGOS ASSOCIATED WITH LEGISLATURE-CENTRIC STRUCTURES. The conciliar model can accommodate a legislature-centric or bureaucracy-centric approach but one would expect SECTOR to correlate with patterns of *balance*. This connection is observed; governmental GGOs are associated with a legislature-centric system. The relationship between government ownership and legislative dominance is less robust than it was for *representation* and *apportionment of influence*. And, of course, the coding based primarily on the frequency of legislative body meetings and the term length of elected leaders provides only one rough measure of the relationship. The reasons for equivocation lie in the realities of legislative participation. As noted above, the representatives often have limited resources and attention span for the workings of global governance organizations. So while the representative bodies are given the opportunities to review budgets and intervene in all sorts of matters, this potential power does not appear to be exercised frequently in most cases.

An interesting complicating factor in evaluating the balance between bureaucratic and legislative influence across organizations is the variation *within* organizations. On some matters, members may be highly engaged. In other areas, the bureaucrats may be largely free to operate without legislative participation. Thus one is left to determine whether the legislative dominance on high-salience issues is more dispositive with respect to the overall dynamic than the tendency to bureaucratic dominance in low-salience arenas.

An interesting example of the variability in balance is found in the World Health Organization. Many of the matters in its bailiwick are high-profile or high-salience public policy issues. Most prominent among these are the distribution of pharmaceuticals in developing countries and the policies on birth control and abortion. Both arouse great interest from some national governments and interest groups but not others. Consequently, the member representatives are deeply concerned with the activities of the WHO secretariat in matters related to issues of particular interest. They scrutinize the budget and publications. They intervene regularly, particularly when alerted by a concerned interest group. On other matters within the WHO sphere, however, they remain relatively silent (Reinalda and Verbeek 1998, 16).

Remember that the consideration of balance is not framed as a contest between branches. The observation of a bureaucracy-centric system reflects the preferences of the members rather than usurpation by the permanent bureaucracy. Greater legislative engagement in issues of importance to members often takes place through focused intermediate bodies. These committees have distinct substantive responsibilities for members thus providing, almost by definition, a prominent legislative role in the organization.

TECHNICALITY AND BUREAUCRATIC DOMINANCE. Given that more technical issues are generally of lower public salience, it is not surprising that bureaucracy-centric operations predominate among technically oriented GGOs. In such issues areas, there is a willingness, even among governmental GGO members, to give the bureaucracy considerable latitude. But this finding is also a function of the treatment of member participation in working groups. Recall that GGOs in more technical areas generally adopt a task-oriented structure. That is, the members play an active role in the crafting of more technical rules. This renders the distinction between bureaucracy and legislature a dubious dividing line in such instances. Substantive representation takes place through the rulemaking process.

Task-oriented organizations therefore challenge the very differentiation underpinning this analysis. For these GGOs, a good portion of the "bureaucracy," the people doing the actual work of the organization, are members! Examples include the organizations cited as exemplars of this type of organization including the ISO, IEC, W3C, and so on. If the members performing this functional role are considered to be part of the bureaucracy when acting in this capacity, their strength certainly cannot be taken as an indicator of legislative weakness. On the other hand, if we regard this participation as a form of legislature-centricity, it begs the question who or what, precisely, is being made peripheral?

The trade-off is clearer when the permanent bureaucracy *does* have a functional role that is supplanted by participating members. In this small set of situations, the deep engagement of members can be seen as a limitation on bureaucratic discretion. It reflects a desire to keep issues in the legislative forum.

FUNDING NOT RELATED TO BALANCE.   Contrary to expectations, no independent relationship is evident between a GGO's source of FUNDING and the *balance* between legislative and bureaucratic influence. It was hypothesized that revenue-generating organizations might display greater bureaucratic independence, but there was no support for this notion. An indirect connection was observed as a result of two relationships. FUNDING and form of representation are connected, because most governmental GGOs are financed through member contributions. And balance and representation are connected as revealed in the absence of legislative dominance among nonconciliar GGOs. Thus an apparent link is suggested, but inspection indicates that it is a second-order effect.

Administrative Structure

Turning to the three characteristics of the administrative structure— bureaucratic role, centralization, and scale—one overarching observation is clear. The patterns across these three aspects of bureaucratic structure are stark with clear clustering of attributes. This makes presentation of the observed patterns quite straightforward.

RULE TYPE AND SECTOR DETERMINE BUREAUCRATIC ROLE.   Variation in the role of the bureaucracy was distilled down to a rather blunt dichotomous choice; is the administration geared primarily toward performance of the functional task of the organization or is it arranged primarily to support members as they engage in the substantive work? This simplification presents the two very different roles played by the permanent staff of all GGOs. This last statement is crucial and must be underscored. *All global governance organizations perform in both capacities.* The analysis here is based on a determination of emphasis in function.

RULE TYPE is the core characteristic with the most intuitive connection to the bureaucratic role variable. This intuition flows from an association between rule type and rule process. In general, the creation of standards is member-participatory. Logically, organizations that place a significant responsibility for rulemaking in members' hands require a permanent bureaucracy in the supportive mode. The association between bureaucratic function and RULE TYPE is strong but not overwhelming. More than half of standards-generating GGOs are identified as having predominantly supporting bureaucracies. There are, however, almost as many functional organizations that produce standards. This is puzzling and leads one to question the strength of connection.

Upon further examination, the intuition is confirmed, albeit with a caveat. Almost all the functional, standards-generating organizations are *governmental.* This finding is consistent with the expectation that governmental GGOs would be organized around a functional bureaucracy. The cases of standard-generating governmental GGOs such as the IAEA, UPU, and ICAO therefore present a clash of two expectations. SECTOR has dominant explanatory power in this area.

Given the rise of standards as a public policy tools, one might suspect that younger organizations are more likely to adopt a supporting model. This inference does not hold up to inspection in either direction. Many of the younger GGOs, such as the Convention on International Trade in Endangered Species (CITES), resemble older functional GGOs. This brings to mind DiMaggio and Powell's (1983) argument that some organizations imitate established organizations as an attempt to establish their legitimacy. Some of the standards-generating GGOs including the IEC and ITU with supporting bureaucracies are considerably older than the average GGO (Claude 1971).

CENTRALIZED STRUCTURE ALMOST PERFECTLY CORRELATED WITH FUNC-TIONAL ROLE. The relationship between these two variables is overwhelming, as one would expect. The centralized structure makes more sense for a functional bureaucracy. To accomplish the substantive work of the organization, employees benefit from working together under a single roof. The distributed structure is well suited to a participatory process that involves members based around the world. Great physical diffusion of people is not as formidable an obstacle to members working together on a common project because of contemporary technology. The emergence of the Internet and other communications technologies has accelerated (but did not create) the use of distributed governance approaches, a trend that may in time spread to functional organizations.

The working groups and technical committees of the standard-setting bodies routinely meet virtually. Drafts of new rules are sent instantaneously around the world. And, when necessary, the secretariat can provide guidance or review drafts without stalling the process. One interview subject recalled the "old days" when drafts were communicated by telex, a slower and more arduous process (interview 29).

In an interesting way, SECTOR and representational structure have explanatory power here aside from their correlations with functional bureaucratic role. Governmental GGOs all adopt the centralized administrative structure. This has practical benefits to many members and implications. Government representatives, particularly those from smaller countries with limited resources, are responsible for "covering" multiple international organizations. This includes representing the member state in meetings of legislative bodies and carrying out any monitoring function. Performing these tasks is made easier if all functions of a GGO are consolidated in one place.

Moreover, there is an efficiency of scale that comes from physically clustering many GGOs in one place. The situation of many global governance organizations (with their large, stable administrative workforces) in one Swiss city allows a lone delegation from one country to maintain responsibility for multiple GGOs. In carrying out research for this volume, the author was able to conduct countless interviews within walking distance from each other by spending time in Geneva, Switzerland, the unofficial world capital of global governance.

BUREAUCRATIC SCALE IS NOT DRIVEN BY SECTOR. Governmental GGOs do not appear to be systematically bigger than their nongovernmental peers. That is not to say that SECTOR does not have explanatory power with respect to the number of people employed by a GGO. This core characteristic once again is correlated with the variation (table 4.8). But this finding is driven more by the nongovernmental organizations—all of which are small (<100 employees)—rather than the governmental GGOs, which show more variation in size.

This data, in fact, *overstates* the connection between larger organizations and governmental membership. Governmental GGOs are less likely

TABLE 4.8 **Organizational Scale by Sector**

	Scale			
Sector	Small	Medium	Large	Total
Government	6	3	4	13
Mixed	0	1	3	4
Nongovernment	8	0	0	8
Total	14	4	7	25
Fisher's exact = 0.005				

to be purely rule-generating than nongovernmental GGOs. So the "head count" for the International Telecommunication Union, for example, includes not just the ITU-T sector responsible for rulemaking but two other divisions as well (Claude 1971; Sands et al. 2001; Cutler et al. 1999). A higher proportion of governmental GGO staff ought to be excluded from any tally of employees for purposes of fair comparison, but this is not possible given the information available regarding the allocation of staff. This observation points to a general truism regarding GGOs. The more tightly circumscribed the mission of the organization, the narrower its purpose, the smaller it will be.

One reason why governmental GGOs are not larger than their nongovernmental peers is the relative stability in many of the policy fields in which government GGOs function. Postal services and customs, for example, are not terribly dynamic and thus do not require large bureaucracies to manage the responsibilities of the organization. The size of such entities—the UPU, for example, employs fewer than two hundred people—may reflect the limit of the organization's mandate or the static quality of the rules promulgated by the organization.

Remember the caution required in the interpretation of scale for organizations with a supporting bureaucratic role. The number of permanent employees may be small but many more people are involved in the rulemaking process compared with functional organizations. The technical committees and working groups that carry out most of the rulemaking work involve the participation of scores of individuals employed not by the GGO but by its members. So if we look at the entire network, the number of individuals engaged in the process under a distributed model likely dwarfs the number involved in a centralized organization.

Two Types of Global Governance Organization

The tendencies in the structure of global governance organizations are not rendered clearly in this characteristic-by-characteristic analysis. To draw fuller portraits, then, one would like to know which characteristics are associated with each other. Latent class analysis is a statistical method utilized to uncover patterns in sets of data. It differs from traditional factor analysis in its applicability to categorical variables like those employed in this study. Latent class analysis allows for identification of "clusters" within the data. These are expressed probabilistically. If there are two clusters, for example, the output of latent class analysis shows the probability of a case within a given cluster displaying a particular characteristic (Vermunt and Magidson 2005).

This methodology can be applied to the dataset comprised of observations on GGOs. Because of the small number of cases, the findings do not often reach levels of statistical significance. Therefore, the results will not consume a great deal of the reader's attention. Still, the output does provide a compelling sense of the general profiles for global governance organizations. Table 4.9 presents the results of cluster analysis of structural characteristics.

Identifying patterns incorporating all six structural characteristics considered in this chapter, two clusters of GGOs emerge. The *traditional* GGO is made up of governmental members organized around a conciliar structure; a large representative body delegates most legislative power to a subset of members that make up one or more intermediate bodies. *Traditional* GGOs apportion voting influence on a one member / one vote basis. The intermediate body oversees a centralized bureaucracy that is primarily functional, carrying out the substantive work of the organization. The well-known intergovernmental GGOs like the World Health Organization or International Civil Aviation Organization are exemplars of this type.

The alternative model is the *hybrid* GGO. This cluster shows more variation, but the standard profile is a nongovernmental or mixed GGO employing a nonconciliar approach to representation. Although this means that apportionment cannot always be thought of in representative terms for these organizations, the formal system of apportionment grants equal influence to all members. With the members involved in the rulemaking process, the permanent staff of a *hybrid* GGO is likely to play a supporting role in the context of a distributed organizational structure. Most of

TABLE 4.9 **Cluster Analysis of Structural Features**

Variable Cluster size	Traditional (percent) 66	Hybrid (percent) 34
Representation model		
Conciliar	85	45
Nonrepresent	1	54
Specialized	14	1
Apportionment		
Nonrepresent	7	27
OMOV	78	72
Proportional	7	0
Select powers	7	0
Balance		
Bureaucracy-centric	43	70
Legislative-centric	57	30
Bureaucratic function		
Functional	92	4
Supporting	8	96
Centralization		
Centralized	99	5
Distributed	1	95
Scale		
Large	35	30
Medium	22	14
Small	43	56

TABLE 4.10 **Two Aggregated GGO Profiles**

GGO Type	Structure	Apportionment	Bureaucracy	SECTOR
Traditional GGO	Conciliar	OMOV	Centralized, functional	Government
Hybrid GGO	Specialized / nonrep.	Nonrep. / OMOV	Distributed, supporting	Mixed / nongov.

the standards-generating GGOs are *hybrid* GGOs. The two profiles are summarized in table 4.10.

The age of organizations in each cluster provides some sense of the trend in global governance. The average *traditional* GGO is fifty-six years old. The average for *hybrid* GGOs is half that, twenty-eight years. This pattern is entirely consistent with general trends in administration. There is little appetite for the creation of government bureaucracies even in domestic contexts. Governance responsibilities are shifting to nongovernmental bodies. So it appears to be in the transnational context as well.

Implications

The sketched portraits of two GGO structure types—*traditional* and *hybrid*—and the patterns in the distribution of these types (and individual structural characteristics) provide support for aspects of competing theories of international organization. SECTOR and TECHNICALITY clearly offer the most explanatory power in the area of structure, a finding that jibes with realist, functionalist, and constructivist accounts. Governmental GGOs are driven by strong normative expectations. The democratic models of representation and other aspects of bureaucratic design seem practically obligatory. The relationship between SECTOR and structure is revealed most vividly when all the core characteristics are considered as predictors of structure type.

Only TECHNICALITY has explanatory power comparable to SECTOR (table 4.11). This characteristic accounts for much of the variation that does not seem to be a function of governmental membership, predicting variation within the groups defined by sector. More technical rule content demands a task-oriented form of representation and member participation. For nongovernmental GGOs, this takes the form of specialized or nonrepresentative structure. For governmental GGOs that seemingly *must* adopt a conciliar structure, the reliance on focused intermediate bodies seems to accomplish the same purpose. TECHNICALITY is associated with a less bureaucracy-centric system and a smaller staff acting in a supporting mode.

TABLE 4.11 **GGO Structure Type by Sector, Technicality**

Sector	Structure Type		Total
	Traditional	Hybrid	
Government	11	2	13
Nongovernment	4	4	8
Mixed	1	3	4
Total	16	9	25
Fisher's exact = 0.048			
Technicality			
High	5	8	13
Low	11	1	12
Total	16	9	25
Fisher's exact = 0.011			
1-sided Fisher's exact = 0.008			

It is something of a surprise that RULE TYPE provides little explanatory power outside its association with SECTOR and TECHNICALITY. Treaties are made only by governments, thus any body capable of this approach must have the structural attributes of a governmental GGO. Standards are more common for technical subject matter, thus such rules are associated with a distributed, task-oriented approach to governance. Even with those correlations observed, the data show that *traditional* and *hybrid* structures are adaptable enough to handle different rule types.

Legitimacy and the Incorporation of Safety Valves

The emergence of the two GGO model types is consistent with the theory presented in the opening chapters. One would expect SECTOR to be the organizational characteristic with the most potent correlation with structure. Governmental GGOs must conform more closely to expectations borne from the democratic domestic political contexts of its founding and most influential members. As a consequence of the governmental membership, they are seen by many as extensions of national governments. These GGOs face unambiguous demands for normative legitimacy.

The structures adopted by *traditional* GGOs are more consistent with representational and bureaucratic norms from the domestic, democratic context. Their conciliar representative structure emphasizes and reinforces the primacy of the state by organizing representation around the national governments. Expectations for equality are met by granting each member nation equivalent voting power. This arrangement not only creates a familiar-feeling legislative system with established rules of participation and deliberation, it also reinforces the Westphalian system of nation-states.

The associated bureaucratic structure places functional responsibility in the hands of a permanent, professional bureaucracy bound by formal rules. This creates an oversight function for the representative and intermediate bodies that is familiar to legislatures around the world. When necessary, the *traditional* GGO provides avenues for deeper participation by its members through intermediate bodies or working groups. These organizations clearly lean toward *responsibility*-type accountability.

The structures of *hybrid* GGOs offer greater latitude to depart from the normative expectations confronted by *traditional* GGOs in order to meet demands for responsiveness. *Hybrid* GGOs are more likely to have a representational structure that deemphasizes institutional affiliation in

favor of substantive interests, for example. Representation is even disconnected from institutions entirely in some cases without any implicit
statement regarding the relative importance of each member. Members
of *hybrid* GGOs are less concerned with broader policy interconnections,
and therefore their efforts will be focused within areas of substantive interest. Among *hybrid* GGOs, the bureaucracy is more likely to play a
supporting role consistent with the participatory, distributed model. The
lion's share of rulemaking responsibility is placed directly in the hands of
organizational members.

One layer beneath the GGO structures that satisfy normative demands
of democratic legitimacy, both *traditional* and *hybrid* GGOs incorporate
features that violate these very same norms. In stark contrast to the assignment of voting rights on a one member, one vote basis, for example,
the selection of members for intermediate bodies is, more often than not,
quite unequal. Most GGOs ensure that the most powerful members have a
place in the intermediate body, the organ most engaged in GGO activities.
As noted above, the United States is not a member of any GGO that does
not include a US representative in its intermediate body.

The intermediate-body selection process is a safety valve incorporated
into GGO structure to make participation of the more powerful actors
possible; it ensures them an outcome no worse than the status quo. While
the predetermined selective membership of the intermediate bodies is not
as glaring a violation of democratic norms as membership on the UN Security Council, it clearly represents a departure from a philosophical ideal.
This concession sacrifices some claim on legitimacy in a bid to secure organizational authority, and yet it is accepted noncontroversially by GGO
members, even by those members not granted such status.

Only One Scene of the Balancing Act

The analysis of representational and bureaucratic structure of GGOs demonstrates the multiplicity of factors that shape global governance organizations. Mechanisms are mixed to build normative legitimacy but protect
the interests of key members. The tension between these two goals is not
fully resolved by the compromises described in this chapter. Indeed, the
observations suggest that in this arena, legitimacy has greater weight than
authority. This conclusion should reassure readers who were concerned at
the outset that governmental participation in international organizations
was underappreciated as a distinguishing feature.

The adaptations required to manage the legitimacy / authority tension are not confined to a single area of GGO design, however. It is important to consider the institutional features as part of a whole system that also includes the rulemaking process and adherence regime. The emphasis on legitimacy in representation—where the normative expectations are clearest and most universal—can be balanced with features in other areas. For instance, the safety valves incorporated in the rulemaking process, as discussed in the next chapter, are clearly linked to the GGOs' approach to representation and administration.

This analysis of structure also demonstrates that the concern with legitimacy and authority is far from the only consideration in shaping a global governance organization. The technical demands of the task have a profound influence on the shape of the organization, as one would expect. This is a critical observation that should reassure those who fear that the claim of this book is overstated. Managing the tension between legitimacy and authority is one consideration in the design of GGOs—and a distinctive one—but it is not the only one.

CHAPTER FIVE

Rulemaking in Global Governance Organizations

The process for drafting and approving new treaties, standards, and regulations is a key feature of every global governance organization. As the mechanism by which general preferences are translated into concrete rules, the rulemaking process determines who has access and influence, how conclusions are reached, and under what circumstances the organization can take action. The rulemaking process also reflects the demands placed upon the organization. Members and concerned parties naturally want to see a process that guarantees a level of fairness but also one that ensures that their interests will be represented. Failure to meet expectations can undermine the GGO and even drive potential participants away. Thus the GGO's rulemaking process not only affects the nature of the rules it produces, it has implications for the organization's ability to implement and enforce those rules (Zamora 1980).

Each global governance organization generates a unique set of rules. In chapter 2, the three different categories of rules—treaties, regulations, and standards—were described in detail. RULE TYPE is linked with other organizational attributes. The previous chapter noted that treatymaking organizations are always governmental, for instance. One would expect the relationship between RULE TYPE and the rulemaking process to be especially strong. The surprising finding of this chapter is that the examined dimensions of rulemaking processes correlate more closely with other GGO characteristics than RULE TYPE.

TABLE 5.1 **GGO Rulemaking Process Types and Accountability Emphasis**

	GGO Rulemaking Type	
Area	*Club*	*Forum*
Formality	Informal	Formal
Decision calculus	Technocratic	Political
Decision rule	Consensus	Supermajoritarian
Permeability	Less permeable	More permeable
Accountability emphasis	Responsiveness (authority)	Responsibility (legitimacy)

This chapter is structured like the three other empirical chapters. The first section establishes the key differences among rulemaking processes. Four dimensions of global rulemaking regimes are described and considered in the analysis—*formality, decision calculus, decision rule,* and *permeability.* In the second section, observed patterns of variation for the set of twenty-five GGOs under study are reported. Based on cluster analysis of the distribution of rulemaking practices, two approaches to GGO rulemaking are identified: *forum* rulemaking and *club* rulemaking.

Forum rulemaking is distinguished by a formalized process in which decisionmaking emphasizes political rather than technical considerations. Although consensus is sought, approval of new rules by a supermajority is formally permissible. Perhaps surprisingly, *forum*-type rulemaking is generally less permeable to nonmembers than *club* rulemaking. The *club* approach to rulemaking is more informal, meaning there is greater flexibility in the process. Decisions are more technocratic in nature and generally outcomes require consensus. *Club* rulemaking processes are often more accessible to interested nonmembers than *forum* organizations.

Consistent with the core theory of this volume, GGOs must satisfy two sets of expectations regarding their rulemaking process. *Forum* and *club* rulemaking processes have much in common; both are guided by rules that provide for participation by members, interested parties, technical experts, and experienced bureaucrats. With more rigid requirements and emphasis on political representation in the decisionmaking process, however, organizations adopting the *forum* approach lean in the direction of *responsibility*-type accountability. This *forum* rulemaking model is more consistent with beliefs adapted from the domestic context regarding participation, due process, and equity that gives rulemaking legitimacy. The *club* model makes it easier to assure key members that their interests are adequately protected in the rulemaking process, a requirement of *responsiveness*-type accountability in the global governance context. One interesting common element is the preference for decisionmaking by consensus, an approach that appears to grant great influence to more powerful players while maintaining a veneer of equality.

The concluding third section of the chapter considers the implications of the observed patterns with emphasis on the relationship between rulemaking and organizational structure, rule adoption, and the legitimacy-authority dilemma.

Variation in GGO Rulemaking

In the details, rulemaking processes are all one of a kind. The number of steps from proposal to approval, the venue for deliberation, the rules of interaction, and many other such characteristics differentiate each GGO from all others. As in the analysis of organizational structure, a step back is required to reveal commonalities across the heterogeneous population of global governance organizations. Data collected on the specifics of each GGO's rulemaking process were combined to characterize each organization on four dimensions. Table 5.2 catalogs the four aspects of the rulemaking process analyzed and the fundamental question at the heart of each. In each case, variation is boiled down to only a few alternatives, described in this section.

Formality

In the domestic governmental context, rulemaking is traditionally a highly formalized affair. The Administrative Procedures Act spells out exacting

TABLE 5.2 **Dimensions of the GGO Rulemaking Process**

Area	Question	Options
Formality	How precisely is the rulemaking process stipulated in organization documents?	Formal Informal
Decision calculus	What is the nature of deliberations regarding proposed rules?	Technical Political
Decision rule	How is the decision to approve a new rule made?	Majoritarian; supermajoritarian; special powers; consensus
Inclusiveness	How open is the rulemaking process to participation by nonmembers?	Self-contained; participatory

requirements regarding the generation of regulations in the United States, for example. Agencies must publish notices of proposed regulation, solicit comments, catalog and respond to said comments, publish draft versions, and so on. Clear requirements regarding timing and format of all aspects must be met. Any agency misstep can result in a legal challenge that will undermine or delay adoption and implementation (Kerwin 2003).

In recent years, rulemaking entities—even governmental entities—have adopted or experimented with a more informal approach to rulemaking (Eisner et al. 2006). The processes are less rigid. They emphasize negotiations among members, interest groups, government officials, and others (Weimer 2006). Decisions are reached through consultation with key parties and bargaining over multiple issues (Coglianese 1997; Langbein and Kerwin 2000). These processes are not as constrained by legal or regulatory requirements, thus giving participants more room to find approaches that are acceptable to interested parties. Proponents of such "reg neg" arrangements argue that these approaches enhance legitimacy of the rules, while critics charge they are unduly influenced by regulated interests (Coglianese 1997; Freeman and Langbein 2000a; Langbein 2002). Both claims resonate in the realm of global governance.

ASPECTS OF THE FORMAL RULEMAKING PROCESS. There is no global administrative code governing rulemaking at transnational organizations, but most organizational charters address the rulemaking process. Thus the distinctive characteristic here is not whether an organization has written rulemaking procedures—they all do—but how much flexibility the rules afford. Organizations are said to have "formal" rulemaking processes when the requirements are specific and inflexible. That is, a formal rulemaking process is one in which the rule must emerge from the precisely stipulated formal process. Not all formal processes cover identical steps to rulemaking. Among the features of the rulemaking process that are typically defined are the following:

- a mechanism by which rulemaking is initiated;
- required steps as rulemaking moves forward;
- requisite parties to any substantive review of a proposed rule;
- parties eligible to participate in consideration;
- fora for participation of members and outside groups;
- mechanisms for approval and opportunities for appeal; and
- voting procedures and decision rules.

There is variance in which organizational body has the power to approve the initiation of rulemaking, ranging from the representative body to a working group. Some GGOs do not require a member proposal at all; the secretariat has the power of initiation. The Financial Action Task Force on Money Laundering is an example of this arrangement. The permanent staff may initiate work (often on an "interpretative note" that clarifies the application of existing "recommendations" to a new phenomenon) when a problem emerges or is brought to the attention of the secretariat by a member or nonmember (interview 48). Intermediate-body approval is sometimes required. In the World Customs Organization, for example, the impetus for new rules or amendments to the existing arrangements comes from member governments following a domestic review. They can propose a new recommendation to be reviewed by an intermediate body. With the approval of this organ, the proposal moves forward through stages of drafting and review (WCO 2007).

Across the population of GGOs, preparation of a new regulation typically requires the circulation of a draft regulation—this requirement is generally met with the provision of document on a website rather than a hard copy document like the Federal Register—before the final regulation is approved. This does not always entail making the draft rule available to the general public, but members are given an opportunity for review. When drafts are available to nonmembers, a comment period is typically observed but reply by the GGO is not required as part of most organizations' formal process. Even when solicitation of comments is not required per the formal process, they are generally accepted as a matter of practice either directly by the GGO or through members.

The rulemaking processes employed by many GGOs for the preparation and approval of treaties and regulations resembles those of domestic government agencies. The methods of the standard-setting GGOs is perhaps more alien in the governmental context. Standards are frequently crafted with members and other interested parties taking a central role, participating in working groups or technical committees. But the rulemaking processes of standard-setting process are not necessarily informal. Standard-setting organizations have rules governing the interaction among participants and the steps required to move a proposed standard to completion (Brunsson and Jacobsson 2000). These procedures reflect the need to balance considerations of efficiency, representation, and technical quality (Tamm Hallstrom 2004; 2000).

Two of the leading standard-setting bodies in the world, the International

TABLE 5.3 **Enumeration of "Stages" in IEC / ISO Standard Making**

	Associated Document	
Project stage	Name	Abbreviation
Preliminary stage	Preliminary work item	PWI
Proposal stage	New work item proposal	NP
Preparatory stage	Working draft(s)[1]	WD
Committee stage	Committee draft(s)[1]	CD
Enquiry stage	Enquiry draft[2]	ISO / DIS IEC / CDV
Approval stage	Final draft International Standard[3]	FDIS
Publication stage	International Standard	ISO, IEC, or ISO / IEC

1. These stages may be omitted, as described in annex F.
2. Draft International Standard in ISO, committee draft for vote in IEC.
3. May be omitted (see 2.6.4).

Organization for Standardization (ISO) and the International Electro-technical Commission (IEC), collaborated in creating a set of procedures for the creation of standards. In a single document, *ISO / IEC Directives*, part 1, "Procedures for the technical work," the steps are carefully laid out (see table 5.3). The document spells out the role of each body involved in the process, the role of the members of that body, and the expectations of each body's members.

In a second document, the ISO / IEC procedures go beyond these general rules and provide great detail regarding the format, terminology, and methodologies to be employed in the crafting of international standards (*ISO / IEC Directives*, part 2, "Rules for the structure and drafting of International Standards.") An annex to this document instructs, for example, "Do not mix information with unit symbols. Write, for example, 'the water content is 20 m/kg' and not '20 ml H_2O/kg' or 20 ml of water/kg" (ISO 2007a, 67). This is perhaps a bit more detailed than the instructions issued by other standards-setting bodies, but it provides a sense of the importance of uniformity. Procedural requirements typically cover:

- rules for forming a working group or technical committee (this generally takes place at the intermediate or representative body level);
- requirements for initiating a standard-setting process;
- selecting member leadership for working groups;
- manner in which members are notified of meetings;
- formats of proposed standards; and
- required steps to approval.

These procedural requirements of standard-setting bodies do not constrain the participants in their interactions with each other. Participatory standard-setting processes are designed to allow for ongoing collaboration among interested parties (Brunsson and Jacobsson 2000). A good portion of the rulemaking deliberation takes place outside the confines of working group meetings in the direct exchanges between members that occur, as a longtime IEC staff member says, "outside the room" (interview 29). The formality only governs part of the process—and some say it is the less important part.

The permanent staff of the standard-setting organizations plays a crucial role in ensuring the consistency of work by the various technical committees and working groups. These "technical officers" offer advice to the leaders of each group but also monitor their work to maintain some level of consistency (interviews 29, 18, 7). This role primarily concerns the "due process" of rulemaking rather than substance although the individual also serves as a liaison with the greater organization and may communicate the concerns of the intermediate body responsible for approving the output of the working group.

The World Trade Organization's Technical Barriers to Trade Agreement includes an Annex specifying the criteria by which standards-setting bodies shall be judged. This "Code of Good Practice for the Preparation, Adoption and Application of Standards" is vitally important, for it determines whether a standard is likely to be judged a barrier to trade (in violation of treaty) or a legitimate effort at standardization. All standards-setting organizations are quick to point out that they meet the WTO's standard as a way to reassure nations considering adoption. The code calls for standards that do not create "unnecessary obstacles to international trade" or replicate existing recognized international standards (WTO 2007a). There are general procedural requirements calling for the publication of proposed standards and provision of comment periods. True to its mission, the ISO goes a step further than the WTO in laying out specific requirements in the ISO / IEC Guide 59 *Code of Good Practice for Standardization* (Barnett and Duvall 2005, 309).

Another organization, the ISEAL Alliance (International Social and Environmental Accreditation and Labelling), has also attempted to standardize rulemaking. ISEAL serves several organizations that promulgate standards to be adopted by specific industries. Three organizations included in this study—the Forest Stewardship Council, Fairtrade Labelling

Organizations International, and the Marine Stewardship Council—are members. ISEAL created its *Code of Good Practice for Setting Social and Environmental Standards* based on ISO 59 to enhance the legitimacy of the rules produced by its members:

> The ISEAL Alliance facilitated the development of a Code of Good Practice for Setting Social and Environmental Standards to strengthen the credibility of social and environmental standards on the basis of how they are developed. By adhering to procedures that constitute good practices, standard-setting bodies help to ensure meaningful results from the application of their standards. In addition, a Code of Good Practice can serve as a minimum bar against which to measure the credibility of voluntary standards. (ISEAL 2007)

All the rulemakers interviewed echoed this sentiment regardless of rule type or organizational sector. The perceived relationship between the rulemaking process and the legitimacy of the rules produced is very strong (Freeman and Langbein 2000b). The approval stage of the rulemaking process is discussed under "decision rule" below.

MORE INFORMAL APPROACHES TO RULEMAKING. One must not put too much emphasis on the definition of the rulemaking process in organizational documents. The de facto rulemaking process may be different than the de jure process. The stipulations of an organizational charter may not be adhered to strictly in form or substance. In other situations, the steps outlined may be followed, but the true process involves much more activity outside the formal process than the documents capture. The quirkiest illustration of this phenomenon involves the World Wide Web Consortium (W3C), a body that develops "protocols and guidelines" that promote the interoperability of software and hardware related to the Internet (W3C 2005). The W3C sets out procedures for rulemaking (much less rigid than those of the ISO) but according to observers the critical juncture in the approval process is not mentioned. Tim Berners-Lee, the director and father of the World Wide Web, has effective authority over the entire process, retaining the power to see which rules make it and which do not (Saint-Laurent 2003).

The very possibility of such disconnects between requirements and practice raises two important considerations. First, attention must be paid to practice and not just the "letter of the law" in characterizing the rulemaking process of any GGO. Second, each GGO's latitude to bend (or even ignore) procedural requirements (as suggested by greater informality and flexibility) represents an area of variation that looms large in the analysis of global rulemaking.

Some organizations are more flexible precisely because the requirements of the rulemaking process are less rigid. As noted, the W3C provides for the creation of working groups on proposed rules with wide latitude granted each group to define its own procedures. There are opportunities to circumvent the prescribed process or suggestions that the process is but one way of adopting rules (Gould 2000; Ostrovsky and Schwarz 2005).

The International Accounting Standards Board is a nongovernmental organization responsible for the creation and revision of International Financial Reporting Standards, a set of accounting norms that allow investors to assess companies around the world in a common framework. It lays out its procedures for considering new standards, but these requirements leave much more latitude than what is spelled out in the ISO guidelines, as these examples suggest. Emphasis is added to highlight the opportunities for discretion:

> Although a discussion paper is *not a mandatory step* in its due process, the IASB *normally publishes* a discussion paper as its first publication on any major new topic as a vehicle to explain the issue and solicit early comment from constituents. If the IASB *decides to omit this step,* it will state its reasons.
>
> If the IASB *decides to explore the issues* further, it *may seek additional comment and suggestions* by conducting field visits, or by arranging public hearings and roundtable meetings (see paragraphs 94–106).
>
> When the IASB is *satisfied that it has reached a conclusion* on the issues arising from the exposure draft, it instructs the staff to draft the IFRS. A preballot draft is *usually subject to external review,* normally by the IFRIC. Shortly before the IASB ballots the standard, a near-final draft is posted on its limited access Website for paying subscribers. Finally, after the due process is completed, *all outstanding issues are resolved,* and the IASB members have balloted in favour of publication, the IFRS is issued. (IASB 2006s, 13)

No normative judgment is intended regarding this approach. The inclusion of such qualifiers may create a better rulemaking process, certainly one that is more responsive. *Traditional* and *hybrid* GGOs employ more flexible processes that grant leaders more discretion to adapt the rulemaking process as they see fit. The International Seabed Authority, for example, calls for open council and assembly meetings but also provides for private sessions at the discretion of the body (ISA 2003, rule 39). The procedures of the International Whaling Commission also grant more latitude to the leaders of the representative and intermediate bodies to shape the deliberation (IWC 2007). Organizations that provide such opportunities for deviation from standard operating procedure are coded as more informal, not because they lack procedural documents but because these organizations grant participants the means to avoid some cumbersome or otherwise undesirable aspects of the process if necessary.

Decision Calculus

The nature of deliberation regarding new rules is a defining characteristic of a GGO: does the rulemaking process seem to give greater weight to technical or political considerations? This distinction may seem subjective, but the answer to the question can be partly found in formal elements of the rulemaking process. Some organizational charters, for instance, identify explicitly the criteria that are to guide decisionmaking in the rulemaking process. In order to determine the decision calculus, analysis centered on the locus of rulemaking and the nature of participants in deliberation and decisionmaking to provide clues. Finally, discussion with participants and secondary accounts of GGO rulemaking inform the characterization of each organization.

TECHNOCRATIC DECISION CALCULUS. Organizations in this category place a large portion of the drafting power in the hands of technical bodies and only turn proposed rules over to general membership when a coherent proposal has been completed. Working groups and focused intermediate bodies (FIBs) generally draw individuals with technical expertise or specific knowledge within a narrowly defined substantive space. Even when the deliberation is limited to members, they are represented by technical experts rather than diplomats. So organizations that put most rulemaking authority in the hands of working groups or focused intermediate bodies are effectively keeping decisionmaking authority in the hands of these individuals, an indication that the decision calculus is primarily technical in nature. Therefore more "technocratic" rulemaking regimes are characterized by the dominance of experts and the (relatively) low profile of political representatives in the process.

One example of a highly technical decision calculus is presented by the Unicode Consortium, a nonprofit organization that generates standards regarding the representation of text in computer systems (Unicode 2006). Its policymaking process accords greatest weight to those individuals with substantive expertise in the area. Indeed, it is difficult to imagine an individual without a high level of technical sophistication being *able* to participate in deliberations (Unicode 2007).

The International Atomic Energy Agency (IAEA), an organization most commonly associated with searches for "weapons of mass destruction," creates standards for the safe operation of nuclear facilities. Notwithstanding the political nature of its inspection work, its rulemaking decisionmaking calculus appears to be dominated by technocratic individuals and consideration (Mathiason 2007; Alvarez 2006). The US representative to IAEA Commission on Safety Standards is, for instance, deputy director of the Nuclear Regulatory Commission with responsibility for the Office of Nuclear Material Safety and Safeguards. His entire career has been devoted to nuclear technology (NRC 2007). This is indicative of the type of deliberations carried out within the Safety and Security Section of the IAEA.

POLITICAL DECISION CALCULUS. More political rulemaking processes are distinguished by a high level of attention to the interests of members and other affected parties in the deliberations. One indicator of a political decision calculus is a meaningful role for the representative body or general intermediate body (as opposed to a FIB) in the rulemaking process. Almost all GGOs place some approval authority in such hands, but the extent to which this constitutes a serious deliberative step is indicated by the number of steps prior to this stage. If the representative body or intermediate-body votes only following several other steps requiring member approval, this stage is more likely symbolic than substantive.

The nature of individuals participating in the rulemaking process provides another signal of political decisionmaking just as it indicated a more technocratic approach. At higher levels of representation, the individuals are more likely to have diplomatic qualifications instead of (or in addition to) technical expertise. This suggests that the member's participation and decisionmaking is at least influenced by political alongside technical considerations.

An example (perhaps an extreme one) of the political rulemaking process is the World Trade Organization. Its rules help apply agreements negotiated by the parties to bilateral and multilateral trade agreements (WTO 2007b). Like the treaties themselves, these rules represent delicate balancing of interests. In recent years, the most contentious issues revolve around the differential impact of trade agreements on developed and developing nations. In this context, no rule is seen as purely technical, and the deliberations reflect this environment (Shaffer 2005).

Crises or events that increase the relevance of a GGO's rules might increase their level of politicization. This has arguably been the case for more technocratic organizations like the WHO, IAEA, and ITU. In the 1970s these organizations' decisionmaking processes moved away from technical issues and more toward Cold War topics (Reinalda and Verbeek 1998).

Decision Rule

A key determination in the design of the rulemaking process is the decision rule to transform a proposed rule into an actual rule. Organizations use a variety of approaches to setting the final hurdle to be cleared before adoption. In most cases, in fact, there are multiple decision points at which votes are required. This naturally poses an analytic challenge because it is not clear which stage is the most important. The final vote may be, and often is, a formality. More often than not, the decision rules are constant across bodies of the same organization. For purposes of uniformity, the organizations are characterized based on the decision rule at the final approval point. There are five approaches to be differentiated: majoritarian, supermajoritarian, majoritarian with veto, consensus, and consensus with fallback.

MAJORITARIAN.   The straightforward "majoritarian" approach to decisionmaking first means that a vote of members (or some subset of members empowered) is incorporated into the rulemaking process. The decision rule provides for approval with the agreement of a simple majority of members. Historically, this is an extraordinarily rare means of making final decisions in international organizations (Zamora 1980). And this is the case among contemporary GGOs.

SUPERMAJORITARIAN.   A variation on the majoritarian voting system sets a higher threshold—a supermajority—as the requirement for rule approval. The actual threshold varies from organization to organization, from body to body within an organization, and in a few cases, from decision to decision. The most common required majorities for rule approval are three-quarters or two-thirds.

Some organizations adopt a different type of supermajoritarian decision rule that is less familiar. These GGOs set a negative threshold for objections in addition to the approval requirement. This means that a rule cannot be approved if X percent of the members object to that rule. Note the distinction required as members cast their votes. On any given rule, there are thus three vote possibilities: in favor, neutral, or against. This approach to decision rule guarantees that no rule disliked by a substantial minority can be approved even if the majority vote in favor of it. It also provides a means of expression for participants who are ambivalent or indifferent regarding the fate of a proposed rule.

MAJORITARIAN WITH VETO. The discussion of supermajoritarian decision rules introduces the notion of minority power, a key consideration in the analysis of global governance. Decision rules that protect minority interests can be a crucial mechanism available to ensure that members cannot be compelled to accept rules they find objectionable. In the previous chapter, this idea was introduced in the discussion of APPORTIONMENT.

Organizations that adopt decision rules granting one or more members the opportunity to veto decisions were separated from other one member, one vote systems because they implicitly give some members more than one vote. The prototypical case, of course, is the UN Security Council. It would be strange indeed to suggest that all council members have equal voting power. Naturally, organizations adopting this kind of apportionment would be perfectly correlated with organizations that adopt this decision rule. This is not a problem because, as noted earlier, not a single organization in the population studied formally employs such a system. But this observation is based on formal rules. In practice, many GGOs effectively grant veto power to some members, often but not always the United States or other wealthy nations. Interestingly, the more subtle mechanism by which this safety valve is often incorporated, decisionmaking by consensus, is generally considered a paragon of democraticness.

CONSENSUS. At the opposite end of the spectrum from the majoritarian approach is decisionmaking by "consensus." Many GGOs make decisions—either by formal requirement or informal norm—by consensus. Ironically, as pointed out in the previous chapter, there is little consensus on the actual meaning of consensus! Global governance organizations use the term differently, and there is even inconsistency of understanding within the same GGO. The intuitive view of "consensus" is that all participants in a deliberative process reach universal agreement. Without such agreement, no decision has been made and no rule can move forward. This would give every member the same effective veto power as every other member. Only a minority in the world of global governance understand consensus this way.

Consensus is frequently taken to mean the "lack of strong disagreement." This suggests a gauging of the intensity of any member's disagreement as part of the decisionmaking process. This understanding naturally places a great deal of power in the hands of the party determining whether consensus has been reached. And, in some cases, even this level of unanimity is seen as an impractical standard; consensus is then viewed as "an overwhelming supermajority." The numerical percentage is never concrete, which provides the organization with some flexibility. This also creates an opportunity to informally allot unequal voting strength.

A common notion of consensus can be implemented in this context: agreement by the critical parties. Some members' agreement is more important than others. Answering questions regarding the meaning of consensus for the Financial Action Task Force on Money Laundering, a senior official of the organization said that consensus without American agreement was impossible. On the other hand, Luxembourg's objection would not necessarily undermine consensus (interview 48). In this way, the reliance on consensus can effectively grant more influence to some members, thus rendering a one member, one vote apportionment somewhat misleading.

Consensus is more normatively appealing than a system granting veto powers, but its effects are similarly undemocratic. In the analytic portion of this chapter, the use of consensus as a mechanism to grant some nations more power will be a focal point. Even in its idealized form, however, consensus requirements give a minority (potentially of one) the opportunity to frustrate the will of the majority. As Jean-Jacques Rousseau described in *Government of Poland,* governance by consensus is also a recipe for paralysis (Rousseau and Kendall 1985). A contemporary example illustrates this point. The World Intellectual Property Organization utilizes a one member, one vote structure but carries out decisionmaking with a consensus norm. This gives any country the ability to effectively halt organizational processes. At present, the consensus norm is preventing the organization from moving forward on a patent harmonization agreement as the Brazilian representative (as well as other sympathetic representatives) is demanding action on other unrelated issues of importance *before* the patent matter is taken up (interview 2).

Decisionmaking by consensus also introduces more ambiguity and opacity into the process. The search for consensus is generally hidden, carried out in the hallways during coffee breaks (interviews 7, 8, 29). This leaves unknown the compromises necessary to reach a shared conclusion. There is no requirement that consensus be reached through high-minded discourse. And, in point of fact, consensus is often achieved through the exertion of pressure by influential members or the extraction of payoffs by those voicing objections (interviews 7, 8, 21, 27, 29).

Permeability

The rulemaking process can be more or less limited to the members and bureaucracy associated with each GGO. As examined in the previous chapter, some organizations concentrate rulemaking responsibility in the permanent bureaucracy, with members playing a somewhat secondary role. Members of *hybrid* structure GGOs are deeply involved in the rulemaking process, participating in working groups or serving on focused intermediate bodies. This dynamic is captured in the "balance" variable.

In this discussion of permeability, the emphasis is on the transparency and accessibility of the process to nonmembers. Critics have argued that delegation of policy responsibilities to GGOs creates undemocratic barriers to participation that effectively exclude the public inappropriately from the process. The variation on the permeability dimension is reduced to two broad categories that is intended to capture the transparency and accessibility of the rulemaking process in relative terms. Each GGO's rulemaking process is characterized as more or less permeable. This crude characterization is based on assessments of four qualities: availability of documents, opportunities to observe, and opportunities to comment and participate in rulemaking proceedings. The relative characterization may be less satisfying than an absolute assessment with more gradation, but it is realistic.

Capturing the participation of external entities requires integration of formal and informal practice and knowledge of the variation within a single body. Once again, the emphasis in measurement is on the relevant formal attributes. Each of the elements of permeability draw upon several variables in the underlying survey of global governance organizations. This allows differentiation of GGOS that provide more opportunities for regular and substantive participation by outside groups from those that are more insulated from external groups, keeping deliberations in-house. Great contradictions between the formal and informal practices were seldom observed.

MORE-PERMEABLE RULEMAKING PROCESS. Participation by nonmembers (including interest groups, individual firms, NGOs, and the general public) is relatively easy and, in some cases, encouraged in more-permeable organizations. This takes several forms, including invitations to testify, opportunities to join deliberations either by application or invitation, and opportunities to submit comments and even offer proposals for new rules.

More-permeable organizations typically make documents easily accessible through websites or other means, providing opportunities for review and comment at multiple stages in the rulemaking process. Publication of rules under consideration is publicized by the organization as are opportunities for interested parties to contribute comments. Comment periods are timed such that there seems to be an opportunity to influence an ongoing process.

Access to materials is not limited to the narrow rulemaking activities in the most inclusive organizations. Data is readily available regarding the implementation of rules, allowing for outside parties to more easily perform analyses that lead to meaningful contribution to ongoing deliberations. Physical archives are open to outside parties or a website maintains an extensive library of documents covering all areas of GGO activity in the past as well as the present.

Finally, the most participatory type of process allows for nonmembers to play some role in the actual deliberations. At a minimum, outsiders are allowed to attend all substantive rulemaking sessions. More participatory procedures allow for testimony or active participation in debates or regular participation in rulemaking working groups. Note that the coding of permeability focused on participation of nonmembers. Thus an organization that has a membership drawing upon a more varied set of interested parties might provide less outside access than organizations with limited membership.

LESS-PERMEABLE RULEMAKING PROCESSES. Within this category, rulemaking processes are characterized by internal decisionmaking with lower levels of accessibility and limited opportunities for nonmember participation. No organization scores a zero on an imaginary scale of permeability; this characterization again must be seen as comparative. Among the GGOs characterized as less permeable, rulemaking processes still may include public observation opportunities for some meetings, publication of rules on the Internet prior to implementation and acceptance of comments from outsiders.

What sets the less-permeable process apart is a relative dearth of opportunities for comment and objection from outside parties (and sometimes even members), particularly at meaningful points in the process. Thus an organization that accepts comments only *after* a rule is approved is not regarded as participatory, *ceteris paribus.* Less participatory organizations restrict opportunities for observation to a subset of total meetings. This makes observation of the most substantive deliberations impossible for nonmembers and often restricts their view to formal votes that only ratify the resolution of controversial matters. In some instances participation is formally possible but logistically quite challenging.

The International Maritime Organization, an entity that creates rules governing safety, pollution, and other concerns of the high seas, has a process that is not conducive to outside participation. Documents related to ongoing deliberations are accessible only to members and "IGOs that have concluded agreements of cooperation with IMO and NGOs in Consultative Status with IMO, through a dedicated password-protected website" (IMO 2007). Many general organizational documents are available through the website but many can only be purchased from the organization. Such provisions make it more difficult for anyone not affiliated with a formal organization to track the IMO than some other GGOs.

Less-permeable GGOs sometimes redirect participation through members. GGOs that involve members are not inherently "participatory" in the terms used here but to the extent that member governments allow outside parties to use them as vehicles for participation—this is common—one *might* consider a member-participatory rulemaking process to occupy a middle ground between more and less inclusive approaches. As discussed in chapter 7, access through members is used more commonly by commercial interests than civil society groups.

Differentiation of global governance organizations on the basis of permeability should not be seen in normative terms. The characterization of a GGO as "more permeable" is not intended to imply that all outside parties participate equally. Corporate interests are generally dominant in the context of global governance, as they are better equipped to take advantage of participatory rulemaking processes. The explanation and implications of this reality are explored extensively in chapter 7. With the variations in GGO rulemaking sketched out, attention turns to the patterns observed in the data.

Patterns of Global Rulemaking

To identify and analyze patterns in the distribution of characteristics, each of the four dimensions of GGO rulemaking—*formality, decision calculus, decision rule,* and *permeability*—was reduced to a small number of alternatives (see table 5.1). As in the previous chapter, analysis focused initially on the relationship between the core characteristics of global governance organizations: SECTOR, FUNDING, TECHNICALITY, MEMBERSHIP, and RULE TYPE. In several instances, linkages were found with other characteristics of a GGO's approach to global governance. Based on a latent class analysis, two GGO rulemaking types are identified that provide a sense of the associations among the four rulemaking attributes and offer sketches of the most typical rulemaking regimes.

Formality

One would expect rule type to drive variations in the rulemaking process, and the requisite steps do vary with the type of rule being produced. Treatymaking organizations emphasize the rules of procedure for the representative body along with the steps followed by the secretariat in preparing materials and the process of ratification and reservation. The Universal Postal Union, for example, establishes clear procedures for its representative body to engage in all business, including its participation in the rulemaking process (UPU 2005). And in this case, the requirements are formal, specifying the voting procedures (including necessary quorum and decision criteria) as well as very specific matters such as seating, admission of observers, and parliamentary procedure. Other treatymaking GGOs catalog a similar set of requirements that would apply to rulemaking situations (as well as other legislative interactions).

Rulemaking procedures associated with regulations generally focus on the requisite steps to be taken by the bureaucracy in preparing regulations, including specification of the points at which member participation is required. Thus the procedures invariably require the approval of some representative body (typically an intermediate body and later the representative body in a more symbolic role) at one or more stages in the process. The attributes of the standard-setting process were described in the previous section.

None of this variation speaks directly to the formality question. Within each rule type, organizations are more or less rigid in the establishment of and adherence to requirements. RULE TYPE was not correlated with formality. Consistent with the findings regarding political and administrative structure, one would also expect SECTOR to have strong predictive power. Governmental GGOs might feel pressure to adopt practices resembling domestic governance practices in the rulemaking process (Kaufman 1977). But SECTOR is only moderately predictive of formality (and not statistically significant). Nongovernmental GGOs are far more likely to have a more informal process but only half the governmental GGOs demonstrated a relatively high degree of formality in rulemaking requirements (table 5.4).

Another core characteristic, MEMBERSHIP, offers more predictive power regarding *formality*. Open-membership GGOs are more likely to follow a formalized set of procedures (table 5.4). This is entirely intuitive. Recall that open-membership organizations essentially lack control over

TABLE 5.4 **Formality and Sector, Membership**

	Formality		
	Formal	Informal	Total
Sector			
Government	6	7	13
Mixed	2	2	4
Nongovernment	1	7	8
Total	9	16	25

Cramér's V = 0.3370
Fisher's exact = 0.293

Membership			
Open	7	5	12
Closed	2	9	11
Total	9	14	23

Cramér's V = 0.4110
Fisher's exact = 0.089
1-sided Fisher's exact = 0.060

admission. The formalized approach to rulemaking is thus necessary to guarantee order and induce nonmembers to join. Potential members are likely to be more comfortable with the future rulemaking activities—and the rules that might emerge—if a binding set of procedures for rulemaking reduce (or eliminate) the likelihood of unexpected outcomes. Closed-membership organizations have less need for rigid procedures because of the higher level of predictability and trust among the participants. With the latitude to be selective in admitting fellow members, there is also greater homogeneity of interests.

This explains the ease with which the Financial Action Task Force on Money Laundering and the Basel Committee on Capital Standards (BCBS) operate with less formal procedural requirements. Consider the BCBS, which focuses on the complex area of capital standards and other issues related to the solvency and security of banks. It is a small organization with a limited membership composed of the world's wealthiest nations, including the United States, the United Kingdom, France, Germany, and Japan (Koenig-Archibugi 2002). Through a series of committees, the representatives of the member institutions work together to address issues and, when deemed necessary, develop standards—the Basel I and II frameworks on capital adequacy are best known (Kapstein 1989). The BCBS process is informal, providing latitude to the members to work out problems and reach compromise (Wood 2005; Kapstein 1994). Like the FATF, the BCBS is restricted to the wealthier, more developed nations of the world. All members have an interest in maintaining the stability of the financial system (Kapstein 1994, interviews 36, 47) Pronounced disagreement among the members is rare, making consensus achievable (Singer 2004; interview 36).

TECHNICALITY also seems a candidate for correlation with *formality*. Technical subject matters seems well suited for a more informal process, allowing for collaboration, dialectic drafting and revision among technically motivated experts. Surprisingly, this relationship does not appear in the data. Informal processes are evenly distributed among organizations working in high- or low-technicality areas. This finding suggests a hierarchy of considerations in the shaping of rulemaking processes. The preference for informality in technical areas is only observed when a minimum comfort level is achieved through closed membership. The relationship among MEMBERSHIP, TECHNICALITY, and FORMALITY stands out in latent class analysis that will define rulemaking regime types (table 5.5).

TABLE 5.5 **Association between Technicality, Membership, and Formality**

	Cluster 1 (percent)	Cluster 2 (percent)
Cluster Size	51	49
Technicality		
High	18	83
Low	82	17
Membership		
Nonmember	0	17
Closed	5	80
Open	95	4
Formality		
Formal	56	18
Informal	44	82

Note: Among organizations with high technicality and closed membership, there is a high likelihood of informal process. This is not true for low-tech, open organizations

High-technicality subject areas *are* associated with informal processes for the set of organizations with *closed membership*.

Only in the context of a closed-membership organization are members comfortable leaving flexibility in the process, allowing technical experts to work together comfortable in their belief that all participants have the same basic background, principles, and goals. Outside the comfort zone of the closed organization, however, a more rigid rulemaking process insures against a free-wheeling process subject to the unpredictable actions of less-familiar parties.

ASTM International is a standard-setting organization dealing in technical matters that is differentiated from the BCBS by its very open approach to membership. Any individual can join as a "participating" member, and institutions can join as organizational members (ASTM 2003). There are fees associated with membership but not a rigorous screening process. Evolved from the American Section of the International Association for the Testing of Materials, ASTM is now independent and promulgates standards in a wide range of areas with technical committees dealing with everything from soap to gaseous fuels to sports equipment. It is the closest rival to ISO as a broad-scope international standards body. Given this notable accessibility, it is not surprising that ASTM has developed a formal rulemaking process spelling out the procedures for technical committees to follow in their deliberations and voting even though the nature of the subjects considered by these committees are highly technical.

Decision Calculus

The relationship between TECHNICALITY and decision calculus might appear to be tautological. One would assume that the basis of decisions in more technical areas is generally technocratic, and there is, in fact, a strong but far from perfect correlation. This finding provides support for the distinction drawn between "pure coordination" and "battle-of-the-sexes" coordination in global rulemaking. Recall that in a pure coordination situation, the benefits to participants derive from the mere fact of coordination, not the choice of a particular rule (e.g., everyone drives on the right side of the street). The tempting assumption is that all technical subject areas create pure coordination situations is not true (Majone 1984). Even in highly technical areas, the choice of a common standard often creates winners and losers. The disconnection between technicality and decision calculus provides some confirmation that technical arguments will not always win the day.

Perhaps the most technical organization in the population examined is the Unicode Consortium, the GGO focused on the digital representations for all linguistic characters. This is coordination in the purest form observed in this study and, not surprisingly, Unicode's decision calculus appears quite technical, as is evident in the indecipherable minutes of its meetings (Unicode 2007). The Internet Corporation for Assigned Names and Numbers (ICANN) also has a highly technical mandate—establishing operating parameters of the Internet's domain name system—but its deliberations and processes can be quite political (Mueller 2002). The decision of whether to add additional "top level domains" (TLDs) provides a good illustration. These three-letter suffixes generally define the type of institution with which a web page or email account is affiliated. The most familiar domains are the *.com*, *.edu*, and *.org* domains. One might regard the decision to expand as technical (will the addition of new TLDs cause difficulties?), but this quickly begets highly political calculation around sensitive questions (interview 50). The most prominent controversy surrounded the potential addition of a *.xxx* domain devoted exclusively to pornography (McCullagh 2005).

SECTOR does not have the predictive power one might expect for decision calculus. One might posit that governmental GGOs are more likely to display political decisionmaking, but this hypothesis underestimates the number of technical issues handled by such entities. The two best predictors of decision calculus are not core characteristics but features of the

GGO drawn from the examination of structure and adherence. The structural feature linked with decision calculus is legislative / bureaucratic *balance*. Organizations with more technocratic decision calculus are likely to see authority delegated to the bureaucracy. This is consistent with our understanding of legislatures as strategic actors (Wood and Waterman 1994). They keep tighter control over matters that are more sensitive and grant the bureaucracy greater latitude in the lower profile areas (Huber et al. 2001; Gruber 1987).

A feature of GGO adherence also shows a firm connection to decision calculus. As explained in the next chapter, a key consideration in the design of GGOs' adherence regime is the manner in which actors are compelled to comply with rules. Almost no GGO has its own enforcement authority; they rely upon agents to carry out this core responsibility. Thus there are two levels of adherence considered: first, the manner in which the GGO compels its agent to carry out enforcement activities (referred to as "primary adherence mechanism"); second, the manner in which the agent compels rule-abiding behavior from the regulated population ("secondary adherence mechanism").

Technocratic decisionmaking is strongly associated with *weak* primary adherence mechanisms. Weak primary adherence mechanisms give the GGO limited ability to compel its agents to carry out enforcement activities. The link between technocratic decision calculus and weak primary adherence mechanisms is consistent with the underlying theory of this book. Because technocratic decisionmaking is indicative of relatively low-stakes rulemaking (pure coordination), we would not expect much resistance from the adherence agent. The agent's interest is in ensuring adherence to a rule, any rule. The more political the decision, however, the more likely an agent will walk away from the rulemaking process dissatisfied and consequently unmotivated to carry out adherence activities. Thus the political decision calculus ought to be associated with somewhat *stronger* primary adherence mechanisms as observed.

Decision Rule

The manner in which new rules are approved is a critical and sensitive consideration in the design of rulemaking systems. It is an organizational feature that highlights the conflict between legitimacy and authority. Alas, the central challenge of this study, treating a heterogeneous population of global governance organizations as a single class of entities, is never more apparent than in this area. For reasons of analytic consistency, the decision rule was coded on the basis of the final approval in what is typically a multistep chain of approvals, but the significance of the final approval varies from organization to organization. In the majority of cases, this final hurdle is a significant barrier to be cleared; thus, the decision rule at this stage is a sensible focal point. In several cases, however, the final approval is typically a formality. The identification of the critical stage, however, is subjective, making the uniformity of "the final approval" the most appealing of imperfect alternatives.

The general problem of bridging the gap between formal rule and informal practice is acute in this area. All observers of organizations know that much of the decisionmaking process occurs outside the confines of the formally prescribed process. The negotiations among participants, the tacit and explicit agreements, the unspoken pressures and inducements, are all critical ingredients that are not enshrined in any document (interviews 8, 29, 18).

Both quantitative and qualitative analysis underscored one key differentiation: does a GGO make rulemaking decisions by consensus? Among those GGOs that do seek consensus, several provide for a majoritarian decision rule as fallback option. In practice, however, all organizations that raise the goal of consensual decisionmaking place a great deal of value in this process and almost never (if ever) resort to the formal majoritiarian vote alternative.

None of these caveats invalidates the observations made in the survey of GGOs. The interviews with participants exposed this gap, however, and so it must be part of the analysis in order to accurately interpret the findings. One accommodation to the diversity of the sample and the challenge of coding was to use multiple approaches to categorizing organizations to ensure that findings were not driven by sorting decisions. An alternative approach to the four categories described in the previous section grouped organizations providing for a vote as a fallback when consensus fails with those that provide only for consensus. This left just two categories: consensus and majoritarian GGOs. The findings were consistent using both approaches.

SECTOR, the core characteristic so important in other facets of organizational design, is not an effective predictor of decision rule. Nongovernmental GGOs are more likely to operate on a consensual basis, but this relationship is not strong. MEMBERSHIP also has a logical connection to decision rule. Theory predicts that the open-membership organizations

TABLE 5.6 **Decision Rule by Membership, Secondary Adherence Mechanism**

	Rule Approval (Reduced)		
Membership	Consensus	Supermajority	Total
Open	3	8	11
Closed	7	4	11
Total	10	12	22
Fisher's exact = 0.198			
1-sided Fisher's exact = 0.099			
Secondary adherence mechanism			
Direct engagement	5	4	9
Market	5	0	5
Engagement and market	4	7	11
Total:	14	11	25
Fisher's exact = 0.078			

are more likely to follow a majoritarian decision rule that allows for action in the absence of consensus and the consensus approach to be more common in the closed-membership organizations. This relationship was observed but at levels short of statistical significance.

Informal practice underscores the manner in which consensus decisionmaking is used to preserve the comity required to maintain closed organizations. The Fairtrade Labelling Organizations International, for example, vests rule approval authority in its Standards Committee. This committee is composed of concerned constituencies with precise criteria regarding the allocation of members (Blowfield 1999). In all organizational documents, the need for agreement is stressed. It is consistent with this notion that the Standards Committee "Terms of Reference" call for decisionmaking by consensus, with simple majority voting as a fallback option if the chair determines consensus in unreachable (FLOI 2007).

Many open-membership GGOs provide for a majoritarian decision rule but either formally or informally require consensus in decisionmaking. The deliberations of the World Health Organization, for example, are characterized by participants as quests for requisite consensus (interview 13). One frustrated WIPO official noted that his organization can be brought to a standstill by the requirement for consensus even though it appears nowhere in the treaties underpinning organization (interview 2).

Although TECHNICALITY does not have a predictive relationship with decision rule, it does appear to influence the locus of final rule approval (table 5.7). More-technical decisions can be resolved by intermediate bodies, while those that are less technical are more likely to require a vote of

TABLE 5.7 **Technicality and Rule Approval Body**

	Final Rule Approval Body					
Technicality	Representative body	Intermediate body	Working group	Member ratification	Leader	Total
High	5	6	0	0	1	12
Low	8	2	2	1	0	13
Total	13	8	2	1	1	25
Fisher's exact = 0.085						

the representative body. The International Civil Aviation Organization provides for different approval procedures depending on the content of the rule. The annexes of the Convention on International Civil Aviation constitute "Standards and Recommended Practices" governing global civil aviation. An amendment to one of these annexes goes through one of the focused intermediate bodies (e.g., the Air Navigation Committee) with final adoption by the council (intermediate body). It need not go to the full assembly of all members. There is a provision allowing for members to "register disapproval." If a majority does so, the amendment is invalidated. More technical changes take the form of "amendments to annexes," and these are also approved by the council (ICAO 2004).

Even when final rule approval is not left in the hands of an intermediate body, representative body consideration is often a pro forma affair. Still, inclusion of even a symbolic vote in the process represents a tip of the hat in the direction of legitimacy, reserving decisions of this type to the members' lead representatives even if the exclusive FIB retains determinative power.

DECISION RULE AND ADHERENCE. Adherence once again seems related to an attribute of the rulemaking process. Recall that almost every GGO relies upon other organizations to implement rules. The actual tool of enforcement utilized by the agent is referred to in the next chapter as the *secondary adherence mechanism*. The multiplicity of adherence mechanisms are reduced to three basic alternatives: direct engagement, market forces, or engagement and market combined. As table 5.6 reveals, decision rule is correlated with secondary adherence mechanism.

In particular, market adherence strategies, which require widespread adoption of rule by market participants in order to have force, are associated strongly with consensus in decisionmaking. This suggests that the perception of broad support is particularly important when the rule must be "marketed" to those responsible for enforcement and those who must comply. A rule that emerges from a fractious decisionmaking process will not be received as definitive, undermining it from its very introduction. Recall the efforts of the ISEAL Alliance to bolster the credibility of its members' standards by introducing a code governing standards development.

GGOs utilizing engagement strategies generally rely upon members to compel adherence. As such, if the member accepts the outcomes under the organizational process, it *may* be willing to act as an effective adherence agent. The situation is complicated by the flexibility regarding member adoption of rules promulgated by a GGO. Consensus may not be required—even for selective organizations—when members are not bound by GGO rules. The analysis in the next chapter focuses on this complex dynamic between the GGO and its members around adherence.

Permeability

There is a logical fear that GGOs are at too great a remove from the citizenry. Diplomats and bureaucrats in faraway places are left to make new rules without the supervision of elected officials and out of public view. Given the implicit argument of such critiques, that GGOs ought to be at least as transparent and accessible as domestic rulemaking bodies, SECTOR is a likely correlate for permeability. Governmental GGOs adopt a conciliar model of organizational structure that mirrors domestic models. Matching norms of participation seems like another important element needed to satisfy the GGOs' normative democratic legitimacy requirements. In fact, there is a relationship between SECTOR and permeability, but it is weaker than one would expect (table 5.8).

One powerful explanation for the tendency of governmental GGOs to adopt relatively less-permeable rulemaking procedures concerns the status of the nation-state in global governance. The inaccessibility of governmental GGOs' rulemaking reinforces the authority of the state. It forces interested parties to access the rulemaking process through national governments. For many GGOs such as the WHO or the ITU, this requirement is formalized (WHO 2006b; ITU 2005). This is not a merely superficial matter. The concerns of an interested nonmember may be a low priority for the GGO member government, cutting off a pathway to the GGO and frustrating efforts to influence the process. For example, a representative

TABLE 5.8 **Permeability by Sector, Technicality**

	Permeability		
	More permeable	Less permeable	Total
Sector			
Government	4	9	13
Mixed	4	0	4
Nongovernment	4	4	8
Total	12	13	25
Fisher's exact = 0.077			
Technicality			
Higher	9	4	13
Lower	3	9	12
Total	12	13	25
Fisher's exact = 0.047			
1-sided Fisher's exact = 0.034			

of the pharmaceutical industry bemoaned the focus of US representatives to the WHO on family-planning issues that result in neglect of intellectual property concerns (interview 12). At the ITU, companies sought to distance themselves from the United States when anti-American sentiments jeopardized any proposal from the US delegation. The software company Oracle participated in ITU deliberations as a German company (interviews 7, 45).

Consistent with this explanation, governmental GGOs provide concrete provisions ensuring the participation of their members' nation-states. They may be more internally participatory (for the members) than their nongovernmental counterparts but that is a difficult refinement to assess. Many mixed GGOs are also highly participatory for members. The International Organization for Standardization (ISO) creates working groups on proposed standards that are composed of experts appointed by members (Mathli and Buthe 2003, 1–42). This is consistent with the observations of governmental GGOs. The ISO is organized around nations. Each nation is represented by its national standards body. These vary in status; some are governmental but many are hybrid organizations, combining features of public and private entities.

The findings regarding permeability also reflect the needs of nongovernmental GGOs. Their members generally do *not* have internal political systems that allow for interest group participation. The only level at which such engagement is logistically possibility is with the GGO itself, making GGO permeability more important.

One must be careful to look at the practical demands of participation. It can be challenging even when the rules create opportunities. The relatively permeable rulemaking approaches offered by standard-setting bodies such as ISO and the IASB are less accessible to parties who are not already "in the know" (interview 37). Many people are not even aware of the existence of international standard-setting GGOs let alone their importance or the mechanisms for participation (Ahrne and Brunsson 2006; Jacobsson and Sahlin-Anderson 2006).

TECHNICALITY, another intuitive correlate of permeability, is the strongest predictor of permeability. It is negative. The procedures of many technical GGOs sound "open," but the opportunity to participate often applies only to members. Rulemaking is dominated by insiders and seems participatory only from the perspective of those with technical knowledge and the resources to get involved. These organizations also generally have less transparency to nonparticipants, and opportunities for public participation and review are limited. Given the tendency of higher-technicality GGOs to make rules that better approximate "pure coordination," the tilt toward less permeability may not arouse concern.

For this reason, the leaders of many GGOs argue that they are performing a technical function as a response to critics calling for more transparency. This argument implicitly invokes the coordination distinction. The normative demands imported from domestic governance contexts should be associated only with "battle of the sexes" rulemaking, it is implied, where the public has an interest in participating (Majone 1984). It has already been observed that many technical rules veer far from the coordination ideal thus explaining the conflict over accountability. Expectations are mismatched. The patterns observed with respect to permeability might be interpreted as an indication of the general acceptance of the technicality argument.

Two Global Rulemaking Types

Latent class analysis defines "clusters" based on the distribution of observations that are not perfectly correlated on multiple dimensions. The cluster analysis results (table 5.9) define two GGO rulemaking types. The percentages indicate the probability that an organization included in each cluster (i.e., rulemaking type) would display the characteristic in question. The higher the percentage, the stronger the association between that characteristic and that rulemaking type. In other words, a higher percentage indicates that the characteristic is more central to the definition of the rulemaking type.

The first rulemaking type, *forum*-type rulemaking, is characterized by a more formal process emphasizing participation of members and the permanent bureaucracy. Of the two types, it more closely approximates domestic government rulemaking (table 5.10). Many of the best-known intergovernmental organizations including the World Health Organization, the International Labor Organization, and the International Civil Aviation Organization, are prototypical forum rulemakers. They follow a precisely defined rulemaking process that channels participation through members first and foremost and provides less flexibility for participants. Consensus is sought in decisionmaking, but the rules do provide for a supermajoritarian decision if necessary (Jacobson 1974; Feld et al. 1994). *Forum* organizations are more likely to handle politically charged matters that push the decision calculus beyond the realm of the technical to include political considerations. Two-thirds of the sample organizations are characterized as *forum*-type rulemakers, meaning there is a great deal of variation within this cluster.

The alternative approach, *club*-type rulemaking, is typified by a more informal rulemaking process, less-strict adherence to a detailed set of rulemaking protocols, and less permeability for interested nonmembers.

TABLE 5.9 **Rulemaking Cluster Analysis (Two-cluster Model)**

Variable	Forum (percent)	Club (percent)
Cluster size	67	33
Formality		
Formal	59	3
Informal	41	97
Decision calculus		
Mixed	32	33
Political	23	27
Technocratic	46	40
Decision rule		
Consensus (major)	0	11
Consensus	1	70
Supermajority	61	10
Permeability		
More permeable	62	33
Less permeable	38	67

Note: The percentages indicate the likelihood that an organization of each type displays a given characteristic. The highlighted boxes call attention to the dominant alternative for each dimension of rulemaking.

TABLE 5.10 **Profiles of Two GGO Rulemaking Types**

Type	Formality	Decision Calculus	Decision Rule	Permeability
Club	Informal	Technocratic	Consensus	Less permeable
Forum	Formal	Political	Supermajoritarian	More permeable

Organizations in this category place emphasis on approving rules by consensus on technocratic grounds. *Club*-type rulemaking naturally resonates with Keohane and Nye's "club model of multilateral cooperation" that sacrifices legitimacy in exchange for efficacy (Keohane and Nye 2002). An example of this type of GGO already mentioned is the W3C, an entity concerned with highly technical matters related to information technology. The small staffs of typical *club* rulemakers support a less-structured collaborative effort among participants, often technical experts employed by firms with a business interest in the area (Mackenzie 1998).

One can see that for both *club* and *forum* organizations, the clustering is more robust around formality, decision rule, and permeability. The differences on decision calculus are less stark. This means that among both types of organizations there is variation in the basis of decisionmaking. This pattern also reflects the reality that within any GGO, the decision calculus varies from decision to decision.

Membership, Technicality, and Rulemaking

One surprise finding is the association between consensus-based decisionmaking and *club*-type rulemaking. It was hypothesized that rule approval by supermajority might be more palatable matched with other *club* characteristics because confrontations among like-minded members are probably not of the "battle-of-the-sexes" type. The implicit assumption is that *club* rulemaking is associated with closed-membership organizations. The relationship is more nuanced.

Being part of a closed-membership organization provides a high level of comfort to members. There is confidence in the alignment of interests and the high level of predictability in organizational outcomes. There is no fear that the organizational agenda will be hijacked by a maverick coalition of members with interests contrary to the dominant players. Therefore many of the safeguards required for other GGOs are not necessary in this context. The more informal, less rigid process better accommodates the deliberation among members.

TABLE 5.11 **Organizations with Rulemaking Type and Variables**

Organization	Formality	Decision Rule	Decision Calculus	Permeability	Rulemaking Type	clu#1	clu#2
ASTM	Formal	Supermajority	Technocratic	More self-contained	Forum	0.993523	0.006477
BCBS	Informal	Consensus	Mixed	More self-contained	Club	0.006792	0.993208
CITES	Formal	Consensus (Super)	Mixed	More permeable	Forum	0.996851	0.003149
FATF	Informal	Consensus	Technocratic	More self-contained	Club	0.007973	0.992027
FLOI	Informal	Consensus (Majority)	Political	More permeable	Club	0.037444	0.962557
FSC	Informal	Consensus (Super)	Mixed	More self-contained	Forum	0.670495	0.329505
IAEA	Formal	Supermajority	Technocratic	More self-contained	Forum	0.993523	0.006477
IASB	Informal	Supermajority	Mixed	More permeable	Forum	0.899694	0.100306
ICANN	Informal	Supermajority	Political	More permeable	Forum	0.886539	0.113461
ICAO	Formal	Supermajority	Mixed	More permeable	Forum	0.997662	0.002338
IEC	Formal	Consensus (Super)	Technocratic	More self-contained	Forum	0.991289	0.008711
ILO	Formal	Supermajority	Political	More self-contained	Forum	0.991282	0.008718
IMO	Informal	Supermajority	Mixed	More self-contained	Forum	0.732843	0.267157
ISA	Informal	Supermajority	Technocratic	More permeable	Forum	0.913358	0.086642
ISO	Formal	Consensus (Super)	Technocratic	More self-contained	Forum	0.991289	0.008711
ITU	Informal	Consensus	Mixed	More self-contained	Club	0.006792	0.993208
IWC	Informal	Consensus (Super)	Political	More permeable	Forum	0.852859	0.147141
MSC	Informal	Consensus	Technocratic	More self-contained	Club	0.007973	0.992027
UC	Informal	Consensus (Super)	Technocratic	More permeable	Forum	0.886621	0.113379
UPU	Formal	Supermajority	Technocratic	More permeable	Forum	0.99801	0.00199
W3C	Informal	Consensus	Technocratic	More self-contained	Club	0.007973	0.992027
WCO	Informal	Supermajority	Technocratic	More permeable	Forum	0.913358	0.086642
WHO	Formal	Supermajority	Mixed	More permeable	Forum	0.997662	0.002338
WIPO	Formal	Consensus (Super)	Political	More permeable	Forum	0.996387	0.003613
WTO	Informal	Consensus	Political	More permeable	Club	0.019106	0.980894

Club organizations are more likely to be closed-membership. With control over the admission of members, the attributes of the *club* rulemaking process—consensus-based decisionmaking and greater informality—are more manageable. But *club* organizations sacrifice *responsibility*-type accountability by virtue of their exclusivity and lack of opaqueness in the process. Members are secure in the knowledge that only they play determinative roles, but normative expectations for public rulemaking are offended.

Some *club*-type GGOs attempt to buy back their legitimacy by creating means of participation that fall short of membership in an explicit effort to win the support of nonmembers. The FATF, for example, has four regional associations that allow for "associate members." Each of these regional organizations seeks the participation of all nations within its jurisdiction (FATF 2006). Through such organs, FATF builds support for the organization—and increases the likelihood of rule adoption—among nonmembers (Held and Koenig-Archibugi 2004; Levi 2002).

But a closer look at the distribution of GGOs suggests that organizations are selective about assuming the legitimacy "costs" incurred by pairing closed membership and *club* rulemaking (table 5.12). Among high-technicality GGOs, there is no relationship between membership and rulemaking type. Most organizations employ a *forum*-type process. Among the low-technicality GGOs, however, the distribution is stark. The closed-membership organizations here are all *club* rulemakers, suggesting greater concern for the content of rules and the uncertainty associated with the *forum* approach. This is what one would expect when rules are more likely in the "battle of the sexes" vein. Given the small numbers of organizations examined, one cannot draw conclusions, but the pattern is suggestive of the interaction among facets of organizational design.

Forum-type rulemaking seems to better satisfy normative expectations carried over from the domestic context. The importance of this legitimacy advantage seems to vary by organization. As one would expect, governmental GGOs do seem to derive value from meeting *responsibility*-type demands in this arena. Ten of thirteen governmental GGOs are forum rulemakers. The three that are *not* (BCBS, FATF, WTO) are all closed-membership organizations, indicating that legitimacy considerations are not paramount. The reason sector is *not* a significant predictor of rulemaking is that many mixed and nongovernmental organizations are also forum rulemakers, suggesting the transcendent value of this approach.

TABLE 5.12 **Rulemaking Type and Membership, Sorted by Technicality**

	Rule-making Type		
Membership	Forum	Club	Total
In higher-technicality organizations			
Open	2	1	3
Closed	6	2	8
Non-member	1	1	2
Total	9	4	13
Fisher's exact = 1.000			

	Rulemaking Type		
	Forum	Club	Total
In lower-technicality organizations			
Open	9	0	9
Closed	0	3	3
Total	9	3	12
Fisher's exact = 0.005			
1-sided Fisher's exact = 0.005			

Many opportunities remain outside the rulemaking process to incorporate safety valves to reassure key members that the worst possible outcome is the status quo. Structural firewalls described in the previous chapter ensure that the rulemaking process does not go astray; disliked rules can be stopped even if preferred rules cannot be forced through. In most organizations, for example, intermediate bodies have an opportunity to stop rules from reaching final consideration (even if they are not the final approval body). Members of the intermediate bodies are thus well positioned to influence disproportionately the rulemaking process. Two-thirds of *forum*-type organizations guarantee representation to the intermediate body. There is no similar pattern for *club* organizations. This safety valve is not necessary in these cases because the *club* approach provides sufficient protection and comfort.

Implications

This concluding section integrates the rulemaking discussion into the broader analysis of global governance and the challenge of accountability. First, the linkages between rulemaking type and structure type are examined. This sets the stage for consideration of the connection between GGO rulemaking and adherence, the subject of chapter 6. Second, the importance of rulemaking safety valves is discussed with particular attention to decisionmaking by consensus. Third, the implications of rulemaking process for the nature of output are considered. Readers will not find assessments of the quality of rules produced by one regime or another. Characterizing rules as "good" or "bad" is hopelessly subjective, and the notion of making such judgments comparable across the diverse range of policy domains under consideration is quixotic. Still, insight into the implications of process can be gleaned from a consideration of rule adoption.

Structure and Rulemaking Process

In the previous chapter, the structural variation among global governance organizations was distilled into two types, *traditional* and *hybrid*. *Traditional* GGOs typically have a conciliar structure, a one member, one vote mode of apportionment, and a centralized, functional bureaucracy. *Hybrid* GGOs employ a nonrepresentative or specialized approach to representation and are more likely to have a distributed, supporting bureaucracy acting in concert with a membership deeply engaged in the rulemaking function. The observed relationship between structure type and rulemaking type was not as robust as predicted. In the most straightforward analysis, the correlation between structure type and rulemaking type is only strong in one direction.

The sample of *traditional* GGOs contains predominantly *forum*-type rulemakers but the *hybrid* GGOs are split evenly between *club* and *forum* rulemaking types. Structure type is a better predictor of rulemaking type than SECTOR, but the correlation is not statistically significant. However, the fact that *traditional* GGOs do *not* uniformly adopt the *forum* formalized approach to rulemaking indicates that there are circumstances under which the demands of SECTOR are relaxed or overwhelmed by other considerations. *Traditional* GGOs with open membership all employ *forum*-type processes, for instance. This suggests that closed-membership organizations face a somewhat relaxed set of normative expectations, allowing them to adopt practices that lean toward responsiveness rather than *responsibility*-type accountability. As noted earlier, MEMBERSHIP also seems to influence the importance of TECHNICALITY as a predictor. Low technicality organizations with closed membership are *club* rulemakers.

These patterns are indicative of the legitimacy-authority dynamic for all global governance organizations. Each GGO has its own complex brew of expectations that have to do with sector, technicality, membership, rule type, and so on. A combination of features approximating the *forum* model appears to put more emphasis on legitimacy, while the *club* model in general affords organizations the flexibility to build and maintain authority.

The rhetoric of global governance fits with the patterns detected in this study. In particular, technicality is used as an instrument to frame expectations. Global governance organizations are eager to frame their activities as highly technical to justify deviations from normatively preferred approaches to decisionmaking. The implicit functionalist argument has two elements. First, technical decisions—because they do not concern political and economic considerations—can be handled in a relatively apolitical fashion. Second, technical decisions require levels of expertise that makes impractical participation by nonexperts (i.e., the general public). Both claims are often met with skepticism because even highly technical decisions can have widespread consequences. Majone dubs the substance of such decisions "trans-science," seemingly scientific issues that require nonscientific decisions for resolution (Majone 1984).

Hidden Safety Valves

The rulemaking safety valves are more difficult to spotlight than the "nondemocratic" devices integrated into the structure of many GGOs for two reasons. First, many of these protections are offered informally; acknowledged by participants but absent from formal documents. Second, much of the protection from rulemaking run amok is found not in the rulemaking process itself but in the organizational structure (addressed in chap. 4) and in the design of the adherence regimes (considered fully in chap. 6). In effect, the rulemaking safety valves are camouflaged in a surface scan of the rulemaking process.

The distance between formal requirements and informal practice means that features appearing to enhance democratic values (like equality among members) actually can serve purposes that are, to put it delicately, orthogonal to these ambitions. The dynamics of consensus decisionmaking is the apotheosis of this phenomenon. In the realm of global governance, decisionmaking by consensus is referred to in tones suggesting it offers a pathway to organizational Xanadu, a place where every party is satisfied with outcomes and the organization moves forward with unanimity in mind and spirit. In fact, consensus has far more subtle implications. The *Oxford English Dictionary* presents a common understanding in its definition of consensus as "agreement in opinion; the collective unanimous opinion of a number of persons." In the organizational decisionmaking context, consensus is implicitly contrasted with a system of decision by vote which is seen as inferior because it creates winners and losers. Absent a consensus requirement, the majority has little incentive to make concessions to the minority. Decisions by vote can create resentment and institutionalize inequity within organizations. Consensus, in contrast, encourages compromise from even the most entrenched majority, thus building stronger organizations and avoiding division (interview 15). There seems to be consensus regarding the desirability of consensus.

Consensus decisionmaking does sometimes give influence to parties who might otherwise be trampled in decisionmaking by vote, but it also affords a great deal of protection to those members whose consent matters far more than their voting power suggests. The natural inequality muted by the one member, one vote apportionment norm can find expression. This aspect of consensus is deemphasized, and the lack of agreement on the meaning of consensus perpetuates the coexistence of contradictory interpretations.

Dictionaries often refer to "unanimity" in defining consensus, but this was rarely suggested in interviews with GGO leaders. In the context of GGO rulemaking, consensus may require a lack of strong opposition. Non-opposition is not the equivalent of support. Also, by tying the existence of consensus to the intensity of any opposition, the door is opened to a somewhat subjective assessment of whether or not consensus actually exists. This decision is typically made by the chairman of the decisionmaking body—either a working group or intermediate body—providing the leader with tremendous influence over the outcome.

Some organizations even allow for "consensus" in the face of opposition, suggesting *near*-unanimous agreement as the standard. This leaves the chairman of the decisionmaking body to determine how far one can get from universal agreement with consensus still intact (Buzan 1981). This is not merely a numerical question—*who* objects is just as important as the *number* of objections. The earlier example of the FATF, where Luxembourg's objection likely would not break consensus, while the United States' would, is illustrative. Further, the BCBS is an example where decisions are often first discussed with the strongest of the strong central banks in the United States and the United Kingdom. Once this approval is established, the topic is opened to general involvement and approval (Simmons 2001).

Consensus-based decisionmaking opens the window to authority-building outcomes *without* requiring an inflammatory explicit override of some members' objections. This lessens the severity of the wounds and the backlash the GGO has to manage. Weaker members benefit as well. Arm-twisting is not the only means of building support. The desire for consensus provides countless opportunities for members to extract goods in exchange for nonopposition. Thus the ambiguity surrounding the meaning of consensus is, in part, willful. This mode of decisionmaking can provide a means to work around opposition—to achieve ends desired by key members—without dramatically undermining organizational legitimacy. Indeed, consensus-based decisionmaking seems to enhance legitimacy (Freeman and Langbein 2000b). Alternative safety valves do not accomplish this impressive two-fer: *higher* levels of legitimacy while accommodating outcomes that favor certain members (Buzan 1981; Langbein 2002; Steinberg 2002).

The consensus device is not costless. It does give less-powerful players a vehicle to slow down or stop disliked initiatives. Indeed, it provides a fulcrum with which members may try to extract concessions in one area by holding an unrelated rule hostage. The World Intellectual Property Organization, an organization without a formal consensus requirement, was brought to a grinding halt as a group of nations led by Brazil denied consensus on matters related to patents for unrelated reasons (interview 2). To understand the tolerance for such situations, consensus-based decisionmaking needs to be appreciated for its strategic and normative utility.

Moreover, such safety valves are best suited to *stopping* rules that are viewed unfavorably. This type of "negative control" is valuable but suboptimal (Koppell 2003). Having the status quo as a baseline outcome is an absolutely crucial assurance, but it falls short of everything a member might hope for and it predisposes every GGO to inertia. The powerful member is denied the ability to move the organization forward, and the GGO bureaucracy has no opportunity to broker logjam-breaking agreement among members.

Even without consensus decisionmaking, GGOs provide powerful members with means to check unpalatable rules. This can be accomplished with dominance of intermediate bodies, informal veto powers, supermajority rules, or ratification requirements. Any country has the opportunity to build a coalition sufficiently large to block outcomes, but this opportunity is more easily exploited by larger, wealthier members who have the resources (carrots and sticks) to influence fellow members (Steinberg 2002).

Resources are always constrained, so members must pick and choose the areas in which their influence will be used. Repeated attempts to unilaterally control a GGO will strain the nation's political capital and ultimately drive away members. In the World Health Organization, the representatives of the United States have concentrated for years on keeping abortion out of the family planning program (Dao 2002). So much political capital is expended in this area that the government has not spoken up loudly on controversial matters regarding intellectual property, much to the chagrin of American pharmaceutical companies (interview 12).

Rulemaking and Organizational Effectiveness

Speculation whether the rulemaking process predicts the caliber of the rules produced is natural but nearly impossible to address in this study. The quality of one rule generated by a single GGO would be difficult to judge *by itself.* The idea of relative quality ratings for the rules produced by twenty-five organizations across subject areas is impractical. Yet this does not take the question of organizational effectiveness completely off the table.

In the next chapter, attention is turned to adherence, a word used instead of enforcement because the tools available to GGOs are not consistent with typical expectations of an enforcement regime. GGOs do not have direct coercive power and rely upon other organizations for implementation. The GGO may approve and disseminate rules but typically they must be adopted by another party (often the members of the GGO) for them to take force. Adoption of GGO rules can be thought of as a proxy measure of rule quality. Well-crafted rules that are not utilized are difficult to see as high-quality.

Rule adoption is still a problematic metric. Substantively, we would worry that adoption merely proves that the rules satisfied the lowest common denominator (Victor 1999). Even overlooking this possibility, one critical obstacle is that organizations with low rates of rule adoption will fail and disappear. In some sense, the organizations included in this study were unavoidably selected on the adoption variable. An organization with critically low levels of rule adoption would have withered and died long ago, thus forgoing inclusion. The existence of a population with diverse approaches to rulemaking is thus a telling observation in and of itself.

Conventional understanding of legitimacy and governance would suggest that the *forum* rulemaking type, one that established parameters more in line with legitimacy expectations, would be likelier to engender adoption. Critiques of GGOs buttress this hypothesis. GGOs have been advised to reduce their "democratic deficit" as a means of making their adoption less offensive to normative expectations and, correspondingly, more likely (Dingwerth 2005). But the diversity of rulemaking types in this set of effective global governance organizations indicates that legitimacy is not the only consideration.

Informal observations do not indicate differential adoption as a function of the rulemaking process type. The IASB, FATF, and W3C, three very different organizations utilizing *club* approaches to rulemaking, all show strong patterns of adoption. These GGOs (and others) have taken an approach to rulemaking that meets the demands of authority, satisfying key interests in order to secure adoption and compliance. *Club*-type rulemaking—with greater flexibility and more opportunities for key concessions—is better suited to achieve *responsiveness*-type accountability even as some normative expectations go unmet. Indeed, the *club* organizations are among the most influential GGOs considered.

In some policy environments, the *club* approach pushes the organization *too* far from legitimacy norms; the violations of *responsibility*-type accountability would be too severe. Organizations in such contexts employ *forum*-type rulemaking processes, meeting the normative demands, but they must incorporate alternative mechanisms to ensure responsiveness. Structural arrangements empowering selective intermediate bodies may provide sufficient opportunities to key members to stifle unwanted rules. Such systems are imperfect because the unequal power distribution is more exposed, undermining efforts to satisfy legitimacy expectations. And, perhaps more importantly, the window is opened for the less powerful—if they have sufficient numbers—to torpedo carefully orchestrated bargains.

In the next chapter, it will be shown that the need for another safety valve can also be met in the realm of adherence. Agreements that states (and other members) make in joining global governance organizations are not truly binding. The costs—in terms of national prestige, goodwill, access to markets—to ignoring the properly adopted rules vary from GGO to GGO. More rigid rulemaking processes are easier to accept when associated with an adherence regime that makes nonadoption relatively painless and inconspicuous. When the costs of nonadoption are higher, the importance of safeguards in the rulemaking process is greater. The correlation between aspects of the rulemaking process and the adherence framework confirms the existence of this relationship, which is explored further in the next chapter. The distillation of such patterns that link structure, rulemaking, and adherence is the unique insight gained from this study. The complex dynamic of global governance is revealed through the interplay of these features.

CHAPTER SIX

The Riddle of Global Adherence

G overnment regulators are typically endowed not only with the power to make rules but also with the ability to enforce said rules. In the American context, for example, the Occupational Safety and Health Administration sends out inspectors to work sites and fines organizations that are out of compliance (OSHA 2007). The same model is common outside American borders. The Brazilian Institute for Environment and Renewable Resources, a government agency, generates standards for sound use of rain forests and also carries out enforcement actions, including assessing fines, to induce compliance (IBAMA 2008).

Global governance organizations almost always lack analogous powers to impose fines, revoke licenses, or apply criminal statutes (Chayes and Chayes 1995). Indeed, the use of the word "enforcement" is awkward with respect to global governance organizations precisely because they almost uniformly lack such tools. And yet by definition, GGOs set forth rules that govern behavior in a variety of fields. Although there is no criminal or civil code enforced directly by a GGO, in most cases there are, by design, consequences for failure to comply with the rules. So it is more accurate to speak of "adherence" even though it lacks the familiarity of "enforcement." The core meaning and purpose of the adherence strategies employed by GGOs are comparable to domestic regulatory bodies. GGOs rely upon alternative tools to induce behavior consistent with the treaties, regulations, or standards they promulgate. The terms "adherence" and "enforcement" are used interchangeably in this chapter.

Almost all global governance organizations face the same daunting adherence challenge. GGOs have limited ability to apply rules to their intended subjects. Thus, the distinguishing feature of adherence for global governance organizations is the delegation of responsibility for compliance. In many cases, GGOs rely upon domestic governments to adopt and enforce the rules they promulgate. In other cases the delegation places responsibility in the hands of market participants, making compliance an economically advantageous behavior. Generally, the GGO has only modest power to alter the consequences for the adherence "agents" of performing the function well or poorly. And often there are additional layers of delegation where a GGO's adherence agent in turn delegates responsibility to *another* party. The most striking finding of this chapter is the transcendent similarity in approaches taken by GGOs to the adherence challenge notwithstanding the heterogeneity of the organizations examined.

Three critical choices or junctures in the construction of a GGO adherence regime do offer meaningful variation (fig. 6.1). First, what entity will implement the rule? Second, what are the means by which the GGO will motivate and monitor its adherence agent (assuming this responsibility is delegated)? Third, what are the means by which the agent will induce the regulated entities to adhere to the GGO rules? All GGOs—governmental and nongovernmental—utilize the entire range of alternatives but two approaches to adherence—*conventional* and *composite*—are identified based on the emphasis in the arrangements associated with the twenty-five GGOs examined (table 6.1).

The catalog of different adherence strategies is not a menu from which GGOs can choose anything from columns A, B, and C. Patterns indicate choices at one juncture limit the options elsewhere. Moreover, GGO leaders or designers obviously do not have the luxury of weighing the pluses and minuses of each option before placing an order. The reference to "choice" indicates the observation of one alternative among a range of alternatives; the strategy is the result of a complex interaction among multiple factors. *Conventional* adherence regimes bear greater resemblance to domestic regulatory arrangements. In general, the GGO delegates enforcement responsibility to governmental entities. On paper, the GGO has some ability to sanction these "adherence agents" if they do not perform this function effectively. In practice, however, these tools (referred to as *primary adherence mechanisms*) are almost never utilized. The adherence agents, in turn, rely upon traditional regulatory tools to enforce rules (this is referred to as the *secondary adherence mechanism*). The alternative model, *composite* adherence, emphasizes market mechanisms to prompt both the adherence agents and the ultimate subject of a GGO's rules.

The structure of the chapter follows the two previous empirical chapters. The first section describes the alternative adherence arrangements focusing on three issues: agent choice (including delegation), agent motivation, and agent's tools. In the second section, the patterns observed in the population of twenty-five GGOs are presented with attention to the relationship between adherence regime features and the core character-

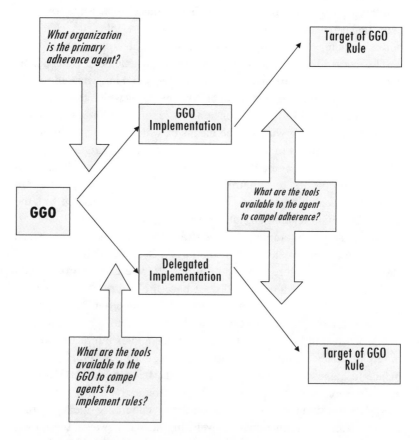

FIGURE 6.1. Critical "Decision Points" in GGO Adherence Regime

TABLE 6.1 **Two GGO Adherence Regime Types**

	Adherence Regime Type	
Area	Conventional	Composite
Agent sector	Government	Both
Primary adherence mechanism	More internal	More external
Secondary adherence mechanism	Regulatory	Regulatory plus

istics of the entities. This includes the identification of *conventional* and *composite* adherence types using cluster analysis.

The third and final section presents implications of the observed patterns for the understanding of GGO legitimacy and authority. This includes a novel account of the critical balancing role adherence plays in viable global governance regimes. Systems granting members a great deal of discretion in implementation—generally *conventional* adherence—can better accommodate more formal rulemaking processes. In the absence of an adherence "safety valve," members will resist rulemaking processes that can yield undesirable outcomes. Therefore, robust enforcement requires a rulemaking process that will not produce rules unwanted by key players. Weak enforcement may be an indicator that the rulemaking process does not grant sufficient latitude to reassure participants.

Variations in Global Adherence Regime

As with the consideration of structure and rulemaking, the analysis of adherence necessarily focuses on key features while glossing over many differences. The alternatives on three dimensions—*adherence agent, primary adherence mechanism, secondary adherence mechanism*—are described in this section (see table 6.2). Note that the delegation question is captured within agent choice and thus does not require a separate field in the reported results.

Delegating Enforcement Responsibility

Global governance organizations' lack of direct enforcement powers is a feature critical to understanding their structure and operations. Most GGOs must delegate responsibility to compel businesses, government

TABLE 6.2 **Three Dimensions of Variation in Adherence Regime**

Dimension	Question	Categories	Options
Agent choice	What entities compel adherence to GGO rules?	GGO	Self-enforcement
		Government	Domestic government
		Market institutions	Market participant
			Auditor/Certifier
		International organizations	International organization
Agent motivation (primary adherence mechanism)	What types of tools are available to the GGO to compel its agent to pursue adherence? (Note: There may not be any.)	Engagement	Suspension of membership
			Suspension of privileges
			Approved bilateral sanctions
			Leverage other orgs.' sanctions
			Comply or explain
			Reporting requirements
			Audit/monitoring
			Contractual requirement
		Market-based	Market-based
		Disclosure/informal	Disclosure/denunciation
Regulatory tools (secondary adherence mechanism)	How does the GGO's agent compel rule adherence from the target organizations?	Engagement	Legal penalty/regulation
			Loss of access
			Comply or explain
			Exposure to liability
			Reporting requirements
		Market-based	Market discrimination
		Disclosure/informal	Disclosure/denunciation

agencies, and individuals to adhere to GGO rules on accounting, nuclear safety, telecommunications, banking, and so on. The term "delegation" here does not connote an explicit transfer of responsibility with contracted terms, as implied by the principal-agent language. It merely describes an enforcement regime as it functions—with responsibility for compelling adherence residing outside the GGO. Broadly speaking, there are three alternative types of agents: domestic government, international organizations, and nongovernmental entity.

SELF-ENFORCING GGOS   The delegated adherence model is not universal. A small set of global governance organizations *does* have adherence powers. Consideration of the "delegation decision" is folded into the agent choice category because, in a sense, self-enforcement also represents a choice of agent. The GGO has "chosen" itself. Self-enforcing GGOs are distinguished by their control (direct or indirect) of some valuable resource. This provides a lever to influence the behavior of parties seeking access. The clearest illustration is provided by the Internet Corporation for Assigned Names and Numbers (ICANN).

ICANN establishes policies for the assignment and management of Internet domain names. All the companies acting as registrars and managers of the top-level domains (e.g., *.com*) must abide by the terms established by ICANN in order to retain their privileges to conduct their business. ICANN's "enforcement power" is more akin to that of a licensing entity than a regulator. It does not impose a civil or criminal penalty for violation of a statute but rather bars the door to noncompliant parties (Marsden 2000; Mathiason 2008). This approach is quite different from the typical GGO. ICANN is in effect governing a self-contained system rather than generating rules to order behavior in the world beyond its bubble. Most GGOs do not have the ability to (directly) deny noncompliant actors access to some service or resource although this dynamic may be simulated with market mechanisms. The subsequent discussion of the tools utilized to compel adherence at the regulatory frontlines—the secondary adherence mechanisms—will elaborate on this.

STATES / DOMESTIC GOVERNMENTS.   In many cases, adherence responsibility is delegated to a national or subnational government agency. This is familiar from domestic regulatory models. Under federal systems of government, for example, national standards are created in anticipation of state / provincial adoption and enforcement. In the United States, for example, the federal government once set motor vehicle speed limits and compelled state and local authorities to carry out enforcement by linking it to federal highway funding (Moore 1999). Environmental regulation in China is thought to be hindered by a model that delegates enforcement to conflicted provincial authorities (OECD 2006; Tang 2003).

Treaties establishing GGOs often enshrine the delegation of enforcement responsibilities to members. These agreements formally oblige member states to adopt and enforce rules promulgated by the organization, but the reality is more complicated. Although treaties create an obligation (or strong expectation) of member participation in the rulemaking process, the member nations are not required to accept every subsequent treaty created within the GGO framework.

Treaties typically specify how many member ratifications are required to bring the new rules into force and nations choosing not to sign are generally exempted. The International Labour Organization, for example, approved the Maritime Labour Convention in 2006, included the provision that its terms enter into force "12 months after the date in which there have been registered ratifications by at least 30 Members with a total share in the world gross tonnage of 33 percent" (ILO 2006, art. 8). Although approved with great fanfare and optimism, only three nations (the Bahamas, Liberia and the Marshall Islands) have ratified to date (ILO 2008). Only nations that ratify a convention are subject to its terms even if it clears the threshold.

Another distinctive feature of the treaty instrument is the validity of reservations. Rare is the GGO treaty that does not provide members of the organization with an opportunity to opt out of specific features at their discretion (Chayes and Chayes 1995). Reservations are issued by nations that approve treaties but object to a part, a section that the signatory intends to disregard (see Aust 2000). One of the most celebrated GGO-driven treaties of recent years—the World Health Organization Framework Convention on Tobacco Control—allows for signatories to exempt themselves from disliked sections (Alvarez 2005, 331).

Treaties sometimes establish two classes of obligations, one more stringently enforced than the other. Rules applicable to the nations themselves (but not requiring an extension of state authority in the name of the GGO) might "bind" each national government without creating an explicit requirement for the member state to implement the rule in one fashion or another. In some cases, the requirements of the treaty are somewhat amorphous, but they are followed by "recommendations" produced by the GGO. The recommendations set a standard, but it is not part of the ratified rule (Alvarez 2005). Treaties are seldom specific regarding consequences of a failure to meet an obligation to enforce. Indeed, there is often no means of assessing whether nations are complying. Informal mechanisms or indirect pressure—discussed in the next section—is generally most meaningful.

Assignment of enforcement responsibilities to governments is not exclusive to treaties. Many GGOs create regulations and standards that governments may choose to adopt and enforce. With respect to discretion regarding adoption, the distinction among rule types rings somewhat hollow. But regulations and standards do not typically require the same level of formal ratification associated with treaties, which is a significant advantage. Some GGOs attempt to attach new rules to existing treaties, building off of previous commitments and speeding the rulemaking process. Members may have the option of incorporating them into domestic law or regulation but to remain perfectly compliant they must do so. The WHO, for example, made revisions to the International Health Regulations (IHR), approved in 1969. These changes were not formally ratified until the whole IHR was overhauled in 2005.

Governments routinely adopt international standards created by nongovernmental entities, incorporating them into their legal codes or common law (Higgins and Tamm Hallstrom 2007). This is seen in areas such as safety, construction, and energy efficiency. Rather than reinventing new standards, governments find it easier to make reference to international standards. Businesses often lobby for the adoption of international standards because it makes expansion to multiple markets a far less costly proposition (interviews 38, 41). Incorporating international standards into domestic law may also create trade advantages for domestic firms by simplifying compliance.

Delegation of enforcement responsibility is not limited to national governments. The function may be assumed by subnational entities (e.g., states, provinces, municipalities) or quasi-governmental bodies including public authorities and governmentally designated private bodies. The rules of the International Maritime Organization and the International Civil Aviation Organization, for example, call upon entities running ports and airports, frequently quasi-governmental bodies, to implement rules (Abbott and Snidal 2000; Reinalda and Verbeek 1998). Distinctions within the governmental category are not core considerations in the analysis (though clearly they may be noteworthy).

MARKET INSTITUTIONS / PRIVATE SECTOR. Many GGOs push further from the classic regulatory model, pursuing a market-based approach that delegates adherence responsibilities to individuals and organizations making purchasing decisions. The core element of adherence strategies that rely upon market participants as agents is the mechanism by which compliance becomes in the self-interest of the regulated parties. Unlike traditional regulation, adherence here is not motivated by fear of government regulation and punishment but by market consequences (Porter and Ronit 2006). Failure to comply may prove harmful or adherence may provide a comparative advantage but there is no coercion in a legal sense (Koski and May 2004, 332, 345). Such approaches to adherence are often characterized as "soft regulation" or "soft law" (Braithwaite and Drahos 2000). This contrasts with the "hard regulation" of government-imposed requirements and penalties. Consistent with this distinction, many GGOs point out that they do not possess enforcement powers. This speaks to their desire to avoid the expectations that accompany "governmental" roles. The very description of market approaches to adherence as alternatives to "enforcement" would raise the hackles of some GGO officials.

The essential element of market-oriented approaches is a rule that differentiates products. In US markets, consumers are familiar with the federal government's EnergyStar label on appliances as an indication of energy efficiency. European efforts to label genetically modified foods for consumers, another type of standard, sparked a trade dispute with the United States. As the typical dynamic revolves around the purchasing decisions made every day by market participants, the consumers are essentially acting as enforcers, "punishing" noncompliant actors by avoiding their products. Manufacturers may prefer to purchase inputs that were created in line with the standards of, say, the Marine Stewardship Council for ethical or marketing reasons. This may present an opportunity to tout this feature to consumers or satisfy a social responsibility requirement of the firm.

Market-oriented GGOs only function if compliance with an international standard—often communicated to consumers by a distinguishing mark—leads purchasers to alter their calculus, perhaps even paying a premium for a compliant product (Blowfield 1999). Many GGOs work to disseminate knowledge about the benefits of products bearing the mark of compliance and delegate this job to the compliant organizations as well (Wessells et al. 1999). Although it is not required, many market-based approaches to adherence involve certification or auditing bodies that can reassure the purchaser of the sellers' claim of adherence. Global governance organizations such as the Forest Stewardship Council or the Fairtrade Labelling Organizations International employ this approach, which involves an explicit delegation (Cashore et al. 2004; Conroy 2007). It is crucial that certifiers faithfully apply the GGOs' rules with rigor and objectivity. Many of these certifiers and auditors are nongovernmental entities including for-profit corporations, international and domestic NGOs, and even individual consumers (Gunningham et al. 1999). GGOs' ability to control them lies in their exclusive authority to recognize bodies as legitimate certifiers.

Civil society organizations also take on important roles in adherence regimes without making purchasing choices. They can be crucial monitors, tracking and reporting on the activities of regulated entities as well as the market decisions of adherence agents (Hutter and O'Mahony 2004). This role complements market-based strategies by making end-consumers aware of the purchasing practices of producers of consumer products.

Socially oriented market-based strategies are receiving more attention of late but the harnessing of market forces to compel adherence with international standards is a venerable approach. All the standard-setting organizations—the ISO, IEC, ITU, and IASB—rely upon similar pressure from market participants to make adherence an attractive course of actions for organizations (Coglianese 2000; Nye and Donahue 2000). Complying with the international rule makes your firm and the products you offer more attractive to customers / investors. Perhaps more importantly, failure to comply with said rules puts your firm at a disadvantage relative to your competitors. For example, standards laid out in IEC 60086-3 specify "dimensions, designation, methods of tests and requirements for primary batteries for watches." If one produces watch batteries that do not meet such standards, they are not likely to sell. Similarly, the appeal of battery-operated watches that require a nonstandardized battery will be limited.

INTERNATIONAL ORGANIZATIONS. One of the most interesting GGO adherence strategies is "piggybacking" on another international organization's adherence mechanism. This leverages existing treaties, particularly those that are backed by some accepted sanctioning authority, to put more force behind a set of rules than a GGO can on its own. Most prominently, this approach to adherence is centered on the World Trade Organization (WTO). A centralized body created to oversee the negotiation and implementation of multilateral and bilateral trade agreements, the WTO's core function is the settlement of trade disputes and the promulgation of rules to avoid such disputes. The WTO does not impose penalties directly. A nation found to have violated an existing bilateral or multilateral trade agreement exposes itself to WTO-approved sanctions by the aggrieved nation (Shaffer 2005; Zweifel 2006). National governments impose sanctions on an offending nation's exporters when the WTO finds that the exporting nation's trade policies violate agreed-upon terms. This arrangement provides real bite (Zweifel 2006). As one senior GGO official put it, the WTO is "the only thing close to a world government" in its ability to compel nations to abide by agreements or unfavorable decisions (interview 23).

Several global governance organizations compel adherence by integrating their rules into the WTO's system. The most straightforward example involves the use of international standards to deciding trade disputes. A requirement drawn from standards of the World Intellectual Property Organization (WIPO) is likely to be seen as consistent with the Agreement on Trade-Related Aspects of Intellectual Property Rights (TRIPS) that is implemented by the WTO. Imposing intellectual property requirements that are *not* consistent with WIPO standards would make a country presumptively "guilty" of violating free-trade agreements (Sell 2003).

In its descriptive literature, the International Organization for Standardization (ISO) emphasizes that its standards meet the WTO requirements. Indeed, the organization does little to disabuse people of the mistaken notion that *only* ISO standards are valid (Adler and Bernstein 2005). This is not the case, as competitors like ASTM International are quick to point out (interview 38). The International Electrotechnical Commission (IEC) and the International Telecommunication Union both produce standards recognized by the WTO, as do socially motivated piggybacking governmental rulemakers like the FSC (Bernstein and Cashore 2007).

The global governance organizations being "piggybacked" do not object to this strategy. Standard-setters vying for recognition under the WTO framework are tacitly reinforcing the legitimacy and authority of the WTO itself. And the proliferation of standards relieves a GGO of the burden of creating such rules. Indeed, several treaties specifically reference international standard-setting organizations to fill out the requirements of their terms. The International Maritime Organization's Safety of Life at

Sea Treaty explicitly references the work of ISO Technical Committee 8, which covers "ships and marine technology." ISO standard 24408, for example, sets "marking requirements for position-indicating lights used in conjunction with various items of lifesaving equipment, including survival craft interior lights . . . for use in ships subject to the requirements of the International Convention for the Safety of Life at Sea, 1974 (as amended)" (ISO 2005).

Motivating the Agent: Primary Adherence Mechanism

Each delegation introduces a challenge to the GGO: what compels the GGO's agent to be an effective enforcer? Most global governance organizations can never be certain that a rule it creates will be enforced by the member countries or any other adherence agent. Adoption is only a partial step; a nation may incorporate global regulations or standards into its laws but forgo actual enforcement activities. Thus the tools available to the GGO to prompt implementation of its rules are an important consideration.

Among the range of potential mechanisms are differential treatment of ineffective agents, loss of membership or participatory rights, market discrimination among members and, finally, informal mechanisms such as public embarrassment (facilitated by the gathering and disclosure of information communicating poor performance). (See table 6.2, *second row*.) These are all referred to in the text as *primary adherence mechanisms*. The list of tactics to spur on the enforcement agents is lengthy, reflecting the variety of approaches incorporated into GGO adherence regimes.

The primary adherence mechanisms are described here individually but for purposes of analysis, they are grouped into five categories that capture the essential differences between tools. The groups of greatest interest are direct engagement, market-based tools, and informal tools. Naturally, the self-enforcing GGOs are set aside in their own category because they have no agent to motivate. And a bin is reserved for the GGOs that do not have any means of compelling enforcement activity by their agents. GGOs frequently employ multiple primary adherence mechanisms. Only "self-enforcing" and "no tools" are exclusive categories.

NO TOOLS.   Treaty-based GGOs present an interesting contradiction. Although their rules are perhaps the most formal and legalistic, the means for promoting adherence are weakest. There is variation in the consequences of *failure* to abide by a treaty requirement but the most common consequence is . . . nothing. The formal implications of a failure to abide by a treaty are not specified or clear, thus calling into question the degree to which they are, in fact, required (Chayes and Chayes 1991, 320). Scholarly accounts of international treaties reveal that there are seldom concrete sanctions for nations that fail to live up to the terms (including enforcement of the treaty's provisions within their jurisdictions) (McNair 1961; Menon 1992). Conventionally, nations not meeting treaty terms are not entitled to the benefits of the treaty.

The treaty obligation may be of consequence for reasons that are not captured in a review of the formal sanctions. Several scholars have argued that nations do take their treaty obligations seriously (Hathaway 2002; Henkin 1979). This may be a function of moral commitments made by national leaders, concerns with national prestige, or the importance of maintaining credibility in future negotiation and commitment (Chayes and Chayes 1991). Leaders of GGOs report that representatives of member nations do seem to take treaty commitments seriously; otherwise there is no reason why they would expend such energy trying to shape them in line with preferences (interview 6).

ENGAGEMENT TOOLS.   These mechanisms involve the GGO taking action that affects its agent in response to adherence activities (or lack thereof). There is a spectrum of primary adherence mechanisms that see the GGO directly engage their agents. These run from the most active (imposition of penalties) to the most passive (reporting requirements). This category of mechanisms is differentiated from market-based or disclosure-based approaches in that the GGO makes some explicit demand of the agent and imposes a cost for failure.

Suspension of membership.   Among governmental GGOs, some treaties call for members to be sanctioned with a suspension of membership—and all associated privileges—for failure to meet the terms of the treaty. In practice, however, this tool is essentially theoretical, as membership is rarely if ever withdrawn or suspended (Chayes and Chayes 1991, 320). The rare cases where such a clause is invoked seem to be mostly about failure to make required financial contributions over a sustained period.

Suspension of voting privileges.   This might be thought of as a milder version of suspended membership. By focusing on the voting, this tool emphasizes the value of participation and influence without the harshness of a general suspension. Again, the imposition of this sanction, as a matter of practice, is related to failure to meet financial obligations rather than substantive performance. It, too, is seldom invoked.

Withhold services or privileges. This approach provides an indication of the value a GGO offers to its members. Voting may not be a central consideration but the service in question is, at least by implication. The International Atomic Energy Agency, for example, uses this strategy to compel adherence with its nuclear power safety standards. Although this agency is commonly associated with weapons inspections, the IAEA has a broader mandate, including development of global standards for the safe operation of nuclear power plants (including transportation of fuel and disposal of waste) and promotion of technological development (including nuclear power plants). The standards are voluntary, but nations that no do not adhere to the safety protocols developed by the IAEA are not eligible to receive technical assistance from the organization (Barretto 2000).

Approved bilateral countermeasures. As noted in the previous discussion, the WTO's ability to approve sanctions imposed by one country (or several) upon another country based upon a finding of treaty violation is one of the most meaningful enforcement tools. Other organizations possess similar authority. The Convention on International Trade in Endangered Species (CITES) has the ability to validate trade restrictions based on violations of its treaty.

Leverage other organizations' requirements. GGOs with limited tools at their disposal to compel adherence activities by their agents sometimes find a resource in the tools possessed by other organizations. Numerous organizations try to leverage the CITES enforcement regime by working requirements from relatively weak treaties (e.g., the International Whaling Commission) into CITES rules (interviews 39, 40). Other international organizations' nonregulatory power can be leveraged as well. For example, the standards of the Financial Action Task Force on Money Laundering (FATF) are linked to an organization not included in this study, the IMF, a multilateral institution created to maintain financial stability that focuses on providing assistance (financial and technical) to struggling nations. Countries are not eligible for IMF loans if they do not adopt the FATF recommendations regarding money laundering (Kirton 2001, interview 48). This requires adoption and enforcement of regulations governing banks and other financial institutions. The IMF requirement thus effectively compels governments to act as the FATF's adherence agents.

Monitor compliance/audit. Organizations can accomplish the goals similar to those achieved through reporting requirements without leaving the responsibility in the hands of the agent by gathering the information independently. This is familiar in the nongovernmental context and is generally associated with market-driven approaches to adherence. Companies approach GGOs to secure recognition as an auditor / certifier, allowing the firm to act as the GGOs adherence agent and charge a fee for this service. To gain and maintain its accreditation, the agent itself is typically subject to audits and compliance requirements. This gives the GGO some control over the adherence process and helps prevent collusion between the agent and the regulated party (Blowfield 1999).

The Forest Stewardship Council (FSC), the Marine Stewardship Council (MSC) and the Fairtrade Labelling Organizations International all use certifiers to compel adherence. Both the FSC and MSC delegate the approval of certifiers to another party, Accreditation Services International, an "independent" organization owned by the Forest Stewardship Council. The Fairtrade Labelling International delegates its accreditation to FLO-CERT, an entity recently separated from FLO. As a vivid illustration of the pervasiveness of international standards, both accreditations bodies note that their certification requirements are consistent with ISO 65, "the leading internationally accepted norm for certification bodies" (FLO-CERT 2007).

These types of reviews are common, although they are rarely called "audits," with the consequence of poor results being one or more of the sanctions described above. The IAEA performs a detailed set of safety reviews and appraisals that evaluate compliance with standards concerning operations, radiation protection, transportation of hazardous materials, and so on. The FATF has one of the more unique approaches, essentially a system of peer review. Member nations prepare and submit a self-assessment of compliance with FATF "recommendations." There is then a "mutual evaluation process" that provides for experts from multiple other countries to provide another assessment (FATF 2008).

Comply or explain requirement. This approach to regulation allows for variation but creates a default behavior that is acceptable and imposes a cost for deviation from the norm. Organizations are left to do whatever they want—there is no formal sanction for failure to adopt and enforce rules—but they must provide some explanation for their actions. This sounds innocuous but does create some sting for nonadoption.

The International Civil Aviation Organization has a "comply or explain" requirement concerning its "international standards and recommended practices." These concern a wide range of critical issues ranging from communications to airworthiness of planes to navigation to air traffic control procedures. The convention requires the following:

> Any State which finds it impracticable to comply in all respects with any such international standard or procedure, or to bring its own regulations or practices into full accord with any international standard or procedure after amendment of the latter, or which deems it necessary to adopt regulations or practices differing in any particular respect from those established by an international standard, shall give immediate notification to the International Civil Aviation Organization of the differences between its own practice and that established by the international standard. In the case of amendments to international standards, any State which does not make the appropriate amendments to its own regulations or practices shall give notice to the Council within sixty days of the adoption of the amendment to the international standard, or indicate the action which it proposes to take. (ICAO 2006, art. 38)

The International Labour Organization uses such an approach in support of its International Labour Code, which is composed of more than one hundred regulations pertaining to labor practices in specific industries (Alvarez 2005, 332–36). Member governments must report to the ILO on the adoption (and nonadoption) of ILO regulations. Required annual reports keep the ILO secretariat abreast of developments in each country and inform and an annual survey of implementation of all labor regulations.

Reporting requirements. Reporting requirements ratchet down the coercive nature of the GGOs toolkit another step from the "comply or explain" approach. This approach creates a member obligation to provide data regarding activities in its jurisdiction. In some cases, this includes reports on regulatory activities. The submission of data does not always lead to the public revelation of any member's behavior with respect to the GGOs' rules, although informally this information is always widely known. In some GGOs (e.g., ILO, WIPO), all reports regarding adherence activities are made public. This soft adherence mechanism builds upon the desire for organization members to avoid embarrassment or shame associated with failure to adopt rules (Young 1992). If no such stigma is associated with nonenforcement, reporting requirements are not a terribly meaningful tool. The International Whaling Commission, with a mediocre record of adherence among the whaling nations of the world, offers an example. Observers have noted a willingness to report activity despite poor adherence (Mitchell 1998).

Contractual Requirements.   A small set of GGOs have contractual relationships with their adherence agents, providing an instrument to impose requirements and sanction poor performance. Many auditing and certifying bodies fit in this category operate under such terms. ICANN is a distinctive case in this category. ICANN oversees the domain names registration system now carried out by private companies under contract. These companies record domain registrations, maintain an accurate directory, and interact with the numerous companies that manage registrations on behalf of individuals and organizations. Without ICANN's approval these businesses cease having a service to offer. Thus ICANN can use the contractual relationship to induce enforcement of its rules. For example, all the registrars must submit to the Uniform Dispute Resolution Protocol, a system by which arguments over the rights to specific domain names can be resolved in a specialized form of binding arbitration (Feldman 2000).

MARKET-BASED APPROACHES.   Under market-based approaches to adherence, producers comply with a rule to secure an economic advantage (or avoid a competitive disadvantage). As a *primary adherence mechanism,* market discrimination reflects the performance of adherence agents. Here, pressure is exerted upon the governments (or other GGO members) by market participants as they make decisions about where to invest, build factories, deploy capital, etc. The adherence regime in a given country or field may influence such choices, creating pressure on adherence agents to perform effectively. The general notion that countries compete in a global marketplace has gained popular recognition in the writing of *New York Times* columnist Thomas Friedman. He describes the power of the "electronic herd," referring to those actors who control capital and can reallocate quickly based upon their assessment of the business climate in different countries (Friedman 1999). His argument regarding the power of the herd to force change is directly analogous and on point. The herd essentially compels adherence behavior from states.

The International Accounting Standards Board sees securities regulators around the world adopt its standards and provide meaningful implementation on the basis of this pressure. The principal activity of the IASB is the creation of the *International Financial Reporting Standards*, envisioned as a global standard for the financial accounting reported by publicly traded companies. To have force, national regulatory bodies must adopt these rules for firms traded in their jurisdiction. Because the US Securities and Exchange Commission (SEC) has not yet recognized IFRS accounting, any company wishing to list on an American exchange must report their finances according to US-approved GAAP accounting standards. If the company is listed in multiple markets, as is increasingly common, it must prepare multiple sets of financial statements, a significant burden. The IASB essentially has no enforcement agent in the United States, but that does not mean that US companies are never compelled to adhere to IFRS rules. An American firm wanting to list in a market that *has* adopted IFRS must prepare financial statements consistent with these rules.

The SEC has recently proposed allowing companies that trade in the United States to comply with GAAP *or* with IFRS standards (SEC 2007). This is a significant change driven by the competitive pressure on US capital markets. As IFRS becomes increasingly recognized as a global standard, firms may decide it is not worth the trouble of preparing a second set of books for US-based investors. Thus the insistence on its own set of standards could be a barrier to entry. Of course, the IASB is willing to satisfy American concerns with IFRS because a US recognition of IFRS would solidify its status as the global rule, accepted in all markets (Demski 2003).

In far less visible ways, many of the organizations included in this study rely upon the market as the *primary adherence mechanism*. There is public pressure to conform with international expectations even when financial consequences are ambiguous. All the standard-setting bodies—those with and without a social agenda—depend on such forces to motivate adherence. The standards produced by the ISO and IEC, for example, have effective adherence agents because the costs associated with poor adherence are significant. If firms do not adhere strictly to IEC standards in the manufacture of electrical components, for example, the end product could be worthless. Thus there is strong reason for an association of producers to ensure that the standards are adopted and complied with by members of their association. There is an equally strong incentive for consumers of the components to ensure adherence. These parties are agents engaged by the market power of rules (Ahrne and Brunsson 2006).

PUBLIC DISCLOSURE (DENUNCIATION). Public disclosure (sometimes including explicit denunciation) gives force to reporting requirements by making information available to market participants. In the absence of such disclosure, reporting requirements and market adherence mechanisms are relatively benign. Collection of data regarding the performance of adherence agents—either through self-reporting or monitoring—does not in and of itself put significant pressure on the agents. Several GGOs make public detailed information regarding the performance of adherence agents, a practice facilitating market discrimination by those who have an interest in prompting vigorous enforcement.

The risk of public denunciation for failure to act as a diligent enforcer may push indifferent or even reluctant members to push GGO rules (Chayes and Chayes 1991, 323). The International Whaling Commission publishes statistics on enforcement that shines a spotlight on nations doing little to implement treaty requirements. It is not likely that this has significant costs to those countries; the electronic herd doesn't care about whales. But it does subject these countries to criticism and may create some embarrassment.

The FATF went a step further by placing nations that are out of compliance with its recommendations on its list of Non-Cooperative Countries and Territories (NCCT), commonly called the "blacklist." Under FATF rules, nations need not ban their financial institutions from interacting with individuals or organizations in blacklisted countries. It simply recommends extreme caution. In its most recent report, the FATF did not list any countries as NCCT, but in the past, several nations have been cited including Egypt, Grenada, Guatemala, Hungary, Indonesia, Israel, Myanmar, Nigeria, and Ukraine (FATF 2007).

Tools at the Regulatory Frontline: Secondary Adherence Mechanisms

None of the variation described thus far concerns the application of the rules to the ultimate objects of regulation: companies, individuals, and associations. The set of tools available to make these entities adhere to GGO rules is obviously a critical consideration. These *secondary adherence mechanisms* include incorporation of global rules into domestic law or regulation (and the application of accompanying legal penalties), market discrimination made possible by systems of audit and certification, loss of access to valued goods and services, exposure to liability and private litigation, and once again, informal sanctions such as exposure or public repudiation (see table 6.1, *third row*). "None" is *not* an option for *secondary adherence mechanism*. Note also that the tools utilized by self-enforcing global governance organizations are considered *secondary adherence mechanisms*. As they target the ultimate object of GGO rules, the adherence tools utilized by *these* GGOs are analogous to those of the enforcement agents.

GGOs often have limited control over the mechanisms employed by their own adherence agents. As a result, the enforcement toolbox varies even among the agents serving the same GGO. Even a single agent may utilize a wide variety of tools requiring some evaluation of the relative importance of each tool. These layers of variation even within a single GGO domain introduce great analytic complexity and the necessity of generalization. For analytic purposes, *secondary adherence mechanisms* are described individually but grouped into the three categories also applied to GGOs' *primary adherence mechanisms*—engagement, market-based adherence, and informal tools. Many of the tools described as *secondary adherence mechanisms* are the same as *primary adherence mechanisms*, but their manifestation in this role is often different.

LEGAL PENALTY. When a government—through an agency, subnational government, or delegated entity—adopts a rule generated by a GGO and enforces it as it would any domestically generated regulation, the typical enforcement resources are available including monitoring, prosecution, penalties, and so on. There is great variation across policy areas—even within countries—with respect to the nature of regulatory enforcement. In some cases, sanctions are limited to fines. In other situations, violations may rise to the level of criminal offenses punished by incarceration. Violators of anti–money laundering statutes (implemented in line with the rules generated by the FATF), for example, are subject to jail time. Violations of worker-safety standards are more likely to face civil penalties.

LOSS OF ACCESS. Although very few GGOs have direct control over some desirable resource, many of the GGOs' *agents* do possess this lever. The implicit image—perhaps a bouncer outside the door of a popular nightclub permitting only the popular to enter—is misleading. Access is denied not by the whim of the enforcer, but by virtue of nonadherence with the GGOs' rules. The World Customs Organization (WCO), for example, sees its conventions implemented by customs agencies that impose requirements on importers and exporters. Without meeting the requirements, movement of goods across borders is not legally possible.

This tool can be "piggybacked" by other GGOs. The WCO's agents provide de facto support for CITES. Under the CITES treaty, each nation designates an authority responsible for issuing import and export licenses in conformity with the CITES rules and the appendices, which designate the protected species. Exports and imports are not permissible under WCO rules without a CITES-approved license.

Access might also be cut off by effective adherence agents, putting pressure on noncompliant counterparties. The International Civil Aviation Organization (ICAO) rules, for example, allow for nations to deny access to aircraft that originate in non-ICAO compliant jurisdictions. This makes the "costs" associated with compliance so onerous as to make adoption universal (Abbott and Snidal 2000).

COMPLY OR EXPLAIN REQUIREMENT. GGO agents may require noncompliant organizations to account for departures from a rule even though there is no penalty for doing so. This may be embarrassing or difficult, particularly if the reason is clearly the morally questionable pursuit of self-interest (for example, with respect to safety requirement). This could have consequences in the marketplace or the court of public opinion and thus is a complement to the more informal adherence mechanisms.

MARKET DISCRIMINATION. Market-based adherence is the core "soft law" approach to compliance. Organizations follow GGO rules to gain market advantage or avoid market penalty. Use of market mechanisms as an alternative approach to regulation has gained wide popularity in recent years. In the environmental arena, cap-and-trade systems for reducing carbon emissions allow firms to get value from reducing pollution. Such strategies are not entirely divorced from the government; "cap and trade" systems require the governmental cap, for instance.

In the context of global governance, market-based approaches generally call for the substitution of marketplace for centralized command-and-control regulation. Using the market to promote rule adherence involves the creation of a market advantage associated with conformity to an international standard or rule. Unlike cap and trade systems, the advantage is not typically the product of a governmental regulatory intervention (i.e., limit on total carbon emissions). Rather, rule adherence is intended to add value relative to nonadherent competing goods and services.

This type of market-based adherence is most commonly discussed in the context of socially motivated standards (e.g., fair trade coffee, dolphin-safe tuna) but the approach is utilized far more extensively. Standards regarding parts, measurement, materials, and processes all rely upon a market preference for standardization—even standardization of laws—to drive adherence. If there is no economic advantage to compliance (through reduced costs, expanded market opportunities, even reduced liability), adherence is far less likely.

There are roles for three types of adherence agents in a market-based regime. First, the market participants making decisions—consumers, producers, suppliers—must act on preferences for rule-consistent goods to create an incentive for compliant behavior. Second, auditors, monitors, and certifiers can verify claims regarding rule adherence. Without a reliable certification system, a market-based system is weaker because there is no way for the purchaser to assess the claim of rule adherence. To ensure that the audit / certification scheme functions effectively, several GGOs take an active role in screening, approving, overseeing, and evaluating the auditors / certifiers. Third, entities with an interest in adherence can promote the rule to parties with market power. This might include generating awareness of an environmentally friendly mark or industry-wide education regarding the desirability of compliant inputs. GGOs can and must play this role, of course, but so can civil society and trade organizations (Wessells et al. 1999).

EXPOSURE TO LIABILITY.   It is perhaps a sign of our litigious times that an available adherence strategy involves private use of the legal system. Organizations may comply with GGO rules because failure to do so exposes them to liability. The liability referred to here is not the threat of criminal penalties by a government agency but civil litigation. For example, a manufacturer of playground equipment that does *not* meet the industry-accepted standards of ASTM International, a US-based standard-setting GGO, would be in a far weaker legal position than a compliant company (CPA 2008). This dynamic can bolster the market pressure to comply, putting legal force behind voluntary standards.

DISCLOSURE (AND OTHER INFORMAL SANCTIONS).   Informal adherence strategies may strike some observers as a default nonstrategy. No document enumerates this tool, and public shaming is arguably part of any punishment. In isolation, disclosure may be of limited consequence, but it complements mechanisms already described. GGOs' agents can disclose the noncompliance of organizations as means of calling nonadherence to the unwanted attention of customers and potential litigants (Morris and Shin 2002). Shaming a company for failure to abide by international rules is most effective when a negative market effect is feared. In some instances, however, the public revelation of a failure to abide by an international rule is the *only* sanction, but the associated embarrassment may impose a modest cost by itself.

Patterns of GGO Adherence

With so many different "agents" and "tools" available to all GGOs, the search for patterns is more complicated in this area compared with structure or rulemaking. There are several approaches to analyzing the dizzying array of adherence mechanisms, each of which has strengths and weaknesses. One can simply look at each individual tool cataloged in the previous section, but given the number of cases and the number of tools, this actually provides little insight. Grouping the alternatives by common character (as suggested in table 6.3) is an improvement. All the mechanisms that require direct engagement of the regulatory target, for example, are grouped and contrasted with market mechanisms. In the case of primary adherence mechanism, this means that the GGO *does something* to the agent. In the case of secondary adherence mechanism, this means that the adherence agent *does something* to the regulated organizations.

This simplifying approach does not solve the additional "problem of many tools." Most GGOs employ multiple primary and secondary adherence mechanisms. One can consider every mechanism employed or focus on the dominant tool. The former approach is comprehensive but obfuscates real variation because every GGO is associated with every tool in some sense. The latter approach sweeps away the complexity—reducing each GGO into a single primary and secondary tool—but also undermines the analysis by drawing stark distinctions where they do not exist.

The solution was to employ latent class analysis to characterize each GGO's primary and secondary adherence mechanism. Every potential adherence tool was coded as a dichotomous variable for each GGO. Clusters

TABLE 6.3 **Different Approaches to Categorizing GGOs by Primary Adherence Mechanism**

Tools	Dominant Tool (by category)	All Tools (by category)
None	None	None
Suspension of membership		Direct engagement
Suspension of voting privileges		Market
Withhold services or privileges		Disclosure / informal
Approved bilateral sanctions	Direct engagement	Disclosure + Market
Leverage other orgs.' requirements		Disclosure + Engagement
Contractual requirements		Market + Engagement
Comply or explain requirement		All
Monitor compliance / audit		Not delegated
Reporting requirements		
Market-based	Market	
Disclosure/informal	Disclosure / informal	
Not delegated	Not delegated	Not delegated

were then identified based on the distribution of tools. The most likely cluster association for each GGO was then used to determine whether differentiable adherence types existed. This analysis yielded the *conventional* and *composite* adherence types that shall be introduced in this section.

Whenever the patterns observed through the latent class analysis differ dramatically from those revealed with other approaches to aggregation, this inconsistency is reported and considered. The challenge of analyzing adherence should be seen as data in and of itself. There is simply no clear distribution because of the variety of adherence regimes.

Agent Choice

One could conceivably draw some link between every GGO and every adherence agent type, an approach that would lead only to an analytical dead end. Organizations are classified on the basis of "dominant" agent because almost all GGOs see their rules implemented by agents from all sectors. In table 6.3, choice of dominant agent is reduced to five categories (one category is added for GGOs who rely equally upon state and market organizations as agents). The observed patterns with respect to agent choice are entirely consistent with intuition. GGO sector is the most powerful predictor of primary adherence agent. Governmental GGOs *all* rely upon governmental entities to implement their rules. In all but two cases, the member nations are responsible for compelling adherence to rules within their own jurisdiction. The exceptions are those GGOs that leverage the power of other international organizations, a formidable tool but one that also ultimately traces back to state action.

The nonintuitive observation to highlight is the fact that *non*governmental entities also utilize states as enforcement agents. The results reported in table 6.4 actually understate this reality by focusing on the *dominant* adherence agent for each GGO. In most cases, there are modes of adherence that involve agents from multiple sectors. The standard-setting bodies (e.g., ASTM, IEC, ITU), for instance, see their rules imple-

TABLE 6.4 **Agent Sector by GGO Sector, Technicality, and Rule Type**

	Sector			
	Government	Mixed	Nongov.	Total
Agent sector:				
Nondelegated	0	0	1	1
States	5	1	0	6
Markets	0	0	4	4
States and market	2	3	3	8
States and int'l. orgs.	6	0	0	6
Total	13	4	8	25
Fisher's exact = 0.001				

	Technicality		
	High	Low	Total
Agent sector:			
Nondelegated	1	0	1
States	2	4	6
Markets	3	1	4
States and market	7	1	8
States and int'l. orgs.	0	6	6
Total	13	12	25
Fisher's exact = 0.004			

	Rule Type			
	Regulation	Standard	Multiple	Total
Agent sector:				
Nondelegated	1	0	0	1
States	3	1	2	6
Markets	0	4	0	4
States and market	0	7	1	8
States and int'l. orgs.	1	0	5	6
Total	5	12	8	25
Fisher's exact = 0.000				

mented by market participants but also national and local governments, international organizations, nongovernmental organizations, and other GGOs. ISO standards are adopted by governments around the world, incorporated into laws on safety, construction, manufacturing, and so on.

In addition to GGO SECTOR, two core characteristics prove powerful predictors of agent sector (table 6.3). Naturally, RULE TYPE is associated with dominant adherence agent; treaties almost universally call for governmental members to play a role in enforcement and standards almost always involve market actors in adherence. Less obvious is the link between TECHNICALITY and agent choice. Higher-technicality GGOs are associated with market agents because such GGOs typically produce industry-sought harmonization standards. Such rules are of vital importance to the affected industries—from oil drilling and transport to production of medical devices—and most logically the province that concerned businesses (Coglianese 2000).

Agent Motivation (Primary Adherence Mechanism)

Choosing the right words to correctly articulate the relationship between the GGO and its adherence "agents" is virtually impossible. Principal-agent language is well understood but is undeniably an awkward fit. This framework implies an explicit "delegation" of responsibility from one party to another that is sometimes, but not always, part of GGO adherence regimes. Principal-agent language is most jarring with respect to market-based adherence regimes. It is hard to see the private actors who compel adherence through their behavior in the marketplace as the objects of a delegation, but through their actions they serve the same purpose as those agents to whom adherence responsibilities are formally assigned. Avoiding the terminological problem is impossible because there is no standard relationship between each GGO and the organization(s) most responsible for compelling adherence.

This heterogeneity is, of course, an extremely important facet of global governance. Global governance organizations have remarkably little control over the organizations responsible for enforcement. Complicating matters, GGOs are associated with multiple primary adherence mechanisms. As noted above, each way of dealing with this challenge is imperfect (see table 6.3). One can treat each tool separately. One can attempt to aggregate the tools into general categories. One can code each organization by the "dominant" tool. One can combine these two approaches by assigning each GGO to a category based on its dominant tool. Finally, profiles can be constructed based on the clustering of tools. The first approach is undermined by the number of tools and small sample size. The second and third approach "work" but throw out meaningful variation. The cluster approach is most promising.

The clustering of primary adherence mechanisms provides a remarkably cogent differentiation of approaches (table 6.5). One set of GGOs are associated with tools that rely on mechanisms *internal* to the GGO-agent relationship. GGOs in this cluster are more likely to promote adherence by withholding some type of service, monitoring adherence activities or requiring reports, or invoking contractual obligations. The other set of GGOs are associated with *external* mechanisms that place a significant burden on actors outside the GGO-agent relationship, principally mar-

TABLE 6.5 **Primary Adherence Mechanism Cluster Analysis**

	External (percent)	Internal (percent)
Cluster size	48	52
Suspension of membership		
No	100	85
Yes	0	15
Approved bilateral countermeasures		
No	94	75
Yes	6	25
Withhold services or privileges		
No	92	54
Yes	8	46
Public denunciation		
No	100	77
Yes	0	23
Comply or explain requirement		
No	92	100
Yes	8	0
Market-based:		
No	1	30
Yes	99	70
Leverage requirements of other orgs.		
No	53	82
Yes	47	18
Reporting requirements		
No	91	63
Yes	9	37
Monitor compliance / audit		
No	97	49
Yes	3	51
Contractual requirements		
No	100	77
Yes	1	23

ket actors or states that impose sanctions on nonperforming agents. It is important to be clear regarding the interpretation of cluster analysis; not every organization assigned to the internal or external cluster displays all of these characteristics. Rather, there is a higher probability that an organization in the internal or external primary adherence mechanisms clusters displays one of these features. The clusters are most useful in the development of adherence profiles.

Sector and Primary Adherence Mechanism

The principal-agent terminology is particularly confusing in the discussion of primary adherence mechanism. One generally sees the global governance organization as the agent of its members. This relationship is reversed in the adherence context. For implementation to occur, member nation-states must adopt and enforce the rules. The natural expectation that the primary adherence mechanism is linked to GGO sector is borne out in the data—but in surprising ways.

One would not expect GGOs to be endowed with coercive tools to compel adherence-oriented activities from member governments. And yet the results suggest otherwise. As table 6.6 indicates, some GGOs are armed with the power to suspend voting privileges and even memberships! This is misleading. The mechanisms associated with governmental GGOs are weaker in practice than they appear on paper. The draconian suspensions of membership or privileges, for example, are almost never invoked. To the extent such sanctions are utilized, it is always linked to a failure to meet financial obligation (i.e., pay dues) rather than a failure of implementation. At the time of writing, no members of any GGO were suspended.

The engagement category of tools also includes more passive mechanisms, such as requiring reports and submission of data. These may cause some chafing but certainly offer a palatable alternative to vigorous implementation when confronted with an unappealing rule. The International Whaling Convention, for example, requires member nations to report statistics on permits granted and whaling activity (IWC 2006). Still this doesn't stop whaling defenders Japan and Norway from continuing their practices, but it does require public recognition of the industry (Mitchell 1998).

The most potent tools associated with governmental GGOs are those that put organizations in the "external" cluster. This is a significant point

TABLE 6.6 **Primary Adherence Mechanism by Sector (Dominant Tool)**

Primary Adherence Mechanism	Government	Mixed	Nongov.	Total
None	1	0	3	4
Suspend membership	2	0	0	2
Suspend privileges	1	0	1	2
Bilateral sanctions	3	0	0	3
Informal	1	1	0	2
Report / audit requirement	4	0	1	5
Market-based	0	3	2	5
Piggybacked	1	0	0	1
Contractual	0	0	1	1
Total	13	4	8	25

Cramér's V = 0.6974
Fisher's exact = 0.034

that must be emphasized. Governmental GGOs may be distinguished from nongovernmental GGOs by *primary adherence mechanisms* that allow direct engagement of their adherence agents, but the most meaningful tools require the cooperation of external actors. Of the primary adherence mechanisms associated with governmental GGOs, the power to approve bilateral sanctions appears the most compelling. Countries inflict real harms on each other through imposition of trade sanctions, but any such actions risks retaliation and an escalating trade war—one of the outcomes global governance organizations are created to avoid. The small set of GGOs with the power to impose sanctions—as a response, say, to unfair tariffs—wield a unique tool. Determining when sanctions are justified, GGOs in this role effectively wield formidable sanctioning authority. Both the World Trade Organization and CITES have already been identified as organizations with this tool. But this type of authority is rare—the IAEA is the only other GGO with a similar power. Most GGOs cannot coerce in this way. What compels adherence activities by the governmental agents of these GGOs?

Market actors can create negative consequences for nations that fail to adopt and enforce international rules; this is often the most potent motivation for implementation of GGO rules. The Basel Committee on Banking Supervision (BCBS) creates recommendations and standards for supervision of banks around the world. In recent years, the BCBS has focused on developing and promulgating capital adequacy standards, setting the capital reserves that banks must maintain as a buffer against losses. Although the BCBS has only thirteen member nations, and the entity with which it is affiliated (Bank for International Settlements) is made up of only fifty-five central banks, its standards are adopted on a global basis. Failure to adopt and enforce the Basel II capital requirements (the name is a reference to the second set of standards to emerge from the committee) is likely to deter private investment. It signals to potential investors that the risks associated with doing business in that market are higher (Morris and Shin 2005; Morris et al. 2006). This effect makes up for the modest sway BCBS has over its members—formally it can suspend privileges—and lack of tools to address nonmembers.

A high-profile incident recently illustrated the sensitivity of nations to the market consequences of noncompliance with GGO rules. At the height of the SARS epidemic, the World Health Organization warned of unsafe conditions in several Chinese cities and Toronto, Canada. These prompted a precipitous decline in travel to these cities, with significant negative consequences for local businesses (BBC 2003). Both the Chinese and Canadian governments objected to the WHO findings but nevertheless satisfied the GGO's requirements. The revealed power made WHO officials nervous, prompting them to codify more precisely the procedures to be followed in such situations (interviews 10, 11).

This type of market motivation for adherence activity is not limited to rules produced by governmental GGOs. There is often economic advantage to implementing rules produced by nongovernmental GGOs. And nongovernmental GGOs sometimes have robust formal tools to exert control over some nongovernmental agents. The certifiers, accreditation bodies, and other auditing entities that must be approved by the GGO (or a third party) as adherence agents depend entirely on the approval of the GGO for their business. Some GGOs use this tool to maintain tighter control of certifiers than others. Fairtrade Labelling Organizations International (FLOI), for example, has a single designated certification body, FLO-CERT, that is wholly owned by FLOI. Several of FLO-CERT's board members were associated with FLOI or its national member bodies. Only products certified by FLO-CERT can carry the registered "mark" of national Fairtrade organizations. Payment of a fee to FLO-CERT is required prior to audit and review, and only then can a producer or seller apply. Subsequent payments are based on sales of certified product. If, for example, a seller of Fairtrade coffee in Canada sells between 10,000 and 12,500 kg of product, Transfair Canada is due a payment of $.25/kg (Transfair Canada 2006). FLO-CERT notes on its website that it follows ISO 65, "the leading internationally accepted norm for certification bodies operating a product certification system" (FLO-CERT 2008).

Other nonstate market-driven GGOs utilize a more open certification system. Six certification bodies have been accredited by the Marine Stewardship Council to ensure that producers applying to use the MSC logo on products are complying with MSC requirements (Highleyman et al. 2004). In practice, however, the MSC has delegated the accreditation of certification bodies to Accreditation Services International (ASI), a body that is wholly owned by, and was created by, the Forest Stewardship Council. Certification organizations—a mix of for-profit and nonprofit bodies—cannot function in the absence of accreditation. Their certification business depends entirely on meeting the requirements of the GGO. Finally, other market participants are motivated to be effective adherence agents by the costs they bear for slack enforcement: competitive disadvantage or added management challenges.

NO STRONG PREDICTORS OF PRIMARY ADHERENCE MECHANISM. Market forces ultimately compel most adherence activities, regardless of the sector of the GGO or the agent. There are a set of mechanisms associated with the internal primary adherence mechanism cluster that do provide real sanctioning ability. Most notably, the few GGOs which feature a contractual relationship between the GGO and its adherence agent (e.g., ICANN) see that as a primary motivator. In some cases, the reporting and monitoring prove a key complement to the informal / market adherence mechanisms.

The strongest predictors of primary adherence mechanisms cluster are RULE TYPE and TECHNICALITY. High-technicality, standards-producing GGOs are likely to see their agents—governmental and nongovernmental—motivated by external primary adherence mechanisms (e.g., market mechanisms). These relationships show up regardless of how the tools are aggregated (as seen in table 6.7). This pattern offers support for hypotheses regarding the varying objectives and incentives of institutions participating in global governance organizations. As described in the previous chapter, higher-technicality rules, most often standards, are generally closer to the "pure coordination" model of rulemaking. When the purpose of the rule approximates pure coordination, adherence agents need no prodding beyond the market advantage to adherence. Organizations with an interest in promoting the universality of the Unicode standards, for example, will insist upon its use—acting as a de facto adherence agent—regardless of which string of digits it "preferred" in the rulemaking process.

TABLE 6.7 **Primary Adherence Mechanism by Sector (Dominant Tool Class)**

	Sector			
Primary Adherence Mechanism	Government	Mixed	Nongov.	Total
None	2	0	3	5
Informal / disclosure	1	1	0	2
Market-mechanism	0	3	3	6
Engagement	10	0	2	12
Total	13	4	8	25

Cramér's V = 0.5896
Fisher's exact = 0.001

When winners and losers in the rulemaking process are readily identifiable—an outcome more likely when rules are of the "battle of the
sexes" variety—arm-twisting of adherence agents through direct engagement may be more necessary. Some participants may be sufficiently
disappointed with the outcome of the rulemaking process that they are
indifferent regarding implementation. To motivate such adherence agents,
the GGOs must be equipped with more coercive tools. Comments of
interview respondents are consistent with the interpretation of the observed pattern linking the rulemaking process and the primary adherence
mechanism (interviews 23, 48).

Secondary Adherence Mechanism (Regulatory Tools)

The most motivated adherence agent is not likely to be effective without
tools to influence the ultimate targets of rules. The prototypical regulatory model endows the state with coercive power to compel rule-abiding
behavior. Government agencies impose fines or otherwise punish rule
violators. In the realm of global governance this traditional vision is not
sufficient. Many of the adherence agents are not governmental and thus
do not possess such coercive tools. Even governmental adherence agents
often rely upon nontraditional tools to implement global rules.

The range of tools employed by adherence agents resembles those
utilized by GGOs to prod those agents into action. The biggest addition to the lineup is, of course, the traditional arsenal of legal / regulatory instruments. "Regulated" entities may also be subject to reporting
requirements, audits, market penalties, incorporation of rules into contractual relationships, and informal sanctions as means of securing their

compliance. This section considers the patterns observed in the agent toolboxes. The key question is whether or not characteristics *of the GGO* predict the toolset utilized by *the adherence agent.*

The most notable finding of this analysis is that the core characteristics of GGOs *do not predict* secondary adherence mechanism well. That is, government and nongovernment GGOs are associated with a remarkably similar set of frontline tools to compel adherence. This speaks not only to the diversity of tools used by all contemporary regulatory bodies but also to the special status many globally crafted rules have in domestic contexts. This is a significant observation, contradicting the expectations of those who assume that government and nongovernment global governance is fundamentally different.

Before delving into observations, a final word is offered as a means of lowering expectations regarding the scope of this insight. The reality of global governance makes analysis in this area very murky. Each GGO has myriad agents working on its behalf in jurisdictions around the world. More often than not, each of these agents employs multiple tools. Almost all GGOs are somewhere associated with every secondary adherence mechanism. Once again, cluster analysis is used to uncover patterns in the distribution of tools among GGOs.

Two general secondary adherence mechanism clusters are identified (table 6.8). These are labeled very simply "regulatory" and "regulatory plus." As the names suggest, GGOs in both sets see their rules backed by the standard tools of regulation with government agencies imposing legal requirements backed by punishments that include fines or other penalties.

TABLE 6.8 **Secondary Adherence Mechanism Cluster Analysis**

	Regulatory Plus (percent)	Regulatory (percent)
Cluster size	51	49
Regulatory tools		
No	16	16
Yes	84	84
Administrative tools		
No	28	53
Yes	72	47
Market tools		
No	4	85
Yes	96	15
Informal tools		
No	62	99
Yes	38	1

The "regulatory" set all have such tools while the "regulatory plus" group sees a quarter without these mechanisms. The key distinction, however, is that the "regulatory plus" group also see a gamut of other tools more frequently including market mechanisms and direct administrative instruments (e.g., control of access to some valuable good or service).

Sector and Secondary Adherence Mechanism

One would expect nongovernmental adherence agents to use market-based enforcement mechanisms, while governmental GGOs have their agents rely upon traditional regulatory tools. This hypothesis is supported if one looks *only* at the dominant secondary adherence mechanism. But the sector of a GGO is *not* a potent predictor of the adherence agents' overall toolset. The explanation for this surprising observation lies in the chain of delegations that make up GGO adherence regimes.

Governmental entities are handed adherence responsibility by GGOs but they, in turn, often delegate the responsibility elsewhere. The full chain of delegation is not captured when analysis is limited to the most prominent secondary adherence mechanism. It is revealed only when one looks across the entire regulatory frontline, where rules are applied to their ultimate targets. Consistent with general trends in public administration, governments often delegate adherence responsibility to nongovernmental entities (e.g., Cherney et al. 2006). Governmental GGOs rely formally and informally upon market mechanisms to compel adherence "on the ground" just as their nongovernmental peers do.

Blurring further the expected differentiation, nongovernmental GGOs often see their rules backed by mechanisms associated with governmental GGOs. The piggybacked approach to enforcement—an organization's standards are integrated into the treaties of the WTO (or other intergovernmental GGOs)—is used by mixed and nongovernmental GGOs. The ISO and the IEC, for example, conform to WTO requirements for recognized standard-setting organizations, and thus adherence with their standards is effectively promoted by the powerful intergovernmental GGO. Even more straightforwardly, governments commonly adopt or integrate standards into regulations. Many European Union nations, for example, explicitly reference ISO standards in regulations. Many of the tests and requirements for evaluation of acoustic materials, for example, are set by ISO 140 (Carvalho and Faria 1998). Japanese building codes also incorporate ISO standards (interviews 31, 32). This approach serves the purposes of the government agencies by reducing workload and making it easier for domestic firms to export without revisions to product specifications.

The interesting heterogeneity of regulatory tools associated with GGOs is obscured by focusing only on the sector of the primary agent. By looking at the tools used where the regulatory "rubber hits the road," the second-order delegation of adherence responsibilities is revealed and the true diversity of adherence approaches is observed. Of course, in this analysis, it is the *non*relationship between GGO core characteristics and secondary adherence mechanism clusters that offers this finding. Consider a few examples that suggest the ways in which governmental adherence agents incorporate other entities and *secondary adherence mechanisms*.

- Intellectual property rights as defined by the WIPO treaties and WTO agreements are incorporated into the law of most nations, but the enforcement mechanisms vary widely. A common nongovernmental approach is to rely upon private litigation as the adherence mechanism. Parties that have a claim of infraction on their intellectual property rights bring suit against the offender. The notion of suing another party for copyright violation is familiar.

- The adherence regime of the International Maritime Organization involves a complex blend of approaches that involve international organizations, national governments, and port authorities (sometimes governmental and sometimes private). Many of the standards for safe shipping are established by private organizations called "classification societies." These bodies trace their origins to the demands of large insurance companies that needed some means to assess the risks posed by underwriting oceangoing vessels (IACS 2006). The need in the marketplace for a standard of fitness bolsters the IMO's goal of adherence to a set of international safety standards. Thus the insurance requirements act as an adherence mechanism.

- Adherence to Universal Postal Union (UPU) standards is driven by an individual or organization's desire to utilize postal services. One might not be punished for failure to abide by the international standards adopted by domestic postal agencies, but your package will not be accepted for service. You may try an alternative carrier—if you abide by *that* company's standards—but this may command a price premium, thus imposing a market penalty for failing to abide by UPU rules. (Alleyne 1994; Zweifel 2006)

The key insight is that GGO sector does not tell you as much as you might expect about how rules are implemented. Sector does not preordain the manner of adherence. Governmental GGOs see adherence promoted through market mechanisms. Nongovernmental GGOs see their rules adopted by governmental agencies and take on the force of law. SECTOR is not the overriding difference many assume it to be.

Technicality and Secondary Adherence Mechanism

The relationship between TECHNICALITY and secondary adherence mechanism mirrors the sector story. Looking only at the "dominant" secondary adherence mechanism, technicality provides a compelling link. Higher-technicality GGOs are likely to incorporate market mechanisms into their adherence regimes (table 6.9). In a few cases, the market mechanism is the only tool associated with a GGO while in many cases it complements a direct engagement mechanism. This observation echoes the findings with respect to primary adherence mechanisms and makes sense for the same reasons.

With respect to rules in the pure coordination vein, regulated parties will find it in their own interests (particularly when buffeted by market penalties) to comply without the threat of legal penalty. Securing adherence to the Unicode or W3C standards is likely to be easier than ensuring compliance with rules promulgated by, say, the FATF or BCBS. This flows from the nature of the rules. Indeed, the rationale for compliance with Unicode and W3C is so apparent that the adherence agents almost certainly do not see themselves as "adherence agents." Any party wishing

TABLE 6.9 **Secondary Adherence Mechanism and Adherence Agent Sector, Technicality**

Area	Secondary Adherence Mechanism			
	Direct engagement	Market	Market and engagement	Total
Adherence agent sector				
Private	1	3	2	6
Public	8	2	5	15
Both	0	0	4	4
Total	9	5	11	25
Fisher's exact = 0.049				
Technicality				
High	2	2	9	13
Low	7	3	2	12
Total	9	5	11	25
Fisher's exact = 0.026				

to produce electronic documents that can be read globally does not require exposure to a whip to see the wisdom of meeting Unicode expectations. Failure to do so will simply lead to rejection by potential users, a real divisible harm to the nonadherent party. The anti–money-laundering standards and capital requirements promulgated by the FATF and BCBS are different. Both organizations promote or protect collective goods. The costs of noncompliance are borne collectively with less *direct* consequence for violators. In some cases, the rules are incorporated into contractual agreements, raising the specter of litigation as an adherence tool, but this underscores the point. The additional coercive push is needed in this case. The toolset required to compel adherence is different.

The technicality–secondary adherence mechanism relationship does not stand up when a more comprehensive view is taken. Technicality is not a strong predictor of secondary adherence mechanism cluster. Indeed, RULE TYPE is the best predictor among the core characteristics. It is associated with the "regulatory plus" secondary adherence mechanism cluster, a relationship driven by the standard-generating GGOs. As was the case with the primary adherence mechanism, the overriding observation is that the diversity of tools is distributed across all categories of GGO.

Adherence Types

Adherence presents a more muddled picture than structure or rulemaking, but the absence of stark patterns does provide insight. The diverse population of GGOs sees their rules "enforced" by a wide variety of means, as the analysis of different aspects of adherence regimes revealed. Still, there are subtle patterns in the distribution of adherence mechanisms. Demonstrating once again that patterns are more visible the further back one stands, relationships consistent with expectations are revealed when two adherence types are defined.

TWO GGO ADHERENCE TYPES.   Using latent class analysis to search for patterns across the three elements of adherence (agent sector, primary adherence mechanism, and secondary adherence mechanism), two clusters are identified, as shown in table 6.10. These are labeled *conventional* and *composite* approaches to adherence. The outlined cells in the far left column indicate that the *conventional* model is distinguished by governmental agents, internal primary adherence mechanisms, and regulatory secondary adherence mechanisms. *Composite* adherence is identifiable by

TABLE 6.10 **Adherence Regime Types (Two-cluster Model)**

Area	Conventional (percent)	Composite (percent)
Agent sector		
Markets	1	26
Nondelegated	10	0
States	58	2
States and intl. organizations	27	22
States and market	5	50
Primary adherence mechanism (cluster)		
External pressure	32	72
Internal pressure	68	28
Secondary adherence mechanism (cluster)		
Regulatory plus	14	84
Regulatory	86	16

TABLE 6.11 **Profiles of Two GGO Adherence Regime Types**

Adherence Regime Type	Agent Sector	Primary Adherence Mechanism	Secondary Adherence Mechanism
Conventional	Government	More internal	Regulatory
Composite	Both	More external	Regulatory plus

the mix of agent sector, the more external approach to primary adherence, and the "regulatory plus" secondary adherence type that features market mechanisms rather than traditional regulatory tools. Table 6.11 summarizes the two adherence profiles.

It is important not to overstate the differences between GGOs in each cluster. GGOs associated with each adherence type do not display all the differentiating characteristics, as is the case with the clusters defined by latent class analysis in previous chapters. More importantly, in the realm of adherence, GGOs have more in common than one would likely expect. Global governance organizations—and their agents—face similar constraints and draw from similar toolkits. The distinctions between adherence types concern the approaches taken by GGOs to the common adherence challenges. The revealed patterns do match our intuition, validating the measures and analysis developed in this chapter, and demonstrating that an organization's approach to adherence is related to its structure and rulemaking.

PREDICTORS OF ADHERENCE REGIME TYPES.   GGO sector has proven critical to understanding patterns of structure and rulemaking. It seems

TABLE 6.12 **Adherence Types with Variables**

Organization	Agent Sector	PAM Cluster	SAM Cluster	Adherence Type	clu#1	clu#2
ASTM	States and market	External pressure	Regulatory	Composite	0.868882	0.131118
BCBS	States	External pressure	Regulatory	Conventional	0.018464	0.981536
CITES	States	Internal pressure	Reg. plus	Conventional	0.103417	0.896583
FATF	States and int'l. orgs.	Internal pressure	Regulatory	Conventional	0.090103	0.909897
FLOI	Markets	Internal pressure	Reg. plus	Composite	0.990061	0.009939
FSC	States and market	Internal pressure	Reg. plus	Composite	0.975981	0.024019
IAEA	States	Internal pressure	Regulatory	Conventional	0.00357	0.99643
IASB	States and market	External pressure	Regulatory	Composite	0.868882	0.131118
ICANN	Nondelegated	Internal pressure	Regulatory	Conventional	0.001648	0.998352
ICAO	States and market	External pressure	Regulatory	Composite	0.995334	0.004666
IEC	States and market	External pressure	Reg. plus	Composite	0.995334	0.004666
ILO	States	Internal pressure	Regulatory	Conventional	0.00357	0.99643
IMO	States and market	Internal pressure	Reg. plus	Composite	0.975981	0.024019
ISA	States and int'l. orgs.	Internal pressure	Regulatory	Conventional	0.090103	0.909897
ISO	States and market	External pressure	Reg. plus	Composite	0.995334	0.004666
ITU	States and market	External pressure	Reg. plus	Composite	0.995334	0.004666
IWC	States	Internal pressure	Regulatory	Conventional	0.00357	0.99643
MSC	Markets	Internal pressure	Reg. plus	Composite	0.990061	0.009939
UC	Markets	External pressure	Reg. plus	Composite	0.998091	0.001909
UPU	States	External pressure	Regulatory	Conventional	0.018464	0.981536
W3C	Markets	External pressure	Reg. plus	Composite	0.998091	0.001909
WCO	States and int'l. orgs.	External pressure	Regulatory	Conventional	0.342049	0.657951
WHO	States and int'l. orgs.	External pressure	Reg. plus	Composite	0.943615	0.056385
WIPO	States and int'l. orgs.	External pressure	Reg. plus	Composite	0.943615	0.056385
WTO	States and int'l. orgs.	External pressure	Reg. plus	Composite	0.943615	0.056385

TABLE 6.13 **Adherence Type and Technicality, Rule Type, and Sector**

Core Characteristic	Adherence Type		
	Composite	Conventional	Total
Technicality			
High	10	3	13
Low	5	7	12
Fisher's exact = 0.111			
1-sided Fisher's exact = 0.082			

	Adherence Type		
	Composite	Conventional	Total
Rule type			
Regulation	0	5	5
Standard	11	1	12
Multiple	4	4	8
Fisher's exact = 0.001			

	Adherence Type		
	Composite	Conventional	Total
Sector			
Government	5	8	13
Mixed	3	1	4
Nongov	7	1	8
Fisher's exact = 0.075			

reasonable to hypothesize a similar relationship in terms of adherence. But sector only predicts variation in an adherence regime for nongovernmental GGOs. As noted in the discussion of agent choice, governmental GGOs do utilize (although not exclusively) governmental agents. But governmental GGOs also rely upon nongovernmental agents and market mechanisms. The strength of the relationship between sector and adherence type is not, in fact, driven by the distribution of adherence regimes among governmental GGOs at all. As table 6.13 shows, the distribution of mixed and nongovernmental GGOs across the conventional and composite types is lopsided. These GGOs are far more likely to be associated with a composite adherence regime, while the governmental GGOs are distributed evenly across the two adherence types.

As this pattern suggests, the most powerful predictor of adherence regime is RULE TYPE. This makes a great deal of sense, of course. Certain rules can logically only be associated with certain adherence mechanisms (e.g., treaties require governmental agents). Any organizations promulgating standards—including governmental GGOs that create multiple rule types—are likely to be associated with *composite* adherence. Organizations that do not craft standards are likely to be associated with *conventional* adherence. This implies a relationship between adherence and TECHNICALITY that is consistent with previous analysis. Lower-technicality GGOs are associated with *conventional* adherence regimes. As rule content approaches pure coordination (i.e., higher technicality), the market mechanisms of the *composite* adherence regimes are more compelling than the *conventional* tools (table 6.13).

These patterns are consistent with the underlying theory of global governance laid out in this book. The tools associated with *conventional* adherence require satisfaction of normative legitimacy considerations. They are logically associated with traditionally structured GGOs. *Composite* GGOs, by relying more on market agents and nonregulatory adherence mechanisms, are more comfortably aligned with hybrid-structure GGOs. These mechanisms do not raise the same legitimacy considerations but place greater emphasis on *responsiveness*-type accountability in order to secure organizational authority.

Implications of Adherence Approach

Global governance skeptics maintain that GGOs' lack of real enforcement powers renders them meaningless, empty vessels used by nation-states to add a gloss of cosmopolitanism to their self-serving behavior. Concomitantly, alarmists decry the loss of sovereignty required for participation in global governance. By their estimation, nation-states are alienating their own power to a group of foreign diplomats. This examination of GGO adherence strategies offers both rejoinders and fuel for this curious combination of contradictory charges. The multilevel structure of GGO adherence provides considerable leeway for nations (or other organization members) that chafe at particular rules. Still, there are plentiful opportunities for motivated agents to achieve meaningful implementation within their jurisdictions.

Are GGOs Destined to Create Weak Rules?

One of the most prominent critiques of global regulation is that only the least-demanding requirements will be enforced. That is, parties will never agree to and implement a rule if it imposes real costs upon them. Thus enforcement or adherence is meaningless even if it is observed, because it merely reflects the creation of a rule without significance (Victor 2000). Determining which GGOs' rules are more rigorous than the rules that *might have been* if the members were not concerned about their narrow self-interest is impossible. Based on interviews, however, there is some support for the notion that only minimal rules are approved, although the dynamic is not as simple as the critique implies (interview 13, 20, 37, 39).

Perhaps the most compelling example of a rule adopted because parties were eager to comply is the Framework Convention on Tobacco Control. This World Health Organization agreement committed nations to take steps combating use of tobacco products. To be sure, there was a great deal of resistance to this initiative, particularly from adversely affected constituencies (tobacco growers and the countries with significant tobacco-related industry). Still, the overwhelming sentiment—and legislative trend within each country—was consistent with the Framework. Thus the Framework was not a precedent. A senior WHO official cautioned not to expect another convention on, say, high-fat or high-sugar foods because there is no consensus in these areas akin to the tobacco consensus (interview 13). Even if an agreement could be rammed through, it would not be adopted by a significant number of members.

By the core logic of this book, global governance organizations will avoid promulgation of rules that will not be adopted or implemented. Repeated demonstrations of a GGO's lack of teeth would lead to the organization being seen as ineffectual or, even worse, irrelevant. Thus the appeal of the Tobacco Convention—it constituted a rule of real import that was likely to be adopted and implemented by members. This logic is not restricted to governmental GGOs. Recall the illustrative anecdote concerning the ISO rulemaking on production standards for bicycles. The technical committee charged with creating this rule reached an agreement with only two members dissenting. When the chairman of the overarching review body, the Technical Standards Committee, learned that the two dissenters were China and India, however, the rule was sent back for modification (interview 16). Promulgating a rule regarding the manufacture of bicycles that would likely be ignored in the two nations comprising 90 percent of bicycle production and consumption would have made ISO look silly. It is simply unthinkable to issue a rule with adherence predestined to fail, for it would undermine organizational authority and legitimacy.

This does not mean that only the rule meeting the lowest common denominator is plausible. First, the distribution of influence among members and adherence agents is not even. Rules disliked by some parties may nevertheless be adopted if key members approve it. Recall the elasticity of the consensus decision rule as discussed in chapter 5. Second, GGOs are wary of *only* producing Potemkin rules. This, too, would threaten legitimacy and authority. Critics of the Forest Stewardship Council, for example, have alleged that industry influence in the rulemaking process has watered down standards to the point of meaninglessness (Wright and Carlton 2007). Thus, GGO leadership has an incentive to push (sometimes) for more meaningful rules. The adherence types provide information regarding the nature of the adherence constraint. *Conventional* adherence will emphasize the support of members while a *composite* approach requires attention to the relevant market.

Does Dependence on Adherence Agents Create Weak GGOs?

GGOs' reliance on adherence agents creates a significant source of potential influence in the rulemaking process. This seems unremarkable for *conventional* GGOs, in which the agents are organization members, because we expect the members to have influence. It would be surprising, for example, for the W3C to adopt a standard opposed by Microsoft, even if the company did not indicate its intention to ignore such a standard. The power of the adherence agent is more striking when the agent is *not* a member of the GGO, as is more often the case with *composite*-type adherence. The IASB is the paradigmatic example. Without adoption and implementation by national securities regulators, the rules produced by the nongovernmental International Accounting Standards Board are meaningless. It is critically important that the enforcers—particularly in key jurisdictions—support new rules. Thus, the opinions articulated by the representatives of the US Securities and Exchange Commission (SEC) and the Financial Accounting Standards Board (FASB) hold a great deal of weight in IASB deliberations though neither are IASB "members." The representatives of other key market regulators are equally important (Jacobsson and Sahlin-Anderson 2006).

Across adherence types, GGOs' need to satisfy adherence agents creates an opportunity for enforcers to exploit their position throughout the process. Critics of the Forest Stewardship Council (FSC), for example, have noted the close relationship between FSC bodies and certifiers, suggesting an undue influence that might water down the standards (Pattberg 2005). This leverage is increased by the competition among standard-setters in many arenas (discussed at length in chap. 8). The balancing act is delicate; bending over too far is damaging as well. Readers may conclude that *conventional* or *composite* approaches are less effective than simply endowing GGOs with their own enforcement powers. The intuitive appeal of this notion—eliminate the dreaded principal-agent problem—does not factor in the demands of the global governance context. The delegated enforcement model has the benefit of providing flexibility and an important safety valve that helps address the ever-present legitimacy—authority tension.

Calculating how much enforcement is "lost" by virtue of the delegated adherence arrangements is only part of a broader equation. If GGOs *did* have more formidable enforcement power, the criticism that only the weakest of rules get adopted would likely be *more* accurate. With a more rigorous enforcement regime, additional safety valves would be incorporated into the structure and rulemaking process, giving members the ability to stop undesirable outcomes. Thus the net result of eliminating safety valves from an adherence regime might be a less meaningful rule with enforcement mechanisms that appear more robust (Hassel 2008). This would be a truly self-defeating outcome when we consider that the market adherence mechanisms prove most significant regardless of the formal powers available to GGOs. Market participants seem less likely to ascribe value to rules emerging from a process designed to thwart rigorous requirements. Thus the net result of eliminating leeway for adherence agents is a rulemaking process that is more tightly constrained and a weaker adherence regime to boot!

Little information is available on compliance, making it hard to assess whether agents are, in fact, compelled to secure adherence. GGOs that publish information regarding the implementation of rules focus on adoption rather than the enforcement. Thus it is difficult to know whether adherence is being pursued with any vigor even when a rule is formally on the books in a given jurisdiction. Moreover, one can never know what percentage of noncompliant behavior is being caught even if the number of citations is reported. Any estimate is speculative. Monitoring and transparency does seem to deter "shirking" by adherence agents. Gross failures of enforcement do have consequences, sometimes through the market's reaction and other times in formal countermeasures. Still, uneven adherence is likely an unavoidable feature of global governance. The dependence on enforcement "agents" means that differential valuation of enforcement will yield differentiated adherence outcomes.

Adherence, Legitimacy, and Authority

The distribution of GGOs across the two adherence types has broad implications for the controversies raised in this book. First, the lack of a strong relationship between sector and adherence type chips away at the notion that government and nongovernmental governance organizations are fundamentally different. Specifically, this observation undermines the intuition that legitimacy expectations ought to be driven exclusively by GGO sector. If rules produced by all types of GGOs end up with equivalent adherence mechanisms, it stands to reason that the bodies that create and implement such rules should be evaluated on similar terms. This matter is explored further in the concluding chapter.

The second critical observation is that adherence, structure, and rulemaking should be viewed holistically. Features in one area likely reflect aspects of organizational design in another. The construction of *conventional* adherence regimes that grant members latitude in carrying out enforcement of GGO rules accommodates an approach to structure and rulemaking that leans in the direction of legitimacy. Far from proving the undoing of global governance, these accommodations result in more robust global governance regimes. Allowing for the adoption of rules without putting nations "on the spot" constitutes a valuable safety valve that maintains organizational authority. Without it, members would be forced to "take it or leave it," creating the very real risk that they will walk away. This would undermine the GGO and yields a very weak form of global governance.

There is no suggestion that the rulemaking process *begets* a particular adherence regime. The direction of causal arrows is forever ambiguous. Even though rule drafting temporally precedes enforcement, rulemakers' foreknowledge of the adherence mechanism may influence the process, for example. The claim is that certain elements logically complement each other. The patterns that emerge tell a story about the demands of global governance for which the causal element is not critical. Excluding coercive primary adherence mechanisms seems necessary to attract participation in GGOs that incorporate mechanisms promoting *responsibility*-type accountability. This adherence safety valve is less appealing than the structural or procedural safety valves described in previous chapters because the failure to pursue adherence is observable and stains the noncompliant agent—something that no one likes. But incorporating the safety valve at the adherence rather than the rulemaking stage allows for the production of more meaningful rules.

This observed relationship helps unravel a problem in theoretical accounts of intergovernmental organizations. Neoliberal accounts suggest that if it is too easy for a nation to opt out of an international organization, it will not be worthwhile for any state to participate. On the other hand, realist accounts would suggest that nations will never be bound by the rules of an international organization such that self-interest is not assured. Understanding the evolved solution requires an appreciation for the entirety of the regimes of which the formal adherence mechanisms are only a part. Critics of global governance focus on the weak formal sanctions for recalcitrant members of intergovernmental organizations. In practice, the market-oriented primary adherence mechanisms are as important, if not more important, than the formal tools at the disposal of the GGO. But market participants will not ascribe any value to adherence if the rule is simply a statement of the lowest common denominator, the type of rule created through a process that is riddled with safety valves. Thus it makes sense to compromise the rigidity of formal primary adherence mechanisms (in the *conventional* approach) to preserve the integrity of the rulemaking process. In the long run, this adherence "sacrifice" actually maintains the more compelling market adherence mechanisms and results in a more robust regime.

In the next chapter, attention turns to the alignment of interest groups and their participation in GGOs. The dominant observed pattern, dubbed global concertation, is strongly correlated with *composite* adherence. This makes sense for concertation is distinguished by the intimate participation of interested parties in the rulemaking process and governance of GGOs more generally. GGOs that rely on a wide range of market actors as part of their adherence regime would be especially dependent on the support of external constituencies. This again provides support for vision of GGO structure as a complex framework balancing competing imperatives.

CHAPTER SEVEN

Interest Groups and Global Governance

As aggregators and advocates, interest groups are integral to understanding any policymaking process. Historical and contemporary popular usage has transformed interest groups into enemies of the common good, promoters of a narrow set of concerns at the expense of the public welfare. But organized interests help shape and articulate the views of citizens, mobilize voters, support and oppose candidates for public office, gather information and research problems, and shape policy debates. They are vital to political systems that exist to hammer collective decisions out of the disparate demands of individuals. Interest groups—sometimes referred to as pressure groups or lobbying groups—play a significant role in global governance. In every substantive arena, the rules and regulations generated by GGOs have profound consequences for multiple constituencies. The effectiveness of the formal organizations representing their interests, and the factors that determine whether such organizations exist at all, shape the outcomes of all GGO decisionmaking processes.

Comparative examination of domestic interest group activity has demonstrated that structure of interest group participation in the policymaking process varies quite a bit across national contexts with significant consequences (Ehrmann 1958a; Thomas 1993). In Germany, for example, the organization of building trades is concentrated and powerful because access to the relevant ministries is granted only through sanctioned associations. In the United Kingdom, however, firms can access the bureaucracy directly, leading to a diffusion of power (Grant and Streeck in Cawson 1985, 169). Examining interest group activity in Canada, Pross shows that the changes in the distribution of power in the federal system were echoed in the interest group landscape (Thomas 1993, 219). Logically, the structure of interest group participation also has some bearing on the role and influence of interested parties in the global rulemaking process.

Each GGO is embedded in a network of interests, including businesses, NGOs, international organizations, trade associations, and other groups attempting to influence the transnational policymaking process. America's founding fathers famously worried about the "mischiefs of faction" and designed constitutional structures with the explicit goal of curbing interest group power, but designers of global governance organizations have apparently not been motivated by such fears. Far from being shunned, their influence is intended and structurally guaranteed. In some cases, the interest groups are de jure or de facto members of the GGO. This integration of interested parties into the deliberative process is a distinguishing feature of global governance.

It is argued in this chapter that the interest group ecosystem in the global governance environment is distinctive. The notion of *global concertation* is offered to distinguish the observed dynamic from *pluralism* and *corporatism,* the two models (very broadly speaking) offered in the rich political science literature that capture the participation and influence of interest groups in the policymaking process (Ehrmann 1958b). *Global concertation* is marked by a high level of integration of interests into the policymaking process, with influence wielded by individual firms rather than formal interest-based organizations (Harrison 1980; Lehmbruch 1984). Access is skewed toward commercial interests while civil society tends to be marginalized. The emergence of *global concertation* is tied to the legitimacy-authority dilemma that undergirds much of GGO design. The integration of interest groups is a critical means of securing the support GGOs need to thrive. *Global concertation* facilitates *responsiveness*-type accountability.

Three distinctive features of the global governance context offer explanation for the poor fit of domestic interest group models. First, the mobilization challenges and opportunities are unique. The potential members of any global interest group present a diffuse and highly diverse target population. Obstacles to collective action may be unusually severe. Second, many GGOs offer membership to individual firms, making them direct participants in the policymaking process and undermining interest-based organizations. Third, interest groups face a two-stage policymaking process. Interested parties can play a role in setting national policy and subsequently have opportunities to influence affairs at the transnational level.[1] This offers opportunities—interest groups have "two bites at the apple"—but complicates relationships. National governments sometimes depend upon interest groups to provide information regarding the behavior of global governance organizations and even represent the country in policymaking deliberations.

This chapter is organized along the lines of the preceding empirical chapters. First, three core areas of variation are described: interest group *mobilization, alignment,* and *participation* in the policymaking process. Second, patterns are revealed based on empirical research. The relationships between GGO core characteristics and the interest group dynamics around each GGO are explored. Third, the *global concertation* model is introduced to capture the observed dynamics of interest group participation and differentiate it from *pluralism* and *corporatism.* The association between interest group participation and other facets of GGO design are also considered.

Transnational Interest Group Variation

"Interest group" is a somewhat ill-defined term even as used in the political science literature. James Madison's definition of a "faction" in "The Federalist, No. 10" remains an elegant if inflammatory statement: "a number of citizens whether amounting to a majority or a minority of the whole, who are united and actuated by some common impulse of passion, or of interest, adverse to the rights of other citizens, or to the permanent and aggregate interests of the community" (Hamilton and Rossiter 1961, 78). Truman offered a more benign restatement that did not cast interest groups as villains: "any group that, on the basis of one or more shared attitudes, makes certain claims upon other groups in the society for the

---

1. It might be observed that in a federal system interest groups also have two opportunities to influence policy domestically. However, representation in a federal system rarely is managed by the states and policy is not determined for the subnational unit before the deliberations at the national level begin. For GGOs, in contrast, the nation-states generally arrive at a policy position, which is then brought to the organization. This might be analogous to confederative states such as the United Arab Emirates or Micronesia.

establishment, maintenance, or enhancement of forms of behavior that are implied by the shared attitudes" (Truman 1993, 33). Both definitions emphasize the common concerns of group members but leave ambiguous the importance of formal organization. Almond distinguishes interest group types on this basis. This specifies further what is generally meant by the term. He identified four types of groups:

1. "associational interest groups," which correspond to the type of organizations usually referred to as interest groups;
2. "nonassociational interest groups," by which he means family, ethnic, status, and similar groups or aggregates that articulate interests "informally, and intermittently," through individuals, cliques, and the like;
3. "anomic interest groups," referring to "more or less spontaneous breakthroughs into the political system . . . such as riots and demonstrations"; and
4. "institutional interest groups," by which he means organizations or groups such as "legislatures, political executives, armies, bureaucracies, churches, and the like." These are, in his terms, "organizations which perform other social or political functions but which, as corporate bodies or through groups within them . . . may articulate their own interests or represent the interests of groups in society." (Described in Truman, xxxi)

The analysis here focuses on the activities of groups in the first and fourth categories: formal organizations with concrete and durable agendas pursuing legislative, administrative, or electoral strategies. Such groups have the ability to mobilize citizens, raise money, influence elected officials and political parties, establish working relationships with civil servants, influence public opinion, and collect and disseminate information with the goal of securing outcomes favorable to their members.

Transnational Interest Group Mobilization

Any picture of the interest group landscape for transnational governance must account for the presence of some organized interest groups and the absence of others. There are thousands of *latent* interest groups, collections of individuals and organizations whose interests are aligned but not organized. Are the dynamics of group activation and mobilization different in the context of global governance? This is a natural starting point in the story of interest group participation in the transnational policymaking process.

James Q. Wilson introduced a classic model for understanding the dynamics of interest group formation and mobilization. His four-category typology of interest group politics focused on the distribution of costs and benefits associated with policies in a given arena (Wilson 1980). When benefits of a policy are concentrated and the costs are widely distributed, for example, he predicts that the beneficiaries will organize in support of said policy and face little resistance (because no individual suffers enough "harm" to organize the opposition). When the benefits are diffuse and costs are concentrated, the dynamic is different. Here the opposition is likely to be organized, and the approval would depend upon proponents' ability to generate mass support for the proposal. Wilson's schema was developed with the domestic political landscape in mind, but its logic is applicable in the realm of transnational governance.

Global governance policy domains appear to favor *"client politics"* as described in the Wilson framework. The benefits of particular GGO policies are likely concentrated on producers or firms in the regulated area, relatively narrow communities of interest. The International Civil Aviation Organization, for example, produces rules that balance considerations such as safety, security, and cost with respect to aircraft design, staffing requirements, air traffic control, cargo handling and so on. The associated costs are borne by the public at large, a disparate and disorganized population, who must support the global regulatory infrastructure, the requirements for implementation, and (potentially) increased prices. By Wilson's logic, it is unlikely that groups representing the public would mobilize to counterbalance commercial interests because the costs to individuals do not make organizing worthwhile.

Industry and business groups also have advantages (relative to citizen, consumer, or "public interest" groups) because of the greater financial resources available to them. The costs of organizing a transnational interest group are not trivial. This is true in financial terms—information may be more difficult to obtain and disseminate, face-to-face meeting requires expensive travel by participants, documents may require translation for wide accessibility—as well as nonfinancial. Logistical, organizational, and cultural challenges abound. Diversity of opinion and interest is likely greater on a global scale than in even the most heterogeneous domestic context.

The anticipated prevalence of industry and trade groups in GGO activities is found in most policy spheres. This is revealed through interviews with individuals involved in the policymaking process at GGOs as well as examination of the organizational documents (including reports of participation in GGO conferences, meetings, and conventions; records of organizations submitting comments on pending rules; and the rosters of organizations that have official status with GGOs). In the area of aviation, for example, the International Air Transport Association is the dominant interest group although there are other organizations in the area such as the International Air Passengers Association.

In some areas the playing field is more even for commercial and noncommercial interests. GGOs are emerging that seem to thrive in environments of *entrepreneurial politics.* These "nonstate market-driven" governance organizations (NSMDs) take upon themselves the role of standard-setter and attempt to harness market forces to gain compliance (Cashore et al. 2004). The benefits secured by such actions are incredibly diffuse—maintenance of biodiversity, preservation of natural resources, eradication of human rights abuses—while the costs are concentrated on small number of firms. Any account of interest group activity in global governance must explain the emergence of such organizations.

The Conditions for Entrepreneurial Success

Mancur Olson challenged an intuitive assumption underpinning the conventional analysis of interest groups: group formation and collective action stems from the shared interests and objectives of individuals. Common concerns may be a prerequisite to collective action, Olson argued, but they do not stimulate or ensure successful group activation. On the contrary, the provision of selective benefits—excludable items with utility for an individual or organization—attract and bind members into organized groups (Olson 1971, 51). This is a strategic response to the paralyzing "free rider" problem. No individual has a strong incentive to contribute to a group when the benefits are available to all regardless of investment. Moe's description of the "political entrepreneur" starts to put a human face on the actor who initiates the idiosyncratic translation of potential interest groups—or what Almond would call nonassociational interest groups—into organized interest groups (Moe 1980, 37).

The political entrepreneur recognizes a potential group and is able to satisfy sufficiently members' selective demands to create an organization capable of pursuing the collective benefits. She may be willing to bear the costs of organizing and maintaining the group because of the enhanced influence and credibility that are not attainable acting alone (Salisbury 1984). The political entrepreneur recognizes the disproportionate costs she will bear relative to other group members but moves forward none-theless because her net benefits remain positive. Following the logic of Olson, this may be easier when the groups in question are small, because the benefits of group activity are distributed more narrowly and free riders are more readily exposed (Olson 1971). In every context, we would expect groups composed of a smaller number of members to be more robust than larger groups (again favoring commercial interests over public interests).

Moe enumerates several variables that determine the success of efforts to stimulate and maintain interest groups: ease of communication to and among potential members, feasibility of administering collective and selective benefits, facilitation of bargaining and coordination among members, and establishment of relationship with other players (Moe 1980, 72). For each of these aspects of interest group formation and mainte-nance, the transnational governance context offers wrinkles suggesting explanations for observed variation in mobilization.

COMMUNICATION.   The global distribution of potential group members poses a logistical hurdle but given contemporary technology, physi-cal distance may not be the most formidable challenge (Tarrow 2005). Internet-based technology reduces the costs of communication so dra-matically that it may be easier to identify and locate like-minded parties on the Internet than it is in the "real world." Organizing a neighborhood block watch may be more challenging than building a global network. Still, linguistic and cultural difference makes communication awkward and uncertain. Forging trust and rapport among members is time-consuming. Face-to-face interaction is difficult to arrange and expensive for the entrepreneurial individuals or organizations who must bear the costs of organization until the group takes root and can make claims upon its member for financial support.

SELECTIVE BENEFITS.   Many organized interest groups provide magazine subscriptions, discounts, and token items (like calendars or umbrellas) to lure like-minded individuals into group membership. This approach is most suitable for groups made up of individuals that may value such "sym-bolic" goods. Most firms have little use for a tote bag. A corporation con-sidering membership in a group or trade association might value access to data, use of a facility, or provision of benefits that are in turn available to its employees. For example, the National Association of Realtors con-trols access to the Multiple Listing Service, a vital tool for selling homes in the United States (Justice 2005). All real estate sales enterprises face huge competitive obstacles if they forgo membership in the association. Some transnational interest groups seeking individual members do utilize typical Olsonian strategies. The International Air Passenger Association mentioned earlier offers potential members "great deals on hotels, car rental and flights" as an inducement to join (IAPA 2008). But most seek for-profit, nonprofit, or governmental organizations as members. Unless interest groups can devise a selective benefit of value to such entities, the provision of *collective* goods is particularly important.

COLLECTIVE GOODS.   Members of interest groups are not seeking subsidies or tax relief (at least not from this sample of rulemaking GGOs). That does not mean that various interests do not have a great deal at stake as GGOs deliberate, set, and implement policy. Indeed, rules in the fields of accounting, shipping, and communications have profound economic consequences for market participants. Thus the collective good at stake for interest groups in the global governance sphere all revolve around the attainment of preferred rules.

Participants in the international travel and tourism industries, for example, have a lot at stake when the ICAO or the WHO renders cross-border travel more difficult. Rules affect the nature of commodities that can be transported on aircraft and the required quarantine times for individuals infected with contagious diseases. The collective benefit offered by an interest group representing the concerns of these industries lies in the marginal preferability of one policy to another (Murphy 1994, 194; Zweifel 2006, 80).

The collective good often lies in the standardization offered by a rule. Firms participate in the ISO standards process because of the economic value associated with standardization (Haufler 2000; Boli and Thomas 1997). More markets are made accessible. Competition and substitution among suppliers is more likely, bringing down costs. Industry participates in International Accounting Standards Board (IASB) rulemaking in the hopes of reducing jurisdictional differences in accounting standards that boards like FASB are bound to face (Demski 2003; Tamm Hallstrom 2004).

Bargaining and Coordination among Members

The ability of an interest group to create a single position through internal bargaining, offering of selective benefits, coercion, and persuasion is critical to its effectiveness. This poses a serious challenge in the transnational milieu. Potential members must consider their interests in the domestic context in addition to the transnational arena. That is, a concession at the international level could prove harmful in the domestic context where the organization is likely more influenced by public policies. Thus the incentives to make concessions in intragroup bargaining are likely low relative to a domestic interest group environment. Moreover, uncertainty regarding the impact of GGO policy may significantly limit the payoffs to any concession. Finally, there is almost certainly a greater diversity of interests among potential group members distributed around the globe. Building an organization to satisfy all parties is likely to be profoundly difficult.

RELATIONSHIPS WITH RELEVANT PARTIES. Interest groups must be able to sway the rulemaking, enforcement, and adjudicatory proceedings of GGOs to secure collective benefits for members. This could be an area of strength for transnational interest groups. First, many of the groups actually predate the GGO, played a role in their design, and secured formal roles in governance and administration. Second, GGOs have grown to rely upon transnational interest groups as sources of information and intelligence regarding conditions in the field. In some cases, they allow GGOs to get input from nonmembers. Most interest groups also have connections at domestic levels thus providing at least two levels of contact—directly with the GGO and through the members (frequently national governments).

Alignment and Participation

The tremendous variation in the manner of interest group–government interaction has been captured by two broad, competing concepts: *pluralism* and *corporatism*. The pluralist understanding of interest groups is generally associated with the United States, while corporatist theories are generally utilized to explain group participation in the politics of Europe and East Asia. Differentiating pluralist and corporatist systems does not imply that one offers interested parties more or less influence on public policy. The distinction lies in how the groups participate with consequences that may defy generalization. There are reasons to expect the interest group dynamic in the context of global governance to resemble both accounts.

PLURALISM.   Given the American founding fathers' concerns with interest groups, it is ironic that political scientists have offered the normatively positive "pluralist" take on the role of groups in the policymaking process. David Truman's seminal book, *The Governmental Process,* held that there is nothing inherently "undemocratic" about group participation in politics because of the egalitarian nature of group formation and participation. All groups have an opportunity to enter the fray. Ideally, pluralism is marked by the emergence of a robust community of groups representing a variety of interests and perspectives, competing for the attention and favor of elected officials. The resulting process may not be pretty, but it allows for the expression of multiple viewpoints in the policymaking process.

Critiques of the pluralist perspective have challenged this view by focusing on the empirical reality of disparate influence for different interests. E. E. Schattschneider's famous observation remains an elegant statement of this perspective. He observed that "the flaw in pluralist heaven is that the heavenly chorus sings with a strong upperclass accent" (1975, 34). Some interest groups have more money, more connections to leaders, more opportunities to influence public opinion, and more access to valuable information than other groups. In general, the powerful groups represent business and corporate interests—labor unions sometimes represent a prominent exception—and interest groups representing diffuse populations are left at a comparative disadvantage (Lowi 1969; Schlozman and Tierney 1986). Moreover, there exists a persistence of bias, an enduring advantage enjoyed by powerful groups that are able to build victory upon victory by skewing the structure of laws and bureaucracies to their benefit. Given the integration of interest groups into the structure of GGOs, the issue of the persistence of bias is certainly relevant for transnational governance, for the resource inequalities discussed in the mobilization section would be compounded.

CORPORATISM.   In contrast with pluralism, corporatism emphasizes the institutionalization of bargaining between the state and interest groups representing key sectors of society. This manifests itself as structural integration of interests into the policymaking apparatus. Indeed, corporatist policymaking, which has many guises that shall not be differentiated here, is marked by a "process of interest intermediation which involves the negotiation of policy between state agencies and interest organizations arising from the division of labor in society" (Grant 1985). That is, the government and interest groups negotiate state policy as partners in governance. Unlike a pluralist framework, the corporatist model does not treat interests as rivals competing for the attention and favor of policymakers. "Peak associations," bodies that represent all groups in a particular sphere or sector of society, are embedded within the system. Rivalries among policy entrepreneurs of the pluralist world are internalized within the associations and figure less significantly in the analysis of interests' role in policymaking.

Corporatism is associated with strong centralized management and control of the economy. It is most frequently linked with analysis of postwar Europe but has been applied to the state-industrial relationships observed in Asia as well. In recent decades, the return to free-market approaches in Europe has been conflated by some scholars with a decline of traditional corporatism (Goldthorpe 1984).

The corporatist formal inclusion of interest groups in the policymaking structure is not generally evident in the United States. This difference poses an interesting intellectual puzzle and a potential source of explanations for variation across GGOs. Speculation has raised cultural and structural factors (i.e., American individualism and fragmentation make group coherence a challenge) and market realities (i.e., diversity of interests within each sector undermines group coherence) (Salisbury 1979; Wilson 1982; Thomas 1993). Both claims are applicable in the transnational context. If Americans—and others—are culturally resistant to collective international action, the organization of transnational interest groups will be difficult. And naturally, there will be tremendous diversity of interests within any potential group of seemingly like-minded parties when they are distributed around the globe!

Patterns of Interest Group Variation

This section is organized along the lines established in previous chapters. Patterns of interest group mobilization and participation are identified and links are investigated between the observations and GGO core characteristics. *Pluralism* and *corporatism* are explored as descriptive models for the observations, but ultimately the notion of *global concertation* is offered. It is more accurate and also ties the observations to the theoretical argument at the heart of this book. *Concertation* is an institutional arrangement well suited to the accountability balancing act facing GGOs. Overarching questions are addressed throughout this section: Are interest group communities dominated by commercial groups, or do broader civil society groups find equal representation? Have the GGOs evolved to relate with interest groups in a fashion resembling pluralist or corporatist models? These questions drove the data gathering and interpretation of observations.

Mobilization: Variation Defying Easy Explanation

Commercial interests are more organized in most, but not all, GGO policy areas. The robustness of noncommercial—or outright anticommercial— activism in some areas and its near total absence in others is enigmatic. The explanation suggests cracks in the Wilson and Olson accounts of political mobilization, at least when applied in the global governance context, and leads to a more fine-grained understanding of the transnational interest group dynamics.

COMMERCIAL INTERESTS GENERALLY DOMINATE. Participation in GGO activities provides hard evidence of the hypothesized disparity in organization of business and civil society interests. A few examples illustrate the norm. The roster of organizations commenting on proposed regulations under consideration by the International Accounting Standards Board (IASB), for example, is dominated by entities doing business in the financial sector. Consider one rule under review. Responses to the "Proposed Amendments to IFRS 2—Vesting Conditions and Cancellations" are posted on the organization's website. As one would expect, the parties interested in this highly arcane area are specialized organizations and firms including national accounting standards organizations, accounting businesses, professional associations, and some individual corporations (IASB 2006; Lamb 2000). There is no obvious representation of public interest or civil society groups in this list. The IASB's general structure and rule-making process reinforce the mobilization dynamic. The drafting of new rules and regulations takes place through "working groups" composed of industry representatives. Participating firms and organizations must pay their own costs for the work they do on IASB matters. Thus not only is there a natural tendency to emphasize entities with an interest in the field, those organizations with resources "to spare" play a prominent role in the rulemaking process (Tamm Hallstrom 2004).

The International Organization for Standardization (ISO) reveals a similar pattern. Unlike the IASB, the ISO's members are quasi-governmental, the national standards bodies of most countries. Still, the bulk of the work of the ISO—the research and drafting of new standards—is carried out by a series of technical committees whose members typically are drawn from the affected industries in areas like textiles, cast iron, and cement (ISO 2006a). In almost every technical committee, all of the participants represent entities with a commercial intent in the rule (Boli and Thomas 1999). Only one public interest group—Consumers International—is broadly engaged in ISO activities, and even this entity must choose carefully where to expend its resources (interview 37).

A short walk from the ISO's Geneva headquarters is the office of the International Electrotechnical Commission (IEC). It is organized similarly to the ISO, with a central administrative unit overseeing working groups composed of representatives of firms involved in the industries concerned with a particular rule. By and large, there is little participation by public or citizen interest groups—and almost no requests for such participation—with the exception of issues related to product safety (interview 37, 29). Once again, Consumers International is the outlier. There are a few instances of individuals participating on their own (i.e., without sponsorship of any organization), but these can be counted on one hand (interview 29).

There *are* areas in which noncommercial, civil society groups have organized effectively and participate vigorously in the rulemaking process. Around the Internet rulemaking body ICANN, there is an active cluster of organizations and individuals that monitor and protest decisions seen as overly accommodating to commercial interests (Feldman 2000). In several environmental areas, civil society groups have thrived and played a prominent and influential role. Issues related to public health also seem to arouse a response from noncommercial interests. The core characteristics of GGOs were explored as predictors of these significant exceptions to the group formation norm.

SECTOR. Suspicions that the dominance of commercial interests is a function of the nongovernmental character of the IASB, ISO, and IEC are incorrect. The pattern of international group formation and participation is not predicted by SECTOR, a striking finding given the predictive power of this characteristic in most areas. Both the International Maritime Organization and World Customs Organization, to take two governmental GGOs, cultivate participation from a rather rarified population of interested companies who participate independently and through national member bodies. The representation among those entities participating in the activities of the IMO is telling. The IMO offers consultative status to interested organizations. Of the sixty-three groups listed by the IMO, 73 percent are industry or professional organizations. Only nine of the groups (14 percent) are classified as "civil society" such as Friends of the Earth and Greenpeace. This pattern is true across organizations, public and private.

TECHNICALITY.   One would expect more technical areas to be dominated by commercial interests. First, the general public is likely less aware of such GGOs and their activities. Second, even those that are aware will be less equipped to participate around highly technical questions than those issues that are more political and accessible. Finally, the incentives for participation are likely particularly skewed when the subject matter is highly technical. That is, the consequences of the rule matter a great deal to business but are probably quite abstract to the average citizen. Table 7.1 provides some support for this hypothesized relationship. Note that the high-technicality organizations do strongly predict commercial interest dominance but the landscape for low technicality is mixed.

Even arcane technical subjects may have significant general impact. Standards regarding the thickness of pipelines or the requisite safety mechanisms on oil tankers do not attract great interest from the public, but the deliberation over such matters actually holds great significance, determining the impact of commercial activities on the environment. Thus the lack of participation in highly technical areas by civil society organizations may not be surprising, but it reflects such groups' misunderstanding about which GGOs really "matter," a point revisited later in this chapter and the book's conclusion.

TABLE 7.1   **GGO Technicality and Interest Group Mobilization**

Technicality	Mobilization		Total
	Industry	Civil Society	
High	12	1	13
Low	6	6	12
Total	18	7	25
Cramér's V = 0.4708			
Fisher's exact = 0.030			

LACK OF COLLECTIVE GOODS.   The cases that do not meet expectations offer more insight. Why is there a robust community of civil society interest groups around some GGOs but not others? The easiest explanation is that the Wilson model has been misapplied. The nature of the transnational governance climate may not be client-centric in some cases. The "cost" associated with the creation and enactment of some rules may not be diffuse at all. There could, in fact, be reason to expect mobilization by multiple groups if a proposed rule has disparate implications.

The World Intellectual Property Organization (WIPO), a body dedicated to harmonizing rules establishing ownership of intellectual property (e.g., patents, copyrights, and trademarks), is illustrative. WIPO is governmental but does grant "observer" status to a variety of international organizations and nongovernmental organizations, a category into which a wide range of interest groups are placed (WIPO 2006a). This fairly diverse interest group community around WIPO seems consistent with a pluralist vision of competition among conflicting claims (Froomkin 2000; Sell 2003; Shaffer 2005). Explanations may lie in the issues surrounding intellectual property; they do not neatly divide into corporate and consumer camps. There are divisions within the business constituencies related to the diversity of profit-making plans. Some firms derive income from strict control of intellectual property including music and movies, while other companies are more interested in selling hardware (and thus favor more lax standards). Moreover, there are multiple industries with interests in the area whose priorities are simply different. Media companies are joined by software, pharmaceutical, agribusiness, biotech and a host of other businesses as they monitor and attempt to influence WIPO proceedings. All of these constituencies are represented in the list of official "observers" provided on the WIPO website (WIPO 2006b). Examples include the Federation of Scriptwriters in Europe, the Global Anti-counterfeiting Group, the Asia-Pacific Broadcasting Union, and the International Federation of Musicians (WIPO 2006b).

Noncommercial groups have also organized (generally using the Internet as the primary forum for interaction) around WIPO. An example of such a group is IP Justice, "an international civil liberties organization that promotes balanced intellectual property law in a digital world" (IP Justice 2006). Like the commercial interest groups, IP Justice is difficult to evaluate in terms of its membership and activities. Its website does not list the names (or number of) members or an annual budget. Numerous inquiries addressed to the leaders of the organizations went unanswered.

As an interesting aside, this experience reinforces concerns regarding the transparency of the activist groups, many of which criticize international organizations for a lack of transparency (Jordan and van Tuijl 2000).

CPTech is another group active in intellectual property issues related to WIPO and other international organizations. Its head, James "Jamie" Love, is a well-known figure in the field and frequently cited by allies and opponents alike as an influential figure. Its representative in Geneva is a coordinator and source of information for like-minded interest groups and representatives of nations that sometimes object to the intellectual property agenda of developed nations (interview 30). According to its website, the organization is funded by several US foundations including the Rockefeller Foundation, Ford Foundation, the MacArthur Foundation, and the Open Society Institute (CPTech 2008).

The availability of such resources help policy entrepreneurs overcome some barriers to mobilization. As with the Internet denizens who have mobilized in the policy sphere defined by ICANN, the WIPO public interest groups seem to be organized and led by individuals who for intellectual or ideological reasons are willing to make the entrepreneurial sacrifices necessary to stimulate and maintain these organizations. These individuals must derive psychological and / or solidarity benefits that explain this selfless investment of time, energy, and resources, an observation that will be expanded upon below.

RELATIONSHIPS AND STRUCTURE. The International Labour Organization (ILO) has a unique structure that institutionalizes participation for a range of interests. Each nation's delegation to the ILO consists of two government representatives, one representative of workers and one representative of employers. Thus the most concerned constituencies—business and labor—are formally integrated into the organization at its representative level and interaction with interest groups is more evenly distributed as a consequence (Feld et al. 1994). The unique ILO structure is likely a cause and effect of the more balanced distribution of interests in this policy space.

Structure matters in the case of ICANN as well. Unlike almost all GGOs, ICANN itself provides for the formal involvement of individuals in the organization. Individual Internet users now participate through one of ICANN's "supporting organizations," formal bodies focused on specific aspects of the organizations mission (e.g., the Address Supporting Organization [ASO], the Generic Names Supporting Organization [GNSO], and the Governmental Advisory Committee [GAC]). Instead of directly electing board members, "Consumer and civil society groups, selected by the Non-commercial Users Constituency of the Generic Names Supporting Organization," play a role in the selection of this body's nomination of a director (ICANN 2006). There is also an At-Large supporting organization that provides membership opportunities to public interest groups.

Interestingly, the current institutional arrangement represents a version with *reduced* participation for the public at large. The organization experimented with global online elections for several members of its board of directors. For various reasons, the election system was scrapped, to the great displeasure of many ICANN followers.

PSYCHOLOGICAL AND SOLIDARY REWARDS AS SELECTIVE BENEFITS. Revolutionary technology has not made interest group formation universal and evenly distributed across all policy domains and sectors, but the Internet plays a significant role in explaining part of the findings. The emergence of some nonbusiness interest groups does depend on use of contemporary communications technologies, specifically the obviation of costs and logistical difficulties in creating groups. Through message boards, blogs, e-mail, voice-over-Internet-protocol, and other innovations, it is now relatively easy to identify those with shared interests, build relationships, bargain regarding group position, formulate strategy, coordinate activity and sustain relationships.

Olson recognized that groups are easier to form and maintain if the "payoff" to the organizer and participants is likely to outweigh their costs. If the costs of organizing a transnational interest group are truly low, this logic would apply. With the advent of new communications technology, the required investment of an entrepreneurial individual or organization is much lower. But the general prevalence of industry groups suggests that the playing field is still not level. The general dominance of corporate interest groups holds true *except* in areas where affected individuals or groups have sufficient access to and knowledge of technologies that allow them to overcome barriers to mobilization. This distinction explains observations around high-tech GGOs like ICANN and W3C (Gould 2000; Ostrovsky and Schwarz 2005).

Like the IASB and ISO, ICANN provides formal opportunities to constituencies with a business interest in its activities to participate in the rulemaking process. It has several "supporting organizations" with memberships made up of such firms. Unlike the other bodies, however, ICANN is also surrounded by a constellation of interest groups—some of whom are also formally represented in the organizations—who represent more diffuse constituencies, many of whom have no financial interest in the policies created by ICANN.

Prominent among these is ICANN Watch, an organization that monitors and frequently offers critiques of ICANN actions (ICANNWatch.org 2006). One might argue that ICANN Watch is not an interest group at all, as it is essentially a community organized around a website. This definitional matter shall be left unexplored for the moment to focus on the more pertinent issue. Based on the postings and publications authored by ICANN Watch founders and regular participants, it is clear that the members of this community / group are concerned not with their own financial interests but instead a set of beliefs regarding the governance of the Internet and the allocation of political power within and around ICANN.

ICANN Watch is a collection of individuals we would expect to be overwhelmed by the costs of organizing (especially relative to the benefits). And yet they are organized and persistent. This is partially a product, without a doubt, of the relatively low costs of organizing using the Internet. Persons with an interest in the subject area are by definition accessible via the Internet, a communications medium that is relatively immune to problems of distance and cost. It also speaks to the importance of recognizing a wide range of benefits enjoyed by organizers.

The participants in ICANN Watch and other noncommercial interest groups related to GGOs receive psychological and social benefits from their work that are as real and motivating as material rewards (Salisbury 1969; Clark and Wilson 1961). Activists get the satisfaction of working to improve something about which they care deeply and enjoy the camaraderie of laboring alongside like-minded individuals. For those in positions of leadership, there may be an additional boost of psychic satisfaction. Technological and structural explanations for group mobilization miss the somewhat ineffable qualities of certain subject areas that make them more likely to provide psychic and solidary benefits. Internet governance arouses great passion and dedication among a significant community of users. The passion of such individuals is as critical an ingredient as the technology at their disposal (Willetts 1982, 185). Noncommercial communities surrounding the International Maritime Organization or the IASB have access to the same modern communications technologies, but the emotional motivation for potential group leaders and members seems absent.

The Internet / technology area is not unique in its population of group organizers who see opportunities for meaningful participation. The most similar dynamic concern GGOs dealing with environmental issues. A small group of concerned individuals started "FSC-Watch," for example, an organization "concerned about the constant and serious erosion of the FSC's reliability and thus credibility" (FSC-Watch 2008). Around the International Whaling Commission, there is a far greater proportion of civil society organizations than is typical for GGOs (Peterson 1992). The issues addressed by these GGOs are salient to diffuse, financially disinterested parties, an indispensable condition for noncommercial mobilization.

The observations and explanations regarding mobilization are not intended to equate group formation with group influence. Analysis to this point is intended only to understand why groups arise without passing judgment on their participation in the policymaking process. The next section considers the opportunities of interested parties to influence outcomes.

Alignment and Participation: The Need for a Global Concertation Model

How do organized interests influence policy? This question is at the heart of the differentiation of pluralism and corporatism (and other notions of group participation in politics). The presentation of the global concertation model is recognition that neither existing model captures the distinctive properties of interest politics around GGOs.

PLURALISM IS AN AWKWARD FIT.   Interest groups attempt to influence domestic policy in four ways: swaying public opinion, shaping the positions of political parties, participating in electioneering, and getting access to legislative and bureaucratic policymakers. Most of these options are not viable in the global governance context, although other tactics are available as substitutes. Global governance organizations—by and large—are less likely to be influenced by public opinion, given that the public is scarcely aware their existence. The only GGO that has spawned a successful concerted effort to arouse generalized public sentiment is the World Trade Organization (Shaffer 2005; Wilkinson 2008). Targeted campaigns intended to activate specific populations (e.g., animal rights advocates, environmentalists, privacy defenders) are occasionally observed around other GGOs.

GGOs are also of little interest to political parties. Global governance is not of much political interest in most domestic contexts, and there are no meaningful transnational political parties. More broadly, electioneering is generally irrelevant in the context of global governance organizations. Only ICANN has experimented with direct election of organizational leaders and has since abandoned this approach. The only elections in the context of global governance are (typically uncompetitive) internal contests to select members of the intermediate bodies or other governing entities. Issues raised by global governance organizations historically hold limited salience in domestic politics, thus the prospect of influencing national policy vis-à-vis a particular GGO is not promising.

Interest groups are most likely to concentrate their efforts on establishing direct access to the policymaking apparatus through members and bureaucrats. This includes frequent consultation with the leadership and bureaucracy, provision of information and analysis, submission of proposals and critiques, and serving as "fire alarms" on behalf of national governments and domestic interest groups (McCubbins and Schwartz 1984). This approach is driven not only by the limitations on the alternative strategies but also by the natural structural advantages enjoyed by interest groups in the transnational context.

The general structure of GGOs provides interest groups at least two opportunities to influence the policymaking process. Interest groups can attempt to influence the policies adopted by national governments. They may target nations that are particularly influential or pursue relationships with members that are not precommitted to a position on an issue of interest. Interest groups may try to build coalitions among members with similar interests that had not previously considered a strategic alliance. Once the process is initiated at the GGO level, groups can leverage their successes or attempt to compensate for failures in the domestic round by approaching other members. Finally, interested parties can not only lobby the members, staff and leadership of GGOs, they can also be active participants in the rulemaking process as described in chapter 5.

The cumulative analysis suggests that pluralism, in both its positive and negative incarnations, is not the most accurate model to describe most relationships between interest groups and the GGOs. First, as noted in the mobilization discussion, competition between transnational interests is far from equal; business interests generally have advantages in overcoming the barriers to international organization and mobilization. Second, the available means of access to GGOs do not present a level playing field that accommodates pluralist competition among interests. Civil society groups generally do not have the resources to participate in the highly arcane and rarified world of transnational rulemaking.

CORPORATISM DOES BETTER BUT . . . . The theory and language of "corporatism" provides a better fit with the contours of interest group participation in global governance. The mechanisms by which interest groups collaborate with the state in the corporatist framework are more consistent with the patterns of transnational governance. In characterizing the "stable corporatism" of the continent, for example, Offe describes a bureaucracy thoroughly entwined with the interest groups in formal and informal respects (Offe 1981, 150). Thus rather than mobilizing public opinion or influencing political parties, the corporatist model embodies an intimate relationship between state and interests. Indeed, Offe cites the potential cooptation of the groups by the state as a threat to the legitimacy of the corporatist system (1981).

Most global governance organizations provide for formal integration of interest groups into the policymaking structure and process. With respect to each organization, the names and arrangements are somewhat different. Some illustrations of the integration of interest groups into the structure of GGOs were provided in the previous section. Both the IASB and the ISO create working groups around projects to introduce new rules or revise existing regulations (Tamm Hallstrom 2004). The ISO creates technical committees with responsibility for drafting standards in specific areas. Each technical committee consists of representatives from national standardization bodies. Within each committee, groups are assembled to generate specific rules. These committees generally have interest groups participating as "organizations in liaison."

Consider one example. Technical Committee 59 (TC59) is concerned generally with building construction, which is defined to cover

Standardization in the field of building and civil engineering, of:

- general terminology for building and civil engineering;
- organization of information in the processes of design, manufacture, and construction;

- general geometric requirements for building, building elements, and components, including modular coordination and its basic principles, general rules for joints, tolerances, and fits;
- general rules for other performance requirements for buildings and building elements, including the coordination of these with performance requirements of building components to be used in building and civil engineering; and
- geometric and performance requirements for components that are not in the scope of separate ISO technical committees. (ISO 2006b)

Within the portfolio of TC59, the committee addresses specific standards questions and forms working committees to generate standards. In particular, there are groups dedicated to "terminology and harmonization of languages," "dimensional tolerances and measurement," and "jointing products" (ISO 2006b). The group devoted to "Sustainability in building construction" includes representatives of several national standards organizations (who are, in fact, employed by interested firms). It also works "in liaison" with several interest groups, including the Federation of European Rigid Polyurethane Foam Associations, the European Insulation Manufacturers Association, and the International Initiative for a Sustainable Built Environment.

The IASB generally establishes working groups around areas of ongoing research and development. The groups carry out research and draft proposed rules that are ultimately adopted by the board. Membership in these groups is individual rather than institutional. Still, the affiliations of group members provide a sense of the representation. Some groups also name institutional "observers" whose role is formally undefined.

An example of an IASB working group is the body entrusted with the broad topic of financial instruments (IASB 2007a). Its members include personnel from a range of financial institutions including Morgan Stanley, UBS, and Credit Suisse First Boston. There are some associations represented (e.g., Japanese Bankers Association) as well as individual corporations (e.g., Siemens, Johnson & Johnson). Observers include associations representing national public agencies (e.g., International Association of Insurance Supervisors, International Organization of Securities Commissions) which may meet the definition of an interest group but certainly not in a typical sense (because they ultimately represent the "state" rather than the nongovernmental sectors) (IASB 2007a).

Another IASB working group generates standards applicable to "small and medium-sized entities." This group's membership includes individuals affiliated with a variety of institutions including individual companies, accounting firms, government agencies, and some trade groups (e.g., Association of Chartered Certified Accountants, UK) (IASB 2007b). Of course, members of the IASB itself have an opportunity to influence all rules generated by this or any other working group, and they too are affiliated with national accounting standards agencies, private firms, and professional associations.

The integration of interest groups and firms into the deliberative process and structure of the organization is not a practice exclusive to these younger GGOs. The World Health Organization (WHO) also formalizes access mechanisms for interest groups. Through its "collaborating centres," the WHO carries out research and also attempts to leverage national institutions to accomplish its mission. Most collaborating centers are governmental, but the relationship extend to groups as well (e.g., Industrial Accident Prevention Association [Canada] and the Federal Association of Company Health Insurance Funds [Germany]) (WHO 2007). The WHO also has partnerships—generally meaning that the WHO provides financial support to projects administered by NGOs—with a variety of organizations (e.g., International Federation of Fertility Societies, International Medical Informatics Association, and World Confederation for Physical Therapy) (WHO 2006). These collaborations reflect a level of organizational integration although they do not necessarily involve rulemaking functions.

During rulemaking, the WHO provides "observer status" to interest groups at key deliberative conferences where nation-states are the sanctioned participants. For example, the WHO Framework on Tobacco Control is perhaps the most significant rule development undertaken by the organization in its history. Joining national delegations at the meeting of the Open-ended Intergovernmental Working Group were representatives of the International Pharmaceutical Federation, the World Heart Federation, and the International Organization of Consumers Unions (among others), which were designated as "Nongovernmental Organizations in Official Relations with the WHO" (WHO 2005). Still, the corporate participation in global governance is not truly corporatist. Participation is firm-driven, not mediated through interest groups. Peak associations—if they exist—have secondary roles. They act more as coordinators than aggregators of preferences.

In addition, the corporatist emphasis on state power relative to the interest groups is awkward in the GGO context. Many corporatists see the institutional arrangements tying interest groups into the bureaucracy as a strategy for state domination, as opposed to pluralists, who see the political process as a contest for influence on state policy (Williamson 1985). As previous chapters make clear, there is little reason to imagine GGO domination over anyone! To the extent invocation of corporatism implies domination of interests, it is entirely misplaced even if this model is generally a more satisfying model than pluralist approaches.

Finally, corporatist models of interest group participation in politics emphasize economic policies and the groups feeling their effects, business, labor, agriculture, professions (Thomas 1993). The corporatist model is associated with significant state intervention in the economy; "producer groups" bargain with the state to work out the distribution of resources across the economy. This model of policymaking does not fit well with the regulatory governance activities of the GGOs in this study. More contemporary "neocorporatist" models move away from anachronistic visions of centralized control and resemble the policy bargaining of the pluralist approach and illustrate the need for hybrid models.

Global Concertation: Influence without Transnational Interest Groups

Observations indicate that the reality of transnational interest group activity is a blend of *pluralist* and *corporatist* patterns. The *global concertation* model is defined by integration of interests into the GGO process, general dominance of commercial interests over civil society, robust competition among interests with the GGO framework, and emphasis on firm-level behavior (Lehmbruch 1984; Harrison 1980).

THE MODEST ATTRACTION OF TRANSNATIONAL INTEREST GROUPS. The emphasis on the participation of firms rather than groups is not accidental. Organizations' participation in GGO activities is not necessarily mediated through interest groups. This departure from pluralist and corporatist notions of interest group participation makes sense given the theories of interest group formation and mobilization. If participation in an interest group offers an opportunity to influence relevant public policy, the value of participation rises accordingly and more likely outweighs costs associated with membership (Salisbury 1984). If the interest group is powerless, membership is not terribly valuable. One might frame this reasoning in terms of the collective and selective benefits of group membership.

Through this prism the limited appeal of transnational interest groups is evident.

Collective benefits of group membership. Influence on GGO policy can make any transnational interest group's offer of *collective* benefits formidable, leading to robust mobilization of potential members. This is more or less true, depending upon the nature of the operative GGO. The more a GGO's activities "matter," the more valuable influence over the GGO becomes, as is the case with the World Trade Organization (WTO), the best known, and possibly strongest, organization considered in this study. Its unique adherence strategy gives more force to WTO rules and decisions than any other GGO. Not surprisingly, then, the WTO attracts the attention of a wide variety of interest groups with varied concerns and perspectives (Barfield 2001). Although the bottle-tossing protesters associated with WTO gatherings in Seattle and Genoa are easy to visualize, many less visible organized interests are also lobbying the WTO attempting to influence its rulemaking processes from every perspective (Marschner 2001).

Variation in the appeal of transnational interest groups reflects the dynamism of global governance organizations. They are not endowed with authority on the day of creation. As any GGO matures and its rules have greater consequence to the governed, the value of participation and interest group influence should increase. For communities affected by GGO policies that do not have organized interest groups, increases in GGO power raise the incentives to overcome collective action challenges and form organized interest groups.

This claim has some observable support. Maturing GGOs have attracted more interest groups as their influence has increased. WIPO and ICANN illustrate this dynamic. WIPO's website proudly points out, "The roots of the World Intellectual Property Organization go back to 1883, when Johannes Brahms was composing his third Symphony, Robert Louis Stevenson was writing *Treasure Island,* and John and Emily Roebling were completing construction of New York's Brooklyn Bridge." The need to provide protection to this and similar works prompted the Paris Convention and later the Berne Convention to grant patents, trademarks, and copyrights. But this organization was a rather sleepy administrative entity until the digital revolution and the rise of the Internet raised intellectual property (IP) issues to the top of the trade agenda (Sell 1999). For a wide range of industries—entertainment, software, pharmaceuticals—intellectual property was a key issue particularly in terms of international trade. WIPO is involved in debates and rulemaking with implications across the board. Although many of the rules have not been formally adopted by WIPO, their recognition under the WTO's TRIPS agreement gives them real teeth. And the list of organizations granted WIPO observer status grows every day (at last count, over 250 organizations, according to WIPO).

In the short period since ICANN's creation—approximately seven years—a community has grown up around the organization. This is undoubtedly a function of the concrete control ICANN possesses over access to the Internet's "root servers," the phone book and switching room for the Internet. In short, ICANN's rules are unavoidable, and thus firms with an interest in their creation must gain a seat at the table. ICANN has effectively cultivated this community by re-restructuring itself to integrate groups through its "supporting organizations" (Feldman 2000; Lowi 2001).

Influence on group as selective benefit of membership. The notion that GGO power can explain membership only takes us so far. The selective good offered by transnational interest group members must be excludable to overcome the classic free rider problem. There are cases where this takes the form of access to privileged information or some other resource. Still the most valuable good to be shared with members only is the opportunity to shape an interest group's policy preferences and guide its participation in the policymaking process.

If interest group influence in GGO policymaking is significant, the value of being a group member for purposes of participating in the determination of an interest group's position can be high. Free riding permits enjoyment of the collective benefit, but opportunities to influence the policy position of the group are foregone. If the interests of all potential group members are well aligned, this is not a terribly high price. Considering the global scope of GGOs and their concerned constituencies, however, this uniformity seems improbable.

Only a limited number of interest groups clearly draw membership by virtue of its role in GGO policymaking. The clearest case is the International Air Transport Association (IATA). The IATA represents multiple constituencies affected by the rules created and implemented by the International Civil Aviation Organization (ICAO). Among the IATA's members are airlines, travel agents, freight shippers, and suppliers. The provided listing of airline members, for example, covers every continent and seems fairly comprehensive (IATA 2007). According to the association, the airlines it counts as members convey 94 percent of the world air passenger volume.

Put simply, IATA's raison d'être is its relationship with the ICAO. The connection is given central importance in the description of the organization's work and, not surprisingly, its headquarters is located in Montreal, the home of ICAO's secretariat. The precise value of policy influence an airline attains by joining IATA as a selective benefit remains difficult to determine. As no major carrier demurs from joining, it would appear that membership is deemed important.

This interpretation of "selective" and "collective" benefits does strain Olson's theory of collective action. The selective benefit of influence is a function of the differential value of one group policy position over another. Thus the potential member must believe that it can influence the group position *and* that the group position somehow matters in the rulemaking process. Given these conditions, the provision of this *selective* benefit does not seem a terribly strong lure to attract and retain members in most cases.

Some transnational interest groups do offer tangible selective benefits to attract members. Several groups have password-protected "members only" portions of their website that offer access to additional materials that are not publicly available (as is much information provided by interest groups). Recall the IAPA example of an interest group using this approach more conventionally, attracting members by offering discounts on hotels and flights.

Finally, group membership is encouraged by the rules of some GGOs. The World Health Organization, for example, requires firms wishing to lobby the organization to approach through the recognized international interest groups. So, for example, if Pfizer wants to comment on a proposed international rule, it must channel its comments through the International Federation of Pharmaceutical Manufacturers and Associations (interview 12). This is a decidedly *corporatist* feature.

THREATS TO GROUP COHERENCE.   The seemingly low level of transnational interest group formation in some policy areas should not be interpreted as an indication of lack of concern on the part of business or industry. In addition to the weak inducements to form and join groups, there are impediments to be overcome in creating and maintaining transnational interest groups. Transnational interest groups face an unusual array of competitors. Even those groups that do find a toehold face constant threats to group coherence.

As a result, across policy domains, the interest group landscape appears to be populated in larger numbers by national and (to a lesser extent) regional organizations than global groups. International interest groups in most policy areas seem to be secondary in stature to the national organizations or even individual firms. Among the groups affiliated with WIPO, for example, more than half are national or regional in scope.

Diversity of interests. The observed dominance of single-nation interest groups and individual firms stems from the diversity of potential group members. Policies affect members in different countries or regions differently, causing ruptures along national or regional lines. There may be, for example, distinctions based on the level of development of group members' countries. Any division undermines transnational interest groups and reduces their influence with GGOs, which, in turn, diminishes the attractiveness of group membership.

For many global governance organizations, the growing divide between developed and developing nations is palpable. The World Intellectual Property Organization and World Health Organization, for example, are deeply divided on issues of intellectual property related to pharmaceuticals. Developed countries are protecting the intellectual property rights of companies within their jurisdictions. They fear the violation of patents and resist calls to allow marketing of inexpensive substitutes to reach poor populations. Developing countries, on the other hand, see the issues as a public health matter. They push for understandings of intellectual property law that promote availability of "essential medicines" even if the returns to pharmaceutical companies are negatively affected. Pharmaceutical companies with an interest in producing the generic alternatives sought by developing countries obviously have a very different preference than those Western firms that hold intellectual property rights. Thus, the idea of a single interest group representing all pharmaceutical producers would not get very far. The same is true in most policy areas. The nongovernmental GGOs that seek to create market-oriented standards bring producers, marketers, and consumers from around the world under a single umbrella. Forging a stable coalition across these divisions is a formidable challenge.

Observation of firm-level participation and weak interest groups poses an interpretation challenge. Firms might only undertake lobbying *because* the transnational interest groups are so weak. This certainly is not what participants believe. Every interview and secondary source suggest that firms feel they are better off "going it alone" than casting their lot with a diverse set of competitors. This weakens transnational interest groups. The paucity of strong transnational corporate interest groups seems to bolster the contention that the diversity of interests fractured by industry and nationality undermines any collective action.

Low costs of organizing. The low costs of organization are generally cited as a factor encouraging the development of interest groups and thus equalizing the playing field for civil society and corporate interests (Tarrow 2005; Keck and Sikkink 1998). Ironically, the very ease of creating groups may also *undermine* the significance of any single interest group. Several organizations may vie to be an industry's or community's voice, resulting in fractured and weakened representation. Interests seem to play a significant role when one group is dominant. The IATA example is most vivid. It suggests that when, and only when, an interest group can emerge as a "peak association," it can play a prominent role. When groups must compete with one another for recognition, no one wins.

The inside track enjoyed by commercial interests in most GGOs is not a function of superior organizational skills. Influence is often achieved at the firm level; the weakness of transnational interest groups has already been noted. In fact, transnational public interest groups may be more robust than commercially oriented groups. This may be explained by the resource differences between the constituents of civil society and commercial groups. Unlike for-profit businesses with a great stake in the outcome of GGO rulemaking processes, citizen or public interest groups can only afford to participate in global governance by working collectively. Thus transnational interest groups are indispensable to them. Industry-based groups may add something but companies that see the benefits in influencing GGOs are willing and able to bear the costs of going it alone.

GGO as competitor to transnational interest group. One surprising impediment to group formation and influence around global governance organizations is the formidable competition they face from GGOs performing functions typically associated with interest groups and peak associations. Many GGOs act as convenors, aggregators of preferences, and hubs for communications and interaction. Through working groups and other committees, individual firms with competing priorities and preferred outcomes settle their differences in order to arrive at mutually agreeable outcomes, obviating the need for interest groups.

The similarities extend beyond this role. The techniques used by GGOs to attract participation come right out of the interest group playbook. Several GGOs induce membership or affiliation by offering selective benefits, including access to the policymaking process. The International Telecommunication Union, for example, offers special access and discounts to member nations and organizations:

> In addition to publicly-available information such as that found on the ITU Website, Member States and Sector Members have also access to a large volume of restricted data such as draft documents, statistics, development plans, training modules, etc.
>
> As a Sector Member, you will receive the invitations with related documentation to all ITU events (information on new publications, circular letters, vacancy notices, Notifications by Member States and Sector Members, information bulletins, etc). You will be given a TIES (Telecom Information Exchange Services) account that allows you to access restricted databases, documents and technical databases.
>
> Discounts of 15% off the catalogue price are granted to all ITU Sector Members on the purchase of any ITU Publication (except those available from the ITU Electronic Bookshop). (ITU 2007)

Like the ITU, the other standards-setting organizations rely upon participation of concerned companies to drive the policymaking process. Although engagement in the work of the ISO and the IEC is managed through the national standards bodies, the participants in all the technical committees charged with actually writing the standards are representatives of firms with an interest in the subject matter. Thus the lobbying effort of interest groups and individual firms will be directed at other participants rather than at "the bureaucracy" per se. This seems more analogous to setting policy *within* an interest group or peak association. GGOs are creating common goods but providing selective, excludable benefits and aggregating industry-wide preferences in the course of rulemaking.

The *global concertation* model of interest mobilization and participation reveals an environment that is not terribly hospitable to formal transnational interest *groups* even as the welcome mat is put out for interested *firms*. With their group-like behavior, GGOs simultaneously draw concerned parties into the fold while retarding the formation and development of rivals. Transnational interest groups exist but they seem unlikely, in most contexts, to emerge as forces on par with their domestic peers.

GGO Authority and the Satisfaction of Interest Groups

In almost every policy domain, interested parties are integrated into the global governance system, either through groups or more commonly as individual firms. They play a hands-on role in the crafting of rules and regulations (in most areas) and are sometimes formal members, making the rhetorical separation of the governance organization and the interest groups somewhat artificial. The integration of interests is a strategic adaptation of GGOs that reflects the demands of global governance.

Integration as a Source of GGO Authority

Pointing a causal arrow between GGO power and interest group formation is a tricky business. The relationship likely flows in two directions. GGOs seek participation of interested parties as a means of securing their own authority. GGOs with authority are more likely to attract interest group participation. Both stories are consistent with the theoretical framework of this book. Global governance organizations cannot secure "obedience" from the "governed" through force or other coercive measures. To win authority they must satisfy the interests of key constituents. Chapter 4, 5, and 6 show how this consideration shapes the GGO approach to structure, rulemaking, and adherence. The same logic extends to interested parties. Integration of interest groups helps secure their acceptance of GGO rules (Willmott 1985).

This inverts the classical understanding of interest group integration in organizational design. Principles applied to the design of public rulemaking emphasize neutrality, not integration of interest groups. Anderson (1979), for example, articulates seemingly universal principles related to the design of public bureaucracies: organizations should (1) "prevent government from becoming the instrument of some faction of the community," (2) remain impartial among interests, and (3) "complement and enhance popular sovereignty, but not displace it." Being true to such principles, while important to creating an organization that satisfies expectations associated with democratic legitimacy, may alienate key constituencies. This would undermine GGO authority in ways that it would not in most domestic contexts. It would place *responsibility* over *responsiveness*-type accountability.

Clearly normative legitimacy—at least as interpreted in domestic contexts—is not the foremost consideration in the shaping of the GGO-interest relationship. Representatives of multiple organizations raise the importance of keeping key participants "at the table" to maintain organizational credibility and authority. Indeed, most GGOs have explicitly devoted resources and aimed reforms at improving the involvement of interested parties in one way or another (interviews 36, 15, 43, 48).

The instrumental value of interest group integration also sheds light on the firm-specific nature of participation in global governance. Just as the importance of members varies, the distribution of influence across individual firms is far from even. It is more important for some interested parties to buy in than it is for others . While a software standard rejected by Microsoft is not worth the hard drive it is saved on, the value of Acme Software Co. as a supporter is trivial. By focusing on individual firms rather than interest groups, GGOs can be assured that they are satisfying the preferences of the players critical to their success.

The pattern of interest group participation provides support for this interpretation. *Structure* type, the variable defined by the cluster analysis in chapter 4, is correlated with interest group alignment. Seven of nine *hybrid* GGOs are associated with a *concertation*-type alignment of interest groups. This relationship, which falls short of statistical significance, indicates the importance of interest group participation and support for GGOs that are not backed by member governments. Without the authority derived from their relationship with nation-states, the need for such GGOs to ensure commitment by keeping avenues for access and influence open is amplified.

Concertation and the Inequity of Influence

Commercial interests do not have unrivaled sway across all global governance policy domains but business-related interests do enjoy advantages when compared with public interest groups. This reality proceeds from theoretical understanding of interest group formation and influence (in most contexts) and it is reinforced by the specific demands of global governance organizations. The obstacles that stand in the way of noncommercial interest participation are primarily informal. Opportunities to participate are open to multiple constituencies, but there is a self-selection bias that is as powerful as it is predictable. Commercial interests have the benefit of greater resources and the incentives to commit them. Individual firms can bear a significant burden in doing the work of GGOs as policies are researched and developed. Even though they are entitled to participate, public interest groups generally do not have the technical sophistication or financial ability to match this participation. They are hard-pressed to raise the membership fees that are a prerequisite to participation in many GGOs (even the lower fee schedules generally offered for nonprofit organizations).

It is not completely one-sided. In several transnational policy domains, public interest groups have thrived. They have created active, well-informed constituencies that participate in the deliberations of GGO and monitor activities. A picture in which corporate interests *never* face countervailing forces is a misrepresentation. Nongovernmental organizations have proven most effective when pressing for procedural reform, such as demanding greater transparency (Scholte 2002). Given the inherent challenges in organizing on a global level, it is noteworthy how several public interest groups have created global networks and been integrated into GGOs (Zacher and Sutton 1996).

The variation from sector to sector seems to be a function of the nature of the issues, the passion aroused in affected communities and access to communications technology. Internet, technology-related, and environmental policy domains see the most persistent set of public interest groups. Recall the striking contrast in participation of interest groups around the International Maritime Organization (IMO) and the International Whaling Commission (IWC). At IMO meetings, nearly 75 percent of observer organizations represent industry. At the IWC, the percentages were reversed. Almost three-quarters of the participating groups were noncommercial. Clearly something about whales arouses individuals to organize.

Ironically, the IMO may have greater impact on whale welfare than the IWC! The IMO's rules on ship safety and noise and water pollution are, for various reasons, more binding than the IWC's protection of whales. But people interested in whales focus their attention, quite logically, on the organization with "whaling" in its name. Pushing this point even further, ISO Technical Committee 8 (TC 8), which covers "ships and marine technology," plays a large role filling out the specifics of the International Convention for the Safety of Life at Sea and other relevant IMO treaties. The work of TC 8 is explicitly referenced by the IMO, making it a de facto element of the treaty. And yet not a single noncommercial NGO is listed among the organizations in liaison with TC 8. Whale activists have not yet realized that their attention should be focused on TC 8. This may change as activists begin to appreciate the relationship between seemingly disconnected GGOs and the issues of greatest concern to them. For the time being, however, the biases in mobilization may unintentionally undermine public interest group influence.

Conclusion

None of this is completely alien to students of interest groups in domestic contexts, of course. The interaction between governance organizations and interest groups is more complicated than the stylized models offered in popular political discourse. Interest groups do not simply "lobby" bureaucrats and elected officials to get desired outcomes. The relationship is ongoing and multifaceted (see Berger and Joint Committee on Western Europe 1981; Wilson 1990). Government officials often rely upon interest groups to collect information, communicate to members, and even sway public opinion on key matters (McCubbins and Schwartz 1984). Far from being adversarial, the relationship is often derided as being too cozy, prone to the phenomenon of "capture" where the bureaucracy may be *too* influenced by pressure groups (e.g., Bernstein 1977).

But *global concertation* offers something different than even realistic accounts of pluralism or corporatism. Robust competition among divergent interests is often resolved within a process that seats interested parties at the rulemaking table without funneling participation through the powerful associations of classical corporatism. In some policy arenas, noncommercial civil society groups are thriving—transnational public interest groups may be more coherent than business organizations—but corporate or business interests do enjoy advantages in terms of mobilization and participation, as any Gramscian student of international politics would predict (Pattberg 2005). Still, the logic of concertation goes beyond Marxist understandings of political influence. The influence of corporate interests is vital to the effectiveness of global governance organizations.

As seen in other aspects of organizational design, GGOs cannot always afford the luxury of organizational neutrality. If the playing field is kept level at all costs, interested parties (or the countries whose governments they influence) will simply walk away. GGOs strive to meet minimum legitimacy standards, but they maintain authority by ensuring a minimum level of satisfaction for key interested parties. The formalized inequality naturally offends most shared standards of normative legitimacy in the governance context (Bull et al. 2004). This distinctive compromise turns conventional fears that interest group influence can undermine legitimacy on their head.

Addressing the challenge of legitimation for corporatist systems, Schmitter points out that "neocorporatist arrangements" must "justify their existence with respect to existing community, market and state institutions" and also "explain how they are compatible with the norms and procedures of political democracy" (Schmitter 1985, 60). Essentially he is arguing that corporatist arrangements threaten to compromise the legitimacy of democratic regimes by the appearance of insider dealing in the creation of government policy (Bull et al. 2004). In the realm of global governance, this logic is twisted around. The integration of interest groups in transnational governance is similarly at odds with democratic norms. But far from threatening the status of GGOs, the global concertation model actually *enhances* the authority of the GGO. Without it, the global governance organization risks its relevance as a rulemaking body.

CHAPTER EIGHT

Cooperation and Competition in Global Governance

Every GGO effort to balance the demands of legitimacy and authority is complicated by an undeniable reality. Each global governance organization is part of an ecosystem populated by potential partners and potential competitors: other GGOs, nongovernmental organizations, private firms, national and other domestic government agencies, and regional transnational entities. The reality of competition and coordination in global governance ties together two issues of great interest to contemporary students of politics: regulatory competition and the rise of policy networks. This chapter explores the dynamics of competition and cooperation, investigates the conditions under which we should expect to see either, or both, and considers the implications of this dynamic for GGO accountability.

The surprising finding revealed in this chapter is that competition and cooperation are correlated. Unlike the preceding chapters, there is no attempt to define GGO types on the basis of competition and cooperation. But this distinctive feature of the global governance context—simultaneous competition and cooperation—reflects the multifaceted calculus underlying GGO behavior. Illuminating this distinctive dynamic is critical to painting a fuller picture. It is argued that cooperation generally serves GGO interests because the legitimacy and authority of each organization is reinforced. Only when competition is based on substantive disagreement

regarding the content of rules—which is *not* typically the case—is competition (without any cooperation) the likely outcome. Thus the seemingly
peculiar phenomenon of competing GGOs coordinating their actions is
not at all atypical.

Global Governance as a Competitive Marketplace

Regulatory competition is typically framed as a geographic tug of war. The
jury is still out on the implications of two or more jurisdictions competing
to create the most attractive regulatory environment, so it is hard to draw
conclusions regarding the implications of such competition in the global
arena (Vogel 1997; Radaelli 2004). Moreover, we have not yet observed in-
terplanetary regulatory competition, so global governance organizations
do not face competition of this sort, but other forms of regulatory competition make the global milieu as competitive as any other (if not more so).
The analysis here focuses on the dynamics of competition rather than its
effect on the quality of rules but experience suggests both general claims
regarding regulatory competition—that it promotes higher-quality rules
or degrades requirements—are part of global governance.

     This first section offers an overview of the varieties of regulatory com-
petition in the global governance context. GGOs compete with other
GGOs (governmental and nongovernmental), regional and even national
rulemaking bodies, and individual firms with rulemaking power. Each
competitive dynamic is distinctive.

GGO versus GGO

The most universal characteristic of competition among global governance organizations is that no one admits that it exists. Organizations
that are clearly vying for dominance in the same substantive space ve-
hemently deny any rivalry and urge the observer to see cooperation
(interviews 15, 29, 43, 45). The denial of competition belies reality. In
several areas, GGOs issue rules covering the same activities and argue for
their own competence in matters handled by other GGOs. It is *true* that
many GGOs do, in fact, cooperate, but this does not preclude competition (Brandenburger and Nalebuff 1996). Concomitant competition and
cooperation is a distinctive feature of global governance examined later
in this chapter.

GOVERNMENTAL GGO VERSUS GOVERNMENTAL GGO. State-based GGOs generally do not compete with each other. If there had once been competition, the ascendance of one organization seems to end it. In a small number of cases, however, established intergovernmental GGOs compete for authority in novel areas created by technological advances. Issues emerge that are ambiguous with respect to proper jurisdiction. There is no centralized coordination of global governance—even for entities affiliated with the United Nations—to delineate the substantive boundaries of GGOs' authority. Both the Universal Postal Union (UPU) and the International Telecommunication Union (ITU), for example, asserted responsibility for making rules for the Internet—without success.

GGOs frequently deal with intricate issues that transcend jurisdictional boundaries. Within the cooperative efforts required in such arenas, a competition for preeminence is ongoing as each organization strives to keep debate primarily in its own bailiwick. The intellectual property issues surrounding pharmaceuticals are illustrative. As one would expect, the World Intellectual Property Organization (WIPO) stakes a significant claim. But the World Health Organization (WHO) is also deeply involved, most notably its consideration of "essential medicines," a designation that affects the protection of property rights. The World Trade Organization (WTO) enmeshes intellectual property considerations in its trade agreements, making itself a player as well. The jockeying among these organizations is never well hidden even as they coordinate efforts.

GOVERNMENTAL GGOS VERSUS NONGOVERNMENTAL GGOS. Competition between governmental and nonstate GGOs is not terribly robust. Once the governmental GGO establishes itself, it seems the barriers to entry loom large enough to dissuade most potential entrants. So, as in the case of competition among governmental GGOs, the most typical contests pit entities (government and nongovernment) against each other in skirmishes over new terrain.

In its pursuit of authority over the Internet, for example, the ITU focuses its competitive energy on the Internet Corporation for Assigned Names and Numbers (ICANN). ICANN, the nonprofit organization that sets the rules of domain name assignment, is peculiar inasmuch as its power is derived almost completely from its contractual relationship with the US government. Under the guise of the World Summit on the Information Society (and the Working Group on Internet Governance that it spawned), the ITU and others have offered themselves as more appropriate alternatives to ICANN (interview 9). Internet governance is, in general, the most contested governance terrain. Although the UPU has mostly given up, other GGOs continuing to assert themselves in this area include W3C, IEC, and ISO, all of which have technical committees working on issues related to the Internet. Both the IEC and ISO are mixed-sector GGOs.

Nonstate GGOs such as the Forest Stewardship Council (FSC), the Fairtrade Labelling Organizations International, and the Marine Stewardship Council can be seen as rivals to *domestic* governmental regulatory bodies although the very weakness of national regulation and the absence of meaningful global regulation is often the rationale for the creation of such market-driven GGOs (Cashore et al. 2004). There is an intergovernmental organization called the International Tropical Timber Organization, for example, that does not have rulemaking authority and, domestically, forestry is not tightly regulated (or not regulated with meaningful enforcement) (Cashore et al. 2004). Thus nonstate entities like the FSC are typically alternatives to domestic government regulation rather than competitors. In some cases, the rise of nonstate market-driven GGO prompts government entrance into the arena. More commonly, an alternative nonstate organization is started (sometimes by a trade association) to compete with the nongovernmental GGO, a phenomenon discussed in a moment.

NONGOVERNMENTAL GGO VERSUS NONGOVERNMENTAL GGO. Competition among nongovernmental GGOs is the easiest to envision and the most intense. The most common manifestation pits a nonstate market-driven entity against another (or several other) organization promulgating its own set of standards. Cashore (2003) documents in great detail the response of timber industry associations to the introduction of the FSC certification. Several rival standards for sustainable forestry were created and promoted, and weaker requirements offered as alternatives to producers seeking some certification. They also can confuse consumers and reduce the coercive marketplace power of the GGOs. Similar dynamics are observed with respect to "fair trade" and labor standards (Fransen 2008a).

Competition among standards-setting bodies is not limited to these normatively charged contests. GGOs that offer standards in domains that are not of great interest to activists also engage in competition. The International Organization for Standardization (ISO) faces competition from several standards-generating entities, including the ITU and the IEC. The ISO's most formidable nongovernmental competitor is ASTM International, a US-based organization that promulgates standards in a wide range of substantive areas. ASTM began as the American Society for Testing Materials but has expanded its substantive footprint as the ISO became the leading industrial standard-setter in the world. The two developments are related.

Historically, the ISO has been dominated by Europeans. This is due both to greater attention by European firms and governments and and to a general disinterest in standards on the part of Americans and Asians. In the age of globalization, however, standards take on new importance. To the extent that the ISO's standards reflect European preferences, these global rules put American businesses at a disadvantage. Accessing markets where ISO standards are the norm becomes more difficult for firms not already conforming to them. This increases pressure on American firms to meet ISO requirements, even creating different products for US and European markets.

The competition has very real implications for the organizations themselves. Standard-setting organizations like ISO and ASTM are funded by revenues derived from the sale of standards. Every firm that conforms to an ISO standard pays a fee, typically routed through the national member bodies, for the documentation of these standards. The greater the market pressure on firms to conform to an organization's standard, the more revenue that organization generates. When one standard becomes dominant, firms will no longer find it worthwhile to pay for competing standards. Thus the competition for preeminence in a given field affects the bottom line of standard-generating bodies.

For ASTM, competing for market share means convincing industries utilizing standards to use their standards rather than ISO's. Industries are distributed globally, of course, so there may be market opportunities in parts of the world that have not yet settled on a standard. (There are switching costs that make such virgin territory particularly valuable). ASTM is currently moving aggressively to promote its standards in China.

The logic of ASTM's China effort is inescapable. First, widespread adoption of ASTM standards in China would generate substantial revenues (even taking into account intellectual property concerns). More important, Chinese industrial adoption of ASTM standards would change the economies of scale associated with each standard. Any business looking to China as a customer or supplier might adopt the standard that is dominant in China to smooth the road. Thus, ASTM's China strategy, if successful, could produce a major blow to ISO. This example is discussed at greater length when the strategic implications of GGO competition—for GGOs and their constituents—are examined in the final section of this chapter.

Global Governance versus "Something Less than Global"

Joining a regional entity or simply sticking with nation-based regulation can be seen as an alternative to participating in a global regime. Among the GGOs included in this study, several have regional analogs and almost all have analogous bodies at the national level. The "value proposition" offered by GGOs is the promise of efficiencies and opportunities presented by a universal set of rules. Common standards open the doors to cross-border commerce—of potential value to exporting firms and consumers who might benefit from enhanced competition. Regional and national bodies cannot match this advantage, but they can tailor rules to suit local needs and interests. Indeed, they may craft rules precisely to create or preserve barriers to entry for outside firms.

Regional bodies can and do coexist with global entities. Many GGOs attempt to avoid competition by integrating such bodies into the organizational structure. The Financial Action Task Force on Money Laundering, for example, encourages regional bodies to participate in discussions, albeit not as members. The Fairtrade Labelling Organizations International and the Forest Stewardship Council are, in some respects, federations of national bodies rather than central organizations with outlets around the world. To attract such collaboration, GGOs must offer some advantage based on the expansion of a rule's footprint. This again underscores the critical importance of participation in the GGO and adoption. Unless there is significant uptake of a GGO's rules—particularly among the most important nations / markets—the "value proposition" of joining is extremely limited and the organization cannot build authority.

GGOs versus Market Participants

For-profit enterprises can also be rulemakers. Entrepreneurs recognize the need for harmonization and offer rules as products. Or, one firm can become so dominant in its sphere that it effectively dictates standards to other players. Both scenarios offer substitutes for GGO rules.

MARKET DOMINANCE. In some industries, private firms posses market power such that they become de facto rulemakers. Perhaps the most ubiquitous example is the Microsoft Windows operating system. By virtue of its market share, Microsoft effectively sets a standard for the underlying architecture of personal computer software utilized around the world. While many people are not fond of Microsoft—and it has been accused of abusing its monopolistic power—the universality of the Windows operating system (and the ubiquity of Microsoft Office programs such as Word and PowerPoint) allows computer users to seamlessly interact the world over.

PRIVATE RULEMAKERS. Companies have made a sustainable business of promoting and implementing standards. One interesting example is Underwriters Laboratories, a for-profit company founded in 1894 (Underwriters 2008). Known to consumers through the UL stamp on a variety of products, Underwriters Laboratories has focused on issuing standards related to product safety and certifying compliance. The company has extended its reach to ninety-nine countries and its 1,000 standards are utilized by more than seventy-thousand companies (UL 2008).

Some private rulemaking is not motivated by profit. Jewish dietary laws specify what food is kosher and what food is not. These laws deal not only with the identification of permissible and impermissible foods but also the manner in which animals are slaughtered, stored, etc. There is debate among Jewish theologians regarding the purpose of the rules but one consequence is certain: they establish a standard that transcends political boundaries. This allows Brazilian entrepreneur Antonio Russo to build a global beef empire, for example, confident in his products' global acceptability because his staff of rabbis is on hand to certify that his product is kosher (Moffett 2004). As is the case with other standards, organizations implement the kosher rules by certifying compliance to the satisfaction of customers and allowing producers to charge a premium for their product.

The Promise and Peril of Regulatory Competition

There is a tendency to reduce all analyses of regulatory competition to a dichotomous conclusion: "race to the bottom" or a "race to the top." The race-to-the-bottom camp sees competition as a contest that forces jurisdictions to appeal to potential regulatees on the basis of regulatory hospitality, which, in this view, is synonymous with regulatory weakness (Stone 1996; Murphy 2004). The race to the top, in the alternative, sees the same competition but with positive consequences. Jurisdictions compete by offering higher-quality regulation rather than watered-down rules and attract firms eager to distinguish themselves by meeting high standards (Murphy 2004; Vogel 1997).

In the field of American corporate governance, regulatory competition results from corporations' choice regarding their state of incorporation (Vogel 2003; Bratton and McCahery 1996). The two outcomes have been described in *slightly* less judgmental terms based on the regulations offered in two American states. Vogel dubbed one "Delaware competition," while the other is called "California competition." These names avoid the better / worse distinction and instead focus on the basis of attraction for potential regulatees. Delaware competition posits a simple economic model in which regulators are driven to keep lowering the cost of compliance in order to create an environment that is marginally cheaper than that offered by all rivals (Bratton and McCahery 1996). This is not necessarily less rigorous, but critics argue that a downward spiral toward the lowest acceptable requirements is inevitable and difficult to halt. Indeed, it has been argued that some international *cooperation* is intended to avoid just this sort of decline (Kapstein 1989).

But the "race to the bottom" is hardly an accepted interpretation of experience. Indeed, the very example from which the label "Delaware competition" is drawn is not regarded as an instance of weakened regulation by all those who focus on corporate governance. It is argued that the competition among jurisdictions has resulted in an optimal level of regulation, satisfying the needs of market participants without incurring excess costs and inefficiency (Romano 1905; Sunder 2002). Models that posit regulatory competition as a force for *enhanced* regulation in this direction depart from the "race to the bottom" view with two important corrections. First, the notion that all firms seek less onerous regulation imposes a monolithic assumption that is not appropriate (Vogel 1995; Murphy 2004). There are firms that regard more rigorous regulation as preferable, creating the "California effect" of competition that *raises* regulatory quality (Braithwaite and Drahos 2000; Vogel 1995). Companies that can already meet such standards, for example, would prefer more demanding rules as they would function as effective barriers to entry. Second, regulatory competition should be seen in social terms as much as economic terms (Bernstein and Cashore 2007). The "competitors" may together move toward consensus around best practices—creating a dynamic that is the very opposite of a race to the bottom (Cashore et al. 2007).

In policy-oriented conversations about regulatory competition, there is an eagerness to identify the answer, good or bad, but research offers no definitive evidence that one effect of competition is predominant (Radaelli 2004; Murphy 2004). This examination of regulatory competition of among GGOs is certainly consistent with this general finding. Although this study does not attempt to judge the quality of rules produced by each GGO, there is no informal evidence suggesting that any type of competition described above uniformly produces more or less onerous regulations.

Cooperation among GGOs

GGO competition is distinguished by concomitant *cooperation*. Rival GGOs are frequently members in a network that must collaborate in order to be effective. The network metaphor has proven to be a powerful way to describe the interplay of organizations involved in global governance (Slaughter 2004b; Reinicke 1999). GGOs are, of course, prominent members of many transnational policy networks. It is important, however, to recognize that the connections between entities within a network are not uniform.

Some are partnerships of equals while others are clearly hierarchical. There is also variation in the integration of GGOs into networks. Some are connected to many other GGOs, while others are fairly isolated. And finally, there is variation in the nature of coordination. Some GGOs actively partner with other GGOs (and other international organizations), while other relationships are passive, in which reference is made to rules produced by GGOs but where there is no working relationship.

The Nature of the GGO Network

In the realm of global regulation, there are three basic connections between GGOs and other international organizations. Most connections involve 1) reference to another organization's rules, 2) a piggybacking of adherence authority, or 3) joint rulemaking. These are not mutually exclusive, of course, and in some issue areas, relationships of all varieties exist. The network of institutions involved in global financial regulation is particularly dense, for example (Alexander et al. 2006). Organizations included in this study (e.g., IASB, FATF, and BCBS) cooperate with a variety of other entities, including the IMF, IOSCO (the International Organization of Securities Commissions), the G-8, and many others (Held and McGrew 2002; Kirton 2001; Bayne 2001; Slaughter 2004a; Jacobsson 2006; Koenig-Archibugi 2002).

REFERENCE TO OTHER GGO RULES.   One central challenge faced by each and every GGO is the acceptance of the rules it promulgates. Reference by another organization to a rule produced by your own is valuable as a building block. It reinforces the legitimacy of the organization—linking it with the legitimacy of the referring organization—and it also bolsters the authority of the organization. The reference enhances the rewards of adherence to potential rule followers.

As discussed in chapter 6, the most powerful reference comes from the World Trade Organization (WTO) because of its potent enforcement regime. The WTO has the power to ratify the imposition of sanctions, effectively protecting a punishing state from further retribution. Rules created by GGOs can be used in the adjudication of disputes regarding WTO treaties. In the case of the Agreement on Trade-related Aspects of Intellectual Property Rights (TRIPS), the linkage to WIPO is formally codified in the text of the document and takes the form of a joint council. The WTO and WIPO collaborate on some activities (like an annual colloquium). Most important, however, the adjudication of TRIPS cases allows for the invocation of WIPO regulations (and the underlying conventions upon which WIPO is based) as a defense against charges of unfair trade practices. The association with the WTO boosts the credibility and significance of WIPO (Sell 2003; Slaughter 2004a).

The WTO also references other GGO rules in less explicit fashion. The agreement on Technical Barriers to Trade includes language granting presumptive justification to any import restriction consistent with a valid international standard, as defined by criteria for legitimate global rulemaking (including reference to an ISO standard on standard-setting!). Organizations have adapted their structure and process to match these requirements and advertise their validity in WTO contests. Even the International Labor Organization, considered a globalization foe by many critics, has advertised its connections to the WTO to boost its own stature (Wilkinson and Hughes 2002, 155).

PIGGYBACKING ADHERENCE AUTHORITY.   In some cases, the reference to a rule provides more adherence authority than the GGO itself possesses. This is certainly the case for the WIPO. Treaties only take force when a requisite number of nations ratify the document. Thus a treaty can be completed but not implemented for many years. This was true of the WIPO Performances and Phonographs Treaty and the WIPO Copyright Treaty. Even prior to the treaties' entry into force, however, the WTO used the treaties to provide guidance in the interpretation of the TRIPs agreement. In other words, the WTO effectively put these treaties into force years before WIPO.

Other examples of piggybacking do not involve textual reference but still call for implementation of one GGO's rule through another GGO's mechanism. For example, the Convention on Trade in Endangered Species (CITES) requires participating nations to establish permitting entities to approve imports and exports of covered species. The protocols defining how this is to be done are in the province of the World Customs Organization (WCO). Thus the two organizations must be aware of each other's requirements. The WCO is also a formally recognized partner of the WTO. The WTO refers to the WCO's Harmonized System of Classification, which standardizes the names and categories of goods. The relationship extends to other transcendent issues, such as rules of origin and customs valuation.

JOINT RULEMAKING.   The relationship between the WTO and WCO goes deeper than "rule referencing." For some purposes they are intertwined. This is not unusual, but it takes two forms: institutionalized collaboration and ad hoc partnership.

Institutionalized GGO Collaboration.   The WTO and WCO sometimes operate as units of an integrated system. Several WTO agreements delegate rulemaking responsibility to the WCO. In fact, the agreements made in the context of World *Trade* Organization treaty negotiations sometimes call for the creation of new bodies within the World *Customs* Organization.

The standard-setting bodies have gone further down this path than other GGOs. The Joint Technical Committee (JTC), a body that brings together the IEC and the ISO (and, in some cases, the ITU), is devoted to a wide spectrum of information technology issues. Had the organizations not collaborated, they likely would have embarked independently on rulemaking in this area, an outcome regarded by all in negative terms (interviews 9, 15, 43). Within the single JTC, there are about twenty working groups organized around more specific areas such as "documents description and processing languages," "software and systems engineering," and "biometrics" (JTC 1 2008).

The ISO has been the leader in establishing relationships with other GGOs, with the Joint Technical Committee as the model collaborative effort. In other cases, another GGO's rulemaking body is designated as an ISO technical committee or vice versa. The Unicode Consortium (UC) integrates the work of a collaborative effort that brings together three GGOs—ISO / IEC 10646 Information technology—Universal Multiple-Octet Coded Character Set—under the umbrella of the Joint Technical Committee (UC 2005). ISO standards in this area explicitly reference the UC work and treat it as authoritative by formal agreement.

Other GGOs have similar relationships with the ISO. The World Wide Web Consortium (W3C), like the Unicode Consortium, is affiliated with the Joint Technical Committee and it is designated to take a leadership role in some areas. For example, ISO / IEC 15445 deals with the standards for HTML, the language of the Web. ISO / IEC JTC1 (specifically, Working Group 4) recognized W3C's "leadership role" in the development of this standard. This is particularly noteworthy as the W3C also promotes standards that compete with other GGOs, including ISO.

Ad hoc Rulemaking Collaboration. There are numerous instances of joint rulemaking that are not institutionalized. The International Labor Organization and the International Maritime Organization cooperated in the creation of the Maritime Labour Convention, an agreement that creates a comprehensive set of rules governing the conditions for workers on ships (interviews 5, 6). Harmonizing rules produced by both entities in this single document would avoid duplication and conflicting requirements. Alas, the new agreement, approved by the ILO, has been ratified by only a handful of countries, meaning it has not yet taken force. The rulemaking process employed to craft the Maritime Labor Convention required cooperation but certainly did not intertwine the organizations in the manner of the examples above. They remained distinct entities working in concert.

Cooperation with Other Types of Organizations

GGOs are not restricted to cooperation with other GGOs, of course. There are a range of entities that interact with global governance organizations and become part of the rulemaking and adherence regimes. The discussion in chapter 7 of interest group integration into the mechanisms of global governance covered a good portion of this activity. That analysis emphasized the influence of groups on the GGO but the relationship between GGO and outside organizations often is a partnership that transcends attempts at influence. Two sets of organizations are typically entwined with GGOs in this way: NGOs and domestic government agencies.

NGOS. The Convention on International Trade in Endangered Species (CITES) sets rules for the issuing of import and export permits for endangered plants and animals. CITES's primary responsibility in carrying out this function is to determine which species are included in the system as established in appendices to the original agreement that are revised periodically to reflect conditions. The organization judges disputes regarding the adherence to CITES rules and approves the imposition of sanctions based on alleged violations. To evaluate adherence and the need for additional regulation, CITES collects data furnished by member states. This is a critical dependency because nations—particularly exporters—have incentives to withhold or even alter data to hide exports of prohibited commodities. The organization has limited resources to collect its own data or verify the information with which it is provided. This limitation is overcome, in part, with the assistance of a nongovernmental organization, TRAFFIC (Slaughter 2004a; Scholte 2002). TRAFFIC (Trade Records Analysis in Flora and Fauna in Commerce) is a "wildlife trade monitoring network" created by two NGOs, the World Wildlife Fund and the World Conservation Union.

TRAFFIC makes CITES more effective. The relationship between the two organizations was formalized in 1999 with the signing of a Memorandum of Understanding that outlines the scope and terms of cooperation (CITES 2008). The two are so integrated that CITES directs authorities to report information regarding trade in regulated substances such as ivory directly to TRAFFIC (CITES 2004). This collaboration is hardly unique for CITES. It engages a wide range of organizations, including GGOs (e.g., WCO), other international organizations (e.g., FAO, Interpol) and domestic nonprofits (e.g., University of Kent, Royal Botanic Gardens). CITES is also linked to the United Nations Environmental Program (UNEP). UNEP technically "administers" CITES even though it is headquartered in Nairobi and CITES operates completely independently in Geneva.

NGOs also collaborate regularly with nongovernmental GGOs. The Fairtrade Labelling Organizations International (FLOI) is a member of a formal alliance of entities with an interest in promoting fair trade. Under the acronym FINE, these organizations (FLOI, the International Fair Trade Association, the Network of European Worldshops, and the European Fair Trade Association) coordinate advocacy and strive to improve monitoring of trade practices on a global scale. The alliance maintains a website and sponsors meetings to foster a network that leverages the influence of each organization. From the perspective of the GGO, it bolsters the credibility, appeal, and visibility of its rules. With all advocates for fair trade pointing to FLOI standards as a benchmark, the value to producers of adherence with these standards increases.

FLOI is also a member of the ISEAL Alliance, referenced earlier. This group is essentially a trade association for nonstate market-driven governance organizations. The central objective of ISEAL is to increase the legitimacy of members' standards and the attractiveness of adherence to them (including rules produced by the FSC and MSC, two GGOs included in this study). This coordination—and the heightened credibility it lends—gives these GGOs a comparative advantage with respect to other standard-setting bodies competing in the same substantive spaces.

There is a temptation to assume that the attraction of such partnerships is greater for nongovernmental GGOs because they are in greater need of the legitimacy that accompanies such relationships. The observations of this set of GGOs do not provide support for this intuition. Governmental GGOs (like CITES) also have a wide range of collaborations with NGOs. The World Health Organization, for example, is one of the most well-known and established GGOs. It has several formal partnerships, that include NGOs and governmental entities (e.g., the Global Outbreak and Response Network, the Global Buruli Ulcer Initiative, and the International Treatment Access Coalition). Moreover, the WHO receives direct financial support from NGOs, most prominently the Bill and Melinda Gates Foundation (McNeil 2008).

These partnerships are a supplement and not a substitute for "traditional" attempts to lobby the WHO with the goal of influencing policy. In some contexts, relationships between GGOs and NGOs emphasize influence on rulemaking rather than collaboration. The World Intellectual Property Organization (WIPO), for example, provides access to NGOs that are interested in issues before the organization. In particular, WIPO has created a mechanism for deliberation regarding the protection of "Intellectual Property and Genetic Resources, Traditional Knowledge and Folklore." This is a heated topic, and the organization has been criticized for favoring the interests of developed nations in such matters. But this type of "partnership" is more properly conceived of as opening access to the rulemaking process, an issue considered in chapters 5 and 7.

GOVERNMENTS AS PARTNERS OF GGOS. Many GGOs have deep connections with the governmental organizations, of course, that formally comprise them. The object of discussion here is obviously something other than this relationship. Like partnerships with NGOs and other international organizations, it is important to take notice of the collaboration of GGOs and nonmember governmental entities.

One type of interaction has already been discussed in previous chapters. Governmental entities—members and nonmembers—are critical elements of most GGOs adherence regimes. Of greatest relevance to this discussion are the entities that play this role but are *not* members of the GGO. Recall the example of port authorities and their role in the adherence regime associated with the International Maritime Organization (IMO). Local port authorities are central actors in enforcing IMO rules pertaining to safety and environmental requirements applicable to oceangoing vessels. The new maritime labor rules created jointly by the International Labor Organization (and IMO) contemplate a similar role for port authorities. Similarly, the WCO could not function without the performance of customs services that do not typically represent the member government in GGO deliberations.

As noted in chapters 6 and 7, GGOs are effectively dependent on these entities, giving them leverage and influence. The International Accounting Standards Board, for example, is not a membership GGO, but as described earlier, the IASB cannot operate without working in conjunction with governmental bodies responsible for oversight of financial markets.

These bodies, with responsibility for the areas in which IASB's rules are applicable are critical to the success of the IASB. Granting influence to bodies like the US SEC makes sense because their participation is crucial to the overall adoption of the IASB's International Financial Reporting Standards.

Another GGO, the Financial Action Task Force on Money Laundering, has gone a step further, formalizing the relationship with governments that have not been invited to join this closed-membership organization. Leaders of the organization realized that the exclusion of these nations limited FATF effectiveness, so a set of institutions were created to draw nonmember governments closer to the organization (interview 48). There are now a series of regional bodies with broad participation. For example, the Eastern and Southern Africa Anti-Money Laundering Group includes fourteen African nations as well as several international bodies, like the African Development Bank and the East African Community (a five-member regional body). The regional bodies provide a formal venue for collaboration—solicitation of input as well as cooperation in promoting adoption and enforcement of FATF rules—that compensates for nonmembership. Other closed-membership GGOs, such as the Basel Committee on Banking Supervision, have created similar structures.

The most unusual partnership between a government and a GGO is surely the relationship between ICANN and the US federal government. As described in earlier chapters, ICANN's function—maintenance of the root servers for the Internet and the Domain Names System—was delegated under terms of agreement with the US Department of Commerce. The American government had the authority to delegate this power by virtue of its leadership in creating the Internet and its physical control of several servers that constituted the Internet's physical backbone. That exclusivity is now diminished, and so when the current agreement expires in September 2009, renewal is by no means certain.

The relationship between the US government and ICANN is a lightning rod for international criticism of the organization. The governmental "partnership" makes the United States in effect the sole member of a nonmembership body. Interestingly, although the argument surrounding the contractual ties between the federal government and ICANN swirls around the issue of accountability, there are two radically different views of what that means for this organization. US critics fear that without the formal linkage, ICANN will not be responsive to their concerns. Pressure from the US Congress (among other constituencies), for example, led ICANN to reverse course in adding the *.xxx* domain name for Internet pornography. To the contrary, international critics of the organization argue that the continued relationship insulates ICANN from accountability to the many interested business and individual users outside the United States.

WORKING WITH FIRMS.   As made clear in the previous chapter, in many fields the most important constituents are not states or interest groups but individual firms. Cooperation with leading private-sector entities can increase the likelihood of rule adoption and strengthen the GGO (Bull et al. 2004). This explains the general integration of firms in the rulemaking process as described in chapter 5. But the desire for industry support may lead to more focused collaboration. Many firms see a potential advantage in having their protocols adopted as international standards. This not only creates an opportunity to earn revenue from licensing fees, it puts competitors at a distinct disadvantage. Sun Microsystems saw this potential and promoted its Java programming language as an ISO standard (McGowan 2000). Despite the vociferous objections of competitors including Microsoft, ISO voted to recognize Sun Microsystem's authorship of the Java standard. Ultimately, however, the company was unwilling to compromise its control over the standard to a level that satisfied ISO (McGowan 2000).

The experience was not a total loss, however, as some eight years later Microsoft adopted the same strategy it once decried. After a lengthy and acrimonious battle, ISO adopted Microsoft's Open Office XML protocol as a standard in the spring of 2008. The decision reversed the outcome of the previous year and is commercially important for Microsoft as government procurement offices often look to the ISO standards (Paul 2008). The most prominent opponent of this outcome was IBM, but others objected to the ratification of one company's product as an ISO standard (Emigh 2008). The entire episode, critics charge, points to flaws in the ISO process and its openness to manipulation by commercial interests (Paul 2007).

From Strategic Cooperation to Partisan Mutual Coordination

In each of the situations described above, the global governance organizations work in concert to reach some shared substantive objective. The entities working with CITES, for example, have a shared goal of reducing trade in endangered species. But there is also a strategic dimension related to the building and maintenance of organizational authority and legitimacy. Organizations build authority through such collaboration by making it more costly for the targets of rules to eschew adherence. In some cases, cooperation results in a more effective enforcement regime. In other situations, cooperation leads to emergence of a single rule rather than a set of alternatives, making nonadherence more problematic. By joining forces, GGOs sometimes avoid competition that could undermine all rulemakers. Strategic cooperation also builds organizational legitimacy. When two GGOs collaborate at the intersection of two substantive spheres, they effectively reaffirm the stature of each other. Or to turn the logic around, exclusion from a partnership sends a damaging signal to those who might adopt a GGO's rules.

Attention to strategic cooperation should not come at the expense of what might be called noninteractive cooperation of GGOs. Competition that might damage both parties seems to be avoided. Although ISO is the most widely recognized standards organization in the world, it has not entered substantive areas that are clearly the province of other GGOs, even market-oriented standards body. The ISO has not only refrained from developing standards at the heart of the IEC and ITU domains, it also has not pursued standards in the arenas of forest or fishery management—nor, for that matter, has ASTM International (ISO's closest rival), even though it might have something to gain with such an incursion.

This is not the result of secret meetings where the standards pie is divided up. It can be likened to the idea of partisan mutual adjustment, Lindblom's insight that people independently choose paths that serve self-interest but provide opportunities for others to do the same (1965). The classic example is the seamless passage of two opposing crowds at a busy crosswalk. The preferred modus operandi of global governance organizations is to stake out spheres of influence that allow multiple entities to thrive. This is preferable to the alternative, universal failure.

Strategic Behavior in the GGO Environment

Taking stock of the organizations mentioned in the previous pages, it becomes clear that many GGOs were introduced as exemplars of cooperation *and* competition. As illustrated in table 8.1, the most surprising observation is that cooperation and competition are tightly linked. Not only are organizations engaged in competition likely to cooperate, they

TABLE 8.1 **Matrix of Competition and Cooperation among GGOs**

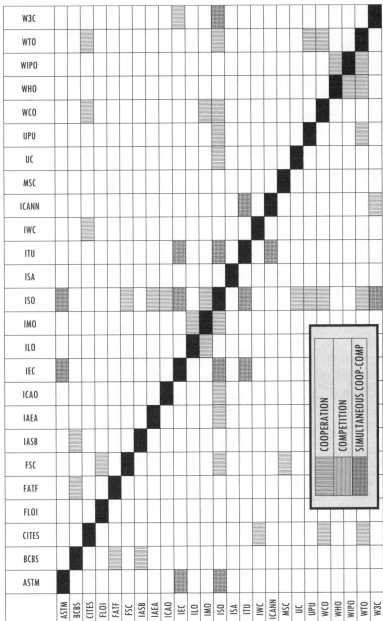

Note: This figure does not capture competition and cooperation with organizations outside this sample. The blue boxes indicate cooperation of two GGOs. Boxes that are half red indicate competition and cooperation. There are no pure red boxes which would indicate competition without cooperation.

are likely to cooperate with the very same entities with which they are competing! This duality reflects the tricky underlying strategic calculus for global governance organizations.

The cooperation-competition phenomenon is most likely in novel issue areas. When several GGOs are making claims to a new jurisdiction, each has strong incentives to cooperate with their competitors. This approach reduces the costs of losing the competition for primacy. Of course, it seems to also reduce the benefits of winning. This reflects an asymmetry in the risks and rewards of competition and cooperation. As GGOs seek to meet legitimacy and authority expectations, they must maximize utility under this condition.

The Conditions of Competition and Cooperation

Although the counterintuitive finding is that the same general conditions are associated with competition and cooperation, they are not perfectly correlated, suggesting that there are distinctive drivers to be identified.

PATTERNS OF COMPETITION. Competition among global governance organizations is most likely when substantive spheres of multiple organizations overlap. The origins of the overlapping jurisdiction vary. In some cases, it is an accident of technological evolution. A collision between the ISO and IEC caused by the digitization of photography provides a nice example. Photography has long been the province of ISO. Indeed, the ISO system of standardized measurement for light sensitivity of photographic film is its most readily identifiable standard (even if most people could not tell you what the ISO in "ISO 400" means). With the transition to digital technology, however, photography has strayed into the terrain of the IEC, the established standard-setter in electronics. Although ISO and the IEC have collaborated in some areas, as described earlier, both entities have produced rules germane to digital photography (e.g., color management).

The second variety of competition arises from geographic overlap. When GGOs offer an alternative to a set of rules produced by an entity with a smaller geographic footprint, a regional organization, bilateral, national, or even subnational body, this type of competition is often unavoidable. Even though many of these organizations participate in the activities of GGOs—one might regard this as a form of hedging—their disposition toward GGOs is likely to be negative. They may offer rules more attuned to the interests of constituencies within their jurisdiction as a tactic to make the GGO regime less (relatively) attractive. Note that new technologies may be *less likely* to produce competition of this sort because there is no historic legacy of local or national regulation.

The third variety of competition is the explicit goal of GGOs created to challenge other rulemaking bodies. "Socially oriented" GGOs encounter this type of competition from two sources: like-minded groups with an alternative emphasis and, more aggressively, from industry-oriented organizations offering a business-friendly alternative set of standards. The emergence of such competition is driven by the dynamics of "pure coordination" versus "battle-of-the-sexes" rulemaking described in previous chapters. Rulemaking in the coordination mode is less contentious because participants see the primary value of a rule—any rule—in terms of harmonization. The substantive terms of the rule are of secondary importance.

In battle-of-the-sexes coordination, the attractiveness of the rule is conditioned upon the content of the rule. This is certainly the case with respect to the socially oriented nonstate market-driven GGOs. The Forest Stewardship Council, for example, was created to promote a standard of conservation through its rules. The creation of standards for forest management and harvesting of timber that do *not* point toward this goal is not attractive in the least for those who believe in the mission. Coordination-oriented rulemaking is less likely to yield competition than the battle-of-the-sexes rulemaking commonly associated with nonstate market-driven GGOs.

PATTERNS OF COOPERATION. The substantive nature of the GGOs' activities is the clearest driver of GGO cooperation. One variety of cooperation emerges when the scope of a particular activity spans the jurisdictions of established GGOs. A second type of cooperation is observed when the subject matter is novel and thus multiple GGOs make claims of dominion in the area. Cooperation of this second type is linked with GGO competition.

Coordination in the face of jurisdictional transcendence is easy to explain as a functional solution to practical problems. Almost every GGO touches upon issues related to the work of other global governance organizations. Trade in goods and commodities ropes in a collection of organizations included in this study: the World Trade Organization (WTO), the World Customs Organizations (WCO), the International Civil Aviation

Organization (ICAO), the International Maritime Organization (IMO), the Convention on Trade in Endangered Species (CITES), and others.

Cooperation among these GGOs (and with other organizations not included in this study) is not surprising. The WTO ought to work with the WCO on development of standardized treatment of imports and exports. And both the WTO and the WCO ought to be connected to CITES, the GGO focused on the import and export of endangered species. And all three GGOs would be expected to interact with the IMO and ICAO, the GGOs responsible for setting rules regarding global sea and air transport, respectively, of the goods and commodities of interest. And CITES naturally interacts with the International Whaling Commission (IWC), a body dedicated to the management of one endangered species.

The intrinsic logic of such coordination in the face of transcendent issues should not lead one to conclude that this cooperation is frictionless. Each GGO has its own priorities; their approaches to rulemaking and adherence vary (as documented in chaps. 5 and 6). Integration of rulemaking activities appears to be more challenging than coordinated adherence efforts. That is why such cooperation is relatively rare. The joint efforts of the ILO and IMO to craft the International Maritime Labour Convention are extraordinary, for example. It required both organizations to determine areas of overlap in their rules and commit to a new agreement that would resolve conflicts. And it is interesting to note that the resulting treaty is nowhere near entering force. The Joint Technical Committee organized by ISO and the IEC is the most institutionalized cooperation among GGOs.

The difficulties notwithstanding, cooperation in the face of boundary-spanning activities is easier than cooperation driven by contested claims to novel issue areas. Indeed, conflicts regarding the appropriate authority of multiple GGOs in a single arena lead one to expect *competition*. So the fact that the very condition identified just a few pages earlier as a predictor of competition is here named a predictor of *cooperation* introduces a conundrum.

THE STRATEGIC CALCULUS OF GGO COOPERATION / COMPETITION. GGOs cooperating with their competitors can reduce the costs of losing the competition for primacy in a new rulemaking space. Of course, cooperation also reduces the benefits of winning. Simultaneous cooperation and competition makes sense when the risks and rewards of competition and cooperation are asymmetric. Referring to Brandenberg and Nalebuff's insight that competing businesses often benefit from cooperation, Esty

TABLE 8.2 **Payoffs of Cooperate and Compete GGO Strategies**

		Likelihood of Payoff by GGO Strategy	
Outcome	Payoff	Cooperate	Compete
Prevail	7	0	0.25
Share	4	1	0.5
Lose	0	0	0.25
Expected Payoff:		4	3.75

and Geradin refer to this approach as "Regulatory Co-opetition" (Esty and Geradin 2001).

The rewards of achieving primacy in a new area are considerable, but the achievement of this goal is improbable relative to some sharing of authority. Moreover, the costs of total defeat—a competing GGO achieves primacy—are quite high. GGO dominance in one area not only encourages adherence in that domain, it creates an incentive for adoption of complementary rules in other areas. Thus a total loss in one arena (although improbable) can spill over negatively into other areas (Brandenburger and Nalebuff 1996, 254–256).

Cooperation, by offering a very high probability outcome of shared authority while reducing the likelihood of total victory, is relatively attractive. Shared authority is the most likely outcome under pure competition anyway but simultaneous cooperation offers the "upside" and lowers the costliness of the "downside." The logic of this approach is illustrated with a simple matrix showing how asymmetric payoffs lead to differential valuation for the two strategies.

Organizations are likely to cheat toward the compete strategy in the hopes of securing the higher payoff associated with total prevalence. So elements of competition will persist, particularly if there is an imbalance between partners. The weaker partner will be wary of "too much" cooperation because with it the distinctiveness of their rules evaporates and the attractiveness of the stronger GGO only increases. The stronger partner will always see the opportunity to create an overwhelming advantage.

There are limits to the logic of concomitant cooperation and competition. When the competition is rooted in the GGO's appeal to different constituencies, organizations will not cooperate. Doing so would be contrary to the rationale for each entity's existence. Battling standards organizations representing social interests versus industry will not cooperate, for example (Fransen 2008b). This logic extends to GGOs competing by crafting rules that serve different *geographic* constituencies. Coordination in that circumstance is contrary to the basis of the competition.

The Significance of Simultaneous Competition and Cooperation

The stability of a network structure featuring simultaneous competition and cooperation provides a powerful indicator of the high value of network embeddedness for GGOs. The advantages of cooperation among global governance organizations extend beyond logistics. The association with other GGOs provides a source of legitimacy and authority for all global governance organizations involved, linking this phenomenon with the core argument of this book.

There is a prima facie case for cooperation and the credibility it creates. It would be nonsensical for the group of organizations crafting rules related to the Internet (e.g., W3C, UC, ICANN, ISO, IEC) to operate without, at a bare minimum, reference to each others' efforts. More coordination among these entities makes the production of a coherent set of rules more likely. And this is not merely an aesthetic achievement. More coherent rules are more likely to engender adherence. The connections among GGOs—and the consequent benefits in terms of rule quality— yield significant secondary and tertiary effects. Greater adoption of rules and more meaningful adherence begins a cascade; more adoption begets more adoption. The pressure for a self-interested actor to adhere grows with each step toward universality; the discretionary quality of adherence fades.

Put in terms of the theory of global governance proposed at the outset of this book, the key differentiating characteristic of global governance organizations—governmental and nongovernmental— is their lack of coercive tools to compel adherence. The potential rule follower must calculate that adoption (and / or adherence) serves its self-interest. In the absence of such a conclusion, one made more likely by more widespread adoption, all GGOs will struggle to build authority. GGO coordination enhances GGO authority.

Network embeddedness also enhances a GGO's ability to leverage the legitimacy of every other GGO. The WTO provides the most dramatic illustration of the attractiveness of association with a highly legitimate GGO. As noted previously, several WTO agreements and rules make reference to international standards as key elements in the adjudication of disputes. This provides a powerful incentive for adherence to a GGO's rules. But in most instances the WTO does not single out any GGO. Rather, it has established the requirements for a GGO that can be regarded as a bona fide standard-setter. Clearing this bar enhances the authority of the GGO and, just as critically, transfers some of the WTO's legitimacy to it. So it is hardly surprising that several GGOs emphasize their acceptance by the WTO.

A Case of Concomitant Cooperation and Competition

Of the organizations included in this study, the ISO and ASTM are two of the most direct competitors, although neither organization would *ever* publicly describe themselves this way. And there is good reason why this description seems peculiar. ASTM is, in a sense, a member of the ISO. ASTM is a member of the American National Standards Institute (ANSI), the body recognized as the American national member of ISO. ASTM participates in ISO meetings; its members are active in ISO technical committees and working groups. For ASTM to eschew ISO would be suicidal; ISO is the leading industrial standard-setting entity in the world. But ASTM actively challenges that dominance in certain substantive areas, safety standards, for example. ASTM standards are universally recognized in this area with greater adoption than ISO rules. And as a competitive strategy, ASTM is promoting its standards in markets that ISO has not yet penetrated deeply, most notably, China.

Encouraging adoption of its standards in China represents a global strategy, not just a regional one. There are two objectives in promoting use of ASTM standards in China. First, of course, China is an enormous market and thus offers a significant economic return. Like other standard-setters, ASTM derives revenue from the sale of its standards, so the prospects of potential sales in China are quite a lure. Second, the global attractiveness of ASTM standards increases exponentially if they emerge as dominant in China. Companies wishing to sell and buy in China will be favorably inclined toward ASTM standards because the costs of adaptation to the market will be much lower. They will, in turn, encourage the use of ASTM standards in *other* markets, looking for a competitive edge.

Still, ASTM is not in a position to offer alternatives to every ISO standard, and logic suggests that attempting to do so would be silly. Companies that participate in and effectively finance the standard-setting process are unlikely to support such duplication, but this alone is not enough to deter competition. Challenging deeply entrenched standards is a losing proposition. Failure is likely and, more important, the self-inflicted damage of failure is significant. Producing a standard that is not used is far worse than producing no standard at all. It is an indication of irrelevance, and the cost is measured in lost credibility and undermined authority. Thus, acceding to ISO dominance is sensible even though it reifies the authority of ASTM's competitor.

Beneficiaries of GGO Cooperation / Competition

Other actors in the global governance context benefit from the competition / cooperation dynamic. With integration, rules produced by multiple GGOs are more likely to be complementary. Thus, participants are less likely to encounter situations where one organization's rules require violation of another's. There are also strategic opportunities associated with GGO competition.

PLAYING GGOS AGAINST EACH OTHER. Competition amplifies the most powerful force working upon GGOs: the pressure to satisfy rule *users*. In areas of intense competition, the nations, interest groups, and firms with an interest in GGO rules have that much more leverage. Essentially, competition promotes *responsiveness*-type accountability. Again, the commonplace critique that regulatory competition results in a race to the bottom is overly reductionist. It assumes all firms have an interest in—and are thus drawn to—lax regulation. This is not always the case; many companies (and even countries) might prefer a more stringent regulatory regime, not for benevolent reasons but because such an environment would provide comparative advantages. This is certainly the case in the realm of global governance.

Competition among GGOs also offers potential rule takers a hedging strategy analogous to the competition / cooperation approach used by some global governance organizations. Joining competing GGOs provides nations with the opportunity to play two strategies simultaneously. Consider the following situation.

Nation Q confronts two GGOs operating in the same substantive sphere, GGO Alpha and GGO Beta. Alpha is the entrenched incumbent. It is dominated by members regarded by Nation Q as hostile to its own interests. GGO Beta is challenging the dominance of Alpha. Beta does not enjoy nearly the same level of acceptance as the established GGO, but its door is open for nation Q to exert its influence. Because Alpha and

Beta must cooperate even as they compete, nation Q can play two strategies at once, attempting to gain influence in GGO Alpha while lending enhanced legitimacy and authority to GGO Beta by participating in its rulemaking.

China is following precisely this course. Chinese firms have become increasingly active in ISO even as it has chafed at the dominance of European (and, to a lesser extent, American) firms in its rulemaking. The secretariats of several technical committees are now located in China, and Chinese participation in working groups has gone from exceptional to typical in a short time. At the same time, ASTM's China strategy has been encouraged by the government. Just as ASTM has a strong incentive to cater to Chinese preferences, Chinese industry (which is, of course, tightly woven in with the state) is keenly interested in seeing ASTM emerge as a global rival to ISO. Chinese influence in ISO is on the rise but it is even greater in ASTM. By building up the threat that ASTM poses to the ISO, China creates a powerful incentive for ISO to grant more influence to the Chinese as a means of dulling their interest in the ASTM.

Conclusion

This preliminary analysis of the dynamics of competition and cooperation in global governance suggests that the substantive matter of rules and the nature of the rulemaking organization are the prime drivers of observed variation. When two established (typically governmental) GGOs confront novel issues that transcend established jurisdictions, there is a high probability of "co-opetition," cooperation even as competition for primacy continues. This observation might be seen as an extension of the analysis of the demand for international regimes (Keohane 1983). In the face of different alignments of interests, the networks of global regulatory entities look different.

Mixed or nongovernmental hybrids—even those that are well established—are more likely to engage in concomitant competition and cooperation than intergovernmental GGOs. This is a function of these organizations' revenue model and their need to maintain the value of rule adherence across issues areas. Global regulatory co-opetition is a hedging strategy, minimizing the risk to the health of the GGO although reducing the likelihood of complete market dominance. In this way, global governance organizations maintain their legitimacy and authority.

Competition without cooperation is observed when GGOs face com-petition on the basis of an ideological or policy-driven divide (Murphy 2004). This typically observed with respect to the nonstate market-driven entities like the Forest Stewardship Council that seek to impose require-ments on a resistant industry. Those industries are likely to sponsor their own rulemaking bodies to offer an alternative and dull the authority of the socially motivated GGO (Cashore et al. 2004). In these situations, coordi-nation by the rulemakers would actually undermine organizational legiti-macy because it would contradict the rationale for the GGO's existence.

The dynamics of competition and cooperation put an additional burden on GGO leaders who must calculate the consequences of their organiza-tions' actions in absolute and relative terms. Other strategic actors—firms and countries—can take advantage of this constraint to gain influence. This may heighten the risk of capture in the global governance context as rulemakers seek to win the patronage the very communities they seek to regulate.

CHAPTER NINE

Conclusion: Models of Global Governance and Accountability

Accountability has become a catchall for everything good in governance and administration. One can never have too much accountability. No one will ever be criticized for excessive emphasis on accountability. Democrats and Republicans, conservatives and liberals, Big-Endians and Little-Endians, all can agree that accountability is worthy of attention and pursuit. But all this bonhomie masks critical disagreement. The meaning of accountability varies with the values of the person using the word and the context in which it is being applied. This claim is central to the explanation offered in this book for the accountability shortcomings of global governance organizations.

The core argument is that the demands of accountability, particularly responsibility and responsiveness, are sometimes incompatible. The empirical observations demonstrate that GGOs attempt to manage this tension across four areas of organizational design—structure, rulemaking, adherence, and interest group participation. But unmet expectations are still inevitable, manifested as charges of unaccountable and undemocratic governance (Kahler 2004). This observation begs the question: do global governance organizations favor one notion of accountability over another? Is there a coherent explanation for the accountability tendencies of GGOs? The answers tie directly into debates between students of realism and liberalism. The former camp asserts that international organizations are designed to institutionalize existing power disparities. In the terms of the argument offered in this book, *responsiveness*-type accountability, focused on key players, inevitably prevails. The liberal institutionalist claims that viable global governance organizations must meet legitimacy expectations, making *responsibility*-type accountability of paramount importance for sustainable international organizations. Both views are right . . . in some cases . . . some of the time. How do we account for the variation?

This question is addressed in three steps. First, the "types" defined in the four areas of organizational design are reviewed and then, mimicking the latent class analysis of key attributes used to define those profiles, three GGO models are identified: *classical* GGOs, *cartel* GGOs, and *symbiotic* GGOs. By virtue of their construction, *classical* GGOs emphasize *responsibility*-type accountability. They have a *traditional* structure and *forum*-type rulemaking, meaning that their practices conform to expectations imported from the domestic governance context. The two other models, *cartel* and *symbiotic* GGOs, lean toward *responsiveness*-type accountability, albeit with radically different approaches. *Cartel* GGOs eschew normative requirements and maintain authority by satisfying the needs of their limited membership. *Symbiotic* GGOs do not possess the coercive tools of the *cartel* GGOs but they emphasize *responsiveness*-type accountability through hybrid structure and participatory rulemaking process, which guarantee satisfaction of key interested parties.

The second section examines the distribution of GGOs across these three types. SECTOR is the most potent predictor of GGO model, but this pattern does not capture more fundamental variation. It is argued that the salience of legitimacy (responsibility) and authority (responsiveness) varies not as a function of organizational sector, but rather as a function of the publicness and constrictiveness, respectively, of the GGO's function. This innovative account helps explain an apparent mismatch. Organizations that one might expect to emphasize legitimacy do not because SECTOR is guiding GGO design, with unintended consequences. While intergovernmental organizations are lambasted for their accountability failures, other entities performing similar tasks are held to less exacting legitimacy standards. Nongovernmental GGOs can emphasize authority over legitimacy, notwithstanding their high levels of publicness. They can be more responsive, building authority and bolstering their constrictiveness. Critics of *classical* GGOs unintentionally push highly public rulemaking to *symbiotic* GGOs that avoid the most onerous legitimacy demands and grow more powerful. This is an ironic and important finding. The push for accountability in global governance may result in a net loss of (*responsibility-*type) accountability.

The final section considers the implications of this study. The findings and observations presented herein complement many existing studies of international organizations, particularly constructivist accounts, and offers an explanation for the structure and processes of GGOs that looks beyond the power of nation-states (Drezner 2007). With an understanding of these dynamics, seemingly paradoxical relationships between structure, rulemaking, and adherence start to make sense. For students of administration, this analysis provides insight into the sources of structure and process by linking organizational design to the underlying demands of legitimacy. Global governance organizations, governmental and nongovernmental, must fall within the scope of research on organizations pursuing public goods. Global governance organizations are a class of entities that transcend conventional dividing lines and, in doing so, offer insight into the implications of features we typically take for granted.

Models of Global Governance

Bringing together the analysis of structure, rulemaking, adherence, and interest group participation, this section mirrors the consideration of organizational profiles in each empirical chapter. Three general GGO models are identified—*classical* GGOs, *cartel* GGOs, and *symbiotic* GGOs—using cluster analysis of the "types" identified in chapters 4–7. Before turning to the cluster analysis, the structure, rulemaking, adherence, and interest group participation "types" are briefly reviewed.

Structure and Administration: Traditional and Hybrid GGOs

The examination of structure in chapter 4 looked at the political and administrative aspects of the organization. It turned out that characteristics on both dimensions are related to each other. Thus the two GGO structure types accommodated differential approaches to representation and bureaucracy.

Traditional GGOs feature conciliar representational structure: a representative body with all members participating in annual or biannual meetings. A subset of this group convenes more regularly in "intermediate bodies" that are more engaged in the day-to-day operations of the organization, oftentimes including rulemaking. At each level, members have equal voting weight, but the key members are guaranteed representation on the intermediate bodies, ensuring greater influence within the organizations. The *traditional* GGO model bears resemblance to a typical domestic government arrangement and has an equally familiar bureaucratic component. The *traditional* GGO tends to be centralized and functional. The role of the bureaucracy is differentiated from the *hybrid* GGO in which the permanent staff often plays a supporting role to members that are prime actors in the rulemaking process.

The *hybrid* GGO model is associated with specialized representation (i.e., entities join the GGO through intermediate bodies defined by their interests) or nonrepresentative arrangements (i.e., the organization is governed by individuals who do not represent member nations, firms, or groups). These arrangements emphasize interests more than nation-states, although geography almost always enters the representation equation. *Hybrid* GGOs often keep rulemaking in the members' hands through working groups or technical committees, giving the bureaucracy a facilitative role. This requires a somewhat less centralized approach to administration as rules are manufactured on a global scale. Naturally members—and the interested parties that are integrated into the rulemaking process—retain a great deal of influence over the organization, thus the functional bureaucracy of the *traditional* GGO is generally more influential.

Given the heightened legitimacy expectations facing governmental GGOs, it makes sense that they typically adopt the *traditional* model, which better satisfies democratic expectations and reinforces Westphalian sovereignty (Krasner 1999). But several nongovernmental organizations are also found in the *traditional* cluster. Given that such GGOs seemingly have greater structural latitude, this observation suggests that legitimacy expectations are not driven solely by SECTOR. Underscoring this point, many nongovernmental GGOs can and do adopt the *hybrid* GGO model, suggesting that normative legitimacy is not as great a concern for them. They build authority by satisfying members' preferences, making a traditional structure a potential encumbrance rather than an asset.

Hybrid GGOs do not have the structural safety valves associated with the *traditional* GGO type. Recall that the democratic structures are balanced by mechanisms—like the skewed representation on intermediate bodies—put in place to avert disaster (Rosendorff and Milner 2001). Structural insurance is less important for *hybrid* GGOs because safety valves are incorporated elsewhere, including the rulemaking process associated with this type.

Rulemaking: Forum and Club Rulemaking

Approaches to rulemaking do not divide as neatly as the variations in structure. Much of what defines each GGO's approach to rulemaking is informal; thus, any picture derived from written procedures must be interpreted through a lens incorporating qualitative data. Two general rulemaking types were identified, *forum* GGOs and *club* GGOs. As with structure, one approach, *forum*-type rulemaking, bears a stronger resemblance to Western domestic models. This process is highly structured with binding formal requirements creating clear opportunities for members to influence the process. The rulemaking process is more permeable for nonmembers compared with *club* GGOs, as norms of transparency and accessibility seem have been integrated in line with normative expectations applied to governmental organizations.

The *forum* model of rulemaking often allows for decisionmaking by supermajority, but this belies practice, which emphasizes consensus (discussed at length in chap. 5). Consensus is normatively highly valued; it is typically seen as a marker of legitimacy (Hurd 2008). But it also provides a mammoth safety valve. Consensus does not require unanimity and it is clear that all members' objections do not undermine consensus equally. The ambiguity of "consensus" endows key parties with greater power to bring rulemaking to a grinding halt.

The *club* approach to rulemaking is more exclusive although the difference is not as dramatic as it might appear. *Club* GGOs are more likely to have closed membership, creating greater confidence among members that their peers will not pursue disagreeable outcomes. This makes a more informal rulemaking process less threatening. Although these organizations are less permeable, the membership of some *club* GGOs spans multiple constituencies, making the member / nonmember distinction less informative than it is when applied to intergovernmental GGOs. *Club* GGOs generally make decisions by consensus to maintain harmony among members and provide the same leeway described above.

The association between rulemaking and structure is less robust than expected. *Traditional* GGOs are associated with *forum* rulemaking but the *hybrid* GGO structure is not a strong predictor of rulemaking type. This observation is suggestive of the complexity in weaving together normatively desirable features with requisite safety valves in a fashion that accommodates the needs of each GGO. One safeguard that offers great insight is the control over membership, mentioned in multiple chapters. By being selective, members can be confident in the fundamental alignment of interests and relax the need for safety valves.

One curiosity is the distribution of standard-generating GGOs, which are sometimes found in the *Forum* category despite similarities to *Club GGOs*. GGOs promulgating standards tend to put rulemaking responsibilities in the hands of members (or, when the members are national bodies, in the hands of firms from those members' jurisdictions). The accessibility of these rulemaking working groups varies, so these GGOs end up coded differently even though this may understate the importance of member participation in rulemaking.

Adherence: Conventional and Composite Approaches

The problems of adherence truly distinguish global governance organizations as a class of entities. All the GGOs considered face a remarkably similar set of constraints in implementing their rules. Indeed, the central finding from the adherence chapter is that GGO sector is not an overwhelming predictor of adherence type. Most GGOs do not have the ability to "enforce" anything, as the word is commonly used, making it difficult to compel adherence. GGOs rely upon their agents—very often the members of the organization—to adopt and implement rules. These agents often delegate adherence responsibility themselves. As a result, GGO adherence presents a nested principal-agent problem. The elements examined to differentiate adherence regimes are the sector of primary agent, the tools available to the GGO to motivate this agent, and the tools available to compel adherence from the ultimate rule target. This sample of GGOs is sorted into two types that reflect the toolsets used to compel adherence: *conventional* GGOs and *composite* GGOs.

Conventional GGOs, as the name suggests, rely more on tools that are typically associated with regulation. The dominant adherence agents are likely to be governmental, the GGOs rely on formal (but weak) hierarchical sanctions to compel these agents to act ("primary adherence mechanism"), and the ultimate target of the rules are more likely to face legal sanctions, including fines or other penalties as the "secondary adherence mechanism." In some cases, the adherence agent might use nonstate sanctions, such as denial of privileges (e.g., access to a resource) or ineligibility for transactions with compliant parties. These can be wielded by nonstate agents as well.

Composite GGOs are associated with adherence strategies that integrate market adherence agents that do not formally engage subjects but "sanction" them with business decisions. Typically, this means customers or potential partners penalize noncompliant parties by taking their business elsewhere. Market-based adherence strategies are often paired with some engagement tools, making the distinction between the two adherence types less dichotomous than those offered in structure and rulemaking. Some publicity regarding the status of the noncompliant entity facilitates the "penalty," for example. The adherence agent may even require the removal of a mark that signals to the market that an organization is complying with GGO rules.

Variation in the sector of the primary agents associated with *composite* GGOs may come as a surprise. Even when GGOs delegate adherence responsibilities to member governments, there is a good chance that adherence will ultimately be compelled by market mechanisms. This is because those governments often establish a market-based adherence system domestically. Moreover, the tools by which a GGO's agent is motivated, referred to as the primary adherence mechanism, vary within GGOs from the same sector. Governments are often more motivated to act as an effective adherence agent by the market consequences of not doing so than any fear of GGO sanctions.

Interest Group Participation: Corporatism, Pluralism, and Global Concertation

The relationship between interest groups and GGOs is distinctive, combining elements of the two dominant understandings of interests in politics. In some cases, the GGO-interest relationship bears a resemblance to *corporatism* with firms tightly integrated into the fabric of the GGO. Unlike classic corporatism, however, there are seldom powerful "peak associations" or other formal organizations speaking for an industry as a whole. The contest of interests happens internally at the GGO. This jostling conjures the image of *pluralism*, which features competition among interested parties as part of the policymaking process. But in only a few cases is the dynamic pluralistic in the mode of classic democratic theory. The limitations on participation, doors that are (practically speaking) more open to industry than to the general public, make the pluralism label an awkward fit.

The notion of *global concertation* is offered to cover the preponderance of GGOs. This model sees interested parties drawn into the organization, particularly through the rulemaking process. Commercial interests have an advantage inasmuch as they have superior resources and access at their disposal. And, most important, the GGO has a deep need to promulgate rules that are acceptable to concerned interests. Without their adherence, the organizations collapse. Conflict regarding this dynamic is increasingly common as socially oriented groups come to understand the importance of GGOs and seek greater influence.

The most novel aspect of the *global concertation* model is that it places the GGO in direct competition with interest groups. The GGO performs a role associated with organized trade groups, an aggregator of member preferences. By internalizing the back-and-forth among companies and national delegations, the GGO effectively cuts the legs out from under transnational interest groups. This helps explain the relative weakness of such groups. The diversity of global interests, even within a single industry, is another formidable impediment.

Putting It All Together: Three Models of Global Governance

Before introducing overall models of global governance, a word of caution is necessary. Aggregating GGO types from the four areas compounds the oversimplification and abstraction required to capture twenty-five very different organizations with one research instrument. Moreover, the definition of GGO clusters is probabilistic, as discussed in the previous chapters, meaning the inclusion of an organization in one type or another represents only a single draw from a distribution. The nested clustering of GGO types embedded in this analysis compounds the inherent uncertainty of characterizing any single organization.

Utilizing the types developed in the four areas, three overarching GGO models, *classical* GGOs, *cartel* GGOs, and *symbiotic* GGOs are defined. The results of the latent class analysis are reported in table 9.1. Cell entries report the likelihood that an organization in a given cluster will be of that model. The highlighted cells indicate characteristics that are strongly associated with a cluster.

The first column of table 9.1 offers a profile of *classical* GGOs. Cells with single outline indicate the predominant types associated with this GGO model. In addition to displaying *traditional* structural characteristics (conciliar representation, centralized bureaucracy), *classical* GGOs

TABLE 9.1 **Models of Global Governance (Three-Cluster Model)**

	Classical (percent)	Cartel (percent)	Symbiotic (percent)
Cluster Size	37	13	50
Structure:			
Traditional	99	37	46
Hybrid	1	63	54
Rulemaking:			
Forum	97	12	69
Club	3	88	31
Adherence			
Composite	14	40	99
Conventional	86	60	1
Interest Model			
Concertation	26	10	98
Corporatism	53	89	2
Pluralism	21	1	0

are associated with the *forum*-style rulemaking process (formalized and self-contained), and *conventional*-type adherence (hierarchical and formally coercive). As the results indicate, this type is not strongly associated with one interest group alignment although *corporatist* alignment is most likely. Within the *classical* GGO group are many of the most venerable and well-known international organizations, including the WHO, IAEA, ILO, UPU, and most governmental GGOs.

The two other GGO types deviate from the *classical* type in important ways. The *cartel* GGO is defined in the second column of table 9.1. The cells marked with double lines indicate the types strongly associated with this model. The *cartel* GGO is associated with *hybrid* structure (nonconciliar and distributed), *club* rulemaking (informal and consensus-driven among closed membership), *conventional* adherence, and *corporatist* model of interest group participation. This is a small cluster that includes only three of the twenty-five organizations, the WTO, BCBS, and FATF, three of the most influential and controversial GGOs. Their rules are widely adopted and implemented with force (including state sanctions as suggested by the *conventional* adherence type), notwithstanding their closed membership and other features that push away from legitimacy expectations (*hybrid* structure and *club* rulemaking). Clearly, the formidable authority of *cartel* GGOs is *not* a product of heightened legitimacy.

The third model is the most populous category, *symbiotic* GGOs. This model is defined in the third column of table 9.1 with the predominant associated types highlighted with dashed lines. These GGOs see structural variation but generally feature *forum* rulemaking, *composite* adherence (with market mechanisms likely playing a significant role) and the distinctive *Concertation* alignment of interest groups. This type is labeled *symbiotic* GGO because the model describes a GGO that derives authority from the participation of a variety of interests, each guaranteed the utility they derive from the rulemaking regime through their direct participation and deference to the market realities shaping the policy arena. As one would expect based on this profile, many of the younger rulemaking bodies currently in the headlines, including the IASB, ISO, ICANN, and the FSC, are in the *symbiotic* GGO cluster.

These three GGO models represent different ways to reconcile the competing imperatives of legitimacy and authority (table 9.2). *Classical* GGOs adopt an organizational structure that hews very close to normative expectations imported from the domestic context. Representation on the basis of geography, with each member assigned an equal vote, is familiar and accepted as legitimate. There are safety valves built into the architecture to assuage concerns of more powerful nations that the organization might produce undesirable outcomes, and additional protection comes through the rulemaking process. Key actors, confident in their ability to waylay an undesirable rule, are willing to cede authority to the GGO. Note that the design of GGOs does not provide the ability to push through a rule over any and all objections. The construction of *classical* GGOs is about negative control, the ability to stop rulemaking that could result in an outcome worse than the status quo. A final bulwark against the imposition of undesirable rules lies in adherence. The *conventional* approach to adherence, associated with *classical* GGOs, provides tremendous leeway to member nations by virtue of weak primary adherence mechanisms and reservation clauses.

TABLE 9.2 **Three Models of Global Governance**

	Structure Type	Rulemaking Type	Adherence Type	Interest participation Type
Classical GGO	Traditional	Forum	Conventional	*
Cartel GGO	Hybrid	Club	Conventional	Corporatism
Symbiotic GGO	*	Forum	Composite	Concertation

* Indicates that there is no dominant type for this cluster. See table 9.1.

The *cartel* and *symbiotic* GGO models represent alternative solutions to the global accountability challenge. Both build authority at the expense of legitimacy but do so in different ways. The *cartel* label is intended to capture the exclusive nature of such organizations. Membership is limited to nations (all three are governmental) that are approved by existing members. The Basel Committee and Financial Action Task Force both have less than forty members. Despite normatively displeasing attributes, the authority of these organizations is unquestionable. It is derived from the unique sanctioning authority associated with the rules produced by these organizations. The *market* consequences of failure to adhere to these organizations' rules are significant. States adopt and implement the rules, putting the force of their governmental tools behind them, rather than risk disadvantage in the global marketplace. Leaders of *symbiotic* GGOs would surely like to wield the same cudgel, but they lack the coercive advantages of *cartel* GGOs.

On the other hand, *symbiotic* GGOs are less constrained on the structural dimension. With no obligation to funnel participation through member states, the mostly nongovernmental *symbiotic* GGOs are freer to build participation around interested constituencies. This approach emphasizes *responsiveness*-type accountability in the structural arena in a way that is not tenable for organizations in the *classical* GGO mode. Most important, interested parties are guaranteed seats at the table—the rulemaking table in particular—through the bottom-up representational schemes and open approach to working group membership. These are the hallmarks of the *concertation* model of interest group participation.

Symbiotic GGOs can accommodate a rulemaking process that is more permeable (at least to knowledgeable and well-funded constituencies). This is not to suggest that the rulemaking process is as accessible as all parties might want. As the profile and mission of *symbiotic* GGOs evolve and expand, the pressure to accommodate a wider range of participants is likely to grow, putting pressure on this model of global governance. The alignment of *composite*-type adherence regimes with the other features of the *symbiotic* model reflects the core goal of building a governance machine that serves the needs of constituents. If industry or consumer interests do not see a global rule serving their purposes, the rule will likely have little impact. *Composite*-type adherence often also involves rule adoption and implementation by governments, as discussed in chapter 6. So it should not be inferred that *symbiotic* GGOs ignore states. The IASB is an

GGO	Structure	Rulemaking	Adherence	Interest Model	GGO Type	clu#1	clu#2	clu#3
ASTM	Hybrid	Forum	Composite	Concertation	Symbiotic	0.996866	0.0009509	0.002183
BCBS	Hybrid	Club	Conventional	Corporatism	Cartel	0.0006806	0.0017013	0.997618
CITES	Traditional	Forum	Conventional	Pluralism	Classical	7.42E-05	0.99949	0.000436
FATF	Traditional	Club	Conventional	Corporatism	Cartel	0.000816	0.179099	0.820085
FLOI	Traditional	Club	Composite	Concertation	Symbiotic	0.970427	0.0055515	0.023921
FSC	Traditional	Forum	Composite	Concertation	Symbiotic	0.921436	0.0771801	0.001384
IAEA	Traditional	Forum	Conventional	Corporatism	Classical	0.0003107	0.98669	0.01902
IASB	Hybrid	Forum	Composite	Concertation	Symbiotic	0.996866	0.0009509	0.002183
ICANN	Traditional	Forum	Conventional	Concertation	Classical	0.0286844	0.66915	0.0044
ICAO	Traditional	Forum	Composite	Corporatism	Classical	0.1059	0.830633	0.063468
IEC	Hybrid	Forum	Composite	Concertation	Symbiotic	0.996866	0.0009509	0.002183
ILO	Traditional	Forum	Conventional	Concertation	Classical	0.0286844	0.66915	0.0044
IMO	Traditional	Forum	Composite	Concertation	Symbiotic	0.921436	0.0771801	0.001384
ISA	Traditional	Forum	Conventional	Corporatism	Classical	0.0003107	0.98669	0.01902
ISO	Hybrid	Forum	Composite	Concertation	Symbiotic	0.996866	0.0009509	0.002183
ITU	Hybrid	Club	Composite	Concertation	Symbiotic	0.965234	6.40E-05	0.034702
IWC	Traditional	Forum	Conventional	Pluralism	Classical	7.42E-05	0.99949	0.000436
MSC	Traditional	Club	Composite	Concertation	Symbiotic	0.970427	0.0055515	0.023921
UC	Hybrid	Forum	Composite	Concertation	Symbiotic	0.996866	0.0009509	0.002183
UPU	Traditional	Forum	Conventional	Corporatism	Classical	0.0003107	0.98669	0.01902
W3C	Hybrid	Club	Composite	Concertation	Symbiotic	0.965234	6.40E-05	0.034702
WCO	Traditional	Forum	Conventional	Corporatism	Classical	0.0003107	0.98669	0.01902
WHO	Traditional	Forum	Composite	Concertation	Symbiotic	0.921436	0.0771801	0.001384
WIPO	Traditional	Forum	Composite	Concertation	Symbiotic	0.921436	0.0771801	0.001384
WTO	Hybrid	Club	Composite	Corporatism	Cartel	0.0651272	0.0004045	0.934468

exemplar. Recognition of International Financial Regulatory Standards by governmental regulators gives them force. Thus it is not surprising that the IASB offers great deference to securities regulators and other accounting bodies from key nations.

The Distribution of Model Types and the Nature of Global Governance

The three models define alternative approaches to the reconciliation of potentially incompatible legitimacy and authority expectations. It is not suggested that one is preferable to the others. The *classical* model places a premium on *responsibility*-type accountability, particularly in its organizational structure and formalized rulemaking procedures, to satisfy legitimacy demands imported from the domestic context of democratic member countries. *Cartel* and *symbiotic* GGOs display features that emphasize responsiveness, allowing these organizations to meet the demands of authority by keeping interested parties satisfied. *Cartel* GGOs do so by restricting membership and keeping decisionmaking power in a limited set of hands. *Symbiotic* GGOs do so by integrating constituencies into the rulemaking process and relying on market forces to prompt and enforce bargains.

In this section, the distribution of GGOs across these three models is explored. Readers may have noted that several GGO characteristics proved powerful predictors of features and type across areas. In particular, GGO SECTOR and TECHNICALITY are seldom far from the top of the list of predictive characteristics. And, as one would expect, these are potent predictors of GGO model. SECTOR is the core characteristic with the most predictive power for GGO type. It is posited, however, that GGOs are sometimes mismatched with their model on this basis; certain areas are entrusted to responsibility-centric GGOs while others are the province of responsiveness-driven GGOs. But does this one characteristic, SECTOR, accurately explain our concern with legitimacy and our wariness of authority? How, then, can we explain the varying salience of legitimacy and authority for governmental and nongovernmental organizations? We don't worry much about the legitimacy of the sanitation department or the neighborhood supermarket, for example. And the question of whether the Post Office or Junior League wields inordinate authority does not keep anyone awake at night. There is something deeper than "governmentalness" at work. Understanding the varying salience of legitimacy and authority allows us to evaluate the accountability solutions adopted by GGOs. Each organization's publicness and constrictiveness is the key.

Patterns of GGO Model

The strong association between GGO Model and SECTOR comes as no surprise. SECTOR is clearly an important factor determining how a global governance organization faces the common GGO challenge—managing the tension between legitimacy and authority. The *classical* model is suited to governmental GGOs because it answers the accountability dilemma in ways that meet demands particular to intergovernmental organizations. In addition to satisfying normative expectations imported from the domestic context, this institutional arrangement does not undermine the preeminence of the state even as a global regime is constructed. The one member, one vote apportionment reinforces the idea of sovereignty and is legitimate on these terms. (Interestingly, geographical apportionment systems are often rejected in the domestic context because individuals are effectively denied equal voting strength.) The *forum* rulemaking process associated with *classical* GGOs channels participation through member states, another gesture affirming the supremacy of the state. In this arena, realism trumps functionalism.

TABLE 9.4 **GGO Model by Sector, Rule Type**

| | GGO Model | | | |
	Symbiotic	Classical	Cartel	Total
Sector:				
Government	3	7	3	13
Mixed	3	1	0	4
Non-government	7	1	0	8
Total	13	9	3	25
Fisher's exact = 0.039				

| | GGO Model | | | |
	Symbiotic	Classical	Cartel	Total
Rule type:				
Regulation	0	5	0	5
Standard	10	1	1	12
Multiple	3	3	2	8
Total	13	9	3	25
Fisher's exact = 0.002				

The *conventional* approach to adherence, associated with the *classical* model, provides a level of comfort to wary participants in global regimes. For members of a *classical* GGO, opting out of any offensive rule is formally costless, although there may be significant market or political pressure to adhere. Participation in a GGO—even if the rules permit reservations—forces a member to publicly acknowledge an unwillingness to abide by an international agreement.

Interestingly, the other core characteristics, even those that proved helpful in understanding patterns with respect to individual characteristics of GGOs, add less insight in the analysis of GGO type. The power of RULE TYPE as a predictor is driven by the strong association between *symbiotic* GGOs and standards. This rule type fits with the *symbiotic* approach to global governance, with its emphasis on collaboration by interested parties and use of market forces to promote compromise and implementation. TECHNICALITY, a core characteristic with explanatory power in many areas, is not a statistically significant predictor of GGO model. The expected relationship is observed—three-quarters of high-technicality GGOs are *symbiotic*—but there is no pattern among low-technicality GGOs. This is what one would expect. For low technicality GGOs, other factors are more important in driving organizational design. MEMBERSHIP has obvious explanatory power with respect to *cartel* GGOs, for example. All three are closed-membership organizations, as noted earlier. FUNDING again has almost no explanatory power beyond its association with SECTOR.

Responsibility, Legitimacy, and Publicness

Responsibility-type accountability, with its emphasis on formal and informal rules in carrying out organizational functions, resonates powerfully with the legitimacy expectations associated with government agencies. Hallmarks of a legitimate process include predictability (according to a set of well-known rules), equality (in treatment of all parties), objectivity, and neutrality in the arbitration of disputes (Kerwin 2003). Legitimate governments—particularly in the democratic context—are expected to be run in accordance with established principles, some enshrined in law and others encapsulated in social, cultural, and professional norms (Kerwin 2003). For a fledgling democracy, for example, the approval of outside election monitors confers legitimacy on new leaders that increases the state's credibility not only with its own people but with the international community. Some even speculated that George W. Bush's ability to govern might be impaired by the controversy surrounding his initial election (e.g., Apple 2000; Woodlief 2000). But we are not equally concerned with the legitimacy of all governmental entities, of course. The legitimacy of the king is of concern but the legitimacy of the dogcatcher generally is not.

And though legitimacy is raised most frequently in the governmental context, making *responsibility*-type accountability important in the arena, the legitimacy of nongovernmental organizations is also questioned by critics. In recent years, for example, the heavy-handed tactics of some environmental NGOs have prompted critics to suggest their methods undermine legitimacy (e.g., Koch-Mehrin 2006). Some NGOs are challenged regarding their representativeness of the group for which they purport to stand. Private contractors are often targets. For-profit prison operators, for example, have been criticized as illegitimate holders of power over inmates (Schmidt 2006; *St. Petersburg Times* 2001; *Washington Post* 1998). Companies that misrepresent themselves to customers or engage in exploitative business practices are often called "illegitimate" in ways that stretch beyond illegality (e.g., Siegel 2004).

These examples are consistent with the idea that there is something other than sector influencing our concern with legitimacy. It is offered here that organizational "publicness" drives concern with legitimacy and that publicness sometimes diverges from sector, or "governmentalness." Some scholars wrestling with the idea of "publicness" have, alas, tied it to governmentalness (Bozeman and Bretschneider 1994). In the most straightforward formulation, to be a public organization is to be of the government. Bozeman and Bretschneider refined this notion to recognize the reality that many organizations (like the government contractors) are funded by governments or derive their authority from governments, making them public as well (1994). Others have looked at the tools employed by an organization, the mechanisms used to control the organization, or the expectations facing an organization as the relevant criteria to determine publicness (Pesch 2008; Antonsen and Jorgensen 1997; Bozeman 1987, 2007). This approach does not disentangle publicness from sector because these aspects of organizational design ultimately trace back to governmentalness (Lan and Rainey 1992; Perry and Rainey 1988).

Remember the observation offered at the start of this book, that governance does not require government (Ruggie 2004). If we believe governance to be public, then logically, public cannot equal government either (Rosenau and Czempiel 1992). To frame publicness as something distinct from sector, the quality of an organization's function, its role in society, and the impact of its activities must be captured (Bozeman and Bretschneider 1994, 219; Haque 2001). "Publicness" should reflect the extent to which organizations draw upon, invoke, and affect the common interests of all members of a society (Wamsley and Zald 1976; Pesch 2008; Nutt and Backoff 1993; Haque 2001). We might capture publicness by looking at three indicators: pursuit of collective goods, effect on individuals, and scope. This is not offered as a definitive list, but is intended to give a sense of the way in which publicness can be divorced from governmentalness.

- Pursuit of common / collective goods—Organizations serving a common interest should be regarded as more public (Haque 2001). Nondivisible public goods are, in this sense, more public than individually consumed goods. Thus, to illustrate with a rather extreme comparison, the UN High Commissioner on Refugees is more public than the Coca-Cola Company even though the beverage maker serves a large percentage of the world's population. Organizations that pursue profits for shareholders are less public than those endeavoring to maintain collective goods such as security. Similarly, control of a common good—by a private or governmental organization—renders an organization more public.
- Affects the "public" side of the individual—State coercion is public not only because it reflects government's monopoly on violence but because the state is depriving individuals of their rights of citizenship. An organization is directly impinging on the "public" side of the individual (Benn and Gaus 1983). Organizations can be differentiated on this basis. Those that affect individuals' purely private interests—say, their product choices—are less public than those that affect civic interests such as voting ability or the right to purchase property. While this distinction is theoretically important, it does not help differentiate the GGOs examined in this study. For the most part, they steer clear of matters affecting individual civil liberties.
- Scope—The size of an organization's jurisdiction—calculated in geographic or human terms—has bearing on its publicness. By design, the organizations examined in this study are uniform in this sense. But there is variation in the total population directly affected by the rules each organization promulgates. In some cases, the number of organizations to which a rule applies is quite small even if this population is distributed globally. This is a tricky point. The rules generated may have universal applicability within a given sphere, making it highly public within, say, an industry or city, but the absolute number of individuals governed is small in global terms.

As *organizations* rise on these three dimensions, legitimacy becomes an increasingly salient issue (Nutt and Backoff 1993). Greater publicness amplifies concerns regarding the justness of an organization's assumption of its role and the manner in which it is carried out (Mathiason 2007). The legitimacy of the police department, for example, a government agency with the authority to deprive people of their fundamental rights, is more important than it is for a municipal sanitation department. Even a governmental entity without the power of violence, such as a municipal zoning board, raises legitimacy concerns because of its ability to curtail enjoyment of property rights. Few have trouble seeing the work of such governmental bodies as public in character, but there are nongovernmental organizations with a high level of "publicness" that arouse legitimacy concerns as a result.

The Educational Testing Service (ETS) is one such organization. Based in Princeton, NJ, this organization is a nonprofit company that creates and administers a range of academic tests that are crucial to thousands of students seeking admission to US universities every year. ETS exams are offered around the world and constitute a gateway to American higher education. Thus the role performed by this private company is public in its effect and broad in scope. Unsurprisingly, the legitimacy of this organization *has* been called into question by teachers, students, parents, and concerned interest groups (Nordheimer and Franz 1997; Jackson 1986). Critics have objected to the unchecked power of the testing agency, the manner in which it produces its exams and the fees it charges test takers.

Nongovernmental contractors engaged by the government are often criticized. Those that rise on the proposed publicness dimensions are often targeted. Halliburton, the massive defense company carrying out billions of dollars of work in Iraq, drew legitimacy questions related to malfeasance (e.g., Gibbons 2004). Private prison operators, companies that have assumed increasing responsibility for housing the nation's inmates, raise legitimacy concerns because of the publicness of their function and its intrusion into the civic life of their inmates. The legitimacy of a private organization assuming this responsibility is often questioned (e.g., Morris 1998).

Global governance organizations are now attracting the attention that enhanced publicness brings (Zweifel 2006; Bodansky 1999; Mathiason 2007). More often than not, however, the intergovernmental bodies responsible for high-profile treaties are targets of criticism. If governmentalness is not a good proxy for publicness, this pressure will yield mismatches, nongovernmental GGOs with high levels of publicness that are not subject to heightened legitimacy expectations. To assess the publicness of the twenty-five global governance organizations, each was assessed on the three dimensions identified above. Establishing a numeric measure would be very subjective. The use of very broad categories—high, medium, or low—is intended to keep the focus on the logic of the argument rather than the characterization of one organization or another. Combining the three aspects offered here to arrive at an overall composite is more art than science, but taken together, they provide some sense of organizational "publicness." Table 9.5 shows the characterization offered for each GGO. Most striking is the low level of variance by sector. The relationship between publicness and sector exists, to be sure, but it is not statistically significant.

This observation is anything but definitive. It is intended to be suggestive of a disconnect between attention to legitimacy and publicness in global governance organizations arising from the habitual focus on sector. There is a similar disconnect between governmentalness and the quality we would expect to predict concern with organizational authority.

Responsiveness, Authority, and Constrictiveness

Global governance organizations are differentiated by their general lack of coercive tools. Without the ability to manipulate preferences that such tools provide, GGOs must align their behavior with the preferences of potential rule adopters. This translates into *responsiveness*-type accountability, which emphasizes the satisfaction of subjects' demands. In the absence of such satisfaction, nations or companies may simply walk away, denying the GGO authority. The GGO must prioritize responsiveness to those parties whose participation is most critical to maintenance of the organization's authority. Put starkly, all GGO members are not created equal and their preferences cannot be treated as such.

How far must a GGO bend to secure authority? Authority considerations are not the same for all organizations. Granting authority to a street sweeper is not terribly controversial. Granting authority to a regulator with the ability to define impermissible activities is another matter. Concerns about endowing an organization with this kind of authority are heightened. Just as we do with legitimacy, there is a tendency to treat authority as a function of sector. This is too simplistic when the underlying quality of the authority being sought actually determines our level of

TABLE 9.5 **Variation in Publicness and Constrictiveness of GGOs**

	Collective Good	"Public side of the individual"	Scope	Overall Publicness	Constraint	Concentration	Latitude	Overall Constrict
ASTM	M	L	M	M	M	L	H	M
BCBS	H	M	H	M	H	H	M	**H**
CITES	H	L	M	M	H	H	M	H
FATF	H	M	H	H	M	H	H	H
FLOI	M	L	L	M	M	L	H	M
FSC	H	L	L	M	M	L	H	M
IAEA	H	L	M	H	H	H	H	H
IASB	H	L	H	M	H	M	M	**H**
ICANN	H	L	M	M	H	H	M	**H**
ICAO	H	L	M	M	M	H	M	M
IEC	M	L	M	M	M	H	H	M
ILO	H	M	L	**H**	M	H	M	M
IMO	H	L	M	M	H	H	M	M
ISA	H	L	L	L	L	M	L	L
ISO	M	L	H	M	H	H	H	H
ITU	H	L	H	H	M	H	H	H
IWC	H	L	L	M	M	M	H	M
MSC	H	L	L	M	M	H	M	M
UC	H	L	M	M	L	H	H	M
UPU	H	L	M	M	H	M	M	M
W3C	H	M	M	M	M	M	M	M
WCO	H	M	M	M	M	H	H	H
WHO	H	M	H	**H**	M	H	M	M
WIPO	M	M	M	M	H	H	M	M
WTO	H	M	H	H	H	H	H	H

concern. This quality is here called "constrictiveness," and it does not coincide perfectly with governmentalness. As the role envisioned for an organization is more constrictive, the salience of authority increases.

Gradations in the constrictiveness of governmental organizations demonstrate this plainly. Some governmental bureaucracies can seize land, freeze assets, and issue or withdraw licenses vital to the operation of businesses. Of course, the police and other law enforcement agencies have the ability to arrest and detain individuals. Courts can sentence individuals to prison or even to death if the accused are found guilty according to prescribed processes. Even bounded by rules, the constrictiveness of these state entities is quite formidable and the salience of authority is high. We are wary of granting license to such powers.

But there are governmental bodies that are not so constrictive. The US Postal Service (USPS) performs a service without imposing severe constraints. It faces competition in much of its business from FedEx, UPS, and even the Internet. It cannot even make key management decisions regarding personnel and rates without Congressional approval. Not surprisingly, no one is terribly concerned with the authority of the USPS. A word of caution before denigrating seemingly banal government agencies: innocuous governmental bodies can be quite constrictive. A state professional licensing agency, for example, serves as the unilateral gatekeeper. There may be little recourse or appeal of its decisions, leaving few options in the event of rejection (Glaberson 2006). Not surprisingly, objections to such panels' actions—and the authority they possess—are voiced regularly, generally by those who receive unfavorable decisions (e.g., Green 2004).

Nongovernmental entities can also be constrictive. Consider Microsoft, a semi-monopolist that has driven out competitors and dominates the market for PC operating systems around the world. Its power is highly concentrated, and the firm has a great deal of latitude in establishing its requirements. One would expect Microsoft's authority to be questioned, as it has been (Alexander 2001). On the other hand, Salvatore the hot dog man, a vendor who competes with many comparably priced substitutes in an evenly divided market, receives little scrutiny or objection. The hot dog man, unlike Microsoft, is highly constrained by competitive forces. Thus the institutionalization of power in Redmond arouses concern, but Sal's prime position at the corner of Fourth Street and D does not. The potential for assertion of highly constrictive power by private-sector organizations is exemplified by the "company town." With a single firm as the sole source of employment and the sole provider of all goods and services for an entire community, residents have almost no ability to disobey the company. Outside critics questioned the moral and political acceptability of such towns in a democratic society but the authority of the company is essentially absolute (Garner 1992).

To differentiate organizations by their constrictiveness, the approach used with publicness is repeated. A rough characterization of an organization's constrictiveness draws on three qualities:

- Constraint—Adherence to some rules imposes a significant constraint; it may even prohibit certain businesses or behaviors. In other cases, rules may impose an additional cost or proscribe one method but not fundamentally alter the range of permissible activities. In this sense, we might say that the level of constraint varies from organization to organization. Note that constraint here refers to the limitations imposed by compliance. We might add to the picture the limitations imposed by noncompliance or the coerciveness of the organization. Coerciveness is typically conceived as a measure of the punitiveness of consequences associated with rule violation. There is a continuum of coerciveness with state violence—capital punishment and incarceration—as the extreme point. Other coercive powers include seizing property, levying fines, or imposing other penalties.

- Concentration—Concentrated power is more constrictive than widely distributed power. Unrivaled organizations can deprive affected parties of any recourse because there is no alternative. A company facing market competition does not pose the threat that the monopolist does because its options are proscribed. Michael Porter identified "forces" that constrain businesses (1998). Monopoly power imposes a high level of constraint upon suppliers, investors, and customers, prompting government intervention. This distinction carries over to the world of global governance. The WTO, for example, is the only venue for adjudication of many disputes within its scope. Parties have no other organization to turn to with similar resources and tools. The International Electrical Commission, on the other hand, faces competitor organizations (e.g., ISO, ITU) that promulgate some overlapping standards in its sphere of specialization.

- Latitude—Organizations vary in the degree to which their range of actions is limited by formal encumbrances, such as those associated with a constitutional regime, and informal restrictions borne of dependence on allies, interest groups, and so on. The extent of limitation is referred to here as organizational "latitude." Organizations with less latitude are less constrictive because the contextual limitations reduce the likelihood of an organization run amok.

Taken together, these elements provide a sense of constrictiveness. Using the same rough "high," "medium," and "low" approach, the constrictiveness of the sample organizations was assessed and is provided in table 9.5. Many of the more constrictive organizations are governmental, but nongovernmental organizations also rise on this dimension.

Global governance skeptics would argue that speaking of GGO constrictiveness is nonsensical given members' ability to opt out. This is arguably less true each day—perhaps explaining why the salience of GGO legitimacy and authority is rising—given the costs of nonparticipation (Barnett and Finnemore 2004). Within its substantive sphere of influence, ICANN is quite constrictive. This nonprofit organization controls the creation of new domains (e.g., .com) and the approval of registrars for new domain names, a lucrative business. Entities unwilling to comply with its rules on domain names or dispute resolution lose access. The World Customs Organization (WCO) sees its rules backed by import authorities armed with the threat of exclusion. The Forest Stewardship Council controls the use of its distinguishing mark, intended to offer a market advantage for compliance. These designs attempt to replace the prototypical governmental sanction by manipulating the interests of the governed.

Moreover, constrictiveness also concerns the nature of authority being sought, the rules the organization produces, and the abundance of options available to the governed. A governance organization approaching monopoly in a given sphere, unconstrained by structures or rival claims, is daunting. When the rules it produces have a material impact on those to which they are applied, and the possibility of exit is increasingly remote, the institutionalization of power is formidable.

Like publicness, the constrictiveness of an organization's authority is not predicted perfectly by its governmentalness. Many nongovernmental GGOs create rules that shape the landscape and leave few options but adherence (without bearing significant costs). The International Accounting Standards Board (IASB) cannot sanction governments that do not adopt its International Financial Reporting Standards (IFRS). Still, the IFRS is the official accounting standard in the EU, and in the coming years even the American securities markets will accept IFRS accounting (Twarowski 2008). The widespread acceptance of IFRS gives the nongovernmental IASB significant constrictiveness (and publicness). Its de facto regulation of the financial commons leaves few options and yet the organization operates relatively unfettered by governments or other constraining forces.

As one would expect, the IASB arouses authority and legitimacy concerns (e.g., Tyrall 2005; Peel 2001).

But the IASB has consistently leaned in the authority direction rather than attempting to satisfy both authority and legitimacy expectations. The board of the organization is not representative of nation-states, and there is no formal guarantee of representation to any constituency. The rulemaking process is accessible to industry professionals who have the knowledge and company support to track developments and join working groups, but noncommercial groups find participation challenging. Requirements fall short of what one might expect of a government rulemaking effort in a constitutional democracy. As one harsh critic judged, "The simple truth is that accounting rules are the outcomes of politics and bargaining among corporate elites populating the IASB. . . . Ordinary people suffering from dubious accounting and losing their jobs, savings, investments, pensions and homes are not in any position to shape IASB standards" (Sikka 2007). The European Parliament issued official complaints, calling for a "public oversight body involving all public stakeholders, including legislators and supervisors, and a body representing market participants" (European Parliament 2008). It also demanded more European representation on the board, given the EU's commitment to IFRS. The leadership has responded to critics with a reform proposal that involves expansion of the board (with formalized geographic distribution requirements) and creation of a "Monitoring Group" to include the heads of the US Securities and Exchange Commission, the World Bank, the European Commission, the International Monetary Fund, the International Organization of Securities Commissioners, and the Japan Financial Services Agency (IASB 2008). Such a change is hardly an abandonment of *responsiveness*-type accountability in favor of democratic responsibility! Rather, this structure formalizes the organizational commitment to keeping key constituents satisfied.

The constrictiveness of the organization would suggest that *responsiveness*-type accountability should be a significant driver of structure and behavior. And it is. But the high level of publicness should arouse significant legitimacy issues (as it did with the one critic quoted above). For the most part, it has not. It is hypothesized here that this is true because attention is incorrectly focused on sector when legitimacy and authority demands are articulated. The IASB is nongovernmental, but it is very public.

Conventional understanding of global governance has yet to catch up with current practice. As discussed in chapter 7, the International Whaling

TABLE 9.6 **GGO Model by Relative Publicness-Constrictiveness, Constrictiveness**

	GGO Model			
	Symbiotic	Classical	Cartel	Total
Relative Publicness-Constrictiveness:				
Low-low	0	1	0	1
Medium-medium	9	3	0	12
High-high	2	2	2	6
More public	2	1	0	3
More constrict.	0	2	1	3
Total	3	9	3	25
Fisher's exact = 0.087				

	GGO Model			
	Symbiotic	Classical	Cartel	Total
Constrictiveness				
Low	0	1	0	1
Medium	12	4	0	16
High	1	4	3	8
Total	13	9	3	25
Fisher's exact = 0.003				

Commission (IWC) is one of the few GGOs that attracts more civic interest groups than industry participants. Seventy-five percent of the registered observer organizations at the last IWC meeting represented groups with an interest in whale welfare. But the IWC is a relatively weak organization. The International Maritime Organization likely has more impact on whale welfare than the IWC. It creates rules pertaining to hull thickness and other safety requirements, which determine the likelihood of a catastrophic oil spill. It regulates the emissions and other polluting activities of oceangoing vessels. It establishes the acceptable noise levels for propellers. All these rules likely affect cetacean quality of life more than the IWC. And yet the participation at IMO meetings is industry-dominated. Even more dramatically, the IMO delegates much of its rulemaking to the International Organization for Standardization. IMO conventions make explicit reference to the standards produced by ISO Technical Committee 8 (TC 8), giving this body the power to write rules that flesh out general agreements. And yet there is not a single civic interest group observing or participating in the work of TC 8!

The mistaken conflation of governmentalness, publicness, and constrictiveness results in a mismatch. *Symbiotic* GGOs are better suited to meeting the demands of authority *because* they are liberated from some legitimacy expectations that accompany *classical* GGOs. They can emphasize *responsiveness*-type accountability over responsibility. For pragmatists interested in creating a robust regime (i.e., one supported by key interested parties), adopting the *symbiotic* GGO model makes sense. As the need for better global governance increases, we should expect more of them.

The proliferation of *symbiotic* GGOs at the same time that calls for GGO accountability are getting louder might represent a perverse outcome. Because publicness is wrongly assumed to be lower in the absence of governmental participation, *symbiotic* GGOs are able to subordinate legitimacy considerations to the requirements of authority, thus enhancing the organization's power. Competition among GGOs—more likely in some arenas than others—intensifies the pressure to make this trade-off. Concomitantly, the governmental GGOs are met with more severe legitimacy demands, making it more difficult for these organizations to build authority. Thus global governance shifts to a less accountable (in the responsibility sense) set of institutions. *Cartel* GGOs are the only governmental GGOs that can deviate markedly from legitimacy expectations. The importance of their rules, their coercive tools, and the corporatist alignment of interests around them put *cartel* GGOs in this unique position (Zweifel 2006).

Implications

Two questions were posed at the outset of this book. First, why do global rulemaking bodies look the way they do? Second, why do all GGOs seem incapable of meeting accountability expectations? The analysis presented in these pages shows that the questions essentially answer each other. Contradictory demands embedded within accountability make some failure inevitable. The architecture of global governance is best understood as a response to this inherent accountability challenge. GGOs are designed to satisfy multiple expectations—indeed, different models of global governance seem to reflect demand sets that vary with context—but the intractability of the basic legitimacy-authority tension in global governance can never be fully overcome.

Legitimacy has both intrinsic value and instrumental importance for GGOs. Members of GGOs require that the organization meet normative expectations familiar in democratic systems. Indeed, organizations can build authority by meeting the demands of normative legitimacy—up to a point. To secure authority, the self-interest of the would-be rule follower must also be served. In the domestic context, there is usually no tension. The coercive powers of the state are sufficient to influence the interest calculus of the populace aligning both considerations.

But most global governance organizations lack such tools. They must secure authority by meeting the demands of potential participants. Of course, the demands of all parties are not equally important. To establish a meaningful global regime, the GGO must pay more attention to key players, nations, or organizations whose participation is critical to the attractiveness of the rules. Such favoritism runs headlong into the normative requirements of legitimacy. *Responsiveness*-type and *responsibility*-type accountability are at odds in such situations. Moreover, this approach gets increasingly complicated as the distribution of power evens out and conflicts amidst core constituencies are more common (Drezner 2007; Bodansky 1999).

Global governance organizations do not "solve" the accountability problem, they manage it with a mixture of structural and procedural features that trade legitimacy for authority, and vice versa. Some balance must be sustained for the organizations to be effective. Pushing too far in either direction is self-defeating. So features like consensus-based decisionmaking are crucial. Although normatively appealing, this approach can be intensely antidemocratic. As discussed in chapter 5, decisionmaking by consensus permits an unequal distribution of real influence, granting key players de facto power that would be difficult to do in formal terms. Incorporating understanding of such trade-offs into our understanding of international organizations is a corrective to realist focus on state power and suggests a fuller set of impediments for constructivist accounts. More legitimacy does not by itself beget more rule adoption—but it cannot be ignored, either. Even if players recognize the differential in influence—and they all do—there is a limit to the "illegitimacy" they can accept and justify to their constituents. How can the formidable expenditures required for participation in global governance organization be justified if the sole purpose of such organizations is simply rubber-stamping the preferences of the most powerful players? For this reason, legitimacy considerations seem to matter more in highly visible aspects of the organization than they do with respect to internal structures. Representative bodies invariably give each member one equal vote, for example. This should hardly be taken as a concession of equal power. The reality of unequal influence is never hidden—as any realist would expect—but it is not pressed to extremes.

The mixture of structural and procedural features that establishes a workable balance is different for each GGO. As discussed in this concluding chapter, *classical, cartel,* and *symbiotic* GGOs constitute alternative responses to the different constraints facing each organization. The analysis in the core empirical chapters makes it clear, however, that transcendent features unite this diverse collection of organizations. One, it is apparent that *negative* control is most attainable and most important for powerful GGO members. That is, influential participants in a global rulemaking regime must be assured of their ability to stop an undesirable rule. But the powerful are not granted *positive* control; they do not possess the ability to compel the GGO to enact a desired rule regardless of other members' preferences. Such a design would push too far on the legitimacy side *and* endanger the self-interest of all other members. Two, the adherence challenge is common to all GGOs. Implementation is almost always delegated, and yet the typical GGO has limited control over its adherence agents. Some would argue that until enforcement is less discretionary, it is hard to take global governance seriously. But the implied prescription—rigid implementation requirements of all GGO rules—would be disastrous. With this safety valve stripped away, GGO constituencies would demand more safety valves in the rulemaking process, resulting in weaker rules. This, in turn, would lower the market value of rule adherence. The net result is to undermine what is the most formidable primary and secondary adherence mechanism, the market preference for compliance. This is the GGO adherence paradox. The seeming weakness of GGO adherence regimes is actually a source of strength (Hassel 2008). Weaker enforcement regimes are associated with more rigorous rulemaking process, a novel observation.

The administrative realpolitik outlined in these pages may invite scorn from those who see the normative demands of democratic governance as nonnegotiable. There are numerous articles prescribing a formula of mechanisms to make global governance more accountable (e.g., Grant and Keohane 2005; Woods 2003; Burall and Neligan 2005; Benner et al. 2004). But the lack of good blueprints is not the obstacle to building accountable GGOs. The dynamics of global governance render accountability a liability at times. Global governance organizations are necessarily constructed with compromised accountability in their very superstructure. There is no argument regarding the justness or appropriateness of the trade-offs identified in these pages. Those contemplating creating, joining, or reforming a global governance organization must determine whether a normatively perfect organization is preferable to one that is sustainably effective. What failure of accountability is more tolerable?

There are strategic implications to the findings. First, given that the design of global governance organizations must incorporate concessions to pivotal actors, it behooves potential members to join or create organizations at the height of their influence. As an actor's power wanes, the vitality of its participation for the legitimacy and authority of the GGO decreases. Advantages should be locked in when its cooperation matters. This logic applies to firms and nations. Moreover, insistence on absolute control is ultimately self-defeating. In most situations, such control cannot be reconciled with effective global governance because it stretches legitimacy too far. Recognizing this dynamic when the need for harmonization is overwhelming is too late. Almost by definition, one's power will have faded at that point and the design of the GGO will be less favorable (Keohane 1983). For the United States of America in 2009, the strategic imperative is fairly clear. In the years ahead, America's economic and political influence will almost certainly decline, particularly in relative terms as new powerhouses like China and India emerge. To maximize American influence in global rulemaking institutions that can respond to worldwide financial crises, climate change, and other transnational issues, the time to promote global governance is now.

Second, the future is promising for *symbiotic* GGOs precisely because they are freer to meet the demands of *responsiveness*-type accountability. As the problems we confront increasingly cross borders, the need for global governance organizations GGOs will only increase. For those who have an interest in normative democratic governance principles (e.g., transparency, equity, etc.), it is imperative to recognize that *classical* and *cartel* GGOs are not the only global rulemakers affecting the common good. This realization is spreading. When ISO undertook creation of standards for "social responsibility," groups that likely had never heard of the organization were suddenly engaged. Indeed, complaints regarding the process to be used in drafting ISO 26000—standard operating procedures for ISO technical committees—were so intense that the organization has created a unique rulemaking process just for this standard (Knight 2008). Episodes like this suggest that GGOs can be compelled to lean back toward legitimacy as more constituencies grasp the importance of global rulemakers (Ougaard and Higgott 2002; Scholte 2004). This ray of hope for those demanding more accountability in global governance is thin. Re-member the observations of chapter 7; mobilization of civil society, espe-cially relative to commercial interests, is unlikely in many areas.

Insistence that GGOs display unbending fidelity to traditional legiti-macy and accountability expectations imported from the domestic sphere is quixotic and self-defeating (Leiken 1996; Haas 2004). *Responsibility*-type accountability can never be the exclusive goal of GGOs. Only by deviating (at times) from the requirements of legitimacy can global gov-ernance institutions effectively address the transnational problems of the twenty-first century.

APPENDIX A

List of Interview Subjects

ID No.	Anonymous Descriptor	Date
1	Senior WIPO executive	16 Oct. 2006
2	Senior WIPO executive	16 Oct. 2006
3	Senior ILO official	16 Oct 2006
4	Senior ILO official	16 Oct 2006
5	Senior ILO official	16 Oct. 2006
6	Senior ILO executive	16 Oct. 2006
7	ITU working group counselor	17 Oct. 2006
8	ITU working group chair	17 Oct. 2006
9	Senior ITU executive	17 Oct. 2006
10	WHO official	17 Oct. 2006
11	WHO official	17 Oct. 2006
12	Pharmaceutical industry representative	17 Oct. 2006
13	Senior WHO executive	18 Oct. 2006
14	Senior WHO executive	18 Oct. 2006
15	Senior ISO executive	18 Oct. 2006
16	Senior ISO official	20 Oct. 2006
17	Senior ISO official	20 Oct. 2006
18	ISO techncial group manager	20 Oct. 2006
19	ISO Member group officer / ISO official	23 July 2007
20	ISO working group participant	6 March 2007
21	Senior WTO official	19 Oct. 2006
22	Senior WTO official	19 Oct. 2006
23	Senior WTO executive	19 Oct. 2006

ID No.	Anonymous Descriptor	Date
24	Senior WTO executive	19 Oct. 2006
25	Senior WTO executive	19 Oct. 2006
26	WTO official	19 Oct. 2006
27	Senior WTO official	19 Oct. 2006
28	Senior WTO official	19 Oct. 2006
29	Senior IEC official	20 Oct. 2006
30	Interest group representative	20 Oct. 2006
31	ISO member body official	5 May 2006
32	ISO member body official	5 May 2006
33	Government official—GGO Affairs	5 May 2006
34	Government official—GGO Affairs	5 May 2006
35	Senior W3C executive	6 May 2006
36	Senior BCBS executive	28 Aug. 2007
37	Interest group executive	21 Sept. 2007
38	Senior ASTM executive	20 Sept. 2007
39	Senior CITES executive	18 Sept. 2007
40	Senior CITES official	19 Sept. 2007
41	Corporate official—GGO Affairs	20 Sept. 2007
42	Government official—GGO Affairs	20 Sept. 2007
43	Senior IEC executive	20 Oct. 2007
44	WHO official	17 Oct. 2006
45	ITU official	17 Oct. 2006
46	Senior ITU official	17 Oct. 2006
47	Senior ITU official	17 Oct. 2006
48	Senior FATF executive	26 Jul 2007
49	FLOI board member	30 Oct. 2007
50	ICANN board member	8 May 2008

References

Abbott, Kenneth W., and Duncan Snidal. 2000. "Hard and soft law in international governance." *International Organization* 54 (3):421–56.

Adler, Emanuel, and Steven Bernstein. 2005. "Knowledge in power: The epistemic construction of global governance." In *Power in global governance*, ed. M. N. Barnett and R. Duvall. Cambridge: Cambridge University Press.

Ahrne, Goran, and Nils Brunsson. 2006. "Organizing the world." In *Transnational governance: Institutional dynamics of regulation,* ed. Marie-Laure Djelic and K. Sahlin-Andersson. New York: Cambridge University Press.

Alexander, Garth. 2001. "A big battle has been won but the war is not over for Microsoft." *Sunday Times*, July 1.

Alexander, Kern, Rahul Dhumale, and John Eatwell. 2006. *Global governance of financial systems: The international regulation of systemic risk.* Oxford and New York: Oxford University Press.

Alleyne, Mark D. 1994. "Thinking about the international system in the 'Information Age': Theoretical assumptions and contradictions." *Journal of Peace Research* 31 (4):407–24.

Alvarez, José E. 2005. *International organizations as law-makers.* Oxford [England]; New York: Oxford University Press.

———. 2006. "International organizations: Then and now." *American Journal of International Law* 100 (2):324–47.

Anderson, Charles W. 1979. "Political design and the representation of interests." In *Trends toward corporatist intermediation,* ed. P. C. Schmitter and G. Lehmbruch. London and Beverly Hills: Sage Publications.

Antonsen, Marianne, and Torben Beck Jorgensen. 1997. "The 'publicness' of public organizations." *Public Administration* 75:337–57.

Apple, R. W., Jr. 2000. "A Shaky platform on which to build." *New York Times,* December 13, A1.

ASTM. 2003. *ASTM By-Laws* 2003. ASTM International 2003. http://www.astm .org/COMMIT/BODBylaws.pdf (accessed January 12, 2007).

Aust, Anthony. 2000. *Modern treaty law and practice.* Cambridge and New York: Cambridge University Press.

Axelrod, Robert, and Robert O. Keohane. 1985. "Achieving cooperation under anarchy: Strategies and institutions." *World Politics* 38 (1):226–54.

Barfield, Claude E. 2001. *Free trade, sovereignty, democracy: The future of the World Trade Organization.* Washington, D.C.: AEI Press.

Barnard, Chester I. 1938. *The functions of the executive.* Cambridge, Mass.: Harvard University Press.

Barnett, Michael N., and Martha Finnemore. 1999. "The politics, power, and pathologies of international organizations." *International Organization* 53 (4): 699–732.

———. 2004. *Rules for the world.* Ithaca: Cornell University Press.

Barnett, Michael N., and Raymond Duvall. 2005. *Power in global governance.* Cambridge and New York: Cambridge University Press.

Barr, Michael S., and Geoffrey P. Miller. 2006. "Global administrative law: The view from Basel." *European Journal of International Law* 17 (1):46.

Barretto, Paulo M. 2000. "IAEA technical co-operation: Strengthening technology transfer." *IAEA Bulletin* 1.

Bayefsky, Anne F. 2007. *The UN and beyond: United Democratic Nations.* [New York, NY]: Hudson Institute.

Bayles, Michael D. 1987. "The justification of administrative authority." In *Authority revisited,* ed. J. R. Pennock and J. W. Chapman. New York: New York University Press.

Bayne, Nicholas. 2001. "Managing globalisation and the new economy: The contribution of the G8 summit." In *New directions in global economic governance,* ed. J. Kirton and G. Furstenberg. Hants, England: Ashgate Publishing Limited.

BBC. 2008. "Toronto back on WHO SARD list." May 27 2003. http://news.bbc .co.uk/1/hi/world/americas/2939136.stm 9 (accessed May 27, 2008).

Beisheim, Marianne, and Klaus Dingwerth. 2008. "Procedural legitimacy and private transnational governance. Are the good ones doing better?" In *SFB governance working papers series.* Berlin: Research Center (SFB) 700.

Benn, S. I., and Gerald F. Gaus. 1983. *Public and private in social life.* London: Croom Helm.

Benner, Thorsten, Wolfgang H. Reinicke, and Jan Martin White. 2004. "Multi-sectoral networks in global governance: Towards a pluralistic system of accountability." *Government and Opposition* 39 (2):191–210.

Berger, Suzanne, and Joint Committee on Western Europe. 1981. *Organizing interests in Western Europe: Pluralism, corporatism, and the transformation of politics.* Cambridge and New York: Cambridge University Press.

Bernstein, Marver H. 1977. *Regulating business by independent commission.* Westport, Conn.: Greenwood Press.

Bernstein, S., and Benjamin Cashore. 2007. "Can non-state global governance be legitimate? Overcoming the conundrum of market-based authority." *Regulation and Governance* 1 (4):2–34.

Bernstein, Steven. 2004. "The elusive basis of legitimacy in global governance: Three conceptions." In *Working Paper Series.* Toronto.

Bernstein, Steven, and Benjamin Cashore. 2007. "Can non-state global governance be legitimate?: An analytical framework" *Regulation and Governance* 1 (1):1–25.

Blowfield, Mick. 1999. "Ethical trade: A review of developments and issues." *Third World Quarterly* 20 (4):753–70.

Bodansky, Daniel. 1999. "The legitimacy of international governance: A coming challenge for international environmental law?" *American Journal of International Law* 93 (3):596–624.

Boli, John, and George M. Thomas. 1997. "World culture in the world polity: A century of international non-governmental organization." *American Sociological Review* 62 (2):171–90.

———. 1999. *Constructing world culture: International nongovernmental organizations since 1875.* Stanford, Calif.: Stanford University Press.

Borzel, Tanja A., and Thomas Risse. 2005. "Public-Private partnerships: Effective and legitimate tools of transnational governance?" In *Complex sovereignty: Reconstituting political authority in the twenty-first century,* ed. E. Grande and L. W. Pauly. Toronto and Buffalo: University of Toronto Press.

Bovens, Mark, Thomas Schillemans, and Paul 't Hart. 2008. "Does public accountability work? An assessment tool." *Public Administration* 86 (1):225–42.

Bozeman, Barry. 1987. *All organizations are public: Bridging public and private organizational theories.* 1st ed. San Francisco: Jossey-Bass.

———. 2007. *Public values and public interest: Counterbalancing economic individualism.* Washington, D.C.: Georgetown University Press.

Bozeman, Barry, and Stuart Bretschneider. 1994. "The "publicness puzzle" in organization theory: A test of alternative explanations of differences between public and private organizations." *Journal of Public Administration Research and Theory* 4 (2):197–224.

Braithwaite, John, and Peter Drahos. 2000. *Global business regulation.* Cambridge and New York: Cambridge University Press.

Brandenburger, Adam, and Barry Nalebuff. 1996. *Co-opetition.* 1st ed. New York: Doubleday.

Bratton, William W., and Joseph McCahery. 1996. "Regulatory competition as regulatory capture: The case of corporate law in the USA." In *International regulatory competition and coordination: Perspectives on economic regulation in Europe and the United States,* ed. W. W. Bratton, J. McCahery, S. Picciotto, and C. Scott. Oxford: Clarendon Press.

Brauninger, Thomas. 2003. "When simple voting doesn't work: Multicameral systems for the representation and aggregation of interests in international organizations." *British Journal of Political Science* 33 (4):681(23).

Brunsson, Nils, and Bengt Jacobsson. 2000. *A world of standards.* Oxford and New York: Oxford University Press.

Buchanan, Allen, and Robert O. Keohane. 2006. "The legitimacy of global governance institutions." *Ethics and International Affairs* 20 (4):405–37.

Bull, Benedicte, Morten Boas, and Desmond McNeill. 2004. "Private sector influence in the multilateral system: A changing structure of world governance?" *Global Governance* 10 (4):481–98.

Burall, Simon, and Caroline Neligan. 2005. "The accountability of international organizations." In *GPPi Research Paper.* Berlin: Global Public Policy Institute.

Buzan, Barry. 1981. "Negotiating by consensus: Developments in technique at the United Nations Conference on the Law of the Sea." *American Journal of International Law* 75 (2):324–48.

Camerer, Colin. 2003. *Behavioral game theory: Experiments in strategic interaction.* Princeton, N.J.: Princeton University Press.

Caron, D. D. 1993. "The legitimacy of the collective authority of the Security Council." *American Journal of International Law* 87 (4):552–88.

Carr, Edward Hallett. 1942. *Conditions of peace.* New York: Macmillan Company.

Carvalho, A. P. Oliveira, and J. Amorim Faria. 1998. "Acoustic regulations in European Union countries." In conference in building acoustics, "Acoustic performance of medium-rise timber buildings," Dublin, Ireland, Dec. 3–4, 1998.

Cashore, Benjamin. 2002. "Legitimacy and the privatization of environmental governance: How non-state market-driven (NSMD) governance systems gain rule-making authority." *Governance—An International Journal of Policy and Administration* 15 (4):503–29.

Cashore, Benjamin, Graeme Auld, Steven Bernstein, and Constance McDermott. 2007. "Can non-state governance 'ratchet up' global environmental standards? Lessons from the forest sector." *Review of European Community and International Environmental Law L* 16 (2).

Cashore, Benjamin William, Graeme Auld, and Deanna Newsom. 2004. *Governing through markets: Forest certification and the emergence of non-state authority.* New Haven: Yale University Press.

Castells, Manuel. 2005. "Global governance and global politics." *PS: Political Science and Politics* 38 (1):9–16.

Cawson, Alan. 1985. *Organized interests and the state: Studies in meso-corporatism.* London and Beverly Hills: SAGE Publications.

Chayes, A., and A. H. Chayes. 1991. "Compliance without enforcement—State behavior under regulatory treaties." *Negotiation Journal-on the Process of Dispute Settlement* 7 (3):311–30.

———. 1995. *The new sovereignty: Compliance with international regulatory agreements.* Cambridge, Mass.: Harvard University Press.

Cherney, Adrian, Juani O'Reilly, and Peter Grabosky. 2006. "The multilateralization of policing: The case of illicit synthetic drug control." *Police Practice and Research* 7 (3):177.

Chesterman, Simon. 2008. "Globalization rules: Accountability, power, and the prospects for global administrative law." *Global Governance* 14 (1):14p.

CITES. 2004. "Notification to the parties: Monitoring of illegal trade in ivory." In *Convention on International Trade in Endangered Species of Wild Fauna and Flora.* Geneva: Convention on International Trade in Endangered Species.

———. 2008a. *The CITES secretariat.* Convention on International Trade in Endangered Species 2008a. http://www.cites.org//eng/disc/sec/index.shtml (accessed April 30, 2008).

————. 2008b. *How CITES works.* Convention on International Trade in Endangered Species 2008b. http://www.cites.org/eng/disc/how.shtml (accessed October 15, 2008).

Clark, P. B., and J. Q. Wilson. 1961. "Incentive systems—a theory of organizations." *Administrative Science Quarterly* 6 (2):129–66.

Claude, Inis L. 1971. *Swords into plowshares; the problems and progress of international organization.* 4th ed. New York: Random House.

Coglianese, Cary. 1997. "Assessing consensus: The promise and performance of negotiated rulemaking." *Duke Law Journal* 46:1255–349.

————. 2000. "Globalization and the design of international institutions." In *Governance in a globalizing world*, ed. J. N. J. Donahue. Washington, D.C.: Brooking Institution Ltd.

Cohen, J., L. E. Hazelrigg, and W. Pope. 1975. "De-Parsonizing Weber—Critique of Parson's interpretation of Weber's sociology." *American Sociological Review* 40 (2):229–41.

Conroy, Michael. 2007. *Branded!: How the certification revolution is transforming global corporations.* Gabriola Island, British Columbia: New Society Publishers.

Cooper, Scott, Darren Hawkins, Wade Jacoby, and Daniel Nielson. 2008. "Yielding sovereignty to international institutions: Bringing system structure back in." *International Studies Review* 10 (3):24p.

Cox, Robert W., and Harold Karan Jacobson. 1973. *The anatomy of influence; decision making in international organization.* New Haven: Yale University Press.

Coy, Peter. 2008. "How new global banking rules could deepen the U.S. crisis." *Business Week* (4081):83–6.

CPA. 2008. "The Implications to the playground designer of the ASTM F1292." Canadian Playground Advisory, Inc. 2008. http://playgroundadvisory.com/Documents/News%20and%20Articles/Implications%20of%20ASTM%20F1292-99%20-designer.pdf (accessed February 8, 2008).

CPTech. 2008. *About.* CPTech.org 2008. http://www.cptech.org/about.html (accessed March 10, 2008).

Cronin, Bruce, and Ian Hurd. 2008. *The UN Security Council and the politics of international authority.* Milton Park, Abingdon, Oxon; New York: Routledge.

Crozier, Michel. 1964. *The bureaucratic phenomenon.* Chicago: University of Chicago Press.

Cutler, A. Claire, Virginia Haufler, and Tony Porter. 1999. *Private authority and international affairs.* Albany: State University of New York Press.

Dahl, Robert Alan. 1971. *Polyarchy; participation and opposition.* New Haven: Yale University Press.

————. 1990. *After the revolution?: Authority in a good society.* Rev. ed. New Haven: Yale University Press.

————. 1999. "Can international organizations be democratic? A skeptic's view." In *Democracy's edges*, ed. I. Shapiro and C. Hacker-Cordon. Cambridge: Cambridge University Press.

Dahl, Robert, and Charles Lindblom. 1992. *Politics, economics and welfare.* New Brunswick, N.J.: Transaction.

Dao, James. 2002. "At U.N. family-planning talks, U.S. raises abortion issue." *New York Times.*

Davies, Howard. 2008. "Five ways to fix our financial architecture." *Washington Post,* October 23.

Davies, Michael D. V. 2002. *The administration of international organizations: Top down and bottom up.* Aldershot, Hants, England; Burlington, VT: Ashgate.

Deloitte. 2008. "IFRS and GAAP in the Kingdom of Thailand." In *GAAP differences in your pocket.* Bangkok: Deloitte.

Demski, Joel S. 2003. "Corporate Conflicts of Interest." *Journal of Economic Perspectives* 17 (2):51–72.

DiIulio, John D. Jr. 1994. "Principled agents: The cultural bases of behavior in a federal government bureaucracy." *Journal of Public Administration Research and Theory* 4 (3):277–318.

DiMaggio, Paul J., and Walter W. Powell. 1983. "The iron cage revisited: Institutional isomorphism and collective rationality in organizational fields." *American Sociological Review* 48 (2):147–60.

Dingwerth, Klaus. 2005. "The democratic legitimacy of public-private rule making: What can we learn from the World Commission on Dams?" *Global Governance* 11 (1):19p.

Drezner, Daniel W. 2007. *All politics is global: Explaining international regulatory regimes.* Princeton, N.J.: Princeton University Press.

Easton, David. 1958. "The perception of authority and political chance." In *Authority,* ed. C. J. Friedrich. Cambridge, Mass. Harvard University Press.

Ehrmann, Henry Walter. 1958a. *Interest groups on four continents,* ed. I. P. S. Association. [Pittsburgh]: University of Pittsburgh Press.

Eisner, Marc Allen, Jeffrey Worsham, and Evan J. Ringquist. 2006. *Contemporary regulatory policy.* 2nd ed. Boulder, Colo.: Lynne Rienner Publishers, Inc.

Emigh, Jacqueline. 2008. "Now an official ISO standard, Microsoft's OOXML invites controversy." In *BetaNews,* April 2.

Esty, D. C. 2006. "Good governance at the supranational scale: Globalizing administrative law." *Yale Law Journal* 115:1490–4562.

———. 2007. "Good governance at the world trade organization: Building a foundation of administrative law." *Journal of International Economic Law* 10 (3): 509–27.

Esty, Daniel C., and Damien Geradin. 2001. "Regulatory co-opetition." In *Regulatory competition and economic integration: Comparative perspectives,* ed. D. C. Esty and D. Geradin. Oxford and New York: Oxford University Press.

Esty, Daniel H. 1998. "Non-governmental organizations at the World Trade Organization: Cooperation, competition, or exclusion." *Journal of International Economic Law* 1 (1):123–48.

European Parliament. 2008. "More transparency and accountability needed in bodies setting international accounting standards." European Parliament website. http://www.europarl.europa.eu/sides/getDoc.do?language=EN&type=IM-PRESS&reference=20080423IPR27465.

Falk, R., and A. Strauss. 2001. "Toward global parliament." *Foreign Affairs* 80 (1): 212–20+.

FATF. 2006. FATF members and Observers. Paris, France, March 1st, 2006.

———. 2007. *NCCT Initiative.* Financial Action Task Force on Money Laundering. http://www.fatf-gafi.org/pages/0,3417,en_32250379_32236992_1_1_1_1_1,00. html (accessed December 27, 2007).

———. 2008. "Monitoring the implementation of the forty recommendations." International Financial Action Task Force on Money-laundering, 2008. http:// www.fatf-gafi.org/document/60/0,3343,en_32250379_32236920_34039228_1_1_ 1_1,00.html (accessed February 7, 2008).

Feld, Werner J., Robert S. Jordan, and Leon Hurwitz. 1994. *International organizations: A comparative approach.* 3rd ed. Westport, Conn.: Praeger.

Feldman, David Lewis. 2000. "Public confidence in cybersystems: Issues and implications for sustainability." *International Political Science Review / Revue internationale de science politique* 21 (1):23–42.

Finer, Herman. 1940. "Administrative responsibility in democratic government." *Public Administration Review* 1 (?):335–50.

Fligstein, Neil. 1990. *The transformation of corporate control.* Cambridge, Mass.: Harvard University Press.

FLO-CERT. 2007. *ISO 65 ACCREDITATION* 2007. http://www.flo-cert.net/flo-cert/main.php?id=16 (accessed December 26, 2007).

———. 2008. *ISO 65 Accreditation.* FLO-CERT 2008. http://www.flo-cert.net/flo-cert/main.php?id=16 (accessed March 14, 2008).

FLOI. 2007. "Terms of Reference: FLO Standards Committee." Fairtrade Labelling Organizations International.

Florini, Ann. 2003. *The coming democracy: New rules for running a new world.* Washington, D.C.: Island Press.

Franck, Thomas M. 1990. *The power of legitimacy among nations.* New York: Oxford University Press.

Fransen, Luc. 2008a. "Understanding dynamics of private regulatory competition: The case of global labour standards." Yale Working Group on Global Governance.

Freeman, Jody, and Laura I. Langbein. 2000a. "Regulatory negotiation and the legitimacy benefit." *New York University Environmental Law Journal* 9 (1): 60–151.

———. 2000b. "Regulatory negotiation and the legitimacy benefit." *N.Y.U. Environmental Law Journal* 9:60–9.

Friedman, Thomas L. 1999. *The Lexus and the olive tree.* Thorndike, Me.: Thorndike Press.

Friedrich, Carl J. 1940. "Public policy and the nature of administrative responsibility." *Public Policy* 1:3–24.

Froomkin, A. Michael. 2000. "Semi-private international rulemaking." In *Regulating the global information society,* ed. C. Marsden. New York: Routledge.

FSC-Watch. 2008. *About.* http://www.fsc-watch.org/about.php (accessed March 11, 2008).

Furth, Dave. 1993a. "Game equillibrium modelling." *De Economist* 141 (3):353–79.

Garner, John S. 1992. *The company town: Architecture and society in the early industrial age.* New York: Oxford University Press.

Gazette, Montreal. 2003. "Who's whining about world bodies now?" *Gazette,* April 25, A22.

Gibbons, James Howard. 2004. "Kuwaiti gratitude? More like a rip-off." *Houston Chronicle,* January 12, 2004, 16.

Gilpin, Robert. 2002. "A realist perspective on international governance." In *Governing globalization: Power, authority, and global governance,* ed. D. Held and A. G. McGrew. Cambridge; Malden, Mass.: Polity.

Glaberson, William. 2006. "How a reviled court system has outlasted many critics." *New York Times,* September 27, 1.

Goldthorpe, John H., ed. 1984. *Order and conflict in contemporary capitalism.* Oxford: Clarendon Press.

Goodin, Robert E. 1996. *The theory of institutional design.* Cambridge and New York: Cambridge University Press.

———. 2000. "Accountability—elections as one form." In *The international encyclopedia of elections,* ed. R. Rose. Washington, D.C.: Congressional Quarterly Press.

Goodnow, Frank J. 1900. *Politics and administration: A study in government.* New York: Macmillan.

Gould, M. 2000. "Locating internet governance." In *Regulating the global information society,* ed. C. Marsden. New York: Routledge.

Grafstein, R. 1981. "The failure of Weber's conception of legitimacy—its causes and implications." *Journal of Politics* 43 (2):456–72.

Grant, R. W., and R. O. Keohane. 2005a. "Accountability and abuses of power in world politics." *American Political Science Review* 99 (1):29–43.

———. 2005b. "Accountability and abuses of power in world politics." *American Political Science Review* 99 (1):29–44.

Grant, Wyn. 1985. *The political economy of corporatism.* New York: St. Martin's Press.

Green, Ashbel S. 2004. "University sues Oregon, says degrees are legitimate." *Oregonian,* August 3, B01.

Greenstein, Shane M., and Victor Stango. 2007. *Standards and public policy.* Cambridge and New York: Cambridge University Press.

Grigorescu, A. 2003. "International organizations and government transparency: Linking the international and domestic realms." *International Studies Quarterly* 47 (4):643–67.

———. 2007. "Transparency of intergovernmental organizations: The roles of member states, international bureaucracies and nongovernmental organizations." *International Studies Quarterly* 51 (3):625–48.

Gruber, Judith E. 1987. *Controlling bureaucracies.* Berkley: University of California Press.

Gruber, L. 2000. *Ruling the world: Power politics and the rise of supranatural institutions.* Princeton, N.J.: Princeton University Press.

———. 2005. "Power politics and the institutionalization of international relations."

In *Power in global governance,* ed. M. N. Barnett and R. Duvall. Cambridge and New York: Cambridge University Press.

Gunningham, Neil, Martin Phillipson, and Peter Grabosky. 1999. "Harnessing third parties and surrogate regulators: Achieving environmental outcomes by alternative means." *Business Strategy and the Environment* 8 (1):211–24.

Haas, Ernst B. 1964. *Beyond the nation-state: Functionalism and international organization.* Stanford, Calif.: Stanford University Press.

———. 1980. "Why collaborate?: Issue-linkage and international regimes." *World Politics* 32 (3):357–405.

Haas, Peter M. 2004. "Addressing the global governance deficit." *Global Environmental Politics* 4 (4):15p.

Hafner-Burton, E. M., J. von Stein, and E. Gartzke. 2008. "International organizations count." *Journal of Conflict Resolution* 52 (2):175–88.

Hall, Rodney Bruce, and Thomas J. Biersteker. 2002. *The emergence of private authority in global governance.* Cambridge and New York: Cambridge University Press.

Hamilton, Alexander, and Clinton Lawrence Rossiter. 1961. *The Federalist papers; Alexander Hamilton, James Madison, John Jay.* [New York]: New American Library.

Haque, M. Shamsul. 2001. "The diminishing publicness of public service under the current mode of governance." *Public Administration Review* 61 (1): 65–82.

Hardin, Russell. 1987. "Does might make right?" In *Authority revisited,* ed. J. R. Pennock and J. W. Chapman. New York: New York University Press.

Harrison, Reginald J. 1980. *Pluralism and corporatism: The political evolution of modern democracies.* London; Boston: Allen & Unwin.

Hassel, Anke. 2008. "The evolution of a global labor governance regime." *Governance* 21 (2):21p.

Hathaway, Oona A. 2002. "Do human rights treaties make a difference?" *Yale Law Journal* 111 (8):1935.

Hatzichronoglou, Thomas. 1997. "Revision of the high-technology sector and product classification." In *OECD science, technology and industry working papers.* Paris.

Haufler, Virginia. 2000. "Private sector international regimes." In *Non-state actors and authority in the global system,* ed. G. U. A. B. Richard Higgott. New York: Routledge.

Hawkins, Darren G., David A. Lake, Daniel L. Nielson, and Michael J. Tierney. 2006. *Delegation and agency in international organizations.* Cambridge and New York: Cambridge University Press.

Healy, Melissa. 1999. "State posts drops in births to single women; welfare: California leads the U.S. in reducing unwed motherhood, which is linked to dependence on aid." *Los Angeles Times,* September 14, 3.

Held, David. 1999. "The transformation of political community: Rethinking democracy in the context of globalization." In *Democracy's Edges,* ed. I. Shapiro and C. Hacker-Cordon. Cambridge: Cambridge University Press.

————. 2004. "Democratic accountability and political effectiveness from a cosmopolitan perspective." *Government and Opposition* 39 (2):364–91.

Held, David, and Mathias Koenig-Archibugi. 2004. Introduction. *Government and Opposition* 39 (2):125–31.

Held, David, and Anthony G. McGrew. 2002. *Governing globalization: Power, authority, and global governance.* Cambridge and Malden, Mass.: Polity.

Henkin, Louis. 1979. *How nations behave: Law and foreign policy.* 2d ed. New York: Published for the Council on Foreign Relations by Columbia University Press.

Higgins, Winton, and Kristina Tamm Hallstrom. 2007. "Standardization, globalization, and rationalities of government." *Organization* 14 (5):685–704.

Higgott, Richard A., Geoffrey R. D. Underhill, and Andreas Bieler. 2000. *Non-state actors and authority in the global system.* London and New York: Routledge.

Highleyman, Scott, Amy Matthews Amos, and Hank Cauley. 2004. "An independent assessment of the Marine Stewardship Council." Anchorage, AK: Wildhavens.

Huber, J. D., C. R. Shipan, and M. Pfahler. 2001. "Legislatures and statutory control of bureaucracy." *American Journal of Political Science* 45 (2):330–45.

Hulsse, Rainer. 2007. "Creating demand for global governance: The making of a global money-laundering problem." *Global Society: Journal of Interdisciplinary International Relations* 21 (2):24p.

Hulsse, Rainer, and Dieter Kerwer. 2007. "Global standards in action: Insights from anti-money laundering regulation." *Organization* 14:625–42.

Hummel, Ralph P. 1987. *The bureaucratic experience.* 3rd ed. New York: St. Martin's Press.

Huntington, Samuel P. 1973. "Transnational organizations in world politics." *World Politics* 25 (3):333–68.

Hurd, Ian. 1999. "Legitimacy and authority in international relations." *International Organization* 53 (2):379–408.

————. 2008. "Myths of membership: The politics of legitimation in UN Security COuncil reform." *global governance* 14 (2):199–217.

Hutter, Bridget M., and Joan O'Mahony. 2004. "The role of civil society organizations in regulating business." London: ESRC Centre for Analysis of Risk and Regulation.

IACS. 2006. "Classification societies—what, why and how?" London: International Association of Classification Societies.

IAPA. 2008. *Home.* International Air Passenger Association. http://www.iapa .com/index.cfm/travel/home.welcome (accessed March 11, 2008).

IASB. 2006a. "IASB due process handbook." International Accounting Standards Board.

————. 2006b. *IASB projects—comment, letters: comment letters on proposed amendments to IFRS 2—vesting conditions and cancellations.* IASB 2006b http://www.iasb.org/NR/rdonlyres/BE4FE435-6B03-47AE-8DDC-B390997600A6/0/IFRS2.pdf (accessed June 15, 2006).

————. 2007. *Financial Instruments* 2007a. http://www.iasb.org/About+Us/About+ Working+Groups/Financial+Instruments.htm (accessed March 22, 2007).

————. March 22. *SMEs*. IASB 2007b. http://www.iasb.org/About+Us/About+ Working+Groups/SMEs.htm (accessed March 22, 2007).

————. 2008. "Trustees publish proposals on enhancements to public accountability and to IASB composition." Website of the International Accounting Standards Board. http://www.iasb.org/Home.htm.

IASC Foundation. 2006. *IASC foundation constitution*. International Accounting Standards Committee Foundation 2007. http://www.iasplus.com/resource/ 2007revisedconstitution.pdf (accessed March 12, 2006).

IATA. 2008. *All IATA members*. International Air Transportation Association 2007. http://www1.iata.org/membership/airline_members_list?All=true (accessed June 20, 2008).

IBAMA. 2008. *Quem somos*. Instituto Brasileiro do Meio Ambiente e dos Recursos Naturais Renováveis 2008. http://www.ibama.gov.br/institucional/quem-somos/ (accessed November 2, 2008).

ICANN. 2006a. "Bylaws for internet corporation for assigned names and numbers." http://www.icann.org/general/bylaws.htm#VII (accessed July 1, 2006).

————. 2006b. "Nominating Committee Procedures, 2006." Internet Corporation for Assigned Names and Numbers, 17 April. http://www.icann.org/committees/ nom-comm/procedures-2006.html (accessed 2006).

ICANNWatch.org. 2006. *About us*. http://www.icannwatch.org/about_us.shtml (accessed July 1, 2006).

ICAO. 2005a. *Making an ICAO standard*. International Civil Aviation Organization, August 11, 2004 2004. http://www.icao.int/cgi/goto_m.pl?/icao/en/anb/mais/ index.html (accessed May 5, 2005).

————. 2005b. "Infectious substances: International civil aviation technical instructions for the safe transport of dangerous goods by air, 2005–2006." International Civil Aviation Organization.

————. 2006a. "Convention on international civil aviation." International Civil Aviation Organization.

————. 2006b. "Safety management manual." International Civil Aviation Organization.

————. 2008. *Strategic Objectives of ICAO*. International Civil Aviation Organization. http://www.icao.int/icao/en/strategic_objectives.htm (accessed June 24, 2008).

ICRC. 2007. *Discover the ICRC*. International Committee of the Red Cross. http:// www.icrc.org/web/eng/siteengo.nsf/htmlall/section_discover_the_icrc? OpenDocument (accessed July 18, 2007).

Ikenberry, G. J. 1998. "Institutions, strategic restraint, and the persistence of American postwar order." *International Security* 23 (3):43–78.

Ikenberry, G. J., and C. A. Kupchan. 1990. "Socialization and hegemonic power." *International Organization* 44 (3):283–315.

ILO. 2006. "Structure of the ILO." International Labour Organisation, 09/26 2000 http://www.ilo.org/public/english/depts/fact.htm (accessed June 10, 2006).

————. 2006. "Maritime labour convention." ed. I. L. Organization: International Labour Organization.

————. 2008. "ILOLEX—database of international labour standards." International Labour Organization 2008. http://www.ilo.org/ilolex/english/newratframeE .htm (accessed March 12, 2008).

IMO. 2007a. *Basic facts about IMO.* International Maritime Organization 2000a. http://www.imo.org/includes/blastDataOnly.asp/data_id%3D7983/Basics2000. pdf (accessed March 12, 2007).

————. 2007b. "Frequently asked questions." International Maritime Organization 2000b. http://www.imo.org/about/mainframe.asp?topic_id=774#7 (accessed March 12, 2007).

————. 2007c. "IMO conference (meetings and documents)." International Maritime Organization 2007. http://www.imo.org/home.asp (accessed April 12, 2007).

IP Justice. 2006. "IP Justice." http://www.ipjustice.org/ (accessed June 15, 2006).

Irwin, Alec, and Eva Ombaka. 2003. "Background paper of the task force on major diseases and access to medicine, subgroup on access to essential medicines." New York: United Nations Development Program.

ISA. 2003. "Rules of procedure of the council of the International Seabed Authority." December 12.

ISEAL. 2007. "Why a code of good practice for social and environmental standard-setting?" ISEAL Alliance 2007. http://www.isealalliance.org/index. cfm?fuseaction=Page.ViewPage&PageID=50 (accessed January 29, 2008).

ISO. 2008. "ISO 24408:2005." International Organization for Standardization 2005. http://www.iso.org/iso/iso_catalogue/catalogue_tc/catalogue_detail. htm?csnumber=40732 (accessed March 12, 2008).

————. 2006a. "How are ISO standards developed?" http://www.iso.ch/iso/en/ stdsdevelopment/whowhenhow/how.html (accessed June 15, 2006).

————. 2006b. "TC59 Building construction." http://www.iso.ch/iso/en/stds development/tc/tclist/TechnicalCommitteeDetailPage.TechnicalCommittee Detail?COMMID=1912 (accessed 2006, June 15).

————. 2007a. "ISO/IEC directives, part 2: Rules for the structure and drafting of International Standards." International Organization for Standardization.

————. 2007b. *Overview of the ISO system.* International Organization for Standardization 2007b. http://www.iso.ch/iso/en/aboutiso/introduction/index. html#one (accessed July 19, 2007).

ITU. 2005. "Resolution 1—Rules of procedure of the ITU Telecommunication Standardization Sector (ITU-T)." International Telecommunication Union.

————. 2007. "Sector membership—Benefits of being a sector member." International Telecommunications Union, 2008-02-11. http://www.itu.int/members/ sectmem/benef.html (accessed April 23, 2007).

IWC. 2006. "The schedule to the convention." International Whaling Commission, October 5 (accessed October 5, 2006). http://www.iwcoffice.org/commission/ schedule.htm

————. 2007. "Rules of Procedure and Financial Regulations." International Whaling Commission. http://www.iwcoffice.org/commission/procedure.htm# technical (accessed June 20, 2007).

Jackson, Dan. 1986. "Student testing comes under fire." *New York Times,* June 1, 5.

Jacobson, H. 1974. "WHO: Medicine, regionalism, and managed politics." In *The Anatomy of Influence,* ed. R. C. H. Jacobson. New Haven: Yale University Press.

———. 1979. *Networks of interdependence: International organizations and the global political system.* 1st ed. New York: Knopf.

Jacobsson, Bengt. 2006. "Regulated regulators: Global trends of state transformation." In *Transnational governance: Institutional dynamics of regulation,* ed. M.-L. Djelic and K. Sahlin-Andersson. New York: Cambridge University Press.

Jacobsson, Bengt, and Kerstin Sahlin-Anderson. 2006. "Dynamics of soft regulation." In *Transnational governance: Institutional dynamics of regulation.,* ed. M.-L. Djelic and K. Andersson-Sahlin. New York: Cambridge University Press.

Jordan, Lisa, and Peter van Tuijl. 2000. "Political responsibility in transnational NGO advocacy." *World Development* 28 (12):2051–65.

JTC 1. 2008. "Information technology." ISO/IEC JTC 001. IEC/ISO Joint Technical Committee 2008 (accessed October 15, 2008).

Justice, US Department of. 2006. "Justice Department sues national association of realtors for limiting competition among real estate brokers." Press release. U.S. Department of Justice 2005. http://www.usdoj.gov/atr/public/press_releases/2005/211008.htm (accessed June 27, 2006).

Kahler, Miles. 2004. "Defining accountability up: The global economic multilaterals." *Government and Opposition* 39 (2):132–58.

Kahler, Miles, and David A. Lake. 2003. *Governance in a global economy: Political authority in transition.* Princeton, NJ: Princeton University Press.

Kapstein, E. B. 1989. "Resolving the regulator's dilemma: International coordination of banking regulations." *International Organization* 43 (2):323–47.

———. 1994. *Governing the global economy: International finance and the state.* Cambridge, Mass.: Harvard University Press.

Karns, Margaret P., and Karen A. Mingst. 2004. *International organizations: The politics and processes of global governance.* Boulder, Colo.: Lynne Rienner Publishers.

Kaufman, Herbert. 1977. *Red tape, its origins, uses, and abuses.* Washington: Brookings Institution.

Kearney, Richard C., and Chandan Sinha. 1988. "Professionalism and bureaucratic responsiveness: Conflict or compatability." *Public Administration Review* 48 (1): 571–9.

Keck, Margaret E., and Kathryn Sikkink. 1998. *Activists beyond borders: Advocacy networks in international politics.* Ithaca: Cornell University Press.

Keohane, Robert. 1983. "The demand for international regimes." In *International regimes,* ed. S. D. Krasner. Ithaca: Cornell University Press.

———. 2002. *Power and governance in a partially globalized world.* London: Routledge.

Keohane, Robert O., and Joseph S. Nye. 1974. "Transgovernmental relations and International organizations." *World Politics* 27 (1):39–62.

———. 2000. Introduction. In *Governance in a Globalizing World,* ed. J. N. J. Donahue. Washington, D.C.: Brookings Institution Press.

———. 2002. "The club model of multilateral cooperation and problems of democratic legitimacy." In *Power and governance in a partially globalized world,* ed. R. O. Keohane. London: Routledge.

———. 2003. "Redefining accountability for global governance." In *Governance in a global economy: Political authority in transition,* ed. M. Kahler and D. A. Lake. Princeton, NJ: Princeton University Press.

Kerwer, D. 2005. "Rules that many use: Standards and global regulation." *Governance-an International Journal of Policy and Administration* 18 (4): 611–32.

Kerwin, C. M. 2003. *Rulemaking: How government agencies write law and make policy.* 3rd ed. Washington, D.C.: CQ Press.

Kirton, John. 2001. "Guilding global economic governance: The G20, the G7, and the international monetary fund at century's dawn." In *New directions in global economic governance,* ed. J. K. G. Furstenberg. Hants, England: Ashgate Publishing Limited.

Kirton, John J., and George M. Von Furstenberg. 2001. *New directions in global economic governance: Managing globalisation in the twenty-first century.* Aldershot, Hants, England; Burlington, USA: Ashgate.

Knight, Frank H. 1958. "Authority and the free society." In *Authority,* ed. C. J. Friedrich. Cambridge, Mass.: Harvard University Press.

Knight, Sam. 2008. "Everyone needs standards." *Prospect Magazine,* March, 2008.

Koch-Mehrin, Silvana. 2006. "NGOs lack transparency and should face regulation." *Financial Times.*

Koenig-Archibugi, Mathias. 2002. "Mapping global governance." In *Governing globalization: Power, authority, and global governance,* ed. D. Held and A. G. McGrew. Cambridge; Malden, Mass.: Polity.

Koppell, Jonathan G. S. 2003. *The politics of quasi-government: Hybrid organizations and the control of public policy.* Cambridge; New York: Cambridge University Press.

———. 2005. "Pathologies of accountability: ICANN and the challenge of 'multiple accountabilities disorder.'" *Public Administration Review* 65 (1):94–108.

Koremenos, Barbara, Charles Lipson, and Duncan Snidal. 2004. *The rational design of international institutions.* Cambridge: Cambridge University Press.

Koski, Chris, and Peter J. May. 2004. "Influential interests: Fostering voluntary regulatory actions." *Conference Papers—American Political Science Association:*1.

Krasner, Stephen D. 1982. "Structural causes and regime consequences: Regimes as intervening variables." *International Organization* 36 (2):185–205.

———. 1999. *Sovereignty: Organized hypocrisy.* Princeton, NJ: Princeton University Press.

Kratochwil, Friedrich. 2001. "Politics, norms, and peaceful change: Two moves to institutions." *Review of international studies* 24 (5):193.

Kratochwil, Friedrich, and John Gerard Ruggie. 1986. "International Organization: A State of the art on an art of the state." *International Organization* 40 (4): 753–75.

Krislov, Samuel, and David H. Rosenbloom. 1981. *Representative bureaucracy and the American political system.* New York, NY: Praeger.

Lake, David A. 2007. "Escape from the state of nature: Authority and hierarchy in world politics." *International Security* 32 (1):47–79.

Lamb, Henry. 2005. "Sovereignty no match for WTO." Web page, July 4, 2000. http://www.sweetliberty.org/sovereigntywto.htm (accessed July 27, 2005).

Lan, Zhiyong, and Hal G. Rainey. 1992. "Goals, rules, and effectiveness in public, private and hybrid organizations: More evidence on frequent assertions about differences." *Journal of Public Administration Research and Theory* 2 (1): 5–28.

Langbein, Laura I. 2002. "Responsive bureaus, equity, and regulatory negotiation: An empirical view." *Journal of Policy Analysis and Management* 21 (3):449–65.

Langbein, Laura I., and Cornelius M. Kerwin. 2000. "Regulatory negotiation versus conventional rule making: Claims, counterclaims, and empirical evidence." *Journal of Public Administration Research and Theory* 10, no. 3: 599–632.

Lasswell, Harold D., and Abraham Kaplan. 1952. *Power and society; a framework for political inquiry.* London: Routledge & K. Paul.

Leazes, Francis J. Jr. 1997. "Public accountability." *Administration & Society* 29 (4): 395–412.

Lehmbruch, Gerhard. 1984. "Concertation and the structure of corporatist networks." In *Order and conflict in contemporary capitalism,* ed. J. H. Goldthorpe. Oxford: Clarendon Press.

Leiken, Robert S. 1996. "Controlling the global corruption epidemic." *Foreign Policy* (105):55–73.

Levi, Margaret. 1997. *Consent, dissent, and patriotism.* Cambridge; New York: Cambridge University Press.

Levi, Michael. 2002. "Money laundering and its regulation." *Annals of the American Academy of Political and Social Science* 582:181–94.

Lindblom, Charles Edward. 1965. *The intelligence of democracy; decision making through mutual adjustment.* New York: Free Press.

Lowi, Theodore J. 1969. *The end of liberalism; ideology, policy, and the crisis of public authority.* 1st ed. New York: Norton.

———. 2001. "Our millennium: Political science confronts the global corporate economy." *International Political Science Review / Revue internationale de science politique* 22 (2):131–50.

Mackenzie, Dana. 1998. "New language could meld the web into a seamless database." *Science* 280 (5371):1840–1.

Maitland, Alison. 2002. "Coping with a more influential role: Non-governmental organisations; the higher profile of pressure groups is demanding greater accountability." *Financial Times,* February 13, 2002.

Majone, Giandomenico. 1984. "Science and trans-science in standard setting." *Science, Technology, & Human Values* 9 (1):15–22.

———. 1997. "From the positive to the regulatory state: Causes and consequences of changes in the mode of governance." *Journal of Public Policy* 17 (2):139–67.

March, James G., and Johan P. Olsen. 1995. *Democratic governance.* New York: Free Press.

———. 1998. "The institutional dynamics of international political orders." *International Organization* 52 (4):943–69.

March, James G., Herbert A. Simon, and Harold Steere Guetzkow. 1993. *Organizations.* 2nd ed. Cambridge, Mass. Blackwell.

Marklein, Mary Beth. 2007. "Rankings face backlash from college presidents." *USA Today*, April 9. http://www.usatoday.com/news/education/2007-04-06-backlash-college-rankings_N.htm (accessed June 24, 2007).

Marschner, Andrew. 2001. "The new lobbying: interest groups, governments, and the WTO in Seattle." *SAIS Review* 21 (1):159.

Marsden, Christopher T. 2000. *Regulating the global information society.* London; New York: Routledge.

Martin, Lisa L., and Beth A. Simmons. 1998. "Theories and empirical studies of international institutions." *International Organization* 52 (4):729–57.

Martins, Luis L. 2005. "A model of the effects of reputational rankings on organizational change." *Organization Science* 16 (6):701–20.

Mashaw, Jerry. 2006. "Accountability and institutional design: Some thoughts on the grammar of governance." In *Public accountability: Designs, dilemmas and experiences,* ed. M. D. Dowdle. Cambridge: Cambridge University Press.

Mathiason, John. 2007. *Invisible governance: International secretariats in global politics.* Bloomfield, CT: Kumarian Press.

———. 2008. *Internet governance: The new frontier of global institutions.* Milton Park, Abingdon, Oxon; New York: Routledge.

McCubbins, M. D., and T. Schwartz. 1984. "Congressional oversight overlooked—police patrols versus fire alarms." *American Journal of Political Science* 28 (1): 165–79.

McCullagh, Declan. 2005. "Bush administration objects to .xxx domains; commerce department raises concerns about a virtual red-light district for pornographers and asks that the process be halted." CNET News.com.

McGowan, David. 2000. "The problems of the third way: A Java case study." In *Regulating the Global Information Society,* ed. C. Marsden. New York: Routledge.

McGrew, Anthony. 2002a. "Democratising global institutions." In *Transnational democracy: Political spaces and border crossings,* ed. J. Anderson. London; New York: Routledge.

———. 2002b. "From global governance to good governance: Theories and prospects of democratizing the global polity." In *Towards a global polity,* ed. M. Ougaard and R. Higgott. London: Routledge.

McIntyre, Elizabeth. 1954. "Weighted voting in international organizations." *International Organization* 8 (4):484–97.

McKinney, Jerome B. 1981. "Process accountability and the creative use of intergovernmental resources." *Public Administration Review* 41 (special issue):144–9.

McLaren, Robert I. 1980. *Civil servants and public policy: A comparative study of international secretariats.* Waterloo, Ont.: Wilfred Laurier University Press.

McNair, Arnold Duncan McNair. 1961. *The law of treaties.* Oxford: Clarendon Press.

McNeil, Donald G. 2008. "Billionaires fund fight on smoking." *International Herald Tribune,* July 24.

Mearsheimer, J. J. 1995. "The false promise of international institutions." *International Security* 19 (3):5–49.

Menon, P. K. 1992. *The law of treaties between states and international organizations.* Lewiston, NY: Edwin Mellen Press.

Merriam-Webster Inc. 1998. *The Merriam-Webster dictionary.* Home and office ed. Springfield, Mass.: Merriam-Webster.

Milgram, Stanley. 2004. *Obedience to authority: An experimental view.* New York: Perennial Classics.

Mitchell, Ronald B. 1998. "Sources of transparency: Information systems in international regimes." *International Studies Quarterly* 42 (1):109–30.

Mitrany, David. 1966. *A working peace system.* Chicago: Quadrangle Books.

Mladenka, Kenneth R. 1980. "The urban bureaucracy and the Chicago political machine: Who gets what and the limits to political control." *American Political Science Review* 74: 991–8.

Moe, Ronald C. 1994. "The 'reinventing government' exercise: Misinterpreting the problem, misjudging the consequences." *Public Administration Review* 54 (2):111–22.

———. 2000. "Government reinvention revisited." *Public Manager* 29 (3):37–49.

Moe, Ronald C., and Robert S. Gilmour. 1995. "Rediscovering principles of public administration: The neglected foundation of public law." *Public Administration Review* 55 (2):135–46.

Moe, Terry M. 1980. *The organization of interests: Incentives and the internal dynamics of political interest groups.* Chicago: University of Chicago Press.

Moffett, Matt. 2004. "Growing a steak: How a Brazilian cattle baron shakes up world's beef trade." *Wall Street Journal,* June 24.

Moore, Stephen. 1999. "Speed doesn't kill: The repeal of the 55-mph speed limit." In *Policy Analysis,* ed. 346. Washington, D.C.: Cato Institute.

Morgenthau, Hans J., and Kenneth W. Thompson. 1993. *Politics among nations: The struggle for power and peace.* Brief ed. New York: McGraw-Hill.

Morris, Phillip. 1998. "Is Ohio's private prison safe, legal?" *Plain Dealer* (Cleveland, Ohio), February 17, 9B.

Morris, S., and H. S. Shin. 2005. "Central bank transparency and the signal value of prices." *Brookings Papers on Economic Activity* (2):1–66.

Morris, S., H. S. Shin, and H. Tong. 2006. "Social value of public information." *American Economic Review* 96 (1):453–5.

Morris, Stephen, and Hyun Song Shin. 2002. "Social value of public information." *American Economic Review* 92 (5):1521–34.

Mueller, Milton L. 2002. *Ruling the root: Internet governance and the taming of cyberspace.* 1st ed. Cambridge, Mass.: MIT Press.

Murphy, Craig. 1994. *International organization and industrial change: Global governance since 1850.* New York: Oxford University Press.

————. 2002. "The historical processes of establishing institutions of global governance and the nature of the global polity." In *Towards a Global Polity,* ed. M. O. R. Higgott. New York: Routledge.

Murphy, Dale D. 2004. *The structure of regulatory competition: Corporations and public policies in a global economy.* Oxford [England]; New York: Oxford University Press.

Nordheimer, Jon, and Douglas Franz. 1997. "Testing giant exceeds roots, drawing business rivals' ire." *New York Times,* September 30, A1.

NRC. 2004. "493 part 75 safeguards on nuclear material." Ed. Nuclear Regulatory Commission. http://0-edocket.access.gpo.gov.library.colby.edu/cfr_2005/janqtr/pdf/10cfr74.84.pdf.

————. 2007. *Mr. Martin A Virgilio.* Washington, D.C.: Nuclear Regulatory Commission. http://www.nrc.gov/about-nrc/organization/virgilio-bio.html (accessed January 20, 2007).

Nutt, Paul C., and Robert W. Backoff. 1993. "Organizational publicness and its implications for strategic management." *Journal of Public Administration Research and Theory* 3 (2):209–31.

NYC Dept of Education. 2002. "Chancellor Klein announces first performance based bonus program for community and high school superintendents." NYC Department of Education, September 24. http://www.nycenet.edu/press/02-03/n29_03.htm (accessed April 12, 2003).

Nye, Joseph S., and John D. Donahue. 2000. *Governance in a globalizing world.* Cambridge, Mass.; Washington, D.C.: Visions of Governance for the 21st Century; Brookings Institution Press.

OECD. 2006. *Environmental regulation in China: Institutions, enforcement, and compliance.* Paris: Organization for Economic Cooperation and Development.

Offe, Claus. 1981. "The attribution of public status to interest groups: Observations on the West German case." In *Organizing interests in Western Europe: Pluralism, corporatism, and the transformation of politics,* ed. S. Berger. Cambridge and New York: Cambridge University Press.

Olson, Mancur. 1971. *The logic of collective action; public goods and the theory of groups.* Cambridge, Mass.: Harvard University Press.

Osborne, David, and Ted Gaebler. 1992. *Reinventing government: How the entrepreneurial spirit is transforming the public sector.* Reading, Mass.: Addison-Wesley.

OSHA. 2007. "Frequently asked questions." Occupational Safety and Health Administration. http://osha.gov/as/opa/osha-faq.html (accessed June 15, 2007).

Ostrovsky, Michael, and Michael Schwarz. 2005. "Adoption of standards under uncertainty." *RAND Journal of Economics* 36 (4):816–32.

Ougaard, Morten, and Richard A. Higgott. 2002. *Towards a global polity.* New York: Routledge.

Parsons, Talcott. 1942. "Max Weber and the contemporary political crisis: I. The sociological analysis of power and authority structures." *Review of Politics* 4 (1):61–76.

Pattberg, Philipp. 2005a. "The institutionalization of private covernance: How business and nonprofit organizations agree on transnational rules." *Governance* 18 (4):22p.

———. 2005b. "The Forest Stewardship Council." *Journal of Environment and Development* 14 (3):356–74.

Paul, Ryan. 2007. "ISO reforms proposed in response to OOXML shenanigans." In *ars technica*.

———. 2008. "Microsoft's Office Open XML now an official ISO standard." In *ars technical.*

Peel, Michael. 2001. "The touchy rule-maker: The International Accounting Standards Board has a worthy goal. But it should be more prepared to listen to its critics." *Financial Times*, November 15, 2.

Perry, James, and Hal G. Rainey. 1988. "The public-private distinction in organizational theory." *Academy of Management Review* 13:182–201.

Pesch, Udo. 2008. "The publicness of public administration." *Administration and Society* 40 (2):170–93.

Peters, B. Guy. 1995. "Introducing the topic." In *Governance in a changing environment*, ed. B. G. Peters and D. J. Savoie. Montreal: McGill-Queen's University Press.

———. 2005. *Institutional theory in political science: The "new institutionalism."* 2nd ed. London; New York: Continuum.

Peters, B. Guy, and John Pierre. 1998. "Governance without government? Rethinking public administration." *Journal of Public Administration Research and Theory: J-PART* 8 (2):223–43.

Peterson, M. J. 1992. "Whalers, cetologists, environmentalists, and the international management of whaling." *International Organization* 46 (1):147–86.

Pfeffer, Jeffrey. 1992. *Managing with power: Politics and influence in organizations.* Boston, Mass.: Harvard Business School Press.

Pfeffer, Jeffrey, and Gerald R. Salancik. 2003. *The external control of organizations: A resource dependence perspective.* Stanford, Calif.: Stanford Business Books.

Piven, Frances Fox, and Richard A. Cloward. 1971. *Regulating the poor: The functions of public welfare.* New York: Pantheon Books.

Porter, Michael E. 1998. *Competitive strategy: Techniques for analyzing industries and competitors; with a new introduction.* 1st Free Press ed. New York: Free Press.

Porter, Tony. 2001. "The democratic deficit in the institutional arrangement for regulating global finance." *Global Governance* 7 (4):427–39.

Porter, T., and K. Ronit. 2006. "Self-regulation as policy process: The multiple and criss-crossing stages of private rule-making." *Policy Sciences* 39 (1):41–72.

Powell, Walter W., and Paul DiMaggio. 1991. *The new institutionalism in organizational analysis.* Chicago: University of Chicago Press.

Radaelli, C. M. 2004. "The puzzle of regulatory competition." *Journal of Public Policy* 24 (1):1–23.

Reinalda, Bob, and Bertjan Verbeek. 1998. *Autonomous policy making by international organizations.* London; New York: Routledge.

————. 2004. *Decision making within international organizations.* London; New York: Routledge.

Reinicke, Wolfgang. 1998. *Global public policy: Governing without government?* Washington, D.C.: Brookings Institution Press.

————. 1999. "The other world wide web: Global public policy networks." *Foreign Policy* 117:44–57.

Rhodes, R. A. W. 1996. "The new governance: Governing without government." *Political Studies* 44:652–67.

Risse, Thomas. 2004. "Transnational governance and legitimacy." Freie Universität, Berlin. http://www.polsoz.fu-berlin.de/en/polwiss/forschung/international/atasp/publikationen/4_artikel_papiere/20/index.html.

Romano, Roberta. 1905. "Is regulatory competition a problem or irrelevant for corporate governance?" Social Science Research Network. http://papers.ssrn.com/sol3/papers.cfm?abstract_id=693484.

Romzek, Barbara, and Melvin Dubnick. 1987. "Accountability in the public sector: Lessons from the *Challenger* tragedy." *Public Administration Review* 47 (3):227–38.

Romzek, Barbara S., and Melvin J. Dubnick. 1987. "Accountability in the public sector: lessons from the challenger tragedy." *Public Administration* Review 47, no. 3:227–38.

Rosen, Bernard. 1989. *Holding government bureaucracies accountable.* Second ed. New York: Praeger.

Rosenau, James N., and Ernst-Otto Czempiel, eds. 1992. *Governance without government: Order and change in world politics.* Cambridge; New York: Cambridge University Press.

Rosendorff, B. Peter, and Helen V. Milner. 2001. "The optimal design of international trade institutions: Uncertainty and escape." *International Organization* 55 (4):829–57.

Rothstein, B., and J. Teorell. 2008. "What is quality of government? A theory of impartial government institutions." *Governance—An International Journal of Policy and Administration* 21 (2):165–90.

Rourke, Francis E. 1992. "Responsiveness and neutral competence in american bureaucracy." *Public Administration Review* 52 (6):539–46.

Rousseau, Jean-Jacques, and Willmoore Kendall. 1985. *The government of Poland.* Indianapolis, Ind.: Hackett Pub. Co.

Ruggie, John Gerard. 2004. "Reconstituting the global public domain—issues, actors, and practices." *European Journal of International Relations* 10 (4):499–533.

Russett, Bruce M., and Ian Hurd. 1997. *The once and future Security Council.* 1st ed. New York: St. Martin's Press.

Saint-Laurent, Simon. 2003. *An outsider's guide to the W3C.* http://simonstl.com, 12 January. http://www.simonstl.com/articles/civilw3c.htm (accessed November 5, 2005).

Salisbury, R. H. 1969. "Exchange theory of interest groups." *Midwest Journal of Political Science* 13 (1):1–32.

————. 1979. "Why no corporatism in america?" In *Trends toward corporatist intermediation,* ed. P. C. Schmitter and G. Lehmbruch. London; Beverly Hills: Sage Publications.

———. 1984. "Interest representation—the dominance of institutions." *American Political Science Review* 78 (1):64–76.

Samuels, D., and R. Snyder. 2001. "The value of a vote: Malapportionment in comparative perspective." *British Journal of Political Science* 31:651–71.

Sands, Philippe, Pierre Klein, and D. W. Bowett. 2001. *Bowett's law of international institutions.* 5th ed. London: Sweet & Maxwell.

Scales, Ann. 1999. "Bush raps rivals, own party on education; Urges accountability for schools; rues Democrats' 'despair.'" *Boston Globe,* October 6, 29.

Scharpf, Fritz. 1997. "Economic integration, democracy and the welfare state." *Journal of European Public Policy* 4 (1):18–30.

Schattschneider, E. E. 1975. *The semisovereign people: A realist's view of democracy in America.* Fort Worth: Harcourt Brace Jovanovich.

Schlozman, Kay Lehman, and John T. Tierney. 1986. *Organized interests and American democracy.* New York: Harper & Row.

Schmidt, Steve. 2006. "Exporting State's Inmates; Packed prisons get some relief; critics want reforms." *San Diego Union-Tribune,* November 19, 2006, A1.

Schmitter, Phillippe. 1985. "Neo-corporatism and the state." In *The Political economy of corporatism,* ed. W. Grant. New York: St. Martin's Press.

Scholte, Jan. 2002. "Civil society and governance in the global polity." In *Towards a Global Polity,* ed. M. Ouggard and R. Higgott. New York Routledge.

———. 2004. "Civil Society and Democratically Accountable Global Governance." *Government and Opposition* 39 (2):211–33.

Scott, W. Richard. 1992. *Organizations: Rational, natural, and open systems.* 3rd ed. Englewood Cliffs, N.J.: Prentice Hall.

———. 2008. *Institutions and organizations: Ideas and interests.* 3rd ed. Los Angeles: Sage Publications.

SEC. 2007. "Acceptance from foreign private issuers of financial statements prepared in accordance with international financial reporting standards without reconciliation to U.S. GAAP." Washington, D.C.: Securities and Exchange Commission.

Sell, S.K. 2003. *Private power, public law: The globalization of intellectual property rights.* New York: Cambridge University Press.

Sell, Susan K. 1999. "Multinational corporations as agents of change: The globalization of intellectual property rights." In *Private authority and international affairs,* ed. A. C. Cutler, V. Haufler and T. Porter. Albany: State University of New York Press.

Selznick, Philip. 1957. *Leadership in administration.* New York: Harper & Row.

Sensenbrenner, Joseph. 1991. "Quality comes to city hall." *Harvard Business Review* 69 (2):64–70.

Shaffer, Gregory. 2005. "Power, governance and the WTO: A comparative institutional approach." In *Power in global governance,* ed. M. N. Barnett and R. Duvall. Cambridge; New York: Cambridge University Press.

Shapiro, Ian. 1999. *Democratic justice.* New Haven: Yale University Press.

Shepsle, Kenneth. 1996. "Institutional equilibrium and equilibrium institutions." In

Siegel, Judy. 2004. "Pfizer fights on-line sales of fake Viagra." *Jerusalem Post*, August 5, 16.

Sikka, Premm. 2007. "There's no accounting for accountants." *Manchester Guardian*.

Simmons, Beth A. 2001. "The international politics of harmonization: The case of capital market regulation." *International Organization* 55 (3):589–620.

Simon, Herbert A., Donald W. Smithburg, and Victor Alexander Thompson. 1991. *Public administration*. New Brunswick : Transaction Publishers.

Sinclair, Timothy J. 2005. *The new masters of capital: American bond rating agencies and the politics of creditworthiness*. Ithaca: Cornell University Press.

Slaughter, Anne-Marie. 2004a. "Disaggregated sovereignty: Towards the public accountability of global government networks." *Government and Opposition* 39 (2):159–90.

———. 2004b. *A new world order*. Princeton, NJ: Princeton University Press.

Sohn, Injoo. 2005. "Asian financial cooperation: The problem of legitimacy in global financial governance." *Global Governance* 11 (4):18p.

Spiro, Herbert J. 1958. "Authority, values and policy." In *Authority*, ed. C. J. Friedrich. Cambridge, Mass.: Harvard University Press.

St. Petersburg Times. 2001. "No-protection prisons." *St. Petersburg Times*, December 5, 2001.

Stein, Eric. 2001. "International integration and democracy: No love at first sight." *American Journal of International Law* 95 (3):489–534.

Steinberg, Richard H. 2002. "In the shadow of law or power? Consensus-based bargaining and outcomes in the GATT/WTO." *International Organization* 56 (2):339–74.

Stone, Katherine. 1996. "Labour in the global economy: Four approaches to transnational labour regulation." In *International regulatory competition and coordination: perspectives on economic regulation in Europe and the United States*, ed. W. W. Bratton, J. McCahery, S. Picciotto and C. Scott. Oxford: Clarendon Press.

Suchman, Mark C. 1995. "Managing legitimacy: Strategic and institutional approaches." *Academy of Management Review* 20 (3):571–610.

Sunder, Shyam. 2002. "Regulatory competition among accounting standards within and across international boundaries." *Journal of Accounting and Public Policy* 21 (3):219–34. http://papers.ssrn.com/sol3/papers.cfm?abstract_id=354101.

Tamm Hallstrom, Kristina. 2000. "Organizing the process of standardization." In *A world of standards*, ed. N. Brunsson and B. Jacobsson. Oxford; New York: Oxford University Press.

———. 2004. *Organizing International Standardization: ISO and the IASC in quest of authority*: Cheltenham: Edward Elgar.

Tang, S. Y. 2003. "Environmental regulation in China: Institutions, enforcement, and compliance." *Journal of the American Planning Association* 69 (1):94–5.

Tarrow, Sidney G. 2005. *The new transnational activism*. New York: Cambridge University Press.

Taylor, Paul Graham, and A. J. R. Groom. 2000. *The United Nations at the millennium: The principal organs.* New York: Continuum.

Taylor, Peter F. 2002. "Relocating the demos?" In *Transnational democracy: Political spaces and border crossings,* ed. J. Anderson. London; New York: Routledge.

Thomas, Clive S. 1993. *First world interest groups: A comparative perspective.* Westport, Conn.: Greenwood Press.

Transfair Canada. 2006. "Overview of the licensing process and contract, version 5.1." Ottawa: Transfair Canada.

Truman, David Bicknell. 1993. *The governmental process: Political interests and public opinion.* 2nd ed. Berkeley: University of California, Berkeley.

Tullock, Gordon. 1965. *The politics of bureaucracy.* Washington, D.C.: Public Affairs Press.

Twarowski, Christopher. 2008. "SEC opens debate on adopting international accounting rules." *Washington Post,* August 28, 2.

Tyrall, David. 2005. "Can accountants figure a way to global standards?" *Financial Times,* March 17, 42.

Unicode. 2007. *The Unicode Standard* 3.0. Unicode Consortium, 2005. http://unicode.org/book/uc20ch1.html (accessed February 21, 2007).

UL. 2008. "About UL." Underwriters Laboratories, Inc. http://www.ul.com/about (accessed May 21, 2008).

United Nations. 2006. "United Nations Convention on the Law of the Sea." United Nations 1982. http://www.un.org/Depts/los/convention_agreements/texts/unclos/closindx.htm (accessed February 16, 2006).

Underwriters Laboratories. 2008. "About UL Underwriters Laboratories, Inc." http://www.ul.com/about (accessed May 21, 2008).

Unicode. 2006. *The Unicode Consortium.* Unicode Consortium, 15 September. http://www.unicode.org/consortium/consort.html (accessed September 15, 2006).

———. 2008. *Approved Minutes of UTC 110/ L2 207 Joint Meeting Mountain View, CA—February 5–8,* 2007. Unicode Consortium 2007. http://www.unicode.org/consortium/utc-minutes/UTC-110-200702.html (accessed January 9, 2008).

United Nations. 2008. "Charter of the United Nations." New York: United Nations.

Uphoff, N. 1989. "Distinguishing power, authority and legitimacy—taking Max Weber at his word by using resources-exchange analysis." *Polity* 22 (2): 295–322.

UPU. 2005. "Constitution general regulations." Berne: Universal Postal Union.

Vermunt, Jeroen K., and Jay Magidson. 2005. *Technical guide for latent gold 4.0: Basic and advanced.* Belmont, Mass.: Statistical Innovations Inc.

Verweij, M., and T. E. Josling. 2003. "Special issue: Deliberately democratizing multilateral organization." *Governance-an International Journal of Policy and Administration* 16 (1):1–21.

Victor, David G. 2000. "Enforcing international law: Implications for an effective global warming regime." *Duke Environmental Law and Policy* 10:147–84.

Vogel, David. 1995. *Trading up: Consumer and environmental regulation in a global economy.* Cambridge, Mass.: Harvard University Press.

———. 2003. *Fluctuating fortunes: The political power of business in America.* Washington, D.C.: Beard Books.

Vogel, Steven. 1997. "International games with national rules: How regulation shapes competition in 'global' markets." *Journal of Public Policy* 17 (2):169–93.

W3C. 2005. "About W3C." World Wide Web Consortium.

Waltz, K. N. 1993. "The emerging structure of international-politics." *International Security* 18 (2):44–79.

Wamsley, Gary L., and Mayer N. Zald. 1976. *The political economy of public organizations: A critique and approach to the study of public administration.* Bloomington: Indiana University Press.

Washington Post. 1998. "The problem with private prisons." *Washington Post,* November 1.

WCO. 2007. "The nature of WCO recommendations and the procedure for their acceptance." World Customs Organization.

Weber, Max, Guenther Roth, and Claus Wittich. 1978. *Economy and society: An outline of interpretive sociology.* 2 vols. Berkeley: University of California Press.

Weimer, D. L. 2006. "The puzzle of private rulemaking: Expertise, flexibility, and blame avoidance in US regulation." *Public Administration Review* 66 (4): 569–82.

Weiss, Thomas George, and Sam Daws. 2007. *The Oxford handbook on the United Nations.* Oxford; New York: Oxford University Press.

Wendt, Alexander. 1999. *Social theory of international politics.* Cambridge; New York: Cambridge University Press.

Wessells, Cathy R., Robert J. Johnston, and Holger Donath. 1999. "Assessing consumer preferences for ecolabeled seafood: The influence of species, certifier, and household attributes." *American Journal of Agricultural Economics* 81 (5): 1084–9.

WHO. 2006. "World Health Organization, list of participants, 3 Feb. 2005." http://www.who.int/gb/fctc/PDF/igwg2/FCTC_IGWG2_D2R1.pdf (accessed June 15, 2006).

———. 2006. "List of 182 nongovernmental organizations in official relations with WHO reflecting decisions of EB117, January 2006." http://www.who.int/civilsociety/relations/NGOs_list_rlct_EB117_decsE.pdf (accessed June 15, 2006).

———. 2006b. "Principles governing relations with nongovernmental organizations." Geneva: World Health Organization.

———. 2007. "WHO collaborating centres, general information 2007." http://www.who.int/kms/initiatives/whoccinformation/en/index.html (accessed March 22, 2007).

Wilkinson, Rorden. 2008. "The contours of courtship." In *Global governance: Critical Perspectives,* ed. R. W. S. Hughes. New York: Routledge.

Wilkinson, Rorden, and Stephen Hughes. 2002. *Global governance: Critical perspectives.* London; New York: Routledge.

Willetts, Peter. 1982. *Pressure groups in the global system: The transnational relations of issue-orientated non-governmental organizations.* New York: St. Martin's Press.

Williamson, Hugh. 2006. "Greenpeace, Amnesty and Oxfam agree code of conduct." *Financial Times,* June 3, 2006.

Williamson, Oliver E. 1985a. *The economic institutions of capitalism: Firms, markets, relational contracting.* New York and London: Free Press; Collier Macmillan.

Williamson, Peter J. 1985b. *Varieties of corporatism: A conceptual discussion.* Cambridge; New York: Cambridge University Press.

Willmott, Hugh C. 1985. "Setting accounting standards in the U.K.: The emergence of private accounting bodies and their role in the regulation of public accounting practice." In *Private interest government: Beyond market and state,* ed. W. Streeck and P. C. Schmitter. London; Beverly Hills: Sage Publications.

Wilson, Graham K. 1982. "Why no corporatism in the United States?" In *Patterns of corporatist policy-making,* ed. G. Lehmbruch and P. C. Schmitter. London; Beverly Hills, Calif.: Sage Publications.

———. 1990. *Business and politics: A comparative introduction.* 2nd ed. Chatham, N.J.: Chatham House Publishers.

Wilson, James Q. 1980. *The politics of regulation.* New York: Basic Books.

Wilson, Woodrow. 1887. "The study of administration." *Political Science Quarterly* 2:197–222.

Winner, Langdon. 1977. *Autonomous technology: Technics-out-of-control as a theme in political thought.* Cambridge, Mass.: MIT Press.

WIPO. 2006a. "List of observers." 2006a. http://www.wipo.int/members/en/organizations.jsp (accessed June 13, 2006).

———. 2006b. June 13. "List of observers: International non-governmental organizations." http://www.wipo.int/members/en/organizations.jsp?type=NGO_INT (accessed June 13, 2006).

———. 2006c. "WIPO frequently asked questions." Geneva: World Intellectual Property Organization.

Wood, B. Dan, and Richard W. Waterman. 1994. *Bureaucratic dynamics: The role of bureaucracy in a democracy.* Boulder: Westview Press.

Wood, Duncan. 2005. *Governing global banking.* Hants, England: Ashgate.

Woodlief, Wayne. 2000. "Divide inspiration needed; VP choice key to post-election unity." *Boston Herald,* December 3, 023.

Woods, Ngaire. 2003. "Holding intergovernmental institutions to account." *Ethics and International Affairs* 17 (1):12p.

Woods, Ngaire, and Amrita Narlikar. 2001. "Governance and the limits of accountability: The WTO, the IMF, and the World Bank." *International Social Science Journal* 53 (17):569–83.

Wright, Tom, and Jim Carlton. 2007. "FSC's 'green' label for wood products gets growing pains." *Wall Street Journal,* October 30.

Wrong, Dennis Hume. 1988. *Power, its forms, bases, and uses: With a new preface.* Chicago: University of Chicago Press.

WTO. 2007a. "Annex 3: Code of Good Practice for the Preparation, Adoption and Application of Standards." World Trade Organization.

————. 2007b. "What Is WTO?" http://www.wto.org/english/thewto_e/whatis_e/tif_e/fact1_e.htm (accessed May 26, 2007).

Young, Oran R. 1992. "The effectiveness of international institutions: Hard cases and critical variables." In *Governance without government*, ed. J. N. Rosenau and E.-O. Czempiel. Cambridge; New York: Cambridge University Press.

Zacher, Mark W., and Brent Sutton. 1996. *Governing global networks: International regimes for transportation and communications.* Cambridge; New York: Cambridge University Press.

Zamora, S. 1980. "Voting in international economic organizations." *American Journal of International Law* 74 (3):566–608.

Zurn, Michael. 2004. "Global governance and legitimacy problems." *Government and Opposition* 39 (2):260–87.

Zweifel, Thomas D. 2006. *International organizations and democracy: Accountability, politics, and power.* Boulder: Lynne Rienner Publishers.

Index